GREATEST GUNS OF
GUN DIGEST

Dan Shideler

Published by

Gun Digest® Books, an imprint of F+W Media, Inc.
Krause Publications • 700 East State Street • Iola, WI 54990-0001
715-445-2214 • 888-457-2873
www.krausebooks.com

To order books or other products call toll-free 1-800-258-0929
or visit us online at www.krausebooks.com, www.gundigeststore.com
or www.Shop.Collect.com

Library of Congress Control Number: 2010925143

ISBN-13: 978-1-4402-1414-1
ISBN-10: 1-4402-1414-X

Cover Design by Tom Nelsen
Designed by Tom Nelsen
Edited by Dan Shideler

Printed in the United States of America

Contents

Introduction

Welcome to the *Greatest Guns of Gun Digest!*

I t's been quite a job, selecting the cream of the crop of the greatest gun annual of all time. After all, *Gun Digest* was first published in 1944 and has now reached its 65th edition, which gives us quite a lot of material from which to choose.

In selecting the pieces to appear in this volume, we applied the tried-and-true formula that seems to have guided *Gun Digest's* editors since the beginning: try to include stories about Handguns, Rifles, Shotguns, and Military Arms. Of course there will be some overlapping, and it just wouldn't be a *Gun Digest* publication without the unique blend of history, scholarship, entertainment, and educated opinion that you'll find in the following pages.

Gun Digest has always been about the guns, first and foremost. In fact, *Gun Digest* has always followed a policy of covering as many gunmakers, major and minor, as its pages can possibly accommodate. Few publications indeed would include a feature on the "Rifleman's Rifle," the Winchester Model 70, and then in the same edition discuss the Garcia Bronco, an ultra-utilitarian skeleton-stocked rifle of decidedly unlovely aspect – but that sort of editorial democracy has always been one of the hallmarks of *Gun Digest*. And we intend that it always shall be.

Argument, disagreement, lack of consensus – all these are distinguishing characteristics of the American gun-owning public. Don't be surprised, then, if your favorite great gun has eluded inclusion in these pages. Every gun featured herein is somehow remarkable, whether it is a high-dollar collectible like the Colt-Walker revolver or a more minor celebrity such as Remington's Nylon 66 .22

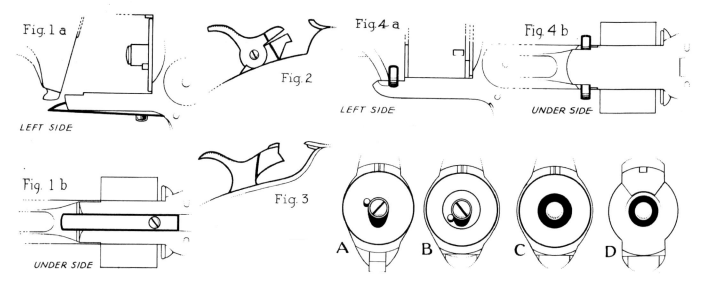

These drawings by the author show characteristic features of the early Smith & Wesson cartridge revolvers described in this article.

employing the same principle as their gun had previously been patented. This may have accounted for the fact that a satisfactory deal was quickly made, whereby Smith & Wesson purchased the rights to White's patent. In November, 1857, Smith & Wesson began the production of the little 22 caliber seven-shot rimfire revolvers.

It would seem that there should be ample data on arms so vitally connected with American cartridge arms history. Such is not the case, however, as the writer found when conducting a brief survey and research on these unique pieces. This survey involved many weeks of writing and checking with leading collectors and authorities for details on actual specimens. The findings presented here are the result of this research. It is hoped that they may prove of help to all who are interested in arms, and incidentally help to clear up some of the confusion which has heretofore surrounded these guns.

Recognizing the First Model and Its Variations

The First Model is easily recognized by these distinguishing features: Oval brass frame with round plate on the left side; a two-piece hammer, the movable top of which operates the cylinder stop spring. In addition to these main features on the First Models, there are other points which the writer feels are important enough to warrant subdividing the arms having them into variations or issues of the First Model. For instance, a very important feature which has escaped many writers is the fact that the first issue of this revolver has a striking point of difference from later issues.

Instead of the conventional thumb catch found on later issues and models, this early rarity has a flat spring type of barrel catch. It was so scarce and unknown that only three specimens of it were believed to be in existence in 1940. The present survey has brought to light eight more; there doubtless are other specimens yet to be found. This flat spring is illustrated in detail (Fig. 1). Early patent papers show the gun with this type of barrel catch, as does also the first instruction sheet issued by Smith & Wesson for these guns. Other items of difference will be found in the suggested classifications given below.

The first issue of the First Model may be found marked "WHITE'S PATENT APRIL 3, 1855" in either one or two lines around the cylinder, or only "PATENTED APRIL 3, 1855." Later issues of the First Model, for the most part, carry a second date, "JUNE 15, 1858," unless the shallow marking has become worn. This last patent applies to the movable thumb piece on the hammer, a feature which was patented by F. H. Harrington, of Springfield, Mass., and assigned by him to Smith & Wesson (Fig. 2). Illustrated on Harrington's patent papers is a gun with the identical lines of the First Model S & W then in production. Whether or not he was employed in the factory operated by Smith & Wesson is not known. The other patent dates generally mentioned in connection with the First Model are July 5, 1859, and December 18, 1860. On the first date was patented a one-piece hammer with a wedge on the top of the nose for operating the cylinder stop spring. This is the type found on the Second and Third Models (Fig. 3). On the second date was patented the conventional thumb catch barrel release (Fig. 4) found on later 22 and 32 caliber models, as well as on many of the First Models. So far the writer has not encountered any First Models carrying these last two patent dates, even though

the thumb catch is found on three of the four issues of the First Model.

Suggested Classifications

Classification of the First, Second, and Third Models has, it is felt, been somewhat confusing. For instance, they have previously been designated as Model No. 1, First Model (oval frame and jointed hammer); Model No. 1, Second Model (flat sides and irregular side plate, western type grips); and Model No. 1, Third Model (similar to Second Model, only with birdshead grips and fluted cylinder). The writer fails to see the necessity of such confusion by adding the "Model No. 1" to each of the three

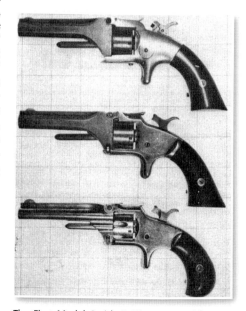

The First Model Smith & Wesson cartridge revolver (top) was placed on the market in 1857. Below it are shown the Second (center) and Third Models of this interesting arm. The author believes that fewer than 20,000 of the First Model arms were produced at S & W's Springfield plant.

models, which incidentally are quite different in design. In this discussion only three simple classifications will be used, the ones in popular use by arms collectors — First Model, Second Model, and Third Model.

As to the variations in the First Model, these will be referred to simply as issues: First Model, first issue; First Model, second issue; and so on. These variations, overlooked so long by writers and dealers, are not only important from a collector's standpoint, but also from the historical angle.

It should be remembered that cartridges, too, went through an evolutionary period. Even Smith & Wesson improved upon their early cartridge in a later patent (No. 27,933 of April 17, 1860), but this improvement was no doubt in use months before that date. Some of the early cartridges bulged at the head upon firing. If they bulged against the frame, it would in all probability lock the cylinder, but by bulging against a revolving plate it would not hamper the revolving of the cylinder for the next shot. So, on the first issue of the First Model is to be found a large size recoil plate (Illus. A). On the back of this plate is a ratchet extending back within the frame, where a hand engages it to revolve the plate. On the face of the plate is a tiny dowel pin, or stud, which fits into a hole in the cylinder to revolve it. As time went by, and ammunition improved, changes were made in the arms themselves. The full size recoil plate gave way to a smaller plate (Illus. B) within a stationary larger plate; next came the hand ratchet but retaining the outer rim of the recoil plate (Illus. C); finally the plain shield as we know it today (Illus. D). The rifling, too, was changed, the three lands and grooves of the left-hand twist being replaced by the five lands and grooves of right twist. While other minor variations may be found in the First Model, it is thought that they are subordinate to the four main issues outlined in this study.

Serial Numbers

Since the records of the Smith & Wesson factory were destroyed by a flood in the early years of the Company, it cannot be stated authoritatively just how many of the First Model were manufactured. It has generally been believed that the First Model and the Second Model were numbered consecutively, and that a total of somewhere around 126,000 were manufactured. It was thought that some 68,000 of the oval-type frame First Model S & W were produced, and 57,400 of the flat-type frame Second Model.

Because of the scarcity of these models, it was the writer's opinion that perhaps not as many were produced as had been thought. This led to the brief survey of existing specimens, from which it would

appear that little more than one-fourth of the original estimated number of the First Model were actually produced. To back up this finding is the fact that in the writer's own collection is a specimen of the Second Model, in its original condition, numbered 18,731. Another known specimen is numbered 20,335, and still another numbered 24,299. So far data on enough specimens has been received to verify the fact that numbers run very consistently upward from the 18,731, the lowest number encountered, to 118,368, the highest number found. If, as hearsay has it, the two Models were numbered consecutively, then it would be logical to assume that the Second Model begins to number somewhere between 11,046, the last number encountered in the First Model survey, and the 18,731 of the Second Model mentioned above. This is some 40,000 fewer than has heretofore been believed to have been manufactured, enough to make quite a difference in the rarity and value of a piece. In any event, the survey indicates that the little First Model S & W, particularly the first issue, is an American rarity of the first order. With the 100th anniversary of their invention less than ten years away, and interest in them increasing, it is hard to predict what price they will bring in a few years.

Many of the First Models were cased in a unique gutta-percha composition box lined with colorful velvet. In the case are holes for holding fifty-six 22 caliber Short rimfire cartridges. The cover, with its high embossing of a miniature reproduction of the First Model and a border design which includes a string of tiny guns and decorative corner motifs, is a work of art. On the cover with the embossed gun is to be found the following wording in relief, "Manufactured only

by Smith & Wesson, Springfield, Massachusetts." While this case is the more familiar, there are at least two other known designs. The cover of one of these has draped flags embossed in the central position. The lid of the other consists only of a very decorative geometrical design. Being as fragile as they are, very few of these unusual cases have survived the more than ninety years since they were made. Fortunate indeed is the collector today who can show his First Model cased in one of them.

In giving the classifications and distinguishing marks of the models and issues, it should be kept in mind that these are from the average manufactured specimens. Specimens will be encountered which do not seem to fill these specifications in every detail. In the transition period between issues, it would be quite possible to have an overlapping either way. Then, too, as in the case with one specimen examined, a later barrel with the five lands and grooves appears to have been installed on an early frame. If so, it was no doubt done not too many years after the gun was issued.

In addition to the number of the gun, found on the butt of the grip and on the inside surface of the wooden stocks, other numbers and letters may be found on various parts of the gun. These are believed to be assembly, inspector's, or fitters' marks.

It seems to be the consensus of leading authorities that the brass frame of the First Model was silver plated rather than nickeled. Examination of specimens retaining at least a part of their finish would seem to verify this opinion. Grips were of rosewood, walnut, ebony, or ivory.

Early Smith & Wessons were often sold in these gutta-percha cases lined with velvet. One type of case has embossed reproduction of pistol on its top. Another shows flags, Masonic emblem, anchor, artist's palette.

(Reprinted by courtesy of *The American Rifleman.*)

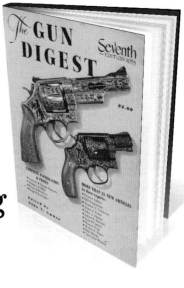

Paterson and Walker Colts

A Few Notes on Gun Collecting

by JOHN S. DU MONT

In 1836, Samuel Colt patented his invention, the first successful revolting-cylinder gun. Cocking the hammer rotated the cylinder at the same time and allowed the user five shots instead of the usual one.

These guns were an immediate success in the Seminole Indian War in Florida, some having been purchased by officers participating. If hen the Indians charged in their usual manner after the first shot hail been fired, they were easily decimated by the remaining four shots, and quickly learned to respect these new weapons.

Colt developed machinery for the manufacture of these guns in order that they could be mass-produced. This called for an investment of $300,000 — an enormous sum in those days. He commenced manufacture at Paterson, N.J., in 1836, continuing until 1842 and producing somewhat over 1,000 guns, in calibers varying from 28 to 40 in the revolvers. Colt also manufactured revolving-cylinder rifles and shotguns of the same elementary design.

Despite herculean efforts, Colt was not successful in interesting the U.S. Army Ordnance Department in his guns, in spite of their obvious advantages over the then standard American military weapons. So, because of lack of large-scale orders, his company failed in 1842. Thus ended the Paterson era.

This picture shows nine variations of the Paterson Colt revolvers in the author's collection, from the large "Texas" models to the "Baby" models with small frames. The early "Texas," or first model, is shown at the top right. These guns all had an English variation — the folding trigger. When the hammer was drawn back to full cock, the trigger was forced out into position by a spring. While this feature had its advantages for holster use, it was found too flimsy for military usage.

As time went on, Colt made various refinements and improvements in design. Not the least of these was the addition of the loading lever, which may be seen on the gun at the top left of the picture.

Today, these guns are extremely rare and are valued collector's items. Prices vary from a few hundred dollars to well over $1,000, depending on the model and its condition. Guns are very much like stamps, and condition is all-important in determining value.

It has been definitely proved that Paterson Colt revolvers were numbered by models, by the existence of three different models all bearing Serial No. 132, and two No. 1's.

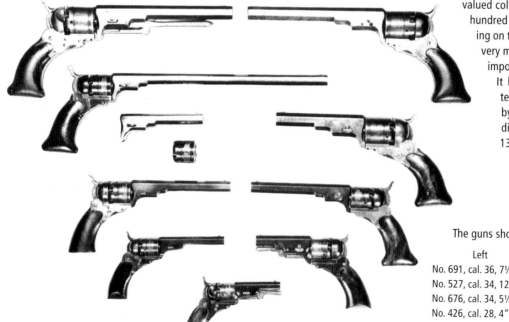

The guns shown left are identified as follows:

Left	Right
No. 691, cal. 36, 7½" bbl.	No. 151, cal. 40, 7½" bbl.
No. 527, cal. 34, 12" and 4½"	No. 950, cal. 40, 5"
No. 676, cal. 34, 5½"	No. 601, cal. 34, 5½"
No. 426, cal. 28, 4"	No. 63, cal. 34, 3"
	No. 111, cal. 28, 2½"

John S. du Mont is President of the Massachusetts Arms Collectors and a member of the Armor and Arms Club of New York. He specializes in collecting Colt handguns, and his collection of these arms is one of the finest in the country. Many of his choicest pieces, with his comments thereon, are illustrated here. His "few notes on gun collecting" are the outgrowth of twenty years' experience in this field. At present he is working on a history of the Custer arms.

Continuing the Colt story, Sam went to work and, through the assistance of Captain Walker of Texas, made many refinements in his original construction and design. After a lapse of five years, in 1847 he produced, with the help of Eli Whitney at Whitneyville, Conn., the so-called "Walker" Colt. This was a massive Dragoon pistol of 44 caliber, weighing over four pounds. This may be considered the gun that "made" Colt: it proved so successful that the Ordnance Department finally became actively interested in the guns. As a result, Colt received government orders for an improved version of the "Walker."

The next three pictures show the Dragoon models that were manufactured at the present home of the Colt Company in Hartford, Conn., circa 1848–1859. They were the first Colts made on government contract, and Colt was finally firmly established.

GUN COLLECTING is a fascinating hobby. Much has been written on the subject — some of it excellent, some passable, and some downright bunk.

The trouble with the "bunk" part is that too many collectors and pseudo-collectors are inclined to believe as gospel anything they see in print.

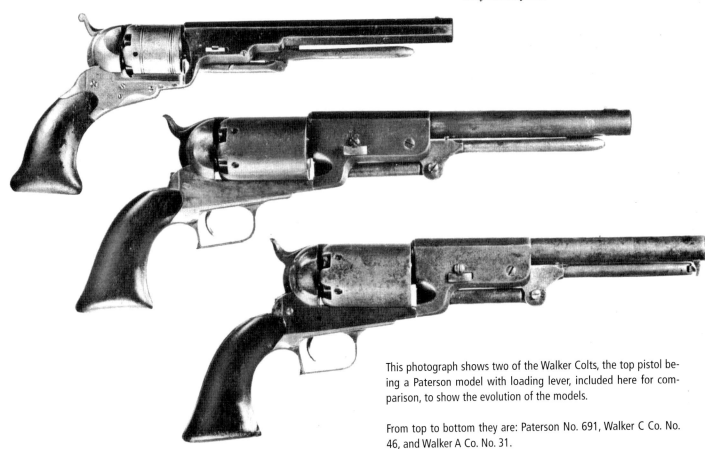

This photograph shows two of the Walker Colts, the top pistol being a Paterson model with loading lever, included here for comparison, to show the evolution of the models.

From top to bottom they are: Paterson No. 691, Walker C Co. No. 46, and Walker A Co. No. 31.

These guns were made to be carried in saddle holsters by mounted Dragoons. Walkers are perhaps the rarest of all Colts from a collector's standpoint, few having survived the rigorous military usage.

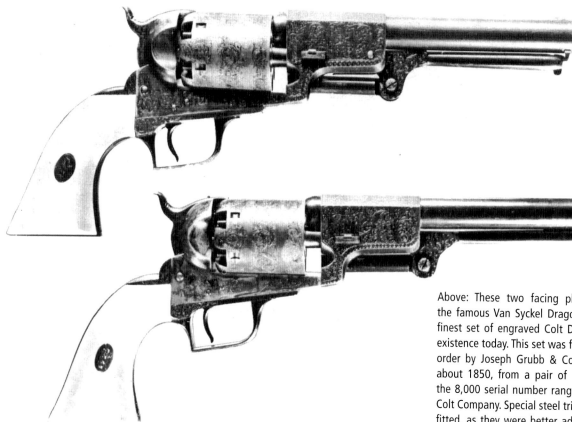

Above: These two facing photographs show the famous Van Syckel Dragoons, possibly the finest set of engraved Colt Dragoon pistols in existence today. This set was finished on special order by Joseph Grubb & Co. in Philadelphia, about 1850, from a pair of Colt Dragoons in the 8,000 serial number range supplied by the Colt Company. Special steel trigger guards were fitted, as they were better adapted to the fine engraving applied.

An advanced collector once told me that the best way to learn guns is to handle and study as many as you can. I believe he is right. Another made the statement that for every gun you buy, you should buy a gun book, and I believe he is right too — if you limit your book buying to those written by authorities.

In gun collecting you are very apt to learn by trial and error. I have, and I know others have too. You can often buy a gun that you later learn to your dismay is not strictly "right" or what you expected. I have heard that there are collectors who have never been stuck by a bad buy, but I have never met these people, and I don't honestly believe I ever will. The "bad buy" is simply the result of lack of collecting knowledge, and we've got to admit it.

We all collect in our own way. Some specialize in certain types or periods of ignition, and the specialist is becoming more and more prevalent. Others simply accumulate, with no plan or program. Unfortunately, these people sooner or later learn that with a few exceptions, their accumulation resembles the local junk merchant's. They find that out definitely when they decide to sell, in order to concentrate on some particular phase of collecting.

I have always felt that the collector should have some definite program in mind, and work with this program.Shooting Master

Protect Your Investment

While you can spend as much or as little as you want to on guns. I have always believed that they are an excellent investment in this world of ever-changing values.

However, it is well to give serious thought to such an investment. Most collectors, over a period of years, wind up with a large amount of money invested in their collections. If the same amount of money was invested in a business, they would watch it like a hawk and give it their full lime. A good collection, therefore, deserves quite a little thought and study. The answer is in books.

With the thousands of books and articles on guns today, we are at last developing some fine and factual writers, of a stature commensurate with the interest in gun collecting — men who base their statements on fact and not on what "Uncle Jeb" said or, worse still, heard.

Inaccuracies have been perpetuated for years, because they were once the statement of some unknowing individual who wrote a book, and someone else copied it.

Writers like John Parsons, James Serven, B. R. Lewis, Cy Karr, Charles Haven, James Hicks, John Amber, Herman Dean, Claud

These guns were made for James Janeaway Van Syckel, a millionaire member of a Philadelphia Militia Regiment. Frames were beautifully case-hardened in colors: backstrap, trigger guard, and rammer were blued, and barrels browned. The guns are completely engraved and have solid ivory grips, inset with gold medallions. The powder flask is sterling silver, made by R. & W. Wilson Co. of Philadelphia, silversmiths of that period. Tools are ebony- and ivory-handled, and the case is made of rosewood, inlaid with brass and German silver.

This beautiful outfit cost $600 in 1850. It was a set fit for a king, and clearly proved that Colt was able to produce a work of art in guns, equal to anything made in the Old World. With Colt's genius, America had forged into the lead in pistol making, a position which it has never relinquished to this day.

Fuller, Richard Steuart, Charter Harrison, and Sam Smith base their statements on fact and exhaustive research. They can be read and believed.

To protect your investment and learn more about guns, read these good books and subscribe to the good collecting papers. It will save heartaches, and pay dividends.

As collectors become advanced collectors, they often become part-time dealers.

Here is the reason. Rare antique guns don't grow on trees. There are only so many, and it is often necessary to buy entire collections to get one or two pieces that are particularly desirable. The balance is then sold, and many smaller collectors benefit.

Dealers — Good, Bad, and Indifferent

I have always believed that reputable dealers were good people to do business with. Over 75 percent of my guns have come through dealers. Their selection is always better — clunkers are usually weeded out — and I have often found their prices lower, contrary to the popular conception.

Dealers are like books — some good, some bad, and some indifferent. But the good, in most cases, predominate. It is rarely that a dealer will knowingly sell a fake. If he does, he is a very poor businessman, for he will shortly have no customers.

Speaking of direct collecting, we all want to find that Paterson Colt in an old trunk for $5, or pick up that "sleeper" in a dealer's stock. It *has* been done, but not as often as you might think.

We all like to brag about the good buys, but there aren't too many these days.

The "Morgan Memorial" Paterson

One classic example is the now-famous "Morgan Memorial" Paterson Colt story. This has been snowballed into a dandy. But the truth must out, so here is the story. I own the gun, and it is illustrated with this article, among the Paterson Colt revolvers in my collection.

This cased Paterson Colt with 12-inch barrel, in new and unfired condition, was enclosed in an old bureau given to the Morgan Memorial, a charity organization in Boston.

The people at the Morgan Memorial did not know what it was, but displayed it for $25. The gun itself, with accessories, did not sell, but a woman thought the case would make a lovely sewing box, and bought it alone.

After a few weeks had passed, a man saw the gun. and thinking it might be valuable, took it to an authority. The latter notified me, and I bought the gun, paying four figures for it, of which the Morgan Memorial got 80 percent.

Two days after this, I took the train to the Ohio Gun Collectors meeting at Columbus, and when I arrived, the story had beaten me there!

I was the hero who bought a mint Paterson for $25. The only unfortunate part was — it wasn't so!

I might add, though, that the Morgan Memorial gets its share of attention these days from local collectors.

Collect with a Plan

If my advice was asked, which it isn't, I would say "Collect with a Plan." Try to get good specimens, or improve on those that you have, but don't start with the mistaken aim of collecting only "mint" pieces. While we all want good ones, the smart boys to whom anything less than "mint" is no good, always wind up missing a lot of good guns and rare guns. I went through this stage, and I have always regretted the time it took me, and the passed-up rarities, to get through it.

The people who originally owned the guns we treasure today *used* those guns. They were made to use, and one hundred years ago, with Indians knocking at your front door, intent on enlarging their scalp collection, you weren't necessarily interested in preserving the finish of a gun someone might collect one hundred years later.

Join a good collecting organization. You can talk guns, see guns, and learn guns. History is a wonderful subject, and guns made American history.

Fifteen years ago, I knew all there was to know about all types of guns — I was an authority. Today, I think there is a remote possibility that I might learn a *little* about certain phases of the Colt guns I collect — if I live long enough!

From a collector's angle, the engraved Dragoons are great rarities. Colt was a very shrewd promoter and presented a number of beautifully engraved models to persons who would be influential in securing him government contracts or notice.

Colt's service to his country through the War Between the States is too well known to be repeated here, and his contribution

to America in mass-producing techniques is part of our heritage.

From a collector's standpoint, there are many variations front the regular lines of manufacture in Colt pistols. Such guns are of great interest; exceptions to the rule and genuine experimental guns are much sought after by collectors. However, it is well, as Serven says, to "beware of the unusual."

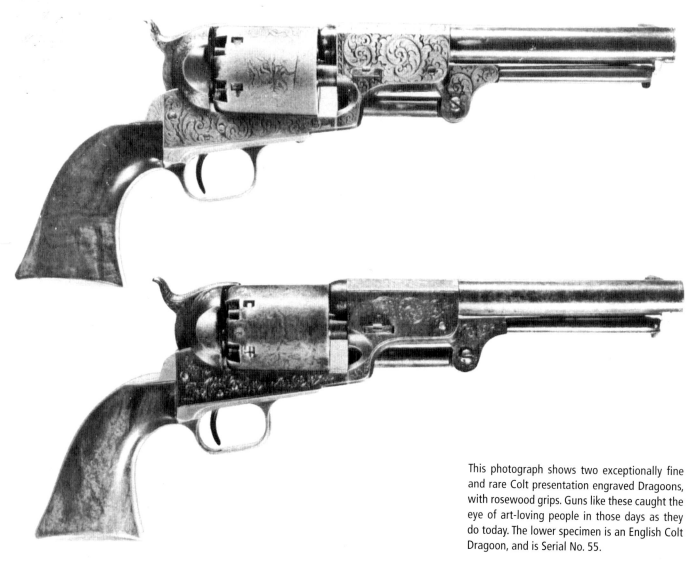

This photograph shows two exceptionally fine and rare Colt presentation engraved Dragoons, with rosewood grips. Guns like these caught the eye of art-loving people in those days as they do today. The lower specimen is an English Colt Dragoon, and is Serial No. 55.

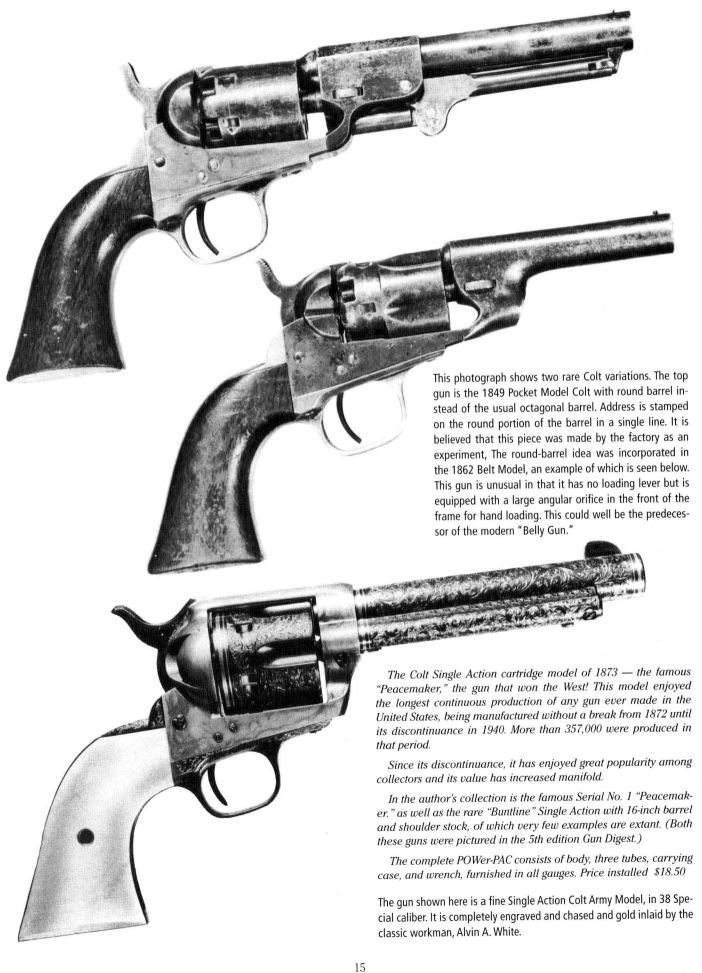

This photograph shows two rare Colt variations. The top gun is the 1849 Pocket Model Colt with round barrel instead of the usual octagonal barrel. Address is stamped on the round portion of the barrel in a single line. It is believed that this piece was made by the factory as an experiment, The round-barrel idea was incorporated in the 1862 Belt Model, an example of which is seen below. This gun is unusual in that it has no loading lever but is equipped with a large angular orifice in the front of the frame for hand loading. This could well be the predecessor of the modern "Belly Gun."

The Colt Single Action cartridge model of 1873 — the famous "Peacemaker," the gun that won the West! This model enjoyed the longest continuous production of any gun ever made in the United States, being manufactured without a break from 1872 until its discontinuance in 1940. More than 357,000 were produced in that period.

Since its discontinuance, it has enjoyed great popularity among collectors and its value has increased manifold.

In the author's collection is the famous Serial No. 1 "Peacemaker." as well as the rare "Buntline" Single Action with 16-inch barrel and shoulder stock, of which very few examples are extant. (Both these guns were pictured in the 5th edition Gun Digest.)

The complete POWer-PAC consists of body, three tubes, carrying case, and wrench, furnished in all gauges. Price installed $18.50

The gun shown here is a fine Single Action Colt Army Model, in 38 Special caliber. It is completely engraved and chased and gold inlaid by the classic workman, Alvin A. White.

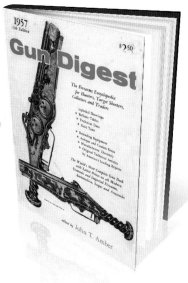

A Man's Sixgun
A Field Test Report on the Ruger and S&W 44 Magnum

by COL. CHARLES ASKINS TECHNICAL DIRECTOR

DURING one somewhat lively decade of an otherwise prosaic life, I worked the Rio Grande as a border patrolman. Every night of that half-score years I wished for just such a shooting iron as this big bruiser, this fine new howitzer, the 44 Magnum. Sometimes we had as many as three separate and distinct gunfights during an 8-hour shift. Had this big Maggie sixgun been around what a lulu of a pacifier it would have been on the border.

This Magnum is a man's gun. It ain't for boys. Word reaches me that some joes, probably with lace on their panties, are putting on gloves to shoot it. I hear that after a few shots your hand feels like you had been swinging at some fast balls with a cracked bat. How soft can we get? I shot the big 44 all one afternoon and found the recoil nothing more than stimulating. The kick kind of reminds me of the existing situation down in Dixie where a certain clientele now buy their white lightnin' over the liquor counter in preference to the smoother and legitimate bourbon. Asked why, they explain it's for the kick. Me, I'm the same way about this big 44 blasting Magnum.

Sure, it kicks. But not enough to hurt your hand, not enough, certainly, to remove any hide. That's for the birds. The re-

---

The new 44 kicks, says Col. Askins, but "not enough to take any hide off."

---

coil is a heart-warming, exhilarating sort of thing. Something like standing behind one of these Nike ground-to-air missiles and setting 'er off with your two sweaty little hands. You feel like you have really done something. I like to shoot the gun. I'm betting you will, too.

When I knew I was going to field test the Magnums for Gun Digest, I scurried about and asked the Kimball Arms Co. for a sample of their 30 (carbine) caliber auto pistol. It appealed to me that it would add a good deal of fillip to the brew if I assembled a modest rack of our more poisonous one-hand guns and then fired 'em all, one against the other. I am still waiting on that Kimball 30 to arrive. Maybe the carbine cartridge doesn't show up too hot in that peewee 5-inch barrel — who knows?

Bill Ruger, after some gentle persuasion sent me the X-2, a strictly pilot model of his soon-to-be-ready 44 Magnum. This is the 357 Blackhawk, essentially, with an especially heavy, non-fluted cylinder. A handsome piece of ordnance.

Bill Wilson, chief *guru* at Great Western, contributed a 7½-inch 357 for the cartridge he likes to call the "Atomic." After the gun got here he wrote me and said he was then making his Single Action for the 44 Magnum cartridge. I'd rather have had it.

I had in my personal battery a 357 S&W Magnum given me by Doug Wesson 20 years ago. I was ready to commence the powder burning ...

The first shot at 25 yards on the Standard American target was an 8 at 7 o'clock with the S&W 44 Magnum. I tinkered with the adjustable rear sight and the remaining four rounds all plopped well within the 10 ring. Despite its three-pound weight the Magnum is easy to hold, and the crisp trigger pull (3 lbs. 3½ oz.) made 10-panning easy. I then switched to ¹⁄₁₆-inch cold-rolled sheet steel stock; the big Maggie ain't intended for target punching, and I felt the sooner we got down to cases the more diverting the afternoon would be.

The big, square-nosed 44 slug plowed a hole through the light metal that measured ⅝-inch in diameter; as this is a bit over 60

The Smith & Wesson
44 Magnum.

caliber it can be appreciated that it mushroomed considerably. The 357 Magnum with standard metal point (Western) loading whipped through the 1/16" plate too, leaving a hole that required a half-inch plug to fill. Likewise quite commendable.

My pardner, George Parker, was over visiting from Arizona and whipping out his favorite equalizer he also poured a slug through the target. He was shooting a 38 Special loaded with a flat-nosed, 150-grain hollow-point ahead of a hefty charge of Bullseye.

At 15, feet the 44 Magnum zipped through a second piece of sheet steel, 1/8-inch in thickness. The 357 Magnum standard factory load did just as well. I slipped a standard factory loaded 44 Special cartridge into the Smith, but it would not penetrate the 1/8-inch plate. Dropping back to the 1/16-inch stuff we found it dented but would not push through this almost paper thin baffle. Small wonder with that pipsqueak charge of 4½ grains of Bullseye! Parker pumped one of his 38 hollow points into the one-eighth-inch piece but it would not cut the mustard.

We switched to plates of 3/16-inch thickness. The big 44 Maggie knocked a sizeable dent in this scrap but it did not break through. The 357 showed less indentation. Thrice more we tested the pair of guns and not during any trial did either perforate the 3/16-inch stock. This, to me, means little. The 240-grain (on my Redding scale it ran as an average 245.4 grains) bullet is as flat and square about the bows as Tugboat Annie. It is almost a complete wadcutter; small wonder, then, that it does not knife through steel plate like a cutting torch. A bit later on in this opus you'll see that it isn't much shakes on wood penetration either, and again the same reason holds true. The big blunt snout commences to mushroom as soon as it meets resistance and as it flattens out it necessarily must push more metal or wood before it, thus slowing down without developing anything very sensational in the way of penetration.

The 357, on the other hand, carried the metal point bullet, a slug with a Lubaloy cap and quite sharply pointed, and should have out-ranged the 44. It did not, at least on metal.

The Ruger X-2 pilot 44 has a 5½-inch barrel, the S&W 44 a 6; there was no perceptible difference in performance between the two. The first 5 shots fired with the X-2 saw the gun throw the cylinder pin back over my shoulder on the 5th and last blast. The cylinder was ready to fall out of the gun. I retrieved the pin, put it back in place and watched it every shot after that. The recoil

is so hot it loosens the cylinder pin latch every shot, and on the experimental Ruger the latch wouldn't hold. This is a prototype gun, of course, and not a production Ruger 44. The company will catch this fault and strengthen the latch, Bill Ruger told me, and that's good enough for me. The production gun will have a 6½-inch barrel, according to Bill.

The first 6 shots with the Great Western 357 Atomic indicated too great headspace. Examination of the cartridges — not those provided by Bill Wilson but standard Western metal piercing stuff — showed the primers were almost pushed out of the primer pockets. The indentation of the firing pin had been completely ironed out, indelible evidence of excessive headspace. I did not fire the GW after this showing.

To get back to the powder burning …

We hied ourselves to the yon side of the pistol butts where a half-dozen old auto engine blocks had been abandoned.

44 Magnum Busts Cylinder Walls and All!

Selecting an old Willys jeep engine I let drive from 15 feet. The 44 Magnum slug cleanly penetrated the waterjacket about the cylinders, and then it struck the true block. A glance inside the cylinder (the head had been removed) was most impressive. A complete selection of the cylinder wall had been broken out. This busted-out portion was 2.1-inches in length and 1.25-inches in width at its widest. The big, flat-ended bullet had never reached the cylin-

der wall at all, but what a hell of a smashing wallop it had delivered there!

I was reminded of fighting tanks that I had seen during WW2 that had suffered in an identical manner. The artillery anti-tank round would not penetrate the fighting compartment but set up such terrific shock waves on the interior surfaces as to create an apalling effect, the metal slabbing off in sections and creating one of the most lethal conditions our crews had to suffer. The 44 Maggie performed in identical fashion on the auto engine.

Three other blocks were fired into and in every case the big bullet broke out metal within the cylinder.

The 357 in standard factory loading would not do this. It never has, despite the hoopla written into advertising these past two decades. The little 357 Magnum will get through the water jacket, which is an integral part of the motor block, but it cannot produce the oomph to do damage to the cylinder walls. I tried some of the so-called 357 Atomic loads of Bill Wilson's, 14.7 grains of #2400 powder as against 13 grains of Western ball powder, and I could see no difference in penetration. The Wilson bullet is the flat-nosed 165-grain all-lead; the Western is the 155 grain metal-capped number; on penetration the latter has the advantage due to the Lubaloy point, at least in my tests.

The next firing was against 3/4-inch selected pine slabs, stacked 1 inch apart, the gun muzzle 18 feet from the first baffle. The 357, standard cartridge, zipped through 12 boards and lodged in the 13th; the 357

"This new 44 Magnum packs a wallop, doesn't it?"

Atomic, 165-grain leaden bullet, 10 boards; the 44 Magnum, 9 boards (both the Smith and Ruger were fired); 44 Special, standard factory cartridge, 6 boards. There was a tiny Walther PPK 22 automatic pistol in the crowd, the barrel only 3½ inches in length. A shot from it penetrated 4 boards. It made the old 44 Special look bad indeed, not that it had been showing up particularly well before that!

We went to 10-lb. sacks of cornmeal. A sack of these grits freely suspended gives an excellent idea of the explosive effect of the bullet. The slug gets inside the sack and as it builds up the mealy substance ahead of the nose a pressure wave bursts out the back side of the sack. The measurement of these ruptured containers, made of a heavily corrugated and treated paper, gives a rough idea of the explosive effect of each bullet.

On the first round, much to our surprise, the 357 outshone the 44. It opened up Snuffy Smith's breakfast mainstay as though a little atomic matter had been riding on the Western slug. But a half-dozen sacks later the 44 Maggie had asserted itself, and clearly it was the more potent of the two. We switched to flour, which is much finer and tends to compress more readily. The results were the same, the 44 does the most damage, the 357 next. The 44 Special punches a hole not much bigger on exit than on entry. There is no explosive reaction whatever.

Tomato Juice Shower

The flour and hominy grits consumed, we switched to what proved to be the most spectacular, all out targets, half-gallon cans of tomato juice. The big 44 Magnum at 18 feet performed on these hermetically sealed tins in a fashion that would have done credit to the new Winchester 458 elephant gun. I put the bullets into the can endways. Struck by the 240-gr., hell-for-leather slug, the can was invariably rent at every seam. The far end was in every instance blown off and lost. The body of the can was not only torn asunder but almost completely straightened of its curved shape. It looked like someone had laboriously opened it and pounded the metal into a flattened sheet. At 18 feet both gunner and photo-man were showered with juice from head to foot. Watching, I could see the red liquid jetted skyward for what looked like at least 20 feet. It was a most impressive display of smashing force, the like of which I had never seen in a handgun before in many years of shooting.

The 357 opened up the tins too, but not in nearly such convincing fashion. The 44 Special poked a hole through either end, the bullet on exit knocking out a drain hole running a little over a half-inch. No seams were opened.

The 44 Magnum is a hunter's gun for sure. I wondered what it would do at 100 yards and maybe out as far as 200. I sighted in for 50 yards, and once I had the bullets printing right over the top of the ⅛-inch, big red patridge-type post, I let drive at 100 yards. The shooting was from a bench rest; the bullets dropped 8 inches. At 200 yards, still with the 50 yard sight-setting, the fall was 20 inches. Once on the paper at 200 yards (I was using the Army "A" target with 12-inch bull) I adjusted my sights and got into the black. The resulting 10 shot score was 47; 7 hits in the black and 3 not-very-wide 4s. This was with a muzzle rest, remember, but even so it was a most convincing demonstration of the long-ranging capabilities of this new cartridge.

Four of our most powerful revolvers. Upper left — Great Western 357 Atomic; upper right — S&W 357 Magnum; lower left — Ruger "X-2" pilot model 44 Magnum; lower right — S&W 44 Magnum.

Even the big heavy S&W gun rears back in recoil when the 44 Magnum load is touched off.

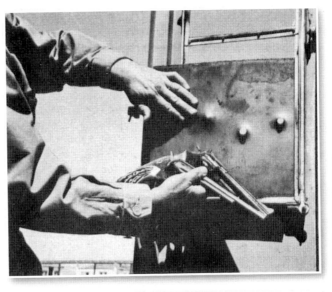

Out on the desert, I set up a Colt silhouette target at a little more than 300 yards. Sitting down with the 44 S&W over one knee, I hit the over-sized man 4 shots out of the cylinder full. The old tradition that the sixgun is strictly an infighting weapon doesn't hold true — not with this new Hellstrom howitzer or the roaring Ruger!

Way down in this end of the world we have a jackrabbit that is the toughest to be found anywhere. This is partly due to the fact that he's a Texas jackrabbit, which makes him all rawhide and tough sinew, but more probably because there are years out here when to get a bellyfull a jack must travel 20 miles in a night. By that time he has found a half-handful of mesquite beans and little else. Ordinary bullets on this class of *conejo* have been known to slip right between the skinny and rope-like gut of this long-eared target, causing him little or no anguish, and leaving the marksman no little baffled and confused.

Sure of Hits on Jacks

Seven big rangy jacks were hit squarely amidships with the 44 Maggie. The bullet lifted them a foot-and-a-half in the air and when they struck, no matter the distance, it sounded just like slapping a pony across the rump with a wet slicker. There is a hell of a plopping sound — no need to turn up your Sonotone to be sure a hit has been registered.

I used to ride the desert and shoot a dozen rabbits every day to feed a pack of kyoodles we had for tracking smugglers. I used every big bore sixgun in the book, but mostly because the hulls didn't cost me anything, I killed my dog meat with the 45 ACP cartridge. More than once I have up-ended a jack rabbit fairly and squarely and, riding over to gather him in, had the hardy rascal recover from the first shock of the heavily jacketed, slow-moving bullet and go galloping off across the mesquite flats.

The desert jack struck with the 44 Magnum does not do that. When he takes one fairly placed between wind and water he folds. The game seasons, unfortunately, are all closed in these hyar parts so nothing but pest game can be tried with the Magnum. The gun will kill much bigger beasties than 12-pound jackrabbit. Just how much larger is going to depend on the shooting skill and hunting know-how of the handgun marksman. ⊕

Firing at $^1/_{16}$" steel plate (above). Big hole in middle made by 44 Magnum. Hole to right from 357 Magnum, standard factory metal point. Indentation to left made by factory 44 Special.

Col. Askins (left) inspects havoc wreaked on half-gallon can of tomato juice struck by 44 Magnum. He was showered by the liquid at a distance of 18 feet.

My velocity checks of the 44 Remington Magnum loads, taken with the *Hollywood* Chronograph show an average velocity over 25 feet of 1520 f.p.s. against 1570 f.p.s. at the muzzle claimed by Remington. This small difference didn't affect the 10-lb. sack of flour used as a target — it was busted wide open.

The Luger Pistol

by FRED A. DATIG

FOR GENERATIONS the most famous name in pistols has been *Luger*. There is no country however small or insignificant in which that name, or its foreign counterpart, *Parabellum*, is unfamiliar. To make the statement that it is the world's finest, most accurate, well designed or generally the "best" pistol would merely be expressing an opinion, but what are the reasons for its popularity? Why has it been accepted as the "best" and what is the story behind its phenomenal success?

To relate the tale from the beginning we must go back to a well known arms designer of his day, Hugo Borchardt, a naturalized American citizen. Borchardt was a mechanical genius of some note, for he not only entered the inventing profession at an early age but also developed many diversified types of mechanical devices.

The earliest record we have of Borchardt, as applied to the weapons field, is a letter written in his own hand to Mr. E. G. Westcott, President and Treasurer of The Sharps Rifle Co. of Hartford, Conn., dated March 18, 1875, when Borchardt was applying for the position of Superintendent of that company:

"… I took the superintendency of a shop in the worst condition at Trenton (New Jersey), designed the tools and finished a contract for 5,000 guns to the entire satisfaction of the Co. Mr. Meecham, who was treasurer of The Pioneer Breechloading Arms Co., hesitated at first in placing confidence in me, owing very likely to my age, I was 24 years old. There were about 60 hands employed. I afterwards had a foremanship in Singer (Sewing Machine Co.?) and several other places…."

His first patent, for a bullet grooving machine, was issued on July 21, 1874. This was followed by a bullet patching machine in 1875, a breech-loading firearm (Sharps-Borchardt) in 1876, a gun sight in 1877, another breechloading firearm, a shirt neck shaper, a magazine; rock driller; wire straightener; recoil magazine pistol (Borchardt Pistol, 1893), and numerous others.

Borchardt was versatile indeed, but it appears that his many patents added few coins to his coffers, for he was constantly changing jobs and addresses. His part in developing the Sharps-Borchardt rifle was his greatest achievement before forsaking his adopted country for Europe, where he remained for the rest of his life. He did not, however, give up his American citizenship.

Georg Luger was born in Steinach in Tirol in 1849. Originally an officer in the Austrian Army and with a decided liking for mechanical things, he became acquainted with Herr Mannlicher, inventor, among countless other designs, of the Austrian Infantry Ordnance Rifle. Together these two wizards produced an automatic, army rifle, (Luger's military career was at an end) opening the door to a new vocation, one that was to make Luger world renowned.

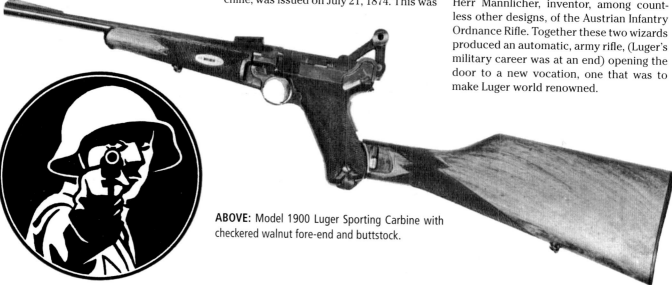

ABOVE: Model 1900 Luger Sporting Carbine with checkered walnut fore-end and buttstock.

In 1891 Luger held a position with the firm of Ludwig Loewe of Berlin, from whence he was sent shortly thereafter to exhibit yet another military rifle in the United States, and where he more than likely first met Hugo Borchardt.

It is known that Borchardt left the United States and took a position as director of the Hungarian Arms Company, but he soon had a disagreement with the Hungarian War Minister, General Fejervary, and undoubtedly through the influence and persuasion of his new friend, Georg Luger, was offered a job with Loewe, which he accepted.

The next we hear of Herr Luger is in the year 1894 when he is once again exhibiting a new weapon before the United States Naval Ordnance Board. That new design was a semi-automatic pistol named after its creator, Borchardt!

The Borchardt Pistol was patented in all of the major countries between 1893 and 1896. Sometime in 1893 the "Automatic Pistol, Borchardt Patent" was offered for sale on the commercial market to the world at large. It was of the finest precision workmanship and only the very best materials were used in its construction. The pistol carried a beautiful, glossy satin finish. The barrel was approximately caliber 30, using a special bottlenecked cartridge. This cartridge was the forerunner of (and interchangeable with) the well known caliber 30 (7.63mm) Mauser round. It is also almost identical to the 7.63mm Mannlicher Pistol cartridge, Model of 1896.

The Borchardt was sold in the United States for $30.00 — that price included a wooden shoulder stock with detachable cheekpiece, leather holster, 3 spare magazines, a wooden dummy magazine which included tools, ramrod and oiler and an instruction manual. For an extra $5.00 a fitted leather case was included. Unfortunately, few of these complete outfits remain intact today although they may be encountered from time to time in some of the larger collections.

The Borchardt Pistol was originally marketed by the Loewe firm but soon after the weapon was placed on the market, that company absorbed the Deutsche Metallpatronenfabrik of Karlsruhe, forming a company thereafter known as the *Deutsche Waffen and Munitionsfabriken* of Berlin-Karlsruhe (January 1, 1897). After that date all weapons were manufactured at the DWM plant in Berlin, and only ammunition was made at the Karlsruhe subsidiary.

On November 22, 1894, the Boston Herald printed a glowing report about Borchardt and his new pistol, noting that Georg Luger exhibited the new gun before a U. S. Navy small arms board at Providence, R. I. on November 21, and "that it had a great future before it." The account went on to say that the "exhibitor fired 24 shots in 43¾ seconds … range 110 feet, and all were hits." The magazine was described as holding "eight cartridges, with nickel jacketed bullets," and these were "the Luger rimless type."

It is interesting to note that it was Georg Luger and not Hugo Borchardt who brought the pistol to this country for these tests. Notice that the cartridge is indicated as being of the "LUGER rimless type" which leads us to believe that Georg Luger might have had more to do with the marketing of the pistol than is generally believed. Also of interest is the fact that although the press gave it an excellent notice the U. S. Navy failed to follow up the tests with any further trials of the Borchardt Pistol.

Georg Luger (1849–1923).

The U. S. Army also tested the Borchardt, for the Chief of Ordnance ordered a board of officers to meet at Springfield Armory on October 20, 1897 "to make a thorough test of, and report upon, a Borchardt Automatic Pistol Carbine." This test was not pursued further so it may be assumed that the pistol did not meet with the complete approval of the officers on the board.

Georg Luger was more than an employee of the new firm of DWM. He received a handsome salary, could patent all of his inventions at company cost and had all of his traveling expenses cared for by the firm. Having no definite office hours, he was more of a partner with a fixed salary and a lengthy contract. After five years his salary was doubled and his contract extended. A point of interest which should be interjected here is that Luger spelled his name exactly that way … LUGER, and not LUEGER or LEUGER as has been erroneously quoted. His personal signature, as early as 1896, bears this out, and members of the Luger family do not recall the name ever having been spelled any other way.

According to close friends and relations, Borchardt and Luger were the best of personal friends though they oftgn had their differences at the factory. Years after the deaths of their husbands the two widows were constant companions. Luger had a son, Georg, Jr., who lives today in Berlin at the age of 81, and who has been of invaluable assistance to the author in bringing to light many of the facts concerning the Luger Pistol and its famous inventor. Herr Luger, Jr. was a famous pistol shot, with a Luger, of course, though he modestly disclaims any outstanding ability. His life was spent with much larger and more complicated weapons than those produced by his sire, namely torpedoes.

Excellent though it was, especially in relations to the other pistols of its day, the Borchardt left a great deal to be desired. The inventor believed his gun to be perfect, though, and so steadfast were his refusals to redesign even the smallest component that DWM, the manufacturers, called upon Herr Luger to make the desired changes. This he did in the following manner. The strong and sturdy action of the Borchardt was retained along with many other of the original features, some being altered slightly and others quite radically. The barrel, though shortened, maintained its long, slim appearance. The grip was inclined at an angle to the receiver and the recoil spring was incorporated in the grip, thereby doing away with two major problems, the angle of the grip and the bulky, protruding, recoil spring housing. The trigger and trigger cover were altered, the latter now completely concealing the rollerpin of the sear and partially covering the sear itself. The position of the ejector was changed from beneath the breechblock to the right side of the receiver, while the extractor remained unchanged. The lanyard ring was moved from the left side of the receiver to the rear, just above the grip safety, a new feature. Buttstock and toggle-knob were completely done away with and all screws, with the exception of the ones holding the wooden grips to the frame, were replaced by pins. The sights remained unchanged.

In the latter part of 1898, November 24 to December 8, a series of pistol trials were

Original Borchardt automatic pistol, Model 1893, cal. 7.65mm Borchardt. Weight 40 oz., overall length 14".

held at Bern, Switzerland by a board of army officers. Other pistols entered were: Mauser with 10-shot magazine, Mauser with 6-shot magazine; Bergmann with 10-shot magazine; Borchardt-Luger with 8-shot magazine; Roth with 10-shot magazine; Mannlicher with 7-shot magazine.

Explanation, assembly and firing of 50 rounds followed; then timing per firing of each weapon; target shooting, 3 frames each at 50 meters; endurance of 400 rounds without cleaning or cooling, etc. The Borchardt-Luger was the only weapon in the endurance test to perform satisfactorily. Then followed dust and water tests, and the firing of 20 rounds in each weapon. Again the Borchardt-Luger was the only weapon without malfunction. The point of greatest interest is the fact that the pistol is referred to as the "Borchardt-Luger." This was a transition piece, a true cross between the Borchardt and the Luger which was to evolve from this and a later Swiss test.

A second series of tests were conducted by the Swiss. They were held at Thun on May 1 to 3, 1899. The Mauser, Bergmann, Roth and Mannlicher Pistols of the previous trials were retested. New models of the Mauser, Hauff and Browning were listed as were the new Mannlicher and a new Borchardt-Luger — these latter two having been modified according to the wishes of the Board. The 1899 tests were conducted in a manner similar to those of the previous year. The Borchardt-Luger of the latter tests was described as "made lighter in weight and fitted with a new safety." It is more than coincidental that the United States patent on this piece was applied for *two days* before the start of these tests!* The patent for the first of the true Luger pistols was filed on March 17, 1900 (British Patent 4399; March 7, 1900) but was not granted in the United States until March 1, 1904 (75,414). This was a remarkably lengthy patent — 7½ pages of text and 10 pages of drawings and diagrams! Georg Luger wanted to be absolutely certain that no one would swipe the slightest detail of his new design.

In contrast to the Borchardt, the "Pistole Parabellum," or "Parabellum Automatic Pistol, Borchardt-Luger System, Swiss Model 1900," was all that had been expected of it. The weight had been decreased from 40 to 30 ounces, the barrel length from 7¼ to 4¾ inches and the overall length from 14 to 9 inches. Also, because greater accuracy could now be got from the pistol, the butt-stock was no longer necessary and thereby lessened the weight by another 15 ounces.

The Model 1900 was the first weapon to bear the famous scrolled *DWM*, trademark of the Deutsche Waffen und Munitionsfabriken of Berlin, where all earlier models were made.

A note of interest is the origin of the name "Parabellum," thought to derive from a Latin phrase, *Si Vis Pacem Para Bellum*. Translated into German this became *Bereite Den Krieg vor Parabellum*, or in English, "If you Want Peace, Prepare For War." Consequently, as the pistol was intended as a military weapon, the "For War" or "Parabellum" name came to be coined.

It is known throughout the world today by that name. In mentioning the name "Luger" to a European, with the possible exception of the English, do not be surprised to be met with only a blank stare! The name "Luger" was first applied to the pistol by Hans Tauscher, first representative for the Borchardt and Luger Pistols in the U.S., and later, after World War I, was registered by the post-war importer, A. F. Stoeger; consequently, the name "Luger," although not an American name has become an American term! In some instances the name "Borchardt-Luger," "Borchardt-Luger Parabellum" and designations such as "P.08" (meaning "Pistol, Model 1908," the year the Germany Army first adopted the Luger), "M943," the Portuguese military title, "Pistole 1900," the Swiss version, etc. may be encountered.

The Model 1900 became a success overnight. On April 2, 1901, the Swiss "Bundesrate," or governing body, officially became the first to adopt it by placing an order with DWM for 3000 pistols. On April 16, 1901, the Commanding Officer of Springfield Armory was officially directed to purchase 1000 Lugers for test by troops of the United States Army! Rock Island Arsenal was directed to fabricate a sufficient quantity of russet or black leather holsters and hardened steel combination tools. The 1000 pieces purchased by the U.S. were marked with small ordnance-bomb proofs, and most of the holsters carried the familiar "U.S." on the flap. These pistols were the original "American Eagle" type, being so marked over the chamber. As far as can be determined these marks were unofficially stamped, and later commercial types carried on with the identical crest. Because these pistols and holsters were issued to and used by U.S. troops, they are considered by some to be U.S. martial weapons!

The Swiss and Americans were not the only ones to test the Model 1900 for in 1903 and 1904 at Rosenburg, Sweden, extensive government trials found the Luger and the Model 1903 Browning in the semi-finals. Although the Swedish report favored the Browning it noted that the Swiss were issuing the Luger to mounted troops. Similar reports indicate that the Parabellum was issued to German officers for use in the Boxer Rebellion in 1901. Other countries to test the Luger in those early days included Austria, Spain, Canada, Russia, Brazil, Luxemburg, Holland, Bulgaria, Norway, Portugal, Chile and several others.

Between 1901 and 1906 rapid advancement was made in making the Luger a better gun, with both military and commercial markets in mind. The first modification of the original was offered in 1902, and was designated the model of that year. Few of these were produced — the type is quite scarce today — but they'll be remembered for one outstanding reason; they were the first weapons to chamber the 9mm Luger cartridge! Now, half a century later, it is by far the most popular and widely used cartridge in the world. This was an unusual situation — the pistol itself was not successful but the cartridge flourished. Probably an accident — or could it have been planned that way?

The first model to be officially adopted by the German Government was the "Marine Modell 1904," or what has become known as the "Navy" Luger. Thus it was the German Navy and not the Army who first realized the merits of the Luger. The Naval Luger has a 6-inch barrel with a 2-position rear sight situated on the extreme rear of the rear toggle link. Caliber was the new 9mm.

One of the most interesting, different, costly and coveted variations of the Parabellum is the "Luger Carbine," which was introduced about 1904 in an attempt to compete with similar weapons marketed at that time by Mauser, Mannlicher and Bergmann. With a barrel too long to be practical as a pistol and too short to meet the requirements of a rifle, it was more nearly the equivalent of a "brush gun." The Luger Carbine is actually a Model 1900 with a heavy 11¾-inch barrel recoiling within a checkered walnut fore-end, and detachable walnut shoulder stock. The 100 to 300 meter rear sight is mounted on the barrel just in front of the chamber. Despite the many rumors of special specimens with assorted differences, all Luger Carbines of the factory production lot are identical and were only produced in caliber 7.65mm Luger. A special cartridge containing one-seventh more powder and having a blackened case was developed for use in the Carbine models.

The German Kaiser, Wilhelm II, because he had difficulty in handling a full sized hunting rifle due to the deformity of his left arm, was extremely fond of hunting deer on his many estates armed with his Luger Carbine. When, prior to the First World War, the President of the United States, Theodore Roosevelt, paid a visit to Germany, he was a guest of the German emperor on at least one of those hunting excursions and was presented with a Luger Carbine by the Kaiser. This gun bears a plaque denoting the presentation, and may be seen today at Roosevelt's home in New York on display with his many other weapons.

The year 1906 brought what was to become known as the "New" Model. This is a colloquial designation, not necessarily an official factory term. The part that was new in the "New" Model was the replacing of the old laminated flat recoil spring with one of coiled type. As all Lugers after 1906 have the coiled spring, they are all designated as "New Models," and consequently all models with the flat recoil spring are called the "Old" Model.

Of even greater historical interest than the U.S. Army Tests of 1901 were the trials that took place in the spring of 1907. These were the tests which led to the adoption by the U.S. Government of the Colt Automatic Pistol, caliber 45, but not before it had successfully competed and won out against the caliber 45 Luger! Records indicate that two, possibly three, of these large Lugers were personally produced by Georg Luger and brought by him to the United States for the Army Tests. Prior to his arrival, Frankford Arsenal supplied him

with 5000 rounds of caliber 45 ammunition with which to experiment. Luger pulled the bullets and, with his own special powder, loaded 11mm Bergmann cases which thereby formed the 45 Luger cartridge. The tests were originally planned for the year 1906 but Luger was ill and the tests were postponed until the following year!

The 45 Luger is merely an enlarged version of the 9mm Model 1902/06 with slight modifications necessitated by the use of the larger cartridge. The only specimen known to exist today bears the serial number "2" and is truly a fine example of Luger workmanship. The initials "GL" appear on the rear toggle link while the absence of proof marks corroborates the fact that this was a super special experimental pistol never intended for sale.

As mentioned earlier, the German Army adopted the Luger in 1908, a move which insured its success for decades to come. The grip safety was omitted from the Model 1902/06 and the first specimens were produced without any accomodation for a "holdopen device." No stock attachments appeared on these early "P.08's."

With the adoption came large orders which could not be filled in the time allot-

ted by DWM. Consequently, the Royal German Arsenal at Erfurt was appointed co-manufacturer. Many thousands of Lugers were turned out of that great establishment, all bearing the insignia of the arsenal, a large crown surmounting the name "Erfurt," stamped on the forward toggle link instead of the DWM trademark. Almost all DWM and Erfurt Lugers produced for the military will bear the date of manufacture and acceptance stamped into the receiver ring. A new system of numbering was initiated wherein the block of numbers never exceeded 9,999. Once that figure was reached a letter was added beneath the numbers beginning with "a" and so on through the alphabet. This letter becomes as much a part of the serial number as the numbers themselves, a point to remember when recording serial numbers on Luger pistols. Without the inclusion of the letter, hundreds of Lugers would carry the identical number and the difficulties which might arise may well be imagined.

In 1914, Germany entered the Great War armed with two basic Lugers, the military Model of 1908/14 and the Naval Model of 1904/14. The military or Army Model is almost identical to the Model 1908. All types have a 4-inch barrel, stock lug, hold-

DWM Lugers with various barrel lengths; left to right: 3⅝", 4", 4¾", 6", 7", and 8".

Disassembling the Luger: remove the magazine (J) and make sure the chamber is EMPTY. With the right hand, grasp the pistol as shown, pulling the barrel and receiver (E) rearward firmly. Rotate the locking bolt (D) 90° downward; the trigger plate (C) will now fall out. The barrel and receiver may be slid forward off frame (A). The breech-block and toggle linkage (F) may be separated from the receiver by pushing out the connecting pin (H). The trigger (B) and the locking bolt may also be removed if desired. To assemble, reverse operations — make sure that the coupling link (G) does not hang into magazine well but drops behind it and in line with link lever (K).

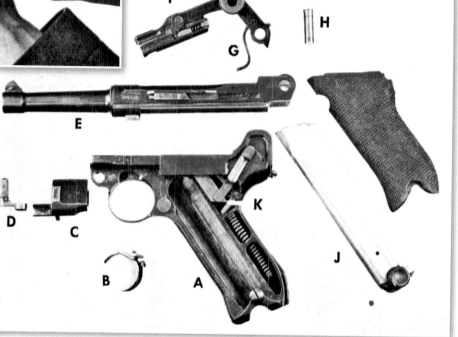

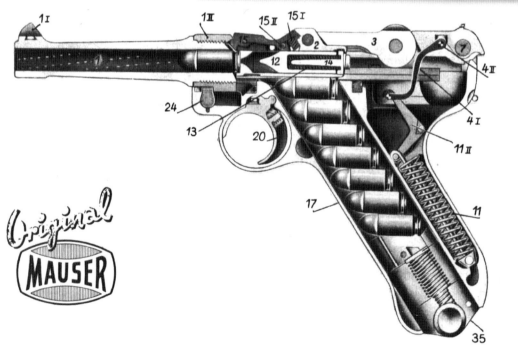

1—barrel.
1'—front sight.
1"—receiver.
2—breechblock.
3—front toggle link.
4'—coupling link.
4"—coupling link pin.
7—connecting pin.
11—mainspring.
11"—coupling link lever.
12—firing pin.
13—firing pin spring.
14—breechblock end piece.
15—extractor.
15'—extractor spring.
15"—extractor pin.
17—grip frame.
20—trigger.
24—locking bolt.
35—magazine.

Original
MAUSER

open device and a letter of the alphabet following the *four* digit serial number. All are caliber 9mm and will have the date of manufacture over the chamber. According to unofficial sources, approximately 2 million 4-inch barrelled Military Models were produced by both manufacturers, DWM and Erfurl, during the First World War period. In addition to this staggering figure, about 50 million replacement parts were supplied. The majority of these pistols and parts were of DWM manufacture.

Like the military Model, the Naval Model was also exactly the same as the earlier Navy Model of 1908 (1904/08), except for having a wartime date over the chamber. All had the 6-inch barrel, stock lug, 2-position rear sight, and a letter following the serial number. Not nearly as many Navy Models were produced due to the much smaller demands of the junior service.

In 1914, a new model was introduced, "new" consisting of the fitting of an 8-inch barrel to the standard Military Model, and the elimination of the rear sight from the rear toggle link. The caliber was 9mm and the back sight, of tangent type, was on the rear of the barrel just forward of the barrel flange. In this respect, it is similar to that on the Luger Carbine, but the sight itself was not the same. It is adjustable from 100 to 800 meters in 100-meter graduations. One unusual thing about this sight is that it has built-in drift allowance to the left. In other words, when the sight is elevated, it not only moves upward but also to the left to compensate for the drift of the bullet over long ranges. Some front and rear sights are adjustable by means of a tiny set screw on the front sights of Naval models. The Model 1914, or "Long Barrelled Model" as it is sometimes called, was issued complete with a long holster, a shoulder stock and a 32-round helical, or snail, drum. It is claimed that these were issued especially to artillery troops, to machine gun units, and to auxiliary cruisers or "Z" boats in place of a rifle or carbine. The reasoning behind this move was, undoubtedly, that a lighter, smaller and more compact side-arm than the rifle was needed — one that could easily be converted into a pistol-carbine for long range firing, and be much handier for the man who had to serve larger weapons. These "Long Barrelled Models" are quite handy and extremely accurate, and all in all, are a pleasure to fire. The loaded drum makes for a rather bulky weapon but not really as bad as one might think.

After World War I

If there is any period in the complete history of the Luger where almost every rule is broken regarding models, variations, se-rial numbers, or anything on which a definite conclusion may be based, it is found in the post-World War I period. Perhaps the most important influence upon Luger production after that war was the Treaty of Versailles. This Treaty limited production to calibers not larger than 8mm and barrels no longer than 100mm, or 3 15/16 inches. These restrictions did not require a complete retooling by Luger manufacturers, however, as the pistol is so designed that by merely changing the barrel, *and no other parts*, the Luger is transformed from one caliber to the other! Because the standard military issue barrel was 4 inches, or 1/16th-inch longer than the terms of the Treaty would allow, the barrel had to be shortened in order to conform. The Germans chose a barrel with a length of 3⅝ inches or approximately 98mm. This model became known as the post-War Model, or the Model 1923.

For all practical purposes, the Model 1923 was a Military Model of the 1908/14 type with the two differences of the short-er barrel and smaller caliber. Strangely enough, this Model 1923 was produced almost exclusively for export outside of Germany. The Germans themselves, theoretically restricted by the Treaty of Versailles, continued not only to use the 4-inch barrelled 9mm weapon but also to manufacture them for military and police use inside Germany.

Also under the terms of the Treaty, Germany was permitted to retain an army of 100,000-man strength. These men had to be armed and they assuredly were. In the days immediately following the war, regular Military Models of 1908/14 were issued to this army. These were pistols that had either seen service during the war or were assembled from parts that had been finished but never issued. The only distinctive marking of these particular guns was a new date of issue added to the one already marked over the chamber. Consequently, we find the "two-date" model. (For example, a Luger that already had the date "1918" over the chamber now had "1920" *above* the "1918," *not superimposed* upon it. Both dates may be easily distinguished.) These pistols were quickly relegated to the police, however, for whom the "second rate" weapons would suffice, and this double-dating became an out-moded practice very rapidly. In a very few instances, the "two-date" Model may be found with police or military markings on the forward part of the frame, just below the trigger guard.

By 1920 the Germans had begun to manufacture or assemble (probably the latter), "as new" Lugers for the Army. These, too, were EXACTLY like the Model 1908/14 except that they were dated "1920," "1921" or "1922." As I recall, I have never seen any with dates other than these three years. These Lugers were of very fine workmanship, for this period, and appear to have been made entirely of new parts.

Somehow the German Navy benefited by this "stretching" of the limits of the Treaty of Versailles, as Naval Model Lugers have been seen, precisely 1908/14 specifications in all respects, also dated "1920," etc. and with no other date. Almost all of these types were caliber 9mm! A few have been encountered in caliber 7.65mm, however.

About 1922 the old, established arms firm of Simson & Co. of Suhl, Germany was given a contract to supply Lugers to the 100,000-man Reichswehr. According to reliable sources, they were the only official suppliers of pistols for the 10-year period 1922 to 1932. These Simson & Co. Lugers were assembled from surplus parts left over in large quantities from World War I. In some cases, the receivers were dated. The only date so far seen on Simson & Co. Lugers, however, is that of 1918; the majority of them have the date ground from the receiver ring, leaving it without markings. A few such pieces have been noted chambered for the 7.65mm Luger cartridge. It is more than likely that such pistols were intended for the commercial market, as were possibly a few of those chambered for the 9mm cartridge. Simson & Co. Lugers are identical with the standard Military Model of 1908/14 type, except for markings. All examples observed have 4-inch barrels, stock lug, holdopen, etc. Instead of the DWM trademark, the words "Simson & Co., Suhl" appear on the forward link of the toggle. Lugers assembled by Simson are relatively uncommon but they can hardly be considered "rare"; let's call them "scarce."

Great numbers of ex-military issue Lugers were "rejuvenated" and heaped upon the commercial market. Some of these were rebarrelled with "as new" surplus military barrels and others were not rebarrelled at all. Almost all had the dates ground from the receiver ring. Original proof marks were often ground away also and replaced by commercial proof marks of that period. In some cases, the old marks were left on, and one or two commercial ones were added.

An extremely interesting and unusual piece, whether it is of this period or not, is the so-called "Baby" Luger chambered for the 7.65mm Browning, or .32 ACP, cartridge! This strange experimental pistol is reported as "smaller in the overall" than

RIGHT: Model 1902 Luger, first to use the 9mm Parabellum cartridge. Note heavy 4" bbl. and magazine cartridge counting strip.

ABOVE: Swiss Model 1929 (06/29) Luger, cal. 7.65mm, 4¾"bbl. Note stepped receiver ring, the "S" above thumb safety, the straight line of the grip, and the grip safety.

LEFT: A. F. Stoeger Luger imported by that firm in the 1930s. (Photo courtesy Sidney Aberman.)

ABOVE: ERMA 22 conversion unit fitted to Luger.

ABOVE: The rare 45 cal. Luger, serial #2, submitted tor U. S. Army test in 1907. (Photo courtesy Sidney Aberman.)

LEFT: Model 1900/06 American Eagle Luger. Note LOADED on the extractor instead of the more common GELADEN. Cal. 7.65mm.

an ordinary Luger, or approximately in the same relation to a standard Luger as the "Baby" Nambu is to a large Nambu Pistol. Very few of these pieces were produced, the number reportedly not more than a dozen. One example has been reported as bearing the serial number "8" and with the DWM trademark on the toggle. No other specifications have been forthcoming.

Another experimental Luger, certainly worthy of special note, is the "5-shot" or "Pocket" Luger, consisting of a shortened (possibly 2-inch) barrel, normal action and shortened frame, housing a 5-cartridge capacity magazine. The "5-shot" was one of extremely limited production, no more than one or two examples having been produced.

Even before the machine pistol, or submachine gun as it is known in this country, first emerged as an accepted military weapon, attempts were made to convert the Luger from semi-automatic to fully automatic fire. Though many attempts were made, none went beyond the experimental stages. This was, undoubtedly, due to the

Experiments were conducted at the factory in an attempt to perfect a silencer for the Luger. These tests called for removing "0.36 gram of powder (from the cartridge) and replacing it with only 0.25 gram of powder." This charge reduction was necessary because the bullet velocity had to be reduced below the speed of sound (1126 feet per second at 68 degrees Fahrenheit) or the silencer could not function efficiently. To further insure the lower velocity the weight of the bullet was increased. However, one problem remained — the silencer functioned as desired, but the pistol would fire only as a single shot. This was because "a Luger with silencer does not function automatically due to the heavier bullet and lesser powder charge, the gas pressure being too small to allow sufficient recoil for normal functioning of the action." No record of further similar tests has been uncovered.

By 1930 the confusion and restrictions of the post-war period had begun to relax and standardization again became the order of the day. Once more DWM changed

military was terminated in 1932, however, and no more Lugers were produced by that firm thereafter.

About 1933, when Adolph Hitler rapidly ascended to power, steps were taken to legally sidestep most of the restrictions placed upon Luger production. The point was argued, and won, that as cylinders of revolvers were not considered to be a part of the length of the barrel, neither then should the chamber of the barrel on an automatic pistol be considered when measuring barrel lengths. It was a small task to completely throw off the remaining restrictions and return to the old proven and desired ways of Luger production without the annoying regulations.

Mauser continued to use the old DWM trademark until late in 1934 but in that year secret code names were given to the major producers of war material, and Mauser was assigned the code name "S." The "S" was replaced almost immediately by "S/42." At the same time, the commercial Mauser Banner trademark first appeared on Luger Pistols. There was a

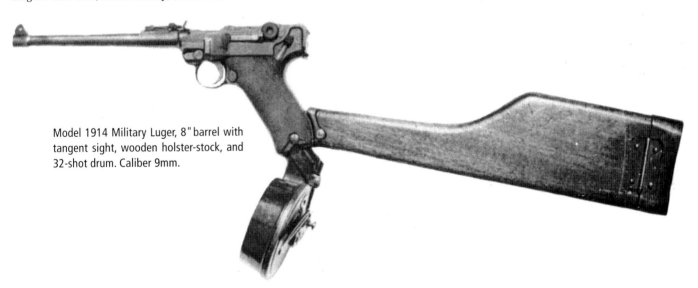

Model 1914 Military Luger, 8" barrel with tangent sight, wooden holster-stock, and 32-shot drum. Caliber 9mm.

delicate trigger mechanism of the Luger and also to the fact that even in normal semiautomatic firing the ammunition used in a Luger must be fairly well standard in power or the various stoppages common to the Luger will occur.

One very unusual Luger is a Model 1908 of World War I vintage, with a 4-inch barrel and a 12-inch silencer about 1½ inches in diameter. A threaded metal disc is permanently attached to the barrel in about the same position as the front sight, which has been removed; the tube, or body, of the silencer screws onto the disc. It is assumed that the tube was filled, at intervals, with rubber or composition baffles and possibly steel wool or some comparable material.

hands, finally becoming a member firm of the same holding company that controlled the famous Mauser-Werke at Oberndorf on the Neckar. On May 1, 1930, 800 machines, tools and technicians were transferred from the Berlin branch of the DWM factory to the Oberndorf location. DWM then concentrated on the production of ammunition and Mauser became the foremost supplier of Lugers from that time until production was finally halted in 1942.

While the changeover from DWM to Mauser was taking place, Simson & Co., continued to supply all Lugers to the German government. Their contract with the

definite reason behind the using of both the code name "S/42" and the commercial Mauser Banner. The former were elements of secret production, employed to confuse the manufacturer's identity. The latter was marked on arms supposedly intended for commercial sales, and a few of them actually reached the commercial market. Most, however, were destined for the rapidly growing German military forces of the early and mid-thirties. To doubly insure their carefully guarded secret from being discovered, pistols were not only marked with the code name but also with a code date of manufacture. Consequently we find "S/42" Lugers carrying the letters "K," indicating manufacture in 1934, and

"G," indicating those made in 1935. Production under these circumstances did not get under way until late in 1934, so few pieces bearing the "K" designation will be encountered. Those marked with the letter "G," or 1935, were in much greater evidence. By the beginning of 1936, the cloak of secrecy was thrown off and Lugers of "S/42" and "Mauser" manufacture, which were in reality one and the same, were marked with the actual dates in numbers over the chamber. It should be noted that the "K" and "G" markings appeared over the chamber in the exact place where the date would normally have been. The names "S/42" and "Mauser" were placed on the forward link of the toggle where the scrolled DWM trademark had previously been encountered. Those few Lugers intended for commercial sale carried only the "Mauser" marking, and were without dates or other stampings over the chamber. Examples were produced in both 7.65mm and 9mm calibers. All had barrels 4 inches long.

Mauser, however, was not the only supplier of Lugers in the 1934–35 period — during that time another name was added to the growing list of Luger producers. It has been said Herman Göring, Marshal of the German Air Force, had a personal interest in weapons produced by the Heinrich Krieghoff Waffenfabrik of Suhl. For one reason or another, Göring decided that his Luftwaffe would be supplied with Lugers produced by that firm. In those days, however, demand far exceeded ability to supply, and the only manner in which any sizable quantity of Lugers could be obtained in a relatively short time was through the assembly of the millions of spare, or replacement parts left over from World War I. Krieghoff acquired the necessary parts, doubtless through his powerful political connections, and began to assemble the Lugers requested by Göring Like the Mausers, these were marked with a code date, but not with a code name. Because their full production did not begin until 1935, Krieghoff Lugers are to be found bearing only one code date, an "S," indicating the year 1935, stamped over the chamber. As Krieghoff's capacity to produce was on a much smaller scale than that of Mauser, and also because he too marketed a small portion of his total output commercially, it was evidently not deemed necessary for the Krieghoff Lugers to employ a code name. Consequently, as did DWM, Krieghoff marked all of his Lugers with his commercial brand. The trademark of Krieghoff was an anchor, the upright body of which was formed by a dagger pointing downward, the letter "H" on the left side of the anchor and the letter "K" on the right. Directly below was the wording, in two lines, "Krieghoff" and "Suhl." Some examples, however, bear only the word "Suhl," the "Krieghoff" having been omitted.

Others, some of which are marked only with the word "Suhl" and still others with both words, are found with the added markings "Heinrich Krieghoff Waffenfabrik, Suhl" in two lines on the left side of the *frame*. Pieces so marked will usually have a letter "P" preceding the serial number. Those Krieghoff Lugers having the letter "P" before the serial number, may not necessarily have the wording on the side of the frame, however. Guns with the "P" are examples of the few commercial Krieghoff Lugers placed for sale in both 7.65mm and 9mm. Areas over the chamber will be unmarked on these commercial pieces. The trademark is, of course, stamped on the forward link of the toggle. Beginning in 1936 Krieghoff, like Mauser, dated his products with the year of manufacture in numbers. Those Krieghoff Lugers with the code date "S," or 1935 over the chamber were probably not serial numbered higher than #5,000. Pieces dated "1936" have been observed from the #5,000 series to the #7,000 series. Unlike those of Mauser manufacture, Krieghoff Lugers do not have a letter following the serial number, though with this one exception, they are numbered in the military system. A few examples may be encountered bearing dates of "1936" and "1937" which do not conform to the proper serial number range. These were pieces assembled from already numbered surplus parts at those later dates.

Some of the Mauser-made Lugers will be found bearing not only the commercial Mauser Banner but also carrying a date-stamp over the chamber. Such arms were originally intended for commercial sale, but when the German military forces demanded more Lugers than normal Mauser production could supply, pistols previously set aside for the commercial market were merely stamped with a date and accepted by the Army as regular issue weapons.

In 1936 the secret code names were augmented. Mauser was assigned the code number "42" in addition to the "S/42" already in use. It is not unusual, then, to find Lugers bearing the code name "S/42" and, for example, the date "1936," and also to encounter "42" pieces having the same date. To add to the confusion, pieces were also produced bearing the same date, "1936," and inscribed with the commercial Mauser Banner.

In 1941 yet another code name was given to Mauser, in this case "byf." Most examples of "byf" Lugers will have black plastic grips, a semi-successful experiment. These "byf" Lugers were in addition to and did not replace the "S/42", "42" and "Mauser" types.

According to reliable sources none of the Luger producing firms were permitted to sell their pistols commercially after 1940 or 1941. All production was claimed by the Wehrmacht, the German Armed Forces, who had the power to dispose of any surplus as they saw fit.

In 1945 and 1946 a small quantity of Lugers were assembled from surplus parts left over from 1942, the year in which official production of the Luger was superseded by that of the Walther "P.38." These were put together at the direction of the French Occupation Forces, in whose zone of occupation the Mauser factory was situated. Exact amounts produced and specifications thereof are not known. Krieghoff, too, assembled a few hundred Luger pistols, in the period following the war, for American occupation troops. It was among these latter that the unusual pieces bearing *no date and no name* were found.

After exactly 30 years of Army service in Germany progress finally caught up with the Luger when that Government adopted the Walther "Heeres Pistole," or "P.38" (Pistol Model 1938), though production continued through necessity until 1942. Switzerland, which since 1924 had produced its own Luger, followed suit in 1948, when the Neuhausen replaced it. The loss of World War II by Germany was the *coup de grace* for the Luger. Countries that had been dependent upon Germany for their supplies of the pistol were forced to turn in other directions when their orders could no longer be filled by the Mauser Werke.

Regardless of the fact that it is no longer produced, the Luger is not a "has been" by any means. Over a period of 40 years literally millions were produced, most of which are today in the hands of the military the world over. There are thousands of soldiers, marksmen and gun fanciers to whom it will never lose its value as a weapon for defense, shooting, or as a collector's item.

Quite possibly Luger production may never again be resumed. Should this prove to be true, all Lugers, especially the rarer ones, will increase in value and the demand will grow. No matter which course the armies of the world pursue, the Luger is now and shall always remain one of the greatest handguns in history.

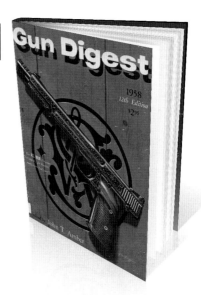

The .44 Magnum... One Year Later

by ELMER KEITH

THIRTY YEARS AGO, I developed the first heavy, safe loads in the 44 Special cartridge. (I had previously found out the hard way that the cylinder walls of the 45 Colt, the 38–40 and the 44-40 were too thin to handle safely as heavy loads as I desired.) My first design was a 260-grain 44 Special bullet for Belding & Mull, followed a short time later by a 280-grain blunt-nose slug of about the same form. Both shot very well at close range and gave plenty of power with 12 grains of No. 80 powder, but they lacked long range accuracy. Determined to get an accurate long range 44 Special load, I designed still another bullet for the Lyman Gun Sight Corp., Ideal 429421, in hollow point and hollow base form as well as solid. The solid bullet weighed 250 grains, the two others 235 grains each. Harold Croft visited me for a month in 1927, when the first mould arrived and we proceeded to do a lot of pest shooting with the new bullets. We used 12 to 12.5 grains of No. 80 powder and found we had a wonderfully accurate long range game load.

Long Range 44 Specials

For ten years I custom loaded this combination and shipped it all over the world, from Fairbanks, Alaska, to Finland and Africa. Harold Criger and John H. McPhee of Fairbanks used it on Alaskan game, and are still using it. One lot of this ammunition, loaded for Dr. Maxwell of Omaha, was taken to Africa on an extended trip. The Doctor had no trouble keeping his whole safari supplied with antelope meat, using an S. & W. 44 Special and these loads. Nearly 20 years later he tested some of the same lot and found they still shot as well as when first loaded. Velocity was around 1200 feet with pressures running around 25,000 pounds. Nearly all species of American big game were killed with this load at one time or another, from elk and moose to grizzly and Alaskan brown bear. Many times, with witnesses, I made from three to five hits out of six shots on a 4' × 4' target at a measured 700 yards. This proved the accuracy of that bullet design beyond any doubt.

The world's most potent handgun cartridge — its history and development, plus notes on handloading and shooting it — by the man whose dream came true!

Later, several others copied and tried to improve this bullet but with poor success. The original design always proved the more accurate. Peace officers along the Mexican border found the bullet and load just what they needed in their numerous gun fights, and were not slow in adopting it. During this time I wrote numerous articles for all the leading sporting magazines, including *The American Rifleman*, on this cartridge and load and strongly urged the ammunition companies to bring it out commercially. Thousands of letters were also written over the years, urging others to bring pressure on the loading companies for just such a powerful 44 Special factory load. The "44 Associates" was an organization formed toward this end, but all our pleas fell on deaf ears.

I worked with Douglas B. Wesson in developing the 357 Magnum cartridge, and strongly urged him to bring out a 44 Magnum instead, but he could not see it at all. Now I think he may have been right. Perhaps the big 44 would have been too long a step to make at that time. Possibly the 357 was necessary to introduce the big 44 Magnum.

DuPont No. 1301 was the powder used when 38 Special velocity and pressure were first stepped up, in what was known as the 38/44 cartridge. I found this powder an improvement over No. 80 in my heavy 44 loads, but before I had time to conduct extensive experiments with it Hercules No. 2400 arrived on the market. It was so much better than No. 80 or No. 1301 in maximum 44 loads that I never loaded either of them again. I went to 20 grains of this powder in S. A. Colts with my 250-grain bullet, finally settling on 18.5 grains of No. 2400 and my 250- or 235-grain bullets as the best and most accurate load for the 44 Special. It proved highly accurate, more stable than No. 80, and was safe in all types of 44 Special arms. Even the old Triple Lock (or New

The buck mule deer that Keith hit twice out of four shots at over 600 yards, using the S & W 44 Magnum.

Century) Smith & Wesson handled the big load accurately and with ease. These loads were covered in my little book, *Sixgun Cartridges & Loads*, published by Samworth in 1936. Periodically, readers of this book and my magazine articles re-discovered my 44 Special loads. They were the inspiration for many 44 Special articles in *The American Rifleman* — without credit.

In spite of all this publicity, we still had no factory load for the 44 Special that even approached my hand load in power. The factories continued to grind out the standard 246-grain 44 Special round-nose-bullet load at 740 to 770 feet. It was a duplicate in velocity and power of the old 44 Russian and a wonderful target cartridge or grouse load but a poor killer on larger game, and a poor man stopper as well.

When I quit custom loading, Dick Tinker of Helena, Montana, and J. Bushnell Smith took over and custom loaded my heavy 44 Special loads for customers all over the country. After their deaths Moody's Reloading Service of Helena, Mont., and J. W. McPhillips, 285 Mastic Ave., San Bruno, Calif., continued the job and still supply their customers with it. When properly loaded with a bullet tempered one to sixteen tin and lead, sized from exact groove diameter to not over .001" larger, and backed by 18.5 grains 2400 in the old semi-balloon head case, no single accident to gun or shooter, to my knowledge, has occurred over all these years. Both S. A. Colt and New Service Colts as well as all available models of Smith & Wessons were used extensively with the big load. An ever stronger demand grew for a factory load that could be bought over the counter. I was no longer alone in asking for a heavy 44 caliber load.

Interest Develops

In 1953 while at Camp Perry, Ohio, I had several long sessions with C. G. Peterson of Remington. He was very much interested when I asked him to bring out a heavy 44 Special load with my bullet at 1200 feet. He asked me to come up to the Remington plant and handload it for pressures and velocity readings. I also had several long talks with Carl Hellstrom, President of Smith & Wesson, and he also urged me to visit his plant after Camp Perry. When I finally arrived at the Remington plant, Mr. Peterson was away on vacation, but Henry Davis took me to Gail Evans, who made notes on all my work and findings and promised to take it up with Mr. Peterson as soon as he returned. They promised me nothing, except to see what could be done about a heavy factory 44 Special load. They were afraid that the old Triple Lock, even though it had been handling my heavy loads for many years, might, in some

instances, blow up. They said, and rightly, that it was made long before the days of heat treatment or magnafluxing, and some could have dangerous flaws. After several days at Remington, I put in a week at the Smith & Wesson plant, urging them to get together with Remington in the production of a heavy factory 44 Special load with my bullet and, if necessary, make a new gun to hold it. If they were afraid of the old gun's strength, I said a new gun could be made with a longer, recessed-head cylinder, the amount of barrel ex-tention through the frame cut to the minimum, but with room for a gas ring.

During my last day at the Smith & Wesson plant Mr. Hellstrom told me he could build a safe gun around any heavy 44 Special load that Remington would make. I then suggested that they could lengthen the 44 Special case until it would not enter any of the older 44 Special guns, and again strongly urged them to get together with Remington and bring out a powerful 44 gun and load. I vamosed then but continued, in letters to both companies, to urge such a load and, if necessary, a gun to handle it. Actually, all this had been covered in my book, *Sixguns*, years before!

From the late summer of 1953 until early in 1956 I had no word from either company on what they were doing about the heavy 44.

In January, 1956, Smith & Wesson phoned me one evening to tell me they had built a big 44, and that the first one finished would be sent to me! This was great news, and I learned also that Remington would ship me some of the new "44 Magnum" ammunition with 240-grain bullet at 1570 foot seconds velocity. I immediately gave General Hatcher — he was also being sent the new gun — the good news.

Well, that's the story behind the Smith & Wesson 44 Magnum gun and the Remington 44 Magnum cartridge, and it's all well documented. Thousands of shooters the country over, their interest spurred by my writings and the articles of others, created the demand. Mr. Peterson and the Remington ballis-ticians put in a lot of hard work designing and perfecting the load, Mr. Hellstrom and his staff of gun makers likewise did endless work on the new gun. At last my dreams of thirty years are a reality. Today we have the world's finest big sixgun and load, and my hat is off to every man in both organizations who had anything at all to do with the development. They did a wonderful job.

First the men behind the gun. Carl Hellstrom, Bill Gunn, Harold Austin, Walt Sanborn, Fred Miller, Harold Steins and many others at the Smith & Wesson plant, had their part in the production of this fine arm.

The first S & W 44 Magnum with 4-inch barrel, engraved and stocked by the Gun Reblu Co., Biltmore, N. C.

The 44 S&W Magnum

The new gun employs the heavy N frame regularly made for the 357 Magnum, 38/44 Heavy Duty, 44 Special and 45 Smith & Wessons, but this gun has all major parts made from a premium lot of special alloy steel, perfectly heat treated for greatest strength in the Smith & Wesson furnaces. The hammer and trigger are case hardened to a new high in this treatment, insuring a perfect and lasting, crisp, clean trigger pull. The heavy barrels are 6½" or 4" in length with a wide rib and encased ejector rod. The top of frame and barrel are grooved along the rib and sandblasted to prevent glare and reflection. All lockwork parts and bearing surfaces are honed to a mirror finish to insure a maximum smoothness, either single or double action. The hammer has a wide target spur and the trigger has a wide flare that perfectly contours the trigger finger for easy cocking and maximum contact area of finger to trigger. The trigger pull runs from three to four pounds, and is as clean and sharp as breaking glass. The S. & W. rear sight, fully adjustable for both elevation and windage and of locking micrometer-construction, has a white-outlined rear notch of adequate width to insure a strip of light on each side of the front sight, a one-eighth inch red-insert ramp, when held at arms length. The red-insert ramp front shows up well on a black target or game in any shooting light. Stock straps are grooved to prevent slippage. Stocks, of Goncalo Alves fancy figured hardwood, are of the S. & W. Target shape and offer a filler behind the trigger guard as well as covering the front strap and the butt of the gun. They are hand filling and the left stock is hollowed out for the right thumb. They are perfectly shaped to fit and fill the hand and distribute the recoil over as wide a surface as possible. They are also finely and attractively checkered. The big gun

weighs 47 ounces empty. Main spring is the standard S. & W. long spring with compression screw in front strap. Cylinder and barrel clearance are held to a minimum, yet the gun has the smoothest possible action. Cylinder locks tight and lines up perfectly. The cylinder is a full 1.75" long and has ample room for my 250 grain bullet reloaded in the one-eighth-inch longer 44 Magnum case, still leaving a sixteenth of an inch clearance when the bullet is crimped in the regular crimping groove.

Shooting the 44 Magnum

The new gun is the finest target arm I have ever fired with standard 44 Special factory ammunition or a light reload with my own, or any, accurate target bullet. It holds steadier than any gun I have used on target. Double action pull for fast work is superb and for the target shooter the broad hammer spur is ideal for fast cocking in single action, timed, and rapid fire matches. The rear end of barrel projects through the frame about ⅛-inch and with the long cylinder adds strength to these, the two weakest parts of a sixgun. The 6½" barrel job is ideal for the hills, for target shooting, or for hunting with a sixgun, and a perfect gun for running cougar with hounds. It gives maximum sight radius as well as maximum velocity. It is a great two-hand weapon for game shooting, as it feels muzzle heavy and hangs well on the object. In a 4" barrel the weight lies more in the hand and is better balanced for emergency double action shooting, hip shooting and fast aerial double action work. The four-inch job will also be the gun for the peace officer as he can stop either man or automobile, and yet it is short enough to ride high on the waist belt where it will not poke the seat of a car or chair. It will also be the faster to get into action. External finish of the new gun is the traditional Smith & Wesson high bright blue. A new high in polish has

Right, Keith 250-gr. bullet cast and plated by Marked, compared with Remington factory 240-gr. gas-check bullet.

been attained on this gun and even the edges of the trigger guard and the hinge of the crane are polished like a mirror. The ramp front sight is pinned through the rib with two pins before polishing, so that careful examination is necessary to detect the two pins. Attractively packaged in a presentation, hinged-lid case of blue leatherette, it sells at $140.00 and is worth every cent of its cost. It all adds up to a finer gun than I thought anyone would ever build.

Remington has produced the greatest and most powerful sixgun cartridge ever made. The new case is an eighth-inch longer than the 44 Special and it will not fully enter any 44 Special chamber we have so far tried, including S. & W., Colt and Great Western. The solid head case is the heaviest sixgun brass I have ever seen. There are no worthless cannelures to cause the case to stretch when fired and resized. The new case appears to be of the same length as the 357 Magnum brass. The bullet is a modification of my design, with two narrow and shallow grease grooves instead of one heavy, wide and deep grease groove, and with the case crimped down into the soft lead of the forward band, leaving a very small full caliber band in front of the case. The crimp is heavy, and so far no bullets have jumped their crimp from recoil. The 240-grain bullet has a shorter nose than my slug, the same wide flat point, slightly larger on the flat surface. It is made of very soft lead, a necessity because it is extruded in long ropes fed to the cutting and swaging machines. The soft bullet requires a gas check cup, not only to prevent deformation of the base but to help hold the soft slug in the rifling at high velocity. The slug upsets

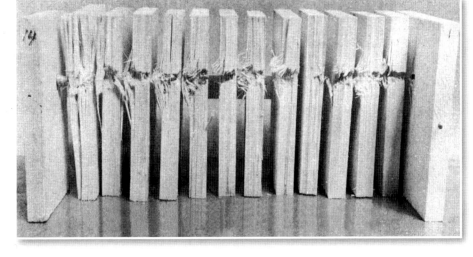

Penetration test—the Remington 44 Magnum factory load went through 13 of the ⅞" pine boards. Note expanded bullet.

to fill the chamber mouths perfectly and the gas check is the best I have ever seen on a bullet, being crimped into the rear grease groove. The factory bullets do not carry as much lubricant in both grooves as my original bullet does in its one grease groove. The slug mikes .431" and the groove diameter of my gun is 429". Pressure is high with factory loads; I would estimate it to be at least 40,000 pounds and possibly 42,000. The gun is made to take it, and the case is made for high pressure; fired cases fall out of my gun with a tap on the extractor rod. Accuracy is high at all ranges and the gun shoots good to a half mile. Once we managed to put five out of six bullets on a rock one foot high by 18 inches long at over 500 yards (two of us paced it), shooting with both hands out of a car window, which is plenty good enough for any sixgun. They would have hit a buck deer at that range five times out of six.

At close range it shot quite small groups on targets and, like my original bullet, cut clean full-caliber holes in the paper. My first shot at game was a big Goshawk in the top of a cottonwood 100 yards away. I used both hands, rested my left arm and shoulder against a post and shot with just his head showing over the front sight. The gas check slug caught him dead center and splattered him all over.

Handloading the 44 Magnum

The powder charge is 22 to 22.2 grains of what looks like Hercules 2400 but may be a duPont version of this powder with similar characteristics. We removed the slugs from a few loads, opened the crimp and put the original charge back in the case with my 250-grain 44 Special bullet, cast hard by Mar-Mur Bullet Co., copper plated and sized to .429". It seemed to shoot in the same group as the factory load but clearly indicated at least 5,000 pounds less pressure, estimated from primer comparisons. With factory bullets the primer is well flattened, the firing pin indentation is not deep or full, and the

primer flows around the perimeter of the firing pin indentation slightly. When the Keith 250-grain hard .429" slug was fired, the firing pin indentation was deep and the primer was not flattened to anything like the extent of the factory load. This clearly shows the value of one to 16 tin and lead, or harder bullets, when reloading this cartridge. We also reloaded the fired factory cases with 22 grains No. 2400 and my 250-grain solid and 235-grain hollow base and hollow point bullets, getting, at an estimate, at least 5,000 pounds less pressure. This is a good way to leave it. Let the factory, with their pressure guns and precision instruments for managing heavy pressures, use the high pressure load. I'm well satisfied with either the factory load or my hand load, which develops far less pressure. It is on the safe side, yet a load substantially as powerful. It penetrates even better in beef, perhaps because it is harder, and gives equal accuracy.

The new 44 Magnum S. & W. does not group all loads of the same bullet weight to the same point as do many 44 Special guns. The new Magnum lighter loads print high and right at 1 o'clock; my heavy 44 Special loads a bit lower and nearer center; 20 grains No. 2400 with the Keith 250-grain slug in the Magnum case, just out of the black at 7 o'clock, while the full hand load of 22 grains 2400 and Keith 250-grain bullet print low and left at 7 o'clock. We settled for the full reload and the factory Remington (as both shoot to the same sighting) and sighted the gun for them. The target shooter wishing to use factory 44 Specials will have to sight for that load and change his sights when using the factory Magnum 44 load. Each load made small groups at all ranges tried. I have fired the big gun at least 600 times, both hand loads and factory hulls.

The factory bullet is soft enough to expand readily on impact with flesh and acts just like a soft nosed bullet from a 45–70 or 38–55. With my hollow point 235-grain bullet and 22 grains of No. 2400 expansion is even more rapid than with the factory bullet. It

disintegrates on large bones and explodes jack rabbits, chucks, torn cats and similar vermin. The tests prove beyond any doubt that the 44 Magnum factory load will penetrate to the brain of the largest bear on earth or the biggest elk or moose if directed right. It will stop any mad cow or bull on the range with one well-placed shot if the cowpoke gets wound up and has to kill a critter. The fisherman or camera hunter, working the Alaskan streams, now has a gun for protection against a suddenly surprised Brownie with which he can stop the animal if he uses his head and shoots for the brain or spine. The prospector can kill all the meat he needs with this gun and factory loads or my heavy reloads.

22 grains No. 2400 and Keilh 250-grain bullet and also factory loads were tried on car bodies, old cook stoves and motor blocks. They'll penetrate a lot of car body material and even get through the heavier steel braces. Each load cracks up motor heads and will penetrate the block and ruin a piston. One shot through a radiator un-corks it and these big heavy slugs placed almost anywhere on a motor will put it out of commission. The peace officer can stop a car with it, or stop the criminal in it by shooting through the body of the car. I only asked for a duplication of my old time tried 44 Special heavy load with 18.5 grains 2400 and the 250-grain Keith bullet, but the boys went me one better by producing a load that is even more powerful!

The big gun is, I would say, pleasant to shoot, and does not jar the hand as much as do my heavy 44 Special loads from the much lighter 4"-barrel 44 Special S. & W. guns. It is definitely not a ladies' gun but I have known women who would enjoy shooting it. The recoil has not bothered me in the slightest, nor have several other old sixgun men complained who have fired it extensively, including Hank Benson and Don Martin. The recoil is not as severe as that of a two-inch airweight Chiefs' Special with high speed 38 Specials. With 44 Special factory loads it is just as pleasant to shoot as a K-22 and with the 44 Magnum loads, which give heaviest recoil, it will not bother a seasoned sixgun man at all. Recoil with my heaviest loads of 22 grains of 2400 and the Keith 250 grain bullet is much less than that of the factory load. The factory load, fired with one hand, flips the barrel up almost to the vertical.

Factory load velocity is claimed to be 1570 feet with 1,314 pounds energy as against 1450 feet velocity and 690 pounds energy for the 357 Magnum factory load. We are a bit skeptical about the claimed 1570 feet velocity. Our own estimate would be somewhere nearer 1400 feet. We base this on a lot of reloading for the 44 Special with 18.5 grains

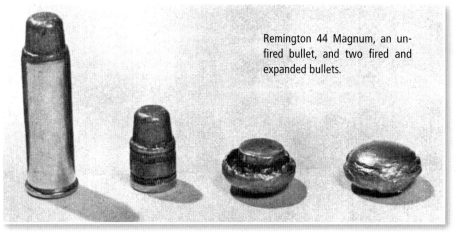

Remington 44 Magnum, an un-fired bullet, and two fired and expanded bullets.

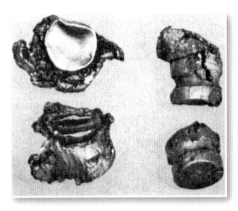

Left, two Remington 44 Magnum bullets found in necks of a big steer and a 1400-lb. cow. Right, two Keith 250-gr. Markell-cast bullets (backed by 22 grs. of No. 2400 powder) taken from necks of two large cows. Skulls were completely penetrated.

2400 which gave the Keith 250-grain slug something over 1200 feet from 6½ barrels. Pressure of the factory load is high, make no mistake on that score. Don't rechamber any 44 Special cylinder to take the big load. Cylinders, as well as guns, should be made especially for this load, and I certainly won't convert any of my 44 Specials to take the 44 Remington Magnum. A Model 1892 Winchester carbine, however, built to handle this load would make an excellent companion gun, especially useful to the peace officer, or to anyone in the back country.

The Remington 44 Magnum is the best case to reload I've seen. With the Keith 250 grain slug cast one to 16 tin and lead and sized exact groove diameter, to cut down pressures, the cartridge gives wonderful accuracy with 5 grains of Bullseye and would shoot accurately with even less of this fast powder. With 8½ grains of Unique it makes a fine medium load of around 1,000 feet or more; with 20 grains of 2400 one gets a good fairly heavy load about equal to my old 44 Special heavy load. If you don't reload you can always buy a box of Remington factory loads and be sure of getting the most powerful and perfect sixgun ammunition ever made anywhere.

I've killed enough beef animals with an 85-pound yew bow, and broadheads that went entirely through the beasts, to know that an arrow gives a slow, painful death with no shock. Now we have a sixgun and load that is infinitely better in every respect as a big game weapon than any bow ever drawn. It kills two-year old steers too dead. They do not bleed well after being hit in the brain with the factory 44 Magnum load. One big porcupine, shot about dead center from the side, was killed instantly leaving a two-inch exit hole on the far side. This gun and load will kill deer just as dead as a 30-30, up to at least

100 yards, if well placed, and the big slug will leave a better blood trail, as it is so soft it expands on contact and continues to expand as it penetrates. Velocity is high enough to carry considerable shock to any animal.

Friends who returned from Korea, after fighting through that unpleasant affair, tell me that they encountered many enemy soldiers with body armor which our 45 auto ammo would not penetrate. The 44 Magnum loads go through quarter-inch dump truck beds like cheese and would penetrate any body armor a soldier would be likely to carry. Loaded with a full metal-jacketed bullet for military use, it would take care of any useful body armor.

After a lifetime of working with all manner of sixguns and loads, answering thousands of letters about them, and the writing of two books on the subject, as well as a great many magazine articles, I consider the 44 Remington Magnum Cartridge and the great Smith & Wesson gun that chambers it the greatest sixgun development of our time! I am happy to have had even a small part in its development.

Since writing this article, Keith has had much added experience in shooting slaughter bulls with the 44 Magnum load. He found that on frontal shots the slugs broke up but got through the skull on into the neck. When shots from above and to the rear were made, aiming at a point just ahead of the scapula and behind the horns, the bullet smashed through several inches of thick hide and heavy muscle, went into and through the brain, and down into the nose or jaws! And some of the bulls weighed a ton. Keith found his handload of 22 grs. of 2400 and his 250-grain solid (cast by G. E. Murphy in both plain and copper coated form) penetrated a bit better than factory loads due to the greater stiffness of his bullets and their slightly lower velocity.

Keith feels that this performance shows that similar results can be surely expected on big bear, elk or moose, and he killed two buck mule deer late in 1956 as a trial. Here's Elmer:

"I shot one small buck for Archie McArthur that he had wounded at around 400 yards with a 270. When the buck came down the mountain to cross the trail I shot him between eye and ear at close range. The factory 240-grain part-jacket bullet went through the skull leaving a 60 caliber exit hole, completely shattering the lower part of the brain. The next chance came at a fairly large four-point buck. Paul Kriley held 18" over this buck's back with the 300 Magnum 180-grain load, breaking the right foreleg and grazing the left foreleg as the buck stood broadside at around 550 yards. The buck fell, then

got up and started following the rest of the band on three legs. That badly wounded we didn't want him to get away, of course, so I dropped prone with the 6½-inch 44 Magnum. Paul shot again from prone. He then shot a third time and as nothing happened I held up all of the red in the front ramp and half of the blade below the red insert and perched the moving buck on top — I shot and nothing happened! Paul shot again without hitting, so I held a trifle more of the front sight up and shot again. Paul said, 'Hell, you hit right at his heels.' My next one would not be low, I said, for his spotting my shot gave me the range. Paul shot again and missed; probably all his shots were low as he had the rifle sighted one inch high at 100 yards. I shot again and this time Paul said, 'I saw that one hit right over his head.' I had held up all of the front sight blade until I could see the shoulders of the front ramp level with top of rear sight blade and the buck running along on top of the front sight. The buck stopped instantly and swapped ends, heading right back toward us and shaking his head. The range must have been 600 yards or over. I wanted to let the buck come as long as he was headed our way but Paul tried him again and missed, and he again turned and ran straight away from us. Paul said, 'I'm empty,' so I held all of the front sight up and perched him on top again and just as I was squeezing the trigger he turned square up the mountain. With all of front sight held up and the buck perched on top I simply moved the width of the front sight over in front of him and squeezed off the shot as he was going slowly uphill. After the gun came back down out of recoil the buck had disappeared. Paul reloaded and ran for the top of the mountain to head him off the other side, while I trailed him around the side hill. He had fallen and rolled down the mountain 50 yards, then got up and started slowly around through a swale and over another low ridge. Just as I reached the next ridge Paul shot twice, and coming out I saw him on the ridge above me. He said his first shot had gone under at about 350 yards, so he'd held four inches higher and killed him. My third shot had hit him in right cheek, and came out his mouth, which was what had made him shake his head and swap ends. My fourth shot had cut a 60 caliber hole square through the middle of both lungs, cutting off a rib on each side. Had we known it no finish shots would have been needed from the rifle. Entrance of both of Paul's shots were about the size of a match head.

"I had turned down many shots at does for two days and would never have fired at that buck with a sixgun had he not been wounded and getting away, but it did prove that the Remington 44 Magnum is effective on a deer at over 600 yards."

The Smith & Wesson 38 Master—

How Good is This New Pistol?

a TESTFIRE REPORT

The factory claims 10-ring accuracy at 50 yards — pistol expert Gil Hebard put 4000 wadcutters through a double brace of these new target pistols, and here's his comprehensive, fact-finding account.

HOW GOOD is Smith & Wesson's new Model 52 38 Special autoloader? This is a logical question on nearly every competitive shooter's lips at this early stage of the 52's career. Time and the heat of stiff competition will dictate the final answer, but I'll venture the following prediction: *If the four production guns I tested are typical of total production, and if S&W continues to hold quality control at its present level, this gun will be a winner!*

Three requisites of any target gun worth its salt in hot competition are functional reliability, fine accuracy and good trigger action. Of lesser importance are precision adjustable sights and good balance or handling quality. The 52 seems to posses all of these desirable features, even when viewed through the most critical target shooter's eye.

Accuracy

S&W claims "ten ring accuracy" when properly machine rest tested — that is, the gun will hold ten consecutive shots within a 3.39-inch circle at 50 yards with good ammunition. To determine if this claim is fact or fiction, I machine-tested four production guns at 50 yards, 300 shots each, with three different brands of factory wad-cutter ammunition. The results are shown in the accompanying chart and to me they were impressively good. The average 10-shot dispersion (group), all guns, all ammo, was 2.60 inches. Average dispersion for Remington ammo was a startling 2.31 inches — more than an inch better than S&W's allowable maximum! Any further doubts about these four particular guns were dispelled when I telephoned the S&W factory and obtained the original test target data (each gun is machine tested before leaving the factory) and found their results had practically co-incided with mine.

S&W asserts that *all* of their 52's are averaging 2 to 2¾ inches at 50 yards. To a rifleman who can hold in one inch at 100 yards *without* the aid of a machine rest this sounds like child's play, but to the pistol-man it approaches the fantastic. He knows that an ill-designed blunt nosed bullet, moving out of a 5-inch barrel that must be locked into position for each shot, is going to be headed toward the moon unless every preparatory condition approaches perfection.

Remington tells me that the best 38 Special wadcutters have inherent accuracy of from 1 to 1½ inches at 50 yards. In developing an autoloader that will shoot as close as 2 inches, S&W has arrived at a pinnacle of achievement heretofore reached only by custom gunsmith James Clark, with his 38 Conversion and Model 61 38 Special; by Fort Benning and their AMU 38 Special, and possibly a couple other custom gunsmiths at most.

In addition to firing thousands of rounds through the Potter machine rest (right foreground), Gil Hebard shot the M52 offhand to check hand fit, sight use, etc.

Factory Ammunition

The four guns tested shot best with Remington, next best with Western and Federal, in that order. The fact that one brand of ammo will shoot better than another in a given gun is pretty well established. The *reasons* for a gun's partiality to a certain load are theoretical and open to argument even among pre-eminent authorities. The fact remains, though, that of the 900 or so Model 52's produced as of this writing, most have demonstrated a definite preference for Remington. This is not a testimonial for Remington. Perhaps Western's next lot of wadcutters will be the favored fodder for the 52 — dies wear, tolerances widen, primer mixtures vary, powder is difficult to stabilize from lot to lot, manufacturers are continually striving for improvement — *things change* and shooters should realize this. A good example here is Federal, whose ammunition did not fare as well as the others in our tests, but they're to be commended on a tremendous improvement in their load from the first lots marketed in mid-1961. It appears that they now have an excellent load and are in the running.

Shoot *any* of the factory wadcutters in this gun and worry naught. But handloads? — this could be a different story!

Handloading the Model 52

2000 various handloads (that's right, 2000) machine-rested through the 52 left me with the impression that the handloader is going to have to use all of the wiles and tricks of his trade to whomp up a match winning load. The 52 seems to be more temperamental than most 38's as to which handloads it will shoot *well*. One contributing factor, doubtless, is that the bullets have to be seated *flush* because of the short magazine. This presents a new problem to the handloading fraternity which, over the years, has developed and perfected wadcutter loads with the bullet seated *beyond* the case mouth.

I was never able to equal factory ammo accuracy-wise but did come close with three loads: 1) Lyman's No. 35863, a 148-grain wadcutter, seated flush, taper crimped to .370" with 2.8 grains Bullseye; 2) North ridge's hollow base pressure-swaged 148-grain bullet, flush seated, .370" taper crimp, 3.8 grains Du Pont 5066; 3) Hensley and Gibbs No. 50, 148-grain wadcutter seated *below* the case mouth with a substantial crimp and 3 7 grains of 5066. All three of these loads averaged slightly over 3 inches.

Trends that became evident in the tests indicated that .3555" was best bullet size; 5066 powder held a slight edge over Bullseye (and is certainly much cleaner); heavier charges such as 2.7 or 2.8 grains Bulls-

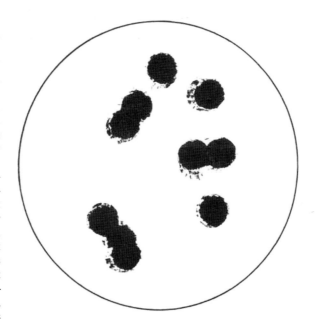

38 Special full wadcutter loads tip slightly, sometimes, from most any handgun, when going through the target at 50 yards. Note "scuff" marks.

eye or 3.7, 3.8, or 3.9 grains of 5066 printed better targets than the lighter loads; light taper crimping (.370"–.372") is superior to roll or heavy (.367") taper-crimp.

Uniform bullet weight and powder charges seemed more critical than usual. It was extremely difficult to get uniform groups when using a standard powder measure. These just won't throw a consistently uniform charge in the 2- or 3-grain area, for the large powder-dispensing hole that is required if the measure is going to throw, say, the 50-grain rifle loads they were originally designed for. Variation of a few tenths of a grain in the powder charge in a 3-grain load can spell the difference between accuracy and inaccuracy with a particular group of components and a given barrel. I cannot emphasize too strongly that a pistol powder measure (one with a small drum that throws from 1 to 20 grains) should *always* be used by a pistol reloader. Owners of Star, Phelps, or Potter tools have no worry as these have very well-designed measures integral with the tool.

H&G's resurrected No. 244 bullet did not do as well as touted. Speer's swaged bullet was a disappointment. Hand swaged bullets were absolutely hopeless (as is usually the case at midrange velocities). H&G's No. 50 loaded backwards is not the answer either. Had I not been plagued by a publisher's deadline, perhaps I would have found a "final" load. But even so, it would have been for *my* gun (or guns) and not *yours*. The variables are just too many and complex to flatly declare that a given load is it, and expect *it* to be the ultimate for all guns. I am well aware that handloads *can* be as accurate as factory and feel confident that it is only a matter of time before excellent loads will be developed for these guns.

Top: M52 barrel breech, showing loading ramp and rim stop.
Bottom: Notched ring on M52 bushing adjusts by means of spanner shown; spring-loaded pin (arrow) locks bushing.

Swelled section of M52 barrel muzzle has near-point contact in bushing for uniform positioning.

Micrometer click rear sight of M52. Sturdy, rugged, sight is quickly, accurately adjustable by means of coin-slotted screws.

Regarding this 1.03" group, Hebard wrote, "... the tightest 10-shot group I have ever gotten at 50 yards with any 38 gun or ammo. "Fired with S&W 52 No. 50817, Remington Targetmaster wadcutters, from the Potter machine rest in April, 1962.

Bullet Tipping

There has been considerable criticism of the 52 in that it tips bullets excessively. Of the 3200 shots we fired at 50 yards about 40% showed a tipping print or "scuff" mark on the target. S&W has tried barrel twists of 12, 14, 16, and 18¾ inches, various barrel lengths, riflings, chambers and reaming to overcome this but without success. This tipping, however, is not confined to the Model 52. Close examination of most any 50-yard target fired from most any gun or barrel (including Mann test barrels) will show some degree of tipping with 38 Special *full wadcutter*, midrange (600 to 900 fps muzzle velocity) ammunition, either factory or handloads. Reming-

ton tells me that tipping is synonymous with the midrange load. This action, perhaps, could be better defined as "yaw," as the base of the bullet is gyrating around its own point (watch a 30-caliber bullet through a scope as it goes down range and you will know what I mean). Trajectory range tests, where the bullet is fired through a series of screens at 5-yard intervals, further proves the point; the "scuff" mark rotates on the successive targets in direct relationship to the barrel twist. Even when fired from a 10" Mann Barrel (closed chamber testing barrel) tipping of wadcutter bullets is still evident regardless of brand of ammunition.

Tipping is something shooters will have to put up with for the time being at least but, if their gun is grouping as tight as 2 or 3 inches, who cares? One unfortunate aspect of this tipping, though, is this: when a shooter throws or jerks a "flier" out in the six-ring and the target hole shows a tipper, he invariably blames his gun rather than himself. In the extensive testing we've just completed, there was no evidence whatsoever that "tippers" were spreading the group.

Tipping should not be confused with lobbing or keyholing, which can be caused by an inaccurate or damaged barrel and/or by poor handloads. Many reloaders do such a poor job that their bullets are actually lobbed out of the barrel, thus may print broadside-on at either 25 or 50 yards! If your bullets are doing this, you can bet your bottom dollar that your loads won't group better than perhaps 15" at 50 yards, even out of the finest gun. In just about every instance, this is the fault of the load, not the gun.

Leading No Problem

The 52 does not seem to suffer from leading — we did not clean the test guns at any time and, although leading developed in the front end of the chamber, accuracy was as good at the end of the test as it had been at the beginning. The chamber leading was easily removed and apparently presents no problem unless, of course, one allows it to build up to the point where malfunctions occur.

Functional Reliability

The four guns function very well with factory loads and a wide variety of handloads, including those made using 38 Colt cases and trimmed 38 Special cases, which allowed the bullet to be seated projecting from the case in the usual manner.

(Here is, possibly, a good avenue of development. More extensive shooting with

These targets represent, approximately, the 100-shot average made with three brands of 38 wadcutter ammo. A – 1.93" for Remington. B – 2.20" for W-W. C – 2.53" for Federal as against 1.830", 2.149" and 2.741" respectively. The M52 will shoot!

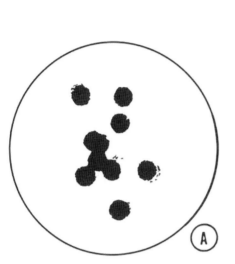

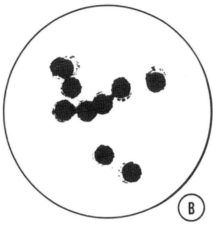

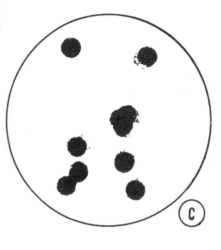

Groups illustrated are shown in 62% scale.

38 Long Colt or shortened 38 Special cases, handloaded, might be rewarding work. Jim Horton, not unknown to these pages, may report on such short-case loads later.)

The gun *is closely* fitted and there was a noticeable slowing down of the normal fast action at the end of the test. A thorough cleaning and oiling again restored the snappy action, a fine tribute to S&W's close fitting and tolerances. To coin a phrase that would be applicable to this or any other finely fitted target arm, "He who shooteth a dirty gun deserveth his alibi."

Life Expectancy

S&W subjected one Model 52 through a "wear and break down" test in which the gun was put through a cyclic operation

The Smith & Wesson M52, disassembled for cleaning and oiling. Takedown is simple, easy, and so is reassembly.

S&W MODEL 52 38 MASTER

CALIBER: 38 S&W Special midrange wadcutter with flush seated bullet
MAGAZINE CAPACITY: 5 rounds
MECHANISM TYPE: Semi-automatic, locked breech, recoiling barrel, detachable magazine
WEIGHT: 41 ounces, empty
OVER-ALL LENGTH: 8⅝"
OVER-ALL HEIGHT: 5¾"
SIGHTS: Front, ⅛" Patridge. Rear, new S&W micrometer-click. Coin slot adjustment screws. Each click ¾" elevation, ½" windage at 50 yards
SIGHT RADIUS: 6-¹⁵⁄₁₆"
BARREL: 5⅛", 5 groove, right twist, one turn in 18.75"
CONSTRUCTION: All steel
TRIGGER REACH: Trigger to backstrap 2⅜"
STOCKS: Checkered walnut with S&W monogram
TRIGGER: ⅜" wide, serrated surface
ACCESSORIES: Bushing spanner wrench, Allen wrenches, cleaning rod with brush and bob
PRICE: $150 with two magazines

100,000 times. 50-yard group accuracy of this particular gun was 2.14" at the start of the test. After 10,000 cycles the gun tested 2.1"; at 25,000, 1.93"; at 50,000, 1.83" and at 100,000 it was back up to 2.14". Considering that a barrel will normally go hundreds of thousands of rounds without showing any appreciable wear (using lead bullets only), it would appear that the 52 would satisfy accuracy requirements for many years, even for an active shooter, barring accidental damage or abuse.

Trigger Action

Some shooters may not like the 52 trigger action; it is a two-stage affair with about ¼" take up before actual sear engagement commences. Of the 15 or so Model 52's that have gone through my hands to date, all seem to have the same general characteristic — a "soft" type of pull. That is, not a clean, crisp break but rather a slight perceptible amount of smooth movement immediately before the trigger breaks away from the sear. This movement is so small that most shooters may not notice it. Nor is it something to be criticized, for it's an excellent example of the soft pull, long recognized by gunsmiths and top target shooters as a very desirable type — *if the shooter happens to like it.* So, this may be an advantage or a disadvantage, depending on your point of view. I personaly don't like a soft trigger, but I must admit that this is one of the finest of its type I've ever seen.

Sights

The rear adjustable sight, new and of excellent design, generally follows the dictates of what our top shooters desire, i.e.: a ⅛" deep notch with large flat sighting surface, uniformity of adjustment with minimum back lash or error and fineness of setting (see specification chart). The sight adjusting screws can be operated with a coin and are marked for direction of movement. The front sight is a ⅛" post and it is fortunate that this size and type is of proven popularity, as it would require the services of a professional gunsmith to change it.

Design and Balance

The Model 52 is basically a target version of the Model 39, the 9mm automatic which S&W introduced in 1954 and which has proven to be more than an excellent weapon. To me the balance seems a little muzzle light, but it does have a feeling of consolidation, which is in line with the present trend toward shorter, more compact guns, among our better shooters.

The angle of the grip to the bore, just slightly more than that of the 45 Colt auto, allows the trigger finger to operate in a line parallel to the arm extension. Contrary to some so-called "authoritative" opinion, I feel that this abrupt stock-to-barrel angle is conducive to better shooting.

I believe the arched mainspring housing, which constitutes the back-strap of the grip, will come up for some criticism, especially from shooters with small hands, as it tends to slip off of the hand and away from the palm when properly gripped. Good custom grips, perhaps, will correct some of this for those shooters who experience this problem; however, there is really not much a custom grip maker can do when the frame is too large (for a given hand) to start with.

Conclusion

The S&W Model 52 appears to me to be the first factory produced 38 Special target autoloader worthy of the name. Its early acceptance by some of our best shooters would indicate that its star will be rising in the target shooting world. Whether this star will be one of first magnitude or not only time will tell. I'll wager a dollar to a doughnut that its future will be brilliant.

50-yard Machine Rest Test of Four S&W Model 52's

Ammunition	Gun No. 50292			Gun No. 50575			Gun No. 50817			Gun No. 50851		
	Rem.	West.	Fed.	Rem.	West.	Fed.	Rem.	West.	Fed.	Rem.	West.	Fed.
50-yard	2.47	2.42	3.89	2.12	2.31	2.53	2.82	2.85	2.20	2.16	2.50	2.80
10-Shot	3.30	3.18	3.57	2.00	2.20	3.08	2.00	2.50	3.25	1.91	2.36	3.92
Machine Rest	2.37	2.59	2.95	1.95	2.95	2.32	2.65	2.33	4.02	2.70	2.74	3.65
Groups,	3.17	2.64	3.06	2.35	1.40	3.10	2.10	3.22	2.70	2.16	2.38	2.00
Measured	3.72	3.49	4.45	1.30	1.62	4.00	1.03	2.25	2.89	2.14	2.28	3.25
in Inches.	3.50	2.92	2.93	1.45	2.50	3.34	1.70	2.35	2.40	2.01	2.25	2.70
	3.21	4.02	2.90	1.55	2.56	1.70	1.42	3.11	3.11	2.95	2.65	4.01
	2.48	2.64	3.77	1.55	1.95	2.42	3.00	2.27	2.73	2.00	2.60	2.47
	2.47	1.89	2.41	2.10	2.25	2.40	2.50	2.43	3.04	1.67	2.55	2.86
	2.87	3.32	3.18	1.93	1.75	2.52	2.81	2.67	2.47	2.90	2.19	2.98
10-Group Av.	2.950	2.921	3.301	1.830	2.149	2.741	2.203	2.598	2.881	2.260	2.450	3.064

All gun average, 3 brands ammunition, 300 shots each gun, total 1200 shots..........2.612
All gun average, Remington ammunition, 100 shots each gun, total 400 shots..........2.310
All gun average, Western ammunition, 100 shots each gun, total 400 shots..........2.529
All gun average, Federal ammunition, 100 shots each gun, total 400 shots..........2.997

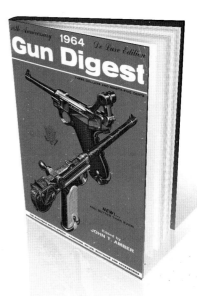

Remington's XP100 and the 221 Fireball

by LES BOWMAN, A TESTFIRE REPORT

EMINGTON'S latest gun — their first handgun in many years — is the XP100, a single shot, bolt action pistol that will probably be the most controversial shooting iron ever. The first production handgun made to handle a cartridge of such velocity, the XP100 was first presented to a group of gun writers at an invitational meeting at Bridgeport last November. To report that some of these gun scribblers were flabbergasted, shocked and generally undone is to put it mildly indeed. Others — the more youthful scribes, of course — were lavish in their praises. There were few fence riders.

The new cartridge for the Remington XP100 is called the 221 Fire Ball, the resultant combination the fastest velocity handgun ever produced commercially. It is also the most accurate and deadly 22 centerfire handgun ever made. The XP100 has moved the handgun into the 100 to 200 yard bench rest class in one step. It's really a holster rifle.

The design of this new Remington pistol is going to make anyone stop and take another look. Shaped somewhat like an International Free pistol, it is a well-balanced handful — the profile of the Borchardt on the cover of this issue resembles the XP100. The new gun will be readily available by the time you read this, as will the ammunition. RCBS loading dies are available, too, and doubtless others soon will be. Bushnell Phantom scopes of 1.3 power and a special mount have been developed for the XP100. A finer crosshair reticle is offered in the Phantom now, and Redfield has a new 2x–4x variable scope designed

especially for the XP100. I'll get round to commenting on these items in greater detail a bit later.

The XP100 is certainly not a combat, quick-draw or "shoot 'em up" sort of gun, nor will it appeal to those who like such arms. Not surprisingly, though, this odd looking gun is in big demand already. Tom Frye, our Remington factory man out this way, a man who knows this gun well and shoots it well, tells me he has taken well over 300 orders for these guns. I've talked to some of these men, and their reaction has been much like my own — while never much of a handgun fan, the really phenomenal shooting of this 10½-inch barreled pistol at ranges up to 200 yards has sold me on it, and it's sold them, too!

> Here's a pistol-carbine/cartridge combination that you may not believe even after you've seen it, but until you shoot it — don't knock it!

The XP100, a far cry from conventional handgun design, is not a light or a small gun. With open sights it weighs 3 lbs. 11 oz., with Bushnell scope and mount 4¼ lbs. With the new Redfield 2x–4x and mount it's a bit heavier. This weight, of course, helps the accuracy of this gun at long distances. Over-all, the XP100 measures 16⅞ inches.

Tom Frye uses the 2-hand hold from sitting, a steady position.

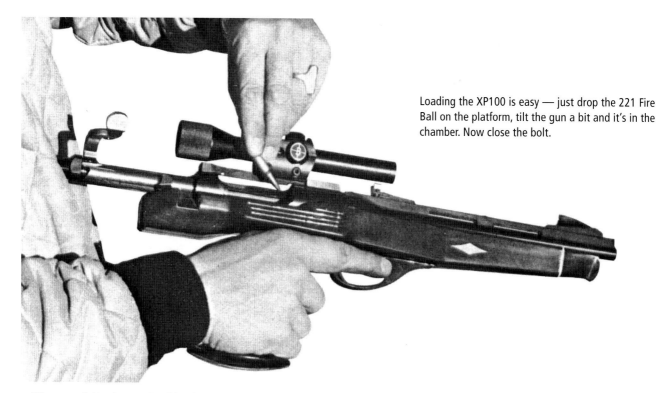

Loading the XP100 is easy — just drop the 221 Fire Ball on the platform, tilt the gun a bit and it's in the chamber. Now close the bolt.

The material in the stock is like that used on the Remington Nylon 22's, moulded into a one-piece structure that is strong, tough and resistant to change in dimension or warpage. The grip is designed to fit right- or left-handed shooters perfectly.

Strong Action

The action, very similar to that used on the latest 700 series Remington rifles, makes this undoubtedly the strongest pistol action ever built. In fact, it may even be stronger than the rifle action because of less cutouts. As in the rifle action the case head in the XP100 is fully enclosed in the bolt head, and the bolt head recesses into the barrel end. No action has ever been made stronger or safer. While the XP100 must be single loaded, fired cases are automatically ejected on opening the bolt.

The XP100 comes equipped with open sights, a flat-top blade front and a rear adjustable for windage and elevation. A ventilated rib is used to improve the sighting plane and the looks. The receiver is tapped for scope mounts. The 10½-inch barrel tapers very quickly from 13/16 (the same as other Remington bolt action barrels) at the receiver ring to 23/32-inch, then gradually reduces to a mere 7/16" at the muzzle. A thumb safety, the same as on the rifles, is used. Instead of the grip being placed at the rear of the action, as in conventional handguns, it is nearly under the center of the action. This helps control muzzle jump better, improves balance and makes for more accurate shooting. Each XP100 comes in a handsome carry-

Les Bowman tries the experimental 2x–4x Redfield scope in the XP100. Note tension sling Bowman designed and the open top holster.

ing case, but with a scope attached a holster is a must for proper carrying, whether on the person, in a car or on horseback. These are available from several sources already. I've also found a shooting sling a big help in improving shooting accuracy. One that we worked out here should be available soon.

The XP100 has features not found in any other handgun. It has the strongest, safest action ever put in a handgun. The trigger is not adjust able except for creep and over travel, but by taking out the counterweight the pull is reduced from 2¾ lbs., which is standard, to 1½ or 1¾ lbs. This lighter pull is the one I like best. There is no creep or jerkiness to the triggers of the guns we've tried — they're velvet smooth and the break is crisp and clean. Lock time

is rifle fast, about 2.75 milliseconds.

The XP100 is chambered for a new cartridge, the 221 Fire Ball. It is similar to the 222 Remington — same case head size, body taper and general conformation — but it's 3/10-inch shorter. It is the hottest handgun cartridge ever offered, muzzle velocity with the 50-gr. factory load being given as 2650, and is does just that on our chronograph. Handloaded it is even better.

I've been enjoying the use of one of these new guns for several months, and I've done a great deal of testing with it. I have put over 4500 rounds through it, chronographing over 400 of them, using bullets from 35 to 70 grains of various makes, and just about every suitable powder-bullet combination.

XP100 Performance

We've killed a lot of small game and varmints around here with the XP100 — and by "we" I mean the numerous ranchers, trappers, hunters, varmint shooters and just plain gun nuts who have visited Martie (Mrs. Bowman) and me over the past year. All but a couple or so of old diehards are sold on the new pistol-rifle — and I think you can tell that I am!

While I've accumulated several handguns over the years, I never did much shooting with them, either at the target or at game. As a big game outfitter, the tool of my trade is a rifle, the more accurate the better. The ordinary handgun just didn't have enough grouping ability to please me, but the potential of the XP100 struck me as soon as I saw it.

A quick check-over of the gun and a study of the 221 Fire Ball ballistics revealed that here could be a real varmint-small game pistol. The iron sights, of course, had to go — there'd be no real accuracy with them on varmints or anything else at 100 yards, let alone 200. A scope it would have to be.

Sometime back Dave Bushnell had sent me one of his new Phantom pistol scopes — I'd set it on a 44 Special, fired it a few times and hung it up — as I said, I'm no big sixgunner. Remembering it now, I dug it out, re-worked roughly an old rifle scope mount to fit the XP100, sat down on the bench and gave the new pistol a trial — the results were honestly startling! I got 1½-inch groups at 100 yards, several under 3 inches at 200, while groups at 27 and 50 yards were sometimes just one ragged hole.

I phoned Bushnell and gave his engineer, Al Akin, the mount dope, asking him for a

The author and a couple of varmints taken with the XP100.

precision-made one, and I also suggested that finer crosshairs be put in the Phantom reticle. Within a week, both arrived at the ranch and were mounted on the XP100. Groups got better, but I wanted Remington's Wayne Leek, who designed the new pistol, to look the new Bushnell mount over, so I sent it on to him. Wayne got in touch with Al Akin, and the Phantom mount now available for the XP100 is a result of that collaboration — and an excellent mount it is.

A reticle with ultra fine crosshairs was also tested, but at 1.3x — the power of the Phantom — the medium fine cross wires are better suited. Bushnell has an adapter coming along that will increase the Phantom magnification about 2½ times; with this the extra fine crosshairs now work out OK.

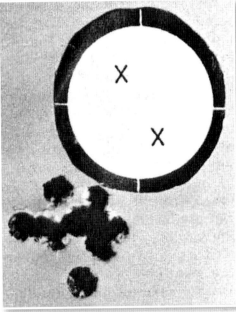

Left: Bowman reports that his tension sling adds to the steadiness of the 2-hand hold.

Right: Bowman's tightest group, 10 shots into .72" at 100 yards, using the Redfield 2x–4x scope, was a handload — 16.1/4227/53-gr. Sierra BR hollow point.

I'm ahead of myself, I see — let's get back to my test-shooting of the XP100.

Testing Starts

First, I gathered together a big batch of bullets — about 1000 from my Biehler & Astels dies, these of 50, 52 and 53 grains; several hundred Sierra 53-gr. bench rest type; a large assortment of Speer, Hornady, other Sierras and some of Dan Hufnail's good heavyweight bullets. These varied from 35 grains — which I wanted for a max. velocity load — on up to 70 grains. All suitable powders and primers were on hand as well.

Assuming that a bullet of around 50 grains would prove most accurate (in view of Remington's choice of that weight) I devoted my initial tests to bullets in the 50- to 55-gr. bracket — I wasn't disappointed.

With the medium fine crosshair in the Phantom and the new mount, groups went as low as ⁷⁄₁₆" at 50 yards. Our tightest 100-yard group was ⁷⁄₈" and at 200 yards we got a group of 1¾". All of these fantastic-for-a-hand-gun groups were made with the Sierra 53-gr. bullet or my own handmade ones, using Sierra jackets, of 50 to 53 grains. All were shot on my range from the bench, using a set of Basil Tuller's Protektor sandbags and a Beecher stand, two-hand shooting for all groups.

Even the 50-gr. factory stuff gave groups down to 1¼" at 100 yards and 2½" groups at 200. Bullets lighter or heavier than the 50–55 gr. range proved less accurate, though good enough for long range varmint shooting.

Next we worked up maximum loads for all weights of bullets, from 35 to 70 grains, then reduced them for best accuracy. The 35-grain bullet really got into high gear, at

Bowman got best accuracy with B&A bullets (made in his RCBS A-2 press) and Sierra 53-gr. BR bullets.

near maximum, with a speed of 3125 fps. I don't believe any such speed has ever before been obtained in a production hand-gun. I also loaded and fired one case twelve times, checking all dimensions and other aspects, such as primer tightness, primer shape, ejection, etc., very closely, after each firing, I am still using that case. The chart of loadings given is our actual chart. Many of these are maximum loadings or near-maximum, and although I have hundreds of fired cases, some of them having as many as 25 loadings, I have not yet junked any of them.

The 50-gr. factory load was excellent on varmints, as was the 50-gr. Sierra Blitz bullet, which really blew the few prairie dogs we were able to catch out this early to small pieces, when we hit them solid. The 53-gr. OP bench rest Sierra bullet and my 53-gr. handmade ones are also good on varmints. The 55-gr. Sierra opens slowly on smaller varmints but works fine on the larger ones.

Small Game

We have lots of cottontail rabbits around here, and during the winter we usually kill some for the icebox as well as for good winter fare. Martie insists on head shots only, in order to save all the meat possible. Using the XP100 with a regular varmint bullet, or even with our OP bench rest ones, we found the velocity and immediate expansion just too severe to save any meat. The

bunnies were blood-shot nearly to the hips, even when shot in the head.

One day, as I was making bullets, I turned some around in the final die and made up a couple dozen full metal pointed ones. Tom Frye took them out and came back in a short time with a bagful of cottontails, all shot in the head and no spoiled meat. A local trapper also found these bullets excellent for killing his trapped animals, and without spoiling any pelts.

On big jack rabbits, any of the 50-to 55-gr. bullets are good, at most any distance. I think the 55-gr. Sierra is about tops for coyotes and such. In states allowing 22 center-fires for deer, the 60-gr. Hornady and 63-gr. Sierra, both giving excellent accuracy in this 1 in 12 twist barrel, should prove to be the right medicine. Sisk makes a special 55-gr. jacketed bullet that should also be good for game. These heavier bullets are slow openers, hence I can't recommend them for prairie dogs and such small animals, but they're fine on bobcats, coyotes and badgers. The 70-gr. Hufnail was the least accurate of those we tested, doubtless because of its great weight and near-instability, but accurate enough to 100 yards for the heavier type predators, however. The 35-gr. bullets were fairly accurate close up, but drifted so badly at 100 yards or more that we didn't continue with them for varmint shooting. The 40-gr. Sierra gave only fair accuracy, but reached close to 3000 fs in near-maximum loads.

Remington 221 Fire Ball Handloading Data

Bullet	Powder, grs.	Primer	Velocity
*35-gr. metal point	16.6/4227	Rem. 6½	2862
35-gr. metal point	17.5/4227	CCI Mag.	3132
35-gr. metal point	17.5/4227	Rem. exp.	3076
40-gr. Sierra	17.2/4227	Rem. 6½	2936
*50-gr. factory	15.8/4227	Rem. 6½	2598
50-gr. factory	16.1/4227	CCI Mag.	2672
†52-gr. B&A	16.1/4227	Rem. 6½	2670
52-gr. B&A	16.1/4227	CCI Mag.	2729
†53-gr. Sierra BR	16.2/4227	CCI std.	2643
*55-gr. Sierra	15.3/4227	Rem. 6½	2564
60-gr. Hornady	15.2/4227	Rem. 6½	2482
*60-gr. factory	15.0/4227	Rem. 6½	2456
63-gr. Sierra	15.2/4227	Rem. 6½	2432
70-gr. Hufnail OP	14.5/4227	Rem. 6½	2339

The loads shown were fired in guns with both 1 in 14" and 1 in 12" twists. They were safe in the guns used, but some were *maximum*, so reduce charges about 5% and work up. A small increase in charge makes a big difference in this small case, so proceed carefully.

* These loads are believed to be safely usable in any production XP100.

† The author's favorite loads.

Factory Ballistics—221 Remington Fire Ball

Range yds.	Velocity fps	Energy fp	Drop in.	MRT in.	Drop 50-yd. zero
0	2650	780	—	—	
50	2420	650	0.7	0.2	—
100	2200	535	2.9	0.8	— 0.6
150	2000	445	7.0	1.9	— 3.6
200	1800	360	13.6	3.9	— 8.1
250	1630	295	23.1	6.9	—17.8
300	1460	235	36.5	11.3	—27.8

Left: The author's loading bench, with himself in attendance.

Below: Trail's end — or the bobcat bobbed.

Handloads

We tried five different powders — H240, 2400, 4227, H4227 and 4759, finally settling on 4227 or H4227. Both gave excellent accuracy and consistency. I think Remington also found this to be true, for a factory load broken down held 15.8 grains of a powder looking much like 4227. Barrel length, bullet weight, case capacity, etc., worked out just right with these powders, for maximum speeds and accuracy.

Primers used were CCI 400, CCI 450, Remington 6½'s and one experimental lot. In maximum loadings the CCI 450 Magnum primer gave higher velocities than the others but less accuracy. As far as we could determine, Remington 6½'s and CCI 400's were the best. Despite the numerous firings our cases received — some as many as 25 or 30 — no more than neck sizing was ever done. After eight to ten firings," cases were trimmed, but even this was not entirely necessary. New factory case length is approximately 1.395" to 1.400" and maximum chamber length is 1.432". So cases can lengthen considerably before trimming.

All handloading was done with RCBS or SAECO stubby dies — Fred Huntington made up our first die set using fired cases.

To speed up reloading accuracy, I ordered one of SAECO's good powder measures with the pistol drum of only 19½ grains total capacity. With this measure and 4227 or H4227 powder I can throw charges consistently within 0.10 gr.

From the beginning of this pleasant chore I thought the XP100 deserved a good holster. Tom Frye had a saddlemaker assemble an excellent one, made with a flap that fully protects it in all kinds of weather, but it's a mite on the heavy side. Now Dave Bushnell has mailed one to me that is only 8 ounces. No flap, just a cross-hold-down strap, with glove fastener. This holster should be available through Bushnell or their dealers.

Scopes and Sling

Wayne Leek of Remington asked me to do some thinking about the possibilities of a carrying strap or sling, and sent me a spare stock to practice on. Well, I drilled here and I drilled there, and finally came up with what I believe is a big help to accurate shooting. This is a loop of leather, more of a shooting sling than a carrying strap, and everyone who has tried it out likes it. Only one QD swivel stud is used, this being screwed into a tapped hole in the rear lower section of the stock. The pictures show how it may be used.

Ed Hilliard of Redfield had told me they would try and have a scope and mount for us to test, and a couple of days ago — just when I'd about given up — they arrived. The mount fit perfectly and after a few sighting in shots, at 50 yards, I shot the first 5 shot group at 100 yards and it came out just a bit less than one inch.

This new scope was a nice surprise. I'd expected a fixed power of about 2½, but the new glass is a 2x–4x variable, patterned after the new Redfield 2x–7x, with the arm's-length eye relief accounting for the drop to 4x at the maximum end. A bit on the heavy side — the gun and scope weigh 4 lbs. 13 ounces, but the outfit really does shoot! I had been getting excellent groups before, but with the new Redfield in position, I got braggin' groups! Yesterday I made two such groups at 100 yards, with a witness — one was 23/32", the other 29/32". Loading used was 16.1 grains of 4227, Remington (experimental) primers and Sierra 53-gr. bench rest OP bullets. These are the tightest 100-yard groups I've ever seen made with a handgun, but I think the XP100 has the potential for even closer ones, using this new Redfield scope.

The sight picture with the 1.3 Phantom, even with the finer crosshair, is a bit vague at this distance if the target is not well defined, so we made up a new style of target to get the best groups.

Here are a few final tips on reloading the 221 Fire Ball — because the case is so small, a 0.10-gr. addition to a maximum charge is equivalent to a 0.50-gr. in a larger case. In the three XP100's I tested, bullets differing by only a few grains invariably shot to a different point of impact.

As I said earlier I'm a rifleman, not a pistol fan, but I've found the new XP100 to be a gun I can shoot well, one that is, with this new cartridge, super accurate and one that will reach out there at long range and still hold that accuracy.

I'm sure that this new handgun will bring real shooting pleasure to many others besides me, shooters who will like the accuracy and speed they get from it, as a varmint, target or plinking gun. It is really the world's first holster rifle.

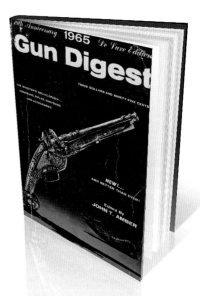

45 Auto Pistol

by ROBERT A. BURMEISTER

THE 45 automatic — enigma of pistols — sturdy companion of our armed forces from the days of Black Jack Pershing hot after Pancho Villa in the deserts of the Southwest, and to the mud and fury of Chateau Thierry, to the shell holes of Anzio beachhead, to the volcanic dust of Iwo Jima, to the frozen night patrols at Pork Chop Hill in Korea. Sometimes carried and not used; sometimes a last defense in some far corner of the world; the choice of FBI man Purvis, nemesis of Dillinger; and the choice of many another law man. Universally admired for pure perfection in engineering, for its flawless functional design, for its brutish power, but always about it one sad doubt — accuracy?

The difficulty of shooting the 45 automatic with passable accuracy has been written about

many times. Ex-servicemen will often make appropriate caustic comments. Target shooters, usually, enjoy only partial or intermittent success with this old war horse, yet the factors or components of accuracy that are responsible for this curious situation are seldom evaluated realistically. Another aspect which confuses and misleads is the all-too-common comment that most of the better handguns will shoot closer than any shooter can hold. True enough, of course, but a lamentable distortion that only conceals a most important fact — that fact is that whatever inaccuracy exists for ammunition or gun will further en- large the group a shooter is capable of holding, and in

the case of the 45 the enlargement may be prodigious. The components of accuracy are three:

1) That of the shooter.

2) That of the ammunition.

3) That of the gun.

These components are cumulative, that is, whatever group size a shooter is capable of making with perfect ammunition and a perfect gun will be enlarged by any inaccuracy of the ammunition and will be further enlarged by the inaccuracy of the gun.

This is shown graphically for one 45 automatic in fig. 1. The largest circle represents a 17.9" group at 50 yards, which is attainable by a shooter who is capable of shooting into a 3.5" group at 50 yards with a perfect gun and perfect ammunition but who in this instance has ammunition capable only of a 3.8" group at 50 yards, and a gun capable only of a 10.6" group at the same distance. The shortest arrow "A" in fig. 1 represents the radius of a 3.5" diameter group and shows how far a bullet can diverge to the right of aiming point due solely to optical error of aim by shooter (for simplicity of treatment it is assumed that the shooter makes no error due to erratic gripping, flinching, or poor trigger release). Arrow "B" represents the radius of a 3.8" diameter group and shows additional possible divergence to the right because of error of ammunition. Arrow "C" represents the radius of a group of 10.6" diameter and shows yet another possible divergence to the right because of error of gun, thus the three arrows accumulate to make a group size of 17.9". While fig. 1 shows only divergences to the right, similar divergences could occur in any other direction. Also divergences can cancel one another in whole or in part. Nevertheless

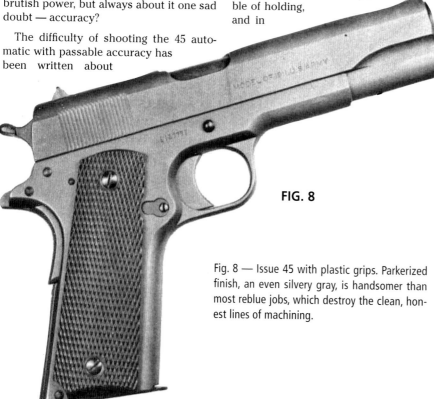

FIG. 8

Fig. 8 — Issue 45 with plastic grips. Parkerized finish, an even silvery gray, is handsomer than most reblue jobs, which destroy the clean, honest lines of machining.

the accumulation in one direction such as shown in fig. 1 expresses the worst that can happen.

Statistical analysis will quickly point out that such an accumulation of errors, all in the same direction, does not happen often. Quite true, but it happens often enough to account for many a poor score. It should be remembered that the foregoing is based on the premise that there is no error due to erratic gripping, flinching, or poor trigger release, etc., which in effect are complementary to "A," the optical error of aim, and if these were included the maximum group size would be still larger.

Values for fig. 1, namely 3.5" for optical error of aim of shooter, 3.8" for error of ammunition and 10.6" for error of gun were obtained as follows:

Error of Shooter

Individual shooting skills vary considerably, but every shooter's performance depends on:

a) How well he can align his sights with the target, which we'll call *optical error of aim*.

b) When sights are aligned how well he can pull the trigger without disturbing alignment (and, of course, how well he resists flinching, accommodates recoil and muzzle blast, etc.).

c) How uniform his grip or hold is from shot to shot.

d) How accurately he can adjust his sights with due regard for ballistics, range, and his hold.

As stated before, items such as (b), (c), and (d) are not treated in this article but item (a), optical error of aim, is considered here as a basic component of accuracy — a principal and assessable error of the shooter. The War Department Basic Field Manual FM 22–35, *Automatic Pistol Caliber 45, M1911 and M1911 A1*, contends that a shooter should be able to make a dime-

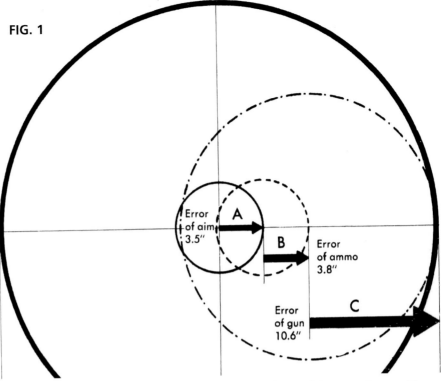

FIG. 1

Fig. 1 – Chart Showing components of accuracy — optical error of aim, error of ammunition, and error of gun — for one 45 automatic. Errors are shown at maximum potential accumulation but all are values based on actual test.

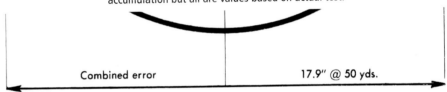

sized group at 30 feet (equivalent to 3.5" at 50 yards) by use of a special fixed rest for the pistol and an aiming test called a sighting exercise. In this "triangulation" test the pistol is held motionless in the fixed rest and an assistant moves a bull's-eye on a blank target until the shooter, looking over his sights, declares alignment has been attained. The position of the center of bull's-eye is then marked and the test

is repeated. After three trials the marks should make a dime-sized group. A seasoned target shot will do better than the criteria specified but the average shooter will do well to equal it. As an interesting comparison the aiming tests made as above and reported by Donald E. Fischer in the March, 1961 *The American Rifleman* showed that his best 5 "shot" groups with a Hammerli free pistol at 50 meters (54.7

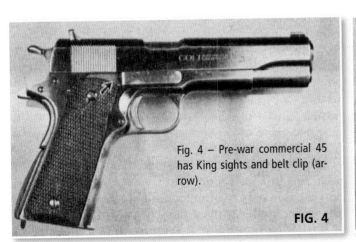

Fig. 4 – Pre-war commercial 45 has King sights and belt clip (arrow).

FIG. 4

Fig. 5 – Government issue hybrid 45 auto. Springfield receiver, Colt slide and barrel; assembled at Rock Island Arsenal. Has low mounted 1/8" Micro sights.

FIG. 5

yards) were approximately ¾" in diameter. Since this free pistol has about double the sighting radius of the 45 automatic, plus precision sights very much superior to the crude military sights of the 45 auto, it is apparent that the criteria of 3.5" at 50 yards for optical error of aim is realistic.

Error of Ammunition

In an excellent article entitled "National Match 45" by Colonel Jim Crossman, U.S.A., and Major Bill Brophy, U.S.A., which appeared in the August 1959 issue of *The American Rifleman*, the following table appears:

FIG. 2   TABLE A

Groups fired from a single accuracy weapon; range 50 yds.; size of 10-shot group measured from center to center of widest holes; selected ammunition lots.

Ammunition	Average Group Size for 3 ten-shot groups
Commercial "A"	0.9"
Handload "A"	1.7"
Service ball, lot 1887	2.4"
Service ball, lot 1806	2.5"
Handload "B"	2.5"
Service ball, lot 18407	3.4"
Service ball, lot 18451	3.4"
Commercial "B"	3.5"
Service ball, lot 1885	3.8"
Handload "C"	7.9"
Handload "D"	8.9"

Same, except 3 groups fired from each lot from each of 3 accuracy weapons.

Ammunition	Average Group Size
Service ball, lot 1854	2.4"
Service ball, lot 6445	2.7"
Service ball, lot 18258	3.0"
Service ball, lot 1686	3.1"

Fig. 2. Accuracy of various lots of ammunition.

Groups were obtained by using a special heavy barrel in a rifle action and firing from a machine rest — hence shooter's error is absent, likewise error of gun is virtually nonexistent. Note variations in group sizes of various lots of ammunition even though these lots (except handloads C and D) were selected for accuracy. Service ball lot 1885, which gave a group size of 3.8" at 50 yards, was chosen for fig. 1.

Error of Gun

In the previous sections it has been shown that at the 50-yard range the optical error of aim and the error of ammunition can account for 3.5" and 3.8" respectively. Error of gun for fig. 1 was derived as follows: Crossman and Brophy tested 5 government issue 45's for accuracy and found that with ammunition rated at 3" the group sizes for the 5 guns were 7.1", 11.8", 6.5", 5.1", and 13.6" respectively. Taking the poorest of these at 13.6" and subtracting ammunition error of 3" the gun is therefore capable of 10.6", the value used for fig. 1. Note that the best of these guns — the 5.1" one, is quite accurate.

Fig. 3 gives the results of the Crossman and Brophy tests on National Match and other accurized guns — of the 281 guns

Fig. 6 — Rear view of guns shown in figures 4 and 5. Note close fit of slide to receiver on pre-war gun at left compared to loose fit (pointer) of slide to receiver on the government issue hybrid Springfield-Colt on right. This looseness of fit is not as important as the fit of barrel, link, link pin, bushing and slide.

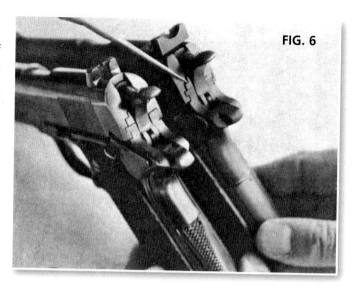

FIG. 6

tested the worst was 16.3" and the best was 2.8".

It is apparent that there is a large variation in accuracy among 45 automatics! This is readily appreciated inasmuch as there have been eight different manufacturers of them in the past 50 years. As to commercial models my first experience was with the one depicted in fig. 4 — a pre-war model. After putting several thousand rounds through this gun (mostly government ammunition) I wrote to the late J. H. Fitzgerald, Testing Engineer for Colt's, telling him that I could do much better with my revolvers than with the 45 automatic and wondered whether I already "shot out" my 45 or whether it was basically inaccurate. His reply sums up the situation admirably!

He stated: "The life of the 45 barrel, for extreme accuracy, is between 5 and 6 thousand shots. In the case of the revolver, the writer has one that has been fired over 150,000 shots, and fired it over 100,000 accurately and without any new parts being installed since the arm left the factory. Extreme accuracy in the 45 automatic requires a match barrel and also a proper fitting bushing that will fit perfectly both slide and outer surface of the barrel. A tight link and link-pin is also necessary. The lower part of the link should correctly fit the slide stop of the pistol. The wear on these parts will, of course, correspond to the wear on the inner surface of the barrel after approximately 5000 shots. For extreme accuracy, they should then be replaced. Trigger pull of not less than 4½ lbs. is recommended by the factory, because after wear the pull may change to about 4¼ lbs."

Fig. 5 shows an issue 45 (equipped with new sights, of which more later); note that in comparing the fit of slide to receiver (fig. 6) of this gun with that of the commercial model (fig. 4) there is a marked difference. Yet the GI 45 of fig. 5 is quite accurate, even with its relatively loose slide.

What to do About Your Issue 45

About this time the reader may want to check out his own 45 to determine how much work may be necessary to improve

FIG. 3   TABLE B

Number of guns tested	Type of gun	Average of 3 groups of 10 shots		Average of all guns, fired 3 ten-shot groups per gun
		Worst gun	Best gun	
106	1959 NM	5.3"	3.3"	4.3"
12	1956 NM	5.7"	3.3"	4.4"
10	1955 NM	6.2"	3.6"	4.7"
8	Gunsmith A	5.7"	3.4"	4.8"
21	Gunsmith B	6.2"	2.8"	4.9"
4	Gunsmith C	8.2"	3.5"	5.6"
21	Gunsmith D	8.7"	3.9"	5.8"
9	Gunsmith E	8.6"	4.2"	5.8"
14	Gunsmith F			6.4"
5	Gunsmith G	9.7"	4.6"	6.6"
5	Gunsmith H	8.4"	5.8"	7.0"
13	Gunsmith I	11.7"	4.4"	7.2"
21	Gunsmith J	10.5"	5.1"	7.5"
6	Gunsmith K	10.8"	4.4"	7.7"
5	Gunsmith L	13.6"	5.1"	8.8"
6	Gunsmith M	15.9"	5.0"	9.5"
15	Gunsmith N	16.3"	4.8"	10.6"

Fig. 3. Accuracy of various guns.

FIG. 7

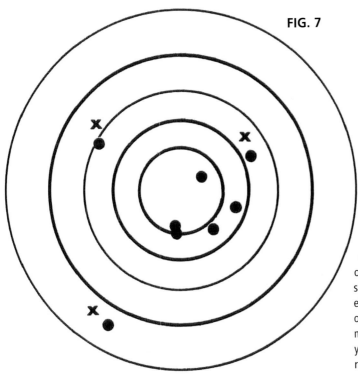

Fig. 7 — A test target showing difference in accuracy of two 45's. One (fig. 5) gave a tight 5-shot 1½" group, all in the black, the other 45 (fig. 10, a strictly issue model), spread 3 shots over 6" (these three marked X). Range 20 yards, forearm bench rest used.

New sights are an absolute *must* on issue 45's, for the old military sights are much too small for accurate sighting. Similarly the trigger pulls on most issue 45's are atrocious — rough, grating and running between 5½ and 7½ pounds. Even an expert cannot shoot such guns well, and it is amazing how much better a 45 will shoot if ⅛" sights are installed and the trigger pull is reduced and smoothed. (Of course target ammunition must be used.) The sight and trigger pull work referred to above for the fig. 5 gun cost $22.50; that included the furnishing and installing of ⅛" Micro sights, the rear sight low-mounted in milled recess, the front staked and silver soldered in place; trigger pull was reduced to 4¼ pounds. This work, done by a custom pistolsmith, is beyond the capability of most home workshops.

For some field work, and as a substitute for a holster, a belt clip may be used as shown in fig. 9. Note that no alteration of the gun is required except for hollowing out the underside of the right grip. The clip is made of 16-gauge steel, shaped and bent as shown. The clip is not as secure as a holster but on the other hand it takes less room, thus preserving one of the salient features of the 45 — its handy, compact, functional design. The writer abhors any alteration of a 45 which clutters it up or makes it unhandy — alterations such as huge, high-mounted sights, ribs, front sights on forward protruding bars and monstrous "anatomical" grips. Maybe these do help in raising the score — but they look like hell and destroy the practicality of the weapon.

Take another look at your old war horse — it may be better than you think.

accuracy. The first step is to run an accuracy test. This is best accomplished by using a machine rest, but if such is not available an improvised forearm rest may be used. An economical and effective rest may be made by constructing a special raised arm rest on a heavy wood lawn chair, or, a bench rest may be utilized. The use of such rests combined with suitable padding, a two-handed hold, and good weather will give results comparable to the machine rest. Testing must be done with ammunition of known accuracy such as commercial target ammunition or high grade custom handloads. (I have found a good load available locally at $3.00/50 having a 185 gr. H&G semi-wad-cutter cast bullet and 3.5 grains of Bullseye powder. There are equally good loads offered in your area, I'm sure.) Don't waste your time with the usually erratic "hard ball" surplus GI ammo or by shooting offhand; the latter will only confuse you as you will be testing a combination of yourself *and* the gun.

Typical tests of two 45's are plotted in fig. 7. Note that at 20 yards one 45 gave a tight five-shot 1½" group, all in the black, whereas the other spread three shots over 6". The first gun is the one shown in fig. 5; it has ⅛" low-mounted Micro sights with front sight staked and silver soldered in place by a custom pistolsmith who also reduced trigger pull to a smooth 4¼ pounds. In other respects this gun is as issued, no "accurizing" as such, so it is suitable for field and target work. The second gun, fig. 8, an issue 45, is obviously not in the same

accuracy class as the first and is therefore subject to an "accurizing" job involving new barrel, new bushing, link, link-pin and possibly tightening slide, in addition to new sights and trigger pull reduction.

Ratings of these guns were based on not one target as shown but also on repeat tests which confirmed results. By testing a gun in this fashion the shooter can determine just how much "accurizing" and improving is desirable. Sometimes a lot of work is necessary, but fortunately some pistols are accurate enough as issued. The writer regards a 45 capable of 2" groups at 20 yards or 5" groups at 50 yards as entirely satisfactory for field work.

FIG. 9

Fig. 9 — Details of belt clip. Grip is hollowed to accommodate clip.

COLT Single Actions

A Detailed Word and Picture Survey of a Legendary Sixgun

by JAMES M. TRIGGS

 UNCE FOR OUNCE there probably has been more unadulterated baloney written, published, and otherwise disseminated about the Single Action Colt revolver than any other handgun ever manufactured. The reason for all this ballyhoo is simple: the old "thumb-buster" was — and still is — one of the finest handguns ever made. It's few disadvantages are often far outweighed by its pure romantic appeal alone.

The Single Action Colt, as we know it, is a development of the first Colt patent of 1836, and the look mechanism of today's Single Acton Colt is virtually identical to that of the Walker model Colt, first manufactured in 1847! The design of the Walker and Dragoon models as further refined in the 1851 Navy and 1860 Army models. The Single Action design, the first large-caliber revolver made by Colt for metallic cartridges, was the logical development from these earlier models.

The Rollin White patent of 1855, which covered bored-through cylinders to take metallic cartridges and which was held Smith & Wesson, delayed the development of cartridge revolvers by other manufacturers until its expirationn in 1869. During this period many systems for employing metallic cartridges and evasions of the White patent were marketed by other arms manufacturers. The Thuer and Richards conversions of the 1851 Navy end 1860 Army models were the Colt company's notable attempts to adapt their revolvers for metallic cartridges yet not infringe the White patent.

It was not until 1872 that Colt could introduce their first large-caliber, conventional-cartridge revolver; this, the 44 rimfire revolver (popularly called the open-top Frontier), was a true transition model, not merely a conversion of an earlier percussion gun.

Single Action Introduction

The Single Action Army revolver, based on the Charles B. Richards patent of July 25, 1871, was introduced in 1873. Later William Mason patents in 1872 and 1875 covered minor improvements in the basic design. Originally designated as Model "P" at the Colt factory, following its adoption by the War Department, the first commercial designation of the new model was the "Peacemaker." It was marketed under this name in 45 Colt caliber by B. Kittredge & Company,

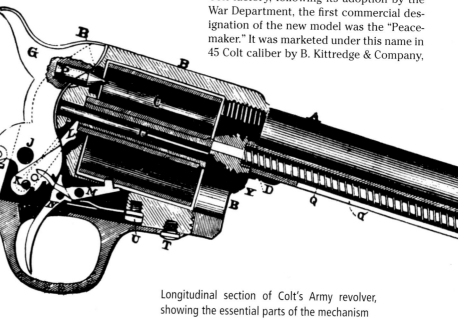

Longitudinal section of Colt's Army revolver, showing the essential parts of the mechanism

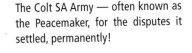

The Colt SA Army — often known as the Peacemaker, for the disputes it settled, permanently!

the Colt agent in Cincinnati, Ohio and by other Colt dealers. It was not until some time later that the designation "Single Action Army" was applied.

In 1878 the Single Action Colt in 44-40 caliber was introduced as the "Frontier Six Shooter" and it was soon thereafter marketed in additional calibers. Between 1875 and 1880, about 1900 Single Action Colts in 44 rimfire Henry caliber were manufactured. These were serially numbered separately from other Single Action models, including the Bisley.

The Single Action Colt was continually manufactured from 1873 until 1941. The highest recorded serial number is 357,859 — a production record for any single action revolver ever made, including percussion models. Following is a list of calibers in which the Single Action Army was made.

Rimfires —

22 Short, Long, Long Rifle	32
22 WRF	44

Centerfires —

32 Colt	41 Long Colt
32 S&W	44 German
32-20	44 Russian
32 44	44 S&W
38 Short Colt	44 S&W Spl.
38 Long Colt	44-40
38 S&W	45 Colt
38–44	45 ACP,
38 Spl.	450 Boxer
357 Mag.	450 Eley
380 Eley	455 Eley
38–40	476 Eley
41 Short Colt	

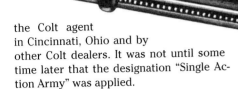

Single Action Variations

Many variations of the Single Action Colt have been made over the years, by both the factory and individual gunsmiths. Only the principal mechanical variations of importance to the shooter and collector will be discussed here.

As originally manufactured, the Single Action Colt was designed for black powder loads. After about number 165,000 (1896) the space for the cartridge head between the rear of the cylinder and the face of the recoil shield (headspace) of the frame was reduced to .060" to prevent primers from backing out because of pressure. Improvement in heat treatment processes and the use of better steel resulted in greater frame strength capable of handling the increased pressures of smokeless powder loads. The original frames were made of wrought iron; about 1883 soft steel was adopted for this part. Modern cartridges should not be used in SA revolvers bearing serial numbers below 165,000.

In the earliest Single Actions, the base pin was secured by a screw which entered the front of the frame at an upward angle. The Mason patent for a tranverse, spring-loaded base pin latch, through the side of the frame, was included in the design at about serial number 150,000 (1893).

Several minor changes to the original Model P were made in the ensuing years. The original ejector rod head had been a disk-shaped button. This was changed to a curved knob which conformed more closely with the under-contour of the barrel and ejector tube. Also, the front sight blade was slightly enlarged, and a small change in rifling design was made at about serial number 273,000.

All the basic Single Action models are detailed in Fig. 2.

The initial acceptance of the Single Action Colt and its continued popularity, particularly on the frontier, were probably results

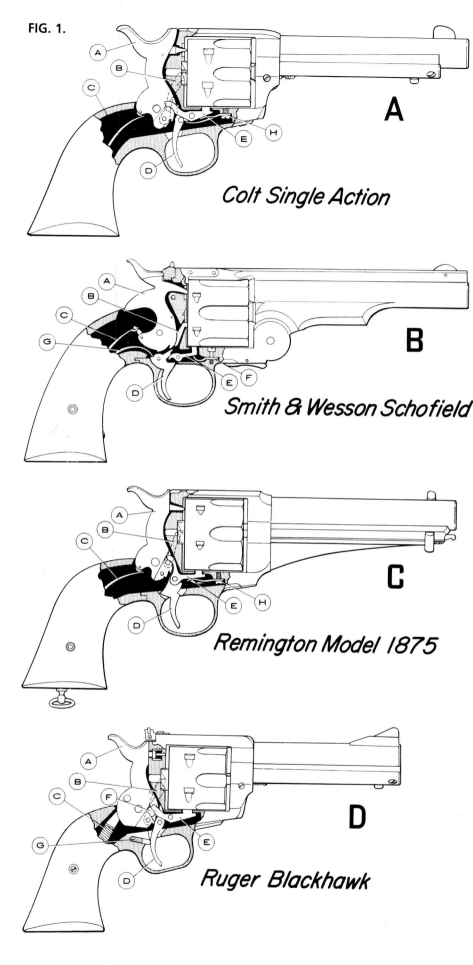

FIG. 1.

Colt Single Action

A

Smith & Wesson Schofield

B

Remington Model 1875

C

Ruger Blackhawk

D

of its ruggedness. mechanical simplicity and dependability. A number of other single action, large-caliber cartridge revolvers were contemporary with the Colt, but none compared with it where these factors were considered. Smith & Wesson's American and Schofield models were break-top types and, while they offered faster reloading, their delicate lock and joint parts would not stand up to the kind of handling demanded. The Forehand & Wadsworth and Merwin & Hulbert revolvers also employed delicate or complicated mechanisms which were subject to malfunction or breakage in hard usage. The sturdy Remington 1875 single action revolver, which closely followed the Colt design, was never made in sufficient quantities to displace the Colt. Shown herewith, for comparison, are cross - section drawings of the Colt, Smith & Wesson, and Remington revolvers (Figs. 1A, B, C, D), as well as the modern Ruger Blackhawk. Other illustrations show all of the basic Single Action Colt revolvers in a graphic form.

Production of the Single Action Colt was discontinued in 1941. After World War II, Colt closed for about nine months for reorganization and, after reopening, announced that this model would no longer be manufactured. Many of the tools, jigs, and fixtures used to produce it, some purportedly dating back to Civil War time, had been placed in storage at some time during the war and could not be found afterwards.

In the late 1940s and early 1950s came a terrific resurgence of interest in the old single action handguns, due in large part to the popularity of Western television shows and the birth of quick-draw competitions. Colt declined to put the Single Action Army back into production, but other manufacturers were busy.

The Great Western Gun Co. introduced about 1955 and sold for a few years a near-duplicate of the Model P. Differing only in using a frame-mounted floating firing pin,

Fig. 1 — These cross-section drawings show the Single Action Colt, Smith & Wesson Schofield, Remington Model 1875, and the Ruger Blackhawk for comparison. All are drawn to the same scale. Note the similarity of the Remington and Colt designs and simplification by the use of coil springs in the modern Ruger. Note the comparative complexity and delicacy of the Smith & Wesson as compared to the Single Action Colt. Parts key: A, Hammer; B, Hand (cylinder pawl); C, Mainspring; D, Trigger; E, Cylinder locking bolt; F, Locking bolt spring; G, Trigger spring; H, Bolt & trigger spring (combined).

these Hy Hunter-made sixguns were of generally inferior quality, and the company did not prosper. Toward the end of the venture. Great Western gun kits were marketed, at a reduced price, but these were hard to assemble in a satisfacory, shootable manner.

It seems likely that the Sturm, Ruger Co.'s greater success was based on their famous Single-Six design. Though their first offering was an excellently designed 22 autoloader, it was not until they began producing a line of single actions that the company really flourished. The Single-Six was patterned after the original Colt Single Action, but incorporated some radical changes for the better, such as a one-piece grip/frame and modern coil springs intsead of flat ones.

New-Old Colts

In late 1947 Colt decided to use the Single Action parts remaining in stock to assemble as many finished SA revolvers as possible. About 300 of these pre-war/post-war guns were produced. They were assigned numbers in serial number gaps in the *original* series.

Colt neither advertised these guns nor offered them for sale. It is a matter of speculation just what did happen to them, but apparently a number found their way into the hands of various persons, either as "gifts" or presentations from the company. It would be impossible to tell if any given high-numbered Single Action were one of these 1947 models, since the workmanship and finish are identical to that of earlier re-

volvers. Accompanying documents which indicated a shipping date after 1947 might mean the gun had been one of these.

Because of increasing demand, Colt resumed manufacture of the Model P in 1955. Calibers were 45 Colt and 38 Special, with the 357 Magnum added in 1960 and the 44 Special in 1962, which was also the introduction date for the new flat-top Frontier. Barrel lengths were 4¾", 5½" and 7½". A 12" model in 45 caliber only was offered as the "Buntline Special," a concession to the television popularity of Wyatt Earp at that time! Regular stocks were checkered hard rubber, as on older models, but two-piece hardwood stocks were also available. In 1960, a version with a 3" barrel was introduced as the Sheriff's Model, to be sold exclusively by one American firearms dealer.

In 1962. a modernized version of the flat-top target models was introduced. Almost identical to the old target guns, the new Single Action has a quick-draw ramp front sight and micro adjustable rear sight.

A 125th Anniversary model was also introduced. It came in 45 caliber only with 7½" barrel, over-all blue finish with the revolver highly polished. Two-piece hardwood grips with the Colt medallion were fitted. Trigger guard and backstrap were gold plated. This revolver was available with a fitted presentation case.

In 1960 Colt had introduced a smaller version of the Single Action design in 22 and 22 Magnum rimfire calibers. Called the

Frontier Scout, this gun had a 4¾" barrel. The trigger guard and backstrap were combined in one casting, similar to the Ruger single actions. Blued over-all or nickel-plated, the Frontier Scout has been offered in many fancy presentation models commemorating various events. While this little single action closely resembles the old Model P, it cannot be properly included as a Single Action Army model for the purpose of this discussion.

Single Action Mechanics

The design and interior mechanism of the Single Action Colt are simple and follow that of the earlier Colt percussion models. The one-piece frame encloses the cylinder, and the barrel is screwed into the frame. The cylinder and cylinder bushing revolve on a base pin, which runs through the frame lengthwise.

Sam Colt, the boy, whittling out the first version of the handgun which was destined to be produced longer than any other model.

FIG. 2 - MAJOR COLT SINGLE ACTION ARMY MODELS

Types	Frame	Barrel	Sights	Stocks	Finish	Calibers†
Standard Army	A	ST	M	E	J	45 Colt
Standard Civilian	A	RST	M	EFGH	JL	45 Colt, 44-40, 38-40, 32-20, 41 Long Colt
Short Bbl. Models	D	Q	M	EFGH	JL	45 Colt
Standard Target	BD	RST	NO	GHI	KL	38 Colt, 45 Colt, 22, 41 Long Colt, 450 Eley
Long Bbl. Models	ACD	V	MNO	EG	J	45 Colt
Standard Bisley	AD	QRST	M	FGI	JL	32-20, 38-40, 45 Colt, 44-40, 41 Long Colt
Target Bisley	BD	RST	NO	FG	JKL	455 Eley, 32-20, 38-40, 45 Colt
Standard (1955)	A	RSTU	M	FG	JK	45 Colt, 38 Spl., 357, 44 Spl.
Short Bbl. (1960)	D	W	M	F	J	45 Colt
Target (1963)	B*	RSTU	P	F	J	45 Colt, 38 Spl., 357, 44 Spl.

Barrel Lengths (ins.)

Q — 2½ to 4
R — 4¾
T — 5½
S — 7½
U — 12 (standard)
V — 8 to 16
W — 3 (standard)

Frame Types

A — Standard
B — Target flat top (Fig. 6, No. 2)
B*— Target flat top (Fig. 6, No. 4)
C — Milled flat top (Fig. 6, No. 3)
D — Without ejector

Stocks

E — 1-piece wood
F — 2-piece wood
G — 2-piece rubber
H — 2-piece rubber, oversize
I — 2-piece ivory or pearl

Sights

M — Fixed square blade front, groove rear
N — Removable square blade front; notch rear, adj. in dovetail
O — Bead front, adj. leaf rear
P — Quick draw ramp front, micro., adj. rear

† Calibers are listed in the order of their popularity. Only the most common are given here; see the text for the others, such as the 32 rimfire, 32-44, 32 S&W, 380 Eley and 45 ACP. See **The Peacemaker and Its Rivals,** John E. Parsons (New York, 1950), for a detailed survey on this point.

Finish

J — Casehardened frame, gate, & hammer, remainder blued
K — Over-all blue
L — Nickel or silver-plated

Note: Throughout the life of the Model P many minor variations were available, usually on special order. These included slight differences in barrel lengths from catalog listings, non-standard combinations of finishes, etc. Also, since some changes were easy to make by owners, they are often seen now, such as different front sight blades in the target models.

FIG. 3.

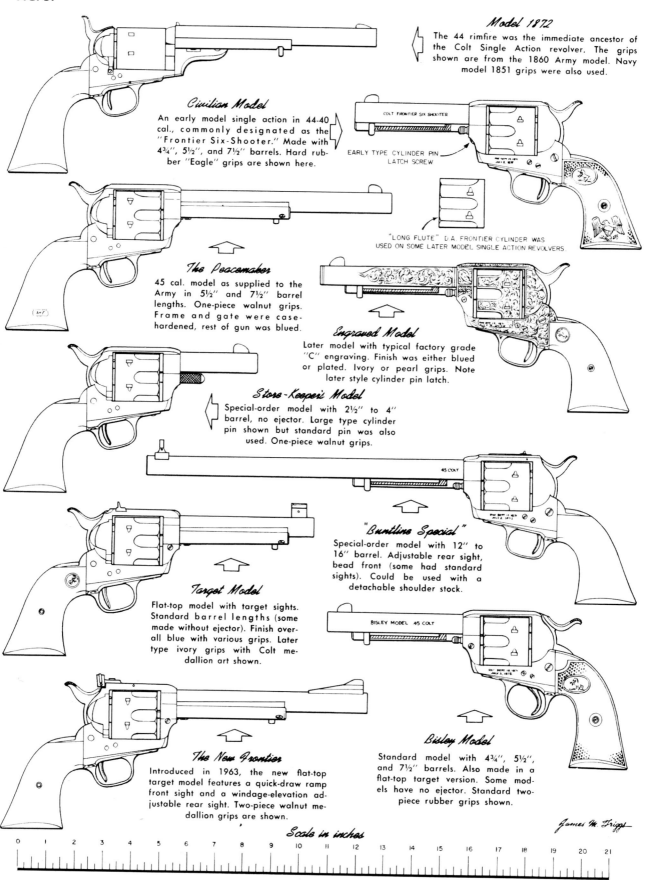

Model 1872

The 44 rimfire was the immediate ancestor of the Colt Single Action revolver. The grips shown are from the 1860 Army model. Navy model 1851 grips were also used.

Civilian Model

An early model single action in 44-40 cal., commonly designated as the "Frontier Six-Shooter." Made with 4¾", 5½", and 7½" barrels. Hard rubber "Eagle" grips are shown here.

COLT FRONTIER SIX SHOOTER

EARLY TYPE CYLINDER PIN LATCH SCREW

"LONG FLUTE" D.A. FRONTIER CYLINDER WAS USED ON SOME LATER MODEL SINGLE ACTION REVOLVERS.

The Peacemaker

45 cal. model as supplied to the Army in 5½" and 7½" barrel lengths. One-piece walnut grips. Frame and gate were case-hardened, rest of gun was blued.

Engraved Model

Later model with typical factory grade "C" engraving. Finish was either blued or plated. Ivory or pearl grips. Note later style cylinder pin latch.

Store-Keeper's Model

Special-order model with 2½" to 4" barrel, no ejector. Large type cylinder pin shown but standard pin was also used. One-piece walnut grips.

45 COLT

"Buntline Special"

Special-order model with 12" to 16" barrel. Adjustable rear sight, bead front (some had standard sights). Could be used with a detachable shoulder stock.

Target Model

Flat-top model with target sights. Standard barrel lengths (some made without ejector). Finish overall blue with various grips. Later type ivory grips with Colt medallion art shown.

BISLEY MODEL 45 COLT

Bisley Model

Standard model with 4¾", 5½", and 7½" barrels. Also made in a flat-top target version. Some models have no ejector. Standard two-piece rubber grips shown.

The New Frontier

Introduced in 1963, the new flat-top target model features a quick-draw ramp front sight and a windage-elevation adjustable rear sight. Two-piece walnut medallion grips are shown.

James M. Triggs

Scale in inches

0 1 2 3 4 5 6 7 8 9 10 11 12 13 14 15 16 17 18 19 20 21

The basic lock mechanism of the Single Action design is shown in Fig. 4. As the hammer (A) is cocked, the hand (B), which is pivoted to the hammer at its lower end, rises through a slot in the frame and engages the ratchet teeth at the rear of the cylinder. The lower point of the hand engages one of the cylinder ratchet teeth just as the revolution of the cylinder has carried the preceeding tooth from the upper part of the hand.

The bolt (E) engages the stop notches in the cylinder to lock it in position for firing. As the hammer is cocked, a small hammer cam (AA), permanently staked into the lower right hand side of the hammer, rises, pressing up the rear end of the bolt and pulling the head of the bolt down and out of the cylinder stop notch. When the revolution of the cylinder is about complete, the beveled lower surface of the hammer cam (AA) comes to the split rear end of the bolt, which slips off the cam, allowing the head of the bolt to snap back against the cylinder wall and slide into the stop notch as the cylinder completes the last few degrees of revolution. The bolt and trigger spring (F) acts both to press the bolt into the stop notch and to keep the trigger (D) forward with its sear end against the hammer.

Single Action Takedown

Figures 5, 6 and 7 show detailed exploded views of the various parts of the revolver. (See illustration captions for identification of parts.) Disassembly of the Single Action Colt is simple. The cylinder is removed by opening the loading gate and pressing in on the left-hand end of the base pin catch, withdrawing the base pin toward the muzzle of the revolver. With the hammer in half-cock position, the cylinder can be dropped out of the frame. On older models, the base pin is removed by unscrewing the base pin screw from the front of the frame.

Remove the stock screw and stocks. On models with one-piece wood stocks, the backstrap must be removed first with the stock attached. Unscrew the backstrap screws and butt screw to remove backstrap. Remove the mainspring screw and mainspring from the rear leg of the trigger guard. Remove front and rear trigger guard screws and pull trigger guard off bottom of frame. Unscrew trigger and bolt spring screw and drop out the spring. Remove the trigger and bolt screws and drop out trigger and bolt. Remove hammer screw and remove hammer to rear of frame, drawing the attached hand and spring out of its slot in the frame. Hand can then be lifted out of hammer. Unscrew gate catch screw and drop gate catch and spring out bottom of frame. Draw gate out of frame toward front.

Unscrew base pin latch screw from nut and draw out of frame with spring.

Remove ejector tube screw and lift front of ejector tube clear of stud in barrel. Pull entire ejector assembly out of frame to front. Ejector rod and spring can be drawn out of ejector tube to rear. Note that the ejector head is screwed tightly to the forward end of the ejector rod and care should be exercised in removing the head.

Reassembly of the revolver is accomplished in reverse order.

The basic stripping procedure has been outlined; however, there are several other steps for complete disassembly which necessitate some degree of skill and special tools. Removal of the barrel requires a suitable wooden clamp to hold the barrel in a vise and a metal block to fit around the front of the frame, for turning the frame off the barrel. Care should be taken to avoid damaging the ejector tube stud at the forward end of the barrel. The threads in this stud are not standard and they are difficult to repair if the stud is damaged. Initial turning of the barrel from the frame is often quite difficult because of the extremely tight fit.

Accurate fitting of a new barrel requires a metal lathe to turn the rear barrel shoulder so that the barrel can be

seated tightly with the front sight properly aligned and ejector tube stud the correct distance from the front face of the frame.

FIG. 4.

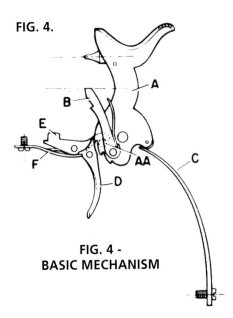

FIG. 4 - BASIC MECHANISM

Fig. 4 — The basic lock mechanism of the Single Action Army revolver is shown here in profile. Parts key: A, Hammer; B, Hand (with hand spring); C, Mainspring; D, Trigger; E, Bolt; F, Cylinder and bolt spring; AA, Hammer/Bolt cam.

TUNING THE SINGLE ACTION COLT

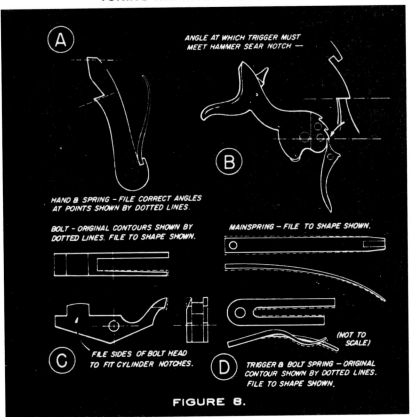

Ⓐ

ANGLE AT WHICH TRIGGER MUST MEET HAMMER SEAR NOTCH —

Ⓑ

HAND & SPRING – FILE CORRECT ANGLES AT POINTS SHOWN BY DOTTED LINES.

BOLT – ORIGINAL CONTOURS SHOWN BY DOTTED LINES. FILE TO SHAPE SHOWN.

MAINSPRING – FILE TO SHAPE SHOWN.

Ⓒ FILE SIDES OF BOLT HEAD TO FIT CYLINDER NOTCHES.

Ⓓ TRIGGER & BOLT SPRING – ORIGINAL CONTOUR SHOWN BY DOTTED LINES. FILE TO SHAPE SHOWN.

(NOT TO SCALE)

FIGURE 8.

This is not a job for an amateur and would be best left to the professional gunsmith or to the factory. Likewise, the installation of a new cylinder often requires precise machine work. Both operations are beyond the scope of this article. If in doubt about replacing these parts, return the gun to the Colt factory where the work can be best accomplished.

The recoil plate set around the firing pin hole in the rear of the frame is a semi-permanent part. To remove it, a proper size punch must be used to drive the plate out through the frame. The new or replacement recoil plate should then be seated in place and staked or punched into place. The factory uses a small, circular edge punch to do this job, but a small center punch can be used, securing the plate in the frame with a circular ring of punch marks. After punching, the front surface of the recoil plate and its surrounding frame area should be filed and polished smooth.

Tuning Up the Action

The Single Action is an excellent design, but its successful functioning depends in large part on the quality of the steel used in its manufacture and in the precision fitting of its working parts. Modern machine production methods have in large measure eliminated the careful hand fitting of years past and leave something to be desired so far as the shooter is concerned. Following are some things the home gunsmith can

accomplish to slick up the action of this model on a do-it-yourself basis:

The Hand: The hand, or cylinder pawl, is pivoted to the lower end of the hammer. It is most often damaged or broken by hard cocking. Fanning the Single Action Colt — that is, driving the hammer back with the heel of one hand while the trigger is held back with the other, and allowing the hammer to fall at the end of its rearward travel — is the most frequent instance of hard cocking. The hammer should be stopped in its rearward motion by the slot in the backstrap, not by the gun's hand ramming again the clinder ratchet after the cylinder has been locked in its firing position by the bolt. A small amount of metal, carefully filed from the two faces of the hand as shown in Fig. 8 (A) will allow the hammer to stop against the backstrap if the hand is too long. Care should be taken not to remove too much metal — it's easy to correct a hand that is to long but impossible to fix one that's too short, unless you resort to welding on more metal.

Hammer and Trigger: Careless or hard cocking, such as "fanning" the Single Action, will also damage the trigger sear and the hammer notches. The only way to repair a cracked or broken hammer notch or sear is to weld on additional metal.

The angle at which the trigger nose or sear meets the full-cock notch of the ham-

mer is critical. Most modern-made guns have a full-cock notch a little too deep for a real crisp trigger-pull. On the other hand, older guns will often have a notch and trigger nose which are badly worn, possibly dangerously. A trigger nose or sear which does not fit the hammer notch correctly will result in either a very hard trigger pull or, what's more dangerous, in having the trigger meet the hammer notch at an open angle which might allow the hammer to slip off of the full-cock position. The correct angle for the trigger and hammer notch is shown in Fig. 8 (B). The trigger nose and hammer notch can be filed carefully to this angle, finished with fine emery paper and polished. It might be necessary to use a stone on the hammer, as it is casehardened. After fitting these parts, have the worked-on areas lightly casehardened by a good gunsmith.

The Bolt: Bolts on many older guns fit quite loosely in the cylinder locking notches and may not engage the hammer cam properly because of wear. Usually it is best to replace the bolt. Since new bolts are made somewhat oversize, careful fitting will be in order.

File the sides of the bolt head to fit into the cylinder notches properly. Note that the contour of the top of the bolt head must also be changed to an angle which will correspond with the cylinder notches. The height of the bolt head is adjusted

FIGURE 5. – LOCK MECHANISM

Parts List

1. Hammer, standard
2. Firing pin
3. Firing pin rivet
4. Hammer roll
5. Hammer roll pin
6. Hand (with spring)
7. Hammer screw
   (Note: Elongated screw used on models designed for use with detachable shoulder stocks)
8. Hammer, Bisley model
9. Stirrup, Bisley model
10. Stirrup pin, Bisley model
11. Mainspring, standard
12. Mainspring, Bisley model
13. Mainspring screw
14. Bolt
15. Trigger, standard
16. Trigger, Bisley model
17. Trigger & bolt screws (2)
18. Trigger & bolt spring
19. Trigger & bolt spring screw

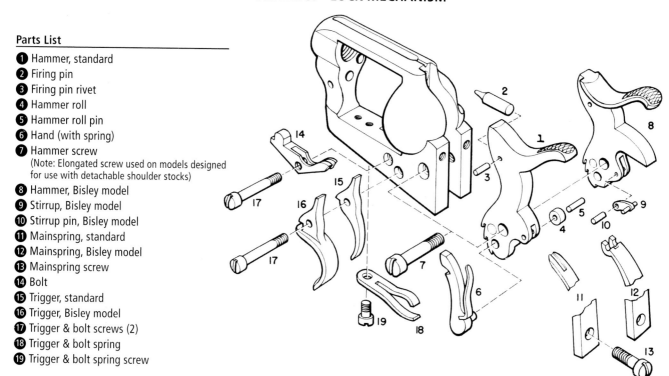

Parts List

❶ Mainframe, standard
❷ Mainframe, standard target with rear sight; flat top, Fig. IB
❸ Mainframe, long barrel models; milled flat top. Fig. 1C
❹ Mainframe, 1963 target model, w. and e. adj
❺ Base pin, standard
❻ Base pin, knurled
❼ Base pin screw (older models, enters front of frame))
❽ Base pin catch screw
❾ Base pin catch spring
❿ Base pin catch nut
⓫ Recoil plate
⓬ Gate
⓭ Gate catch
⓮ Gate catch spring
⓯ Gate catch screw
⓰ Cylinder, standard
⓱ Base pin bushing
⓲ Trigger guard, standard
⓳ Trigger guard, Bisley model
⓴ Front trigger guard screw
㉑ Rear trigger guard screws (2)
㉒ Stock pin (used on models with two-piece grips only)
㉓ Butt screw
㉔ Backstrap, standard
㉕ Backstrap, Bisley model
㉖ Backstrap screws (2)

FIGURE 6. – MAINFRAME COMPONENTS

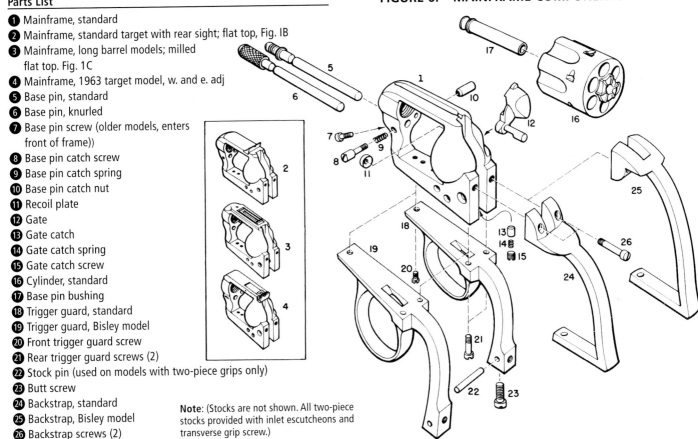

Note: (Stocks are not shown. All two-piece stocks provided with inlet escutcheons and transverse grip screw.)

by filing the lower part of the rear end of the bolt where it rests on the hammer cam. File a bevel on the left-hand rear tip of the bolt as shown in Fig. 8 (C) to allow it to slip over the hammer cam easily. This spring-like rear end of the bolt can also be thinned slightly for smoothness of bolt operation. Do not caseharden the bolt after finishing.

The Springs: The action of the revolver can be smoothed and lightened appreciably by carefully reshaping both the mainspring and bolt and trigger spring as shown in Fig. 8 (D). Do not attempt to grind the springs as this will remove the temper of the metal; rather, use a small stone and fine emery cloth. Although not critical, the hand spring can also be thinned slightly and polished to cut down on friction as it slides in its channel in the frame.

Tuning other single action revolvers of modern manufacture is basically the same as that described above. With revolvers like the Ruger, the action can be smoothed a great deal by reducing the power of the coil springs employed. This is accomplished by clipping a turn or two off of the spring until it seems about right. Don't take off too much!

Customizing the SA Colt

While custom rifle makers, both amateur and professional, have been able to find many varied military and commercial long arms that lend themselves admirably to a number of conversions, handgun enthusiasts have found few such readily convertible arms — with the exception of the Single Action Colt. Its bad points notwithstanding, the fact remains that no other model offers the handgun crank such a wide variety of possibilities for custom alteration as does the reliable old Colt.

The Single Action and Bisley model Colts have one of the strongest revolver frames ever made. This strength lies in the fact that a generous amount of steel has been used throughout. Such beefy construction, free from the weakening cutouts of many more modern revolvers with swing-out cylinders, provides an excellent foundation for a customized handgun. Furthermore, the quality of the metal makes it easy to anneal and to shape. The frame's thickness permits case hardening without risk of ruining it, which is not true of some more modern revolvers.

The Single Action and Bisley models are basically the same gun. Only the hammer, trigger, mainspring, back-strap, and

trigger guard are not interchangeable between the two models. All that is necessary to convert the Bisley frame for use with conventional Single Action grips is to alter the height of the rear face of the frame slightly. Some typical conversions and custom alterations of both the Single Action and Bisley models are shown in Fig. 9.

Both the Single Action and Bisley models offer fine grips, and each lends itself

Samuel Colt

FIGURE 7. – BARREL COMPONENTS

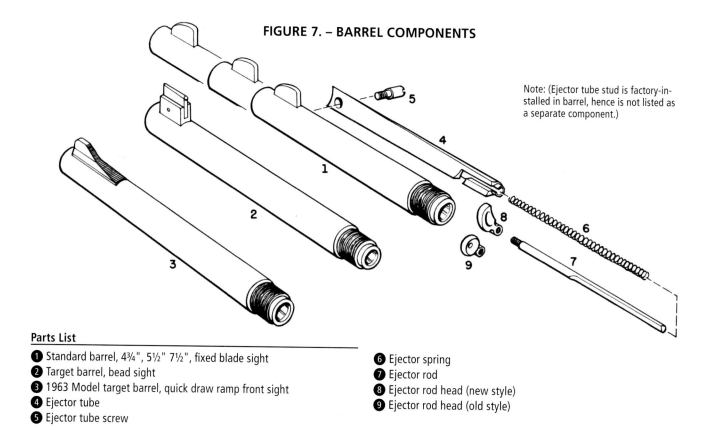

Note: (Ejector tube stud is factory-installed in barrel, hence is not listed as a separate component.)

Parts List

❶ Standard barrel, 4¾", 5½" 7½", fixed blade sight
❷ Target barrel, bead sight
❸ 1963 Model target barrel, quick draw ramp front sight
❹ Ejector tube
❺ Ejector tube screw

❻ Ejector spring
❼ Ejector rod
❽ Ejector rod head (new style)
❾ Ejector rod head (old style)

well to changes according to the whim of the individual shoter. A close look at the Bisley reveals features which are much in demand today for target revolvers, such as the wide-spur hammer and wide trigger. These came "built-in" the Bisley with its introduction in 1895. Technical discussions aside, what other handgun offers these — as well as a built-in bottle opener? The Bisley hammer will do this job very well!

With the combination of a rugged frame and easily disassembled component parts, which make most conversions relatively simple, the desires of the shooter with respect to caliber can be indulged with almost limitless abandon. The Single Action Colt can be converted to virtually every handgun cartridge ever manufactured and can be used with some rifle cartridges as well, such as the 22 Hornet and 30 Carbine cartridges. These latter will necessitate the use of a specially made cylinder to accommodate the long cartridge cases.

New cylinders and barrels in the three standard lengths (4¾", 5½", 7½") are available in a variety of calibers, either from the Colt company or from custom gunsmiths such as Christy and others. Many calibers not presently available can be easily made up by having a cylinder of smaller caliber rechambered to take the desired cartridge. Special or extra-long barrels in the desired caliber can be made up from a wide selection of rifle barrels available at reasonable prices from various arms dealers specializing in old or surplus parts.

Hard Hammer Fall

One of the complaints about the Single Action Colt is the hard hammer fall, which invariably jars even the best shooter slightly off target. The solution to this problem is to have a gunsmith shorten the hammer fall, but since this short action conversion is a tricky and expensive job at best, a good alternative is to "skeletonize" the hammer by drilling holes in it. This operation, combined with lightening the mainspring, as shown in Fig. 8 (D), will considerably lessen the jar of the hammer's fall. This kind of alteration would be considered a sacrilege by the serious collector but it does improve the action of the revolver.

The Single Action hammer can be converted to a wide spur type by welding additional metal to the hammer spur and filing to the shape desired. Or a very practical and good looking conversion can be made from an old Bisley hammer, the spur of which is cut off and welded to a regular Single Action hammer which has been cut and filed to receive the new spur.

Floating firing pins for the Single Action Colt are available from a number of custom gunsmith firms at a nominal cost. This type of firing pin is easily installed by the amateur gunsmith and the alteration of the hammer for use with this type of firing pin consists of a simple grinding operation. A floating firing pin is definitely recommended for use with all rimfire cartridges as well as all high pressure loads.

The Single Action grips offer many possibilities for alteration to fit the hand of the individual shooter. One of the easiest and most practical changes, thought by many to be an improvement over the standard grips, is to install an 1860 Army model Colt trigger guard, backstrap, and grips. This results in a grip which is about ½" longer than standard and provides plenty room for the little finger. These man-size grips are especially desirable when shooting high powered cartridges. The 1860 Army trigger guard is made of brass and the regular iron Single Action trigger guard can be substituted for it by welding a little metal to its underside and filing until it fits the 1860 backstrap. (Back-straps and trigger guards for the models 1851 Navy, 1860 Army, and Single Action Colt are all interchangeable on the Single Action frame.)

These parts for the older percussion Colts are usually available from the many dealers in antique arms and parts. Since most of the original old parts are from unused arsenal stock, they are usually in excellent

FIGURE 9.

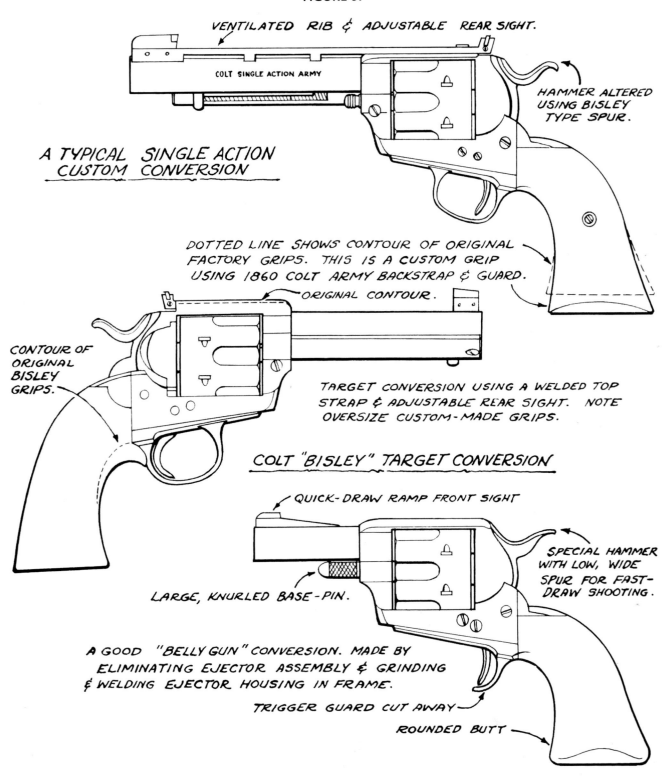

VENTILATED RIB & ADJUSTABLE REAR SIGHT.

COLT SINGLE ACTION ARMY

HAMMER ALTERED USING BISLEY TYPE SPUR.

A TYPICAL SINGLE ACTION CUSTOM CONVERSION

DOTTED LINE SHOWS CONTOUR OF ORIGINAL FACTORY GRIPS. THIS IS A CUSTOM GRIP USING 1860 COLT ARMY BACKSTRAP & GUARD.

ORIGINAL CONTOUR.

CONTOUR OF ORIGINAL BISLEY GRIPS.

TARGET CONVERSION USING A WELDED TOP STRAP & ADJUSTABLE REAR SIGHT. NOTE OVERSIZE CUSTOM-MADE GRIPS.

COLT "BISLEY" TARGET CONVERSION

QUICK-DRAW RAMP FRONT SIGHT

SPECIAL HAMMER WITH LOW, WIDE SPUR FOR FAST-DRAW SHOOTING.

LARGE, KNURLED BASE-PIN.

A GOOD "BELLY GUN" CONVERSION. MADE BY ELIMINATING EJECTOR ASSEMBLY & GRINDING & WELDING EJECTOR HOUSING IN FRAME.

TRIGGER GUARD CUT AWAY

ROUNDED BUTT

shape. In addition to these, many dealers are offering modern-made replacement parts for these older revolvers. If other changes in the shape of grips are desired, the trigger guards and backstraps are easily altered fy forging, or by welding on additional metal which can be filed to shape by hand.

In any conversion or custom job, after the gun has been fitted and polished, the frame, gate and hammer should be re-casehardened, especially when the gun is to be used with one of the more powerful cartridges. While it is possible for the home gunsmith to do this work, it is much better (and much easier) to send the frame back to the factory or to a competent heat-treating plant. They are better equipped to do the job, and incidentally, to bring out the desirable coloring associated with good casehardening. The small cost of having this work done by a professional does not justify the sweat and aggravation the amateur will undergo when he attempts to do it himself.

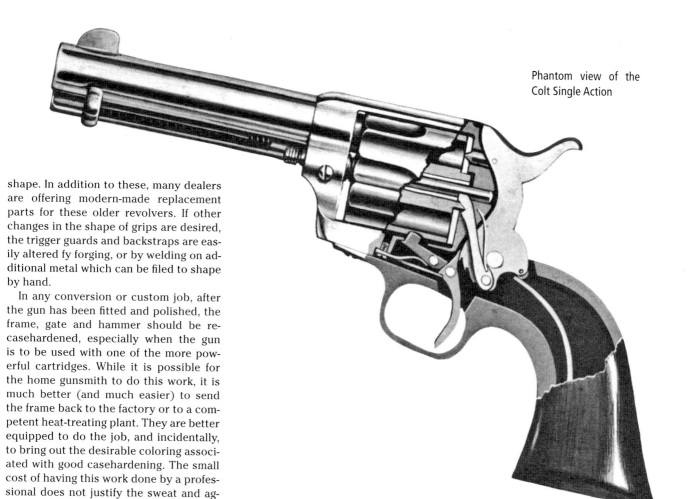

Phantom view of the Colt Single Action

Exotic Alterations

For the shooter who is never quite satisfied with a run-of-the-mill conversion, there are countless changes that can be made in the old hogleg to put the gun into the "exotic" class. Such a novel change

This form of rifling was the design of Alexander Henry, Scottish gunmaker. It is found in his rifles, also in Peabody-Martini rifles and was used in Colt Single Actions for a time.

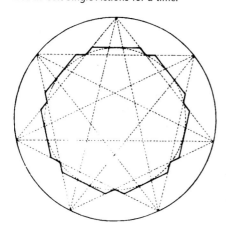

would be the installation of an octagonal barrel, a stunt guaranteed to raise the eyebrows of even the most jaded gunbug! The Sheriff's Model type of Single Action can be made up easily by grinding off the socketed boss that holds the ejector tube on the right-hand side of the frame and welding to match the original contours. A long cylinder pin can be turned on the lathe and knurled appropriately. The home gunsmith should take care, however, in any such operation that he does not attempt to duplicate exactly a rare original model. This practice would most certainly be looked upon as counterfeiting by the serious antique arms collectors. Remember that the purpose of customizing your Single Action Colt is to have an *improved* gun which is unique and suits your personal taste — not to re-create an existing model.

The original Single Action sights can be left as is or various adjustable target-type sights can either be purchased or made up and installed. Full-length ventilated ribs, semi-ribs, etc., can also be installed. Any of these improved, modern sights will usually make quite a difference in your hitting capabilities with the gun and will

improve its appearance as well.

Fitting an adjustable rear sight to the Single Action frame is another one of those jobs which would be better left to a professional gunsmith. This operation usually requires drilling and tapping, either of which can ruin the frame if the job is bungled. (Note: such drilling and tapping should be done before any re-case-hardening is accomplished).

The last item in customizing the gun, and the most important operation where appearance is concerned, is the finish. Regardless of the finish desired — blued, plated or whatever — the quality and appearance of the final product will depend almost 100% on the care with which the gun first was polished. All of the hours spent in customizing a good gun can be canceled by hasty polishing. Over-zealous buffing on a power wheel results in numbers and markings becoming indistinct or lost altogether; sharp edges become rounded and ugly. The best technique is to use progressively finer abrasives, emery paper, and crocus cloths until a high polish is achieved; on flat surfaces use these abrasives with a flat piece of metal such as a file. If a power buffing wheel

E. C. Prudhomme did the engraving and gold inlaying on both these SA's — the basic 5½" model, below, and the Buntline, right.

must be used, *go easy*! Final buffing *can* be done very nicely by hand, using soft cloths. Good results are achieved through lots of patience and painstaking workmanship. Even though the process takes a lot of time and hard work, it is worthwhile in the end.

The Final Touch

As the final touch you might want the gun engraved. All kinds of engravings are available in qualities that vary from excellent to terrible. As a rule, you get just what you pay for. Generally, it is a lot better to pay what it costs to have a first-class job done by a well-known, reputable maker than to spend less money on a poor job. A finely engraved handgun is always a pleasure to own and increases in value in proportion to the quality of the work. Money spent on a bad job is just money thrown away, as it actually decreases the gun's worth.

When the job is all finished and you have stopped admiring your handiwork, take the gun out and shoot it, correcting any minor faults in sighting, grips,

etc. Many custom handgun makers do this after completing all alterations but before the finish or engraving is applied. The more you use a customized or tuned gun the more you will come to appreciate it, especially if you have done a good workmanlike job. Even if you are using a standard, factory-made, unaltered, simon pure Single Action Colt, the more you shoot it the more you will appreciate its rugged dependability. It is truly one gun that is here to stay.

New Colts

by the EDITORS of GUN DIGEST®

AVING LONG SINCE reconciled themselves to the re-adoption of their single-action, Colt has gone on to offer it in a profuse assortment of commemorative versions, absorbing the profits from such sales with a brave smile. The most recent of such souvenir editions is the "Golden Spike," a 6-inch barreled "Scout" model in caliber 22 Long Rifle to celebrate the centennial of the meeting of the Central Pacific and Union Pacific railroad lines at Promontory Point, Utah, on May 10, 1869. The metal of the Golden Spike is blued and gold-plated, with the walnut grips being sand-blasted to bring out the grain, producing an unusual weathered appearance. The presentation case, of simulated mahogany, is lined with plush green velvet. In the lid is a reproduction of an old tintype depicting the historic completion of the nation's first transcontinental railroad. Included in the case with the gold and blue gun is a gold-plated replica, full size, of the final spike which, like the right side of the gun's barrel, is inscribed with the legend, "1869 — Golden Spike — 1969."

As with all commemorative Colts, the Golden Spike has been issued in a limited edition and is available through registered Colt's dealers.

In a somewhat more modern vein, Colt announces the fourth and final edition of the 45 auto commemorating outstanding U.S. victories of the first World War. The first three were the Chateau-Thierry, Belleau Wood and the second Battle of the Marne. The last of the series observes the Meuse-Argonne offensive, which took place between September 26th and November 7th, 1918, effectively assuring victory for the Allied forces. The limited edition of the Meuse-Argonne Colt auto consists of 7,500 units, 25 custom-engraved at $1,000 a copy,

75 deluxe engraved at $500 and the remainder at $220, with standard engraving and the khaki-lined, glass-fronted display case.

Getting on down to the world at hand, it is reassuring to observe that the folks at Hartford are not neglecting the concept of handguns designed to be fired with live ammunition. Their newly announced "Trooper Mk III," caliber 357 magnum, appears to have been conceived by the realization that those people over in Massachusetts had been selling a lot of hardware to police departments without the benefit of hardly any gold plating. As with Colt's Python and Diamondback models, the ejector rod is protected by a solid metal shroud or housing, integral with the lower surface of the

Far Right: Meuse-Argonne WW I commemorative 45 auto is the fourth and final issue of Colt's series — $500 model is shown.

Right: Golden Spike Centennial is Colt's Frontier Scout revolver commemorating the 100th anniversary of America's first transcontinental railroad.

barrel. However, unlike the reptilian models, the Mk III's housing comes to a graceful end a short distance ahead of the rod rather than continuing to the end of the barrel. There are, somewhere, peace officers who still cover many miles each day on foot, men who appreciate the weight saving of an ounce, or even a fraction thereof. Weight of the empty Mk III, with 4-inch barrel, is 40 ounces on the nose; an excellent compromise heft for the lusty 357 cartridge. The 6-inch version weighs in at two extra ounces.

Scanning the vital statistics for the Mk III (including such optional features as target hammers and stocks — improved, adjustable Accro rear sights are standard), the seasoned student of handgun lore encounters a really startling bit of data; the rifling pitch is one turn in 16 inches — quite normal for the caliber — but, *right hand twist?*

It's dim in the memory, but I think left-hand twist is said to have had something to do with the torque of bullets going up the barrel acting to tighten the threads rather than loosening them in the frame. At any rate, it's been traditional for Colt handguns to have left-hand rifling. As you view the fired bullet, with the nose away from you, the marks left by the lands start at the base and spiral to your left. Nearly all other handguns, and, for that matter, rifles, use right-hand rifling. Offhand, I don't know of anyone but Colt using left-hand rifling. I say "nearly" only as a hedge against the inevitable erudite reader poised to point out (crushingly) that they made three Rast-Gassers in 1911 with left-hand rifling when the polarity of the house current was reversed accidentally. For years, it has been a devastating ploy of the fairly well-versed ballistics expert to pick up a fired bullet and remark, "Hmm. Fired from a Colt." Or,

"Obviously, not fired from a Colt," after a glance to see which way the rifling marks veered. But, alas, no more can this be pulled upon the open-mouthed layman. To me, this is the most startling piece of news in the world of handguns for this and several other years. Upon learning about it, I was surprised that the great metropolitan dailies didn't scarehead the news across their front pages in red ink: "COLT GOES NORTHPAW!" Ah well ....

In the meantime, levity aside, the Mk III looks like an excellent piece of ordnance when viewed from any angle. Its double-action trigger pull is a source of deep-dish delight and, with the growing realization that handguns that work for a living are apt to be fired that way in a clutch, that's worth a solid touchdown plus point-after in any evaluator's score-book. Also to the good is the fact that Colt's hasn't been so carried away as to give up their clockwise cylinder rotation. What this means, in essence, is that the thing can be set up so that the notch that locks the cylinder can be offset slightly to bring it to one side of the thinnest spot in the chamber wall. Counterclockwise cylinder rotation, for some odd reason, positions the little semi-circular notch right above the thin place, creating a weak spot. So long as the timing of hand and pawl is faultless, clockwise rotation is much to be preferred, though a small discrepancy can set off the primer with the chamber slightly out of alignment with the barrel; that state of affairs can knock out a hunk of cylinder wall. You pays your money and you takes your choice.

If the sample seen and handled is representative of production guns, the Mk III

Cutaway view of Colt's Trooper MK III DA revolver.

Colt's Diamondback revolvers in 22 caliber are now made with 2½- and 4-inch barrels and a choice of standard or target grips.

looks like a most promising entry in the sweepstakes for working handguns. It is an encouraging sign for those who believe that handguns are for shooting as much, if not more, than for admiring.

Architectural rendering of Colt's Rocky Hill plant

Astra 400
A Legacy of Guernica

by DENNIS RIORDAN

THE ARMED FORCES of Spain adopted their first automatic pistol in 1913. Designed by the Spanish Count of Campo Giro and named in his honor, the gun was manufactured under contract by Esperanza y Unceta at Guernica. The Campo-Giro was a straight blowback pistol, chambered for the powerful 9mm Bergmann-Bayard, known in Spain as the 9mm Largo (long). Several modifications were incorporated into the gun during its life, but it was superseded in 1921 by a new pistol, designed and manufactured by Esperanza y Unceta. This pistol, to become commercially known as the Astra 400, was the largest and most powerful of a series of similar automatic pistols; the model 300 chambered in 32 and 380, the model 200 in 25 caliber and, eventually, the model 600 in 9mm Luger, developed for sale to the German military as the Model 1943.

Astra was the company's trade name, and most Model 400 pistols, both commercial and military, carry the Astra trademark on slide and magazine floorplate. The device consists of the word "Astra" superimposed over a starburst and enclosed within a circle. Esperanza y Unceta was to become Unceta y Compania, probably about 1925. The firm is still registered under that name.

The Astra 400 is a straight blow-back pistol in caliber 9mm Largo. It shares other characteristics of the Campo-Giro, such as a cylindrical slide moving within frame grooves and a barrel-mounted recoil spring. However, many Astra features apparently derived from Browning guns, particularly one F.N. Military Pistol of 1903. Like the F.N., the Astra has a grip safety operated by a flat spring. The hammer is located internally, the barrel secured to the frame by a series of lugs. The Astra's breechblock is

A thoroughly researched, definitive study of this famous Spanish service pistol. Included are three excellent drawings and other illustrations, plus a parts legend, detailed takedown instructions and full bibliography.

an integral section of the slide forging, and a removable barrel bushing is fitted to the slide's forward end. Other features, such as the sliding sear located at the rear of the hammer, the clever grip-safety ratchet that locks the sear, the vertically-moving

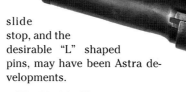

slide stop, and the desirable "L" shaped pins, may have been Astra developments.

The Model 1921 marked a great advance over the Campo-Giro. It is a stronger, safer pistol, far more rugged and reliable, infinitely simpler to strip and clean. The excellence of the design is indicated by its long military life, during which no modifications or improvements were found necessary. The Astra remained the standard Spanish military pistol until after World War II, when it was finally replaced by the Super Star from Echeverria of Eibar. The Star is also in 9mm Largo, but has a fully locked breech and is externally similar to the 1911 Colt 45.

Straight blowback systems are rarely found in pistols chambered for ammuni-

tions more powerful than the 9mm Browning Long. The Astra Models 400 and 600 are the only ones that have proved completely successful, both empirically and commercially. These pistols, totally unlocked at the moment of discharge, rely solely on the inertia of their heavy recoiling parts to prevent premature opening of the breech. To supply the necessary weight, Astra 400 slides are particularly massive forgings, yet while the pistols are heavy, they still run 3 ounces lighter than 1911 Colts.

The Astra's long, heavy slide is not entirely a liability, the weight and its distribution promotes steady holding and good muzzle control; the massiveness offers a great margin of safety; the length permits a long sighting radius.

Trigger Pull and Safeties

W.H.B. Smith has said that the Astra 400 won many European awards for accuracy. There are several good reasons why the pistol should produce good target scores. Beyond the weight and long sighting radius, the slide is well guided within grooves running the length of the Astra's frame. These grooves were fitted quite closely for a military pistol. Because the barrel is not required to move in firing, its lugs were made to engage their frame recesses tightly. For the same reason, the barrel bushing was given a close-tolerance fit to the barrel. Finally, the pivoted trigger operating a freely moving trigger bar, and the sliding sear engaging the rear of the hammer, combine to produce a smooth and unchanging trigger pull. Because the sliding sear is the vulnerable part of the trigger mechanism, it is important that the contacting surfaces between frame and sear be kept clean and smooth.

The grip safety is the primary safety device of the Astra 400. Its pivoting ratchet locks the sear and, resultantly, the hammer. Regardless of the condition of the manual safety, the sear is always locked until the pistol is actually held in the hand with the grip safety depressed by the palm.

The manual safety blocks the trigger's movement. Unlike most safety catches of this type, it does not lock the slide closed. An arm on the safety is used as an aid to field stripping, and it can be employed to lock the slide in open position at any time.

The magazine safety is also a trigger block, engaging automatically as the magazine is withdrawn. Should the magazine become lost or damaged, the magazine safety can be easily removed without otherwise affecting the pistol's operation. The large ejection port, the extractor design, and the ability of the manual safety to function as a hold-open device make single loading practicable.

The disconnector is comprised of a vertical arm of the trigger bar, which seats into a rounded slide notch. As the slide moves to the rear following discharge, the disconnector is cammed downward, breaking contact between trigger bar and sear and positively preventing multiple fire. The trigger bar cannot recapture the sear until the trigger is released and the disconnector again rises into the slide notch. Therefore the pistol cannot be fired unless the slide is fully closed. All of the Astra's safety devices are simple, rugged and dependable.

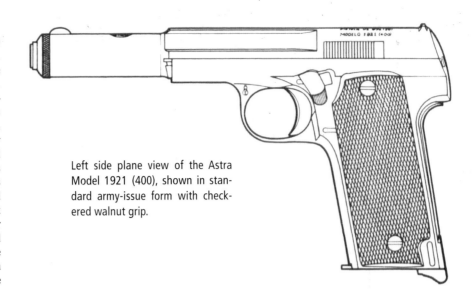

Left side plane view of the Astra Model 1921 (400), shown in standard army-issue form with checkered walnut grip.

The independent slide stop signals that the pistol is empty. It is operated by a step on the magazine follower. The Astra's heavy gauge steel magazine is of seamless construction.

Field stripping the Model 400 is not difficult and it requires no tools. Such takedown results in 7 parts, none so small as to be easily lost. Complete disassembly presents no special problems and is facilitated by the slip fits given the pins, all of which can be pushed or pried out with little effort. All pins are mechanically retained within the assembled pistol.

Few Faults

Unfavorable characteristics are not particularly serious. The pistol is heavy and somewhat awkward to carry. The powerful recoil and hammer springs require a considerable effort to cycle the slide manually. The fixed sights cannot be knocked out of plumb and are virtually indestructable, but they do not allow of adjustment except by filing or brazing. There is no external indication of a chambered round. The manual safety is located a bit too far forward for thumb release in firing position. The Astra's safety devices are not foolproof, but they do provide a reasonable degree of safety. Though the hammer is not equipped with a safety notch, the sear engages its full-cock notch deeply, is unlikely to jar off, even without the added security of the grip safety. Whether the lack of an outside hammer is a point against the Astra is perhaps a matter for theory and opinion. An external hammer can be a mixed blessing, because it exposes a vital part of the firing mechanism to outside influences. The Astra's hammer cannot be struck a direct blow.

Probably the worst problem with this Astra is the difficulty of obtaining proper ammunition. The Model 400 has acquired a reputation for some reason, as having been designed to fire a variety of cartridges. This is a misconception; the pistol was designed and chambered for the 9mm Largo and no other. The use of substitute ammunitions has never been anything more than a matter of expediency.

Dimensions of the 9mm Steyr cartridge are so close to the Largo's that this ammunition has been used in the Astra pistol with great success. The rear of the case bulges slightly to conform to the Astra's chamber, but not to a serious degree. Unfortunately, Steyr ammunition is no less elusive than the Spanish Largo.

The 38 ACP round is nearly identical in length, but where the Largo and Steyr cartridges chamber on the case neck, the straight-sided Colt case simply wedges in the Astra's tapered chamber, driven home through the blow delivered by the heavy slide. When loading 38 ACP ammunition, it is therefore necessary that the slide be slammed closed to fully seat the cartridge. Manual extraction can be quite difficult in tightly chambered pistols. 38 ACP ammunition will operate satisfactorily in most Astra pistols, not at all in others, depending on whether the counterbore in the breech face is of sufficient diameter to accept the larger rim of the 38 case.

While the dimensions of the 38 Super case are the same as those of the 38 ACP, this round is too powerful for use in the Model 400. The 400 pistol does not use a recoil buffer, so 38 Supers cause excessive battering between slide and frame at the end of the recoil stroke.

The 9mm Luger cartridge can be dangerous. Much shorter than the Largo round, it must wedge at the rear of the chamber to operate properly. Some types of Luger ammunition, such as U.S. commercial and Canadian surplus, don't have a big enough base diameter to do this. As a result the extractor cannot snap over the case rim, but rather pushes the cartridge ahead of it, deep into the chamber. The Astra firing pin has a long reach and will usually fire a round so located, under a condition of grossly excessive headspace. Even with Luger ammunition that chambers adequately, the shorter cartridge has stacking difficulties in the magazine, with resultant jams.

If extensive shooting is wanted with the Astra 400, the 38 ACP is the logical choice. If necessary the counterbore can be opened up slightly to accommodate the larger rim.

Astra 400 Variants

Astra 400 pistols have evoked collector interest because of the variations reported. The standard Spanish model with moulded black composition or checkered walnut grips is by far the most common, though pistols displaying *Guardia Civil* markings are available in plenty. A mechanical variant has long been known, this version bearing a side-mounted magazine catch similar to that of the Astra 600. Astra pistols marked with German ordnance stamps, models with various commercial markings and special grips, and contract types carrying distinctive markings for individual Spanish services have all come to light in recent years. Additionally, copies of the Model 400 by other Spanish makers have been recognized, ranging in quality from poor to excellent.

But the big Astra is not essentially a gun for collectors; it has been brought into the country in numbers sufficient for distribution among shooters, and it is a gun well worthy of use. Fine quality steels, properly hardened, were used throughout its construction. The quality of finish and fit is on a uniformly high level. The parts are rugged and strong, direct acting and simple. The action is very well enclosed against the entry of dust and sand. Above all, the gun has rock solid dependability. It is weighty, but that weight means also strength and safety; homely, but absolutely the functional machine it was designed to be, a man's gun without compromise.

Bibliography

Study of Astra Model 400, Nos. 89188 and 103453, by Unceta y Compania S. A., Guernica, Spain.

Study of Astra Model 600, No. 37028, as above.

Dean A. Grennell, "Grand Olde Gun," Gun World magazine, September, 1968, p. 39. (F. N. Browning 1903)

E. J. Hoffschmidt, "Astra Models 400 and 600 Pistols," N.R.A. Firearms Assembly Handbook, vol. 2, p. 32.

Maj. Dick Keogh, "An Orphan Astra," The Gun Report magazine, August, 1970, p. 27. (Astra 400 copy)

Harold Murtz, "Astra Condor," Guns magazine, December, 1970, p. 42.

Maj. George C. Nonte, Jr., "Star's Modelo Super," Gunfacts magazine, July, 1969, p. 31.

Maj. George C. Nonte, Jr., "The Versatile Astra 400," Gun World magazine, September, 1969, p. 72.

Dale T. Shinn, "Campo-Giro — Spain's First Automatic Military Pistol," The American Rifleman magazine, November, 1969, p. 78.

Donald M. Simmons, Jr., "In Defense of a Tarnished Trio," Guns magazine, April, 1968, p. 24. (Astra 400)

Donald M. Simmons, Jr., "High-Power Blowback Pistols," The American Rifleman magazine, November, 1967, p. 61.

W. H. B. Smith, Book of Pistols and Revolvers, 6th ed. Harrisburg, 1965, "Astra 400," p. 370; "Browning 1903," p. 326.

W. H. B. Smith and Joseph E. Smith, Small Arms of the World, 7th ed., Harrisburg, 1964, "Spanish Pistols," p. 543.

Capt. Robert D. Whittington, III, "Astra Pistols in the German Army," Guns magazine, November, 1968, p. 41.

J. B. Wood, "Viva Astra," Gun World magazine, February, 1966, p. 26. (Astra 400)

J. B. Wood, "The Adaptable Astra," Shooting Times magazine, September, 1968, p. 39. (Astra 400)

J. B. Wood, "The Count of Campo-Giro," Guns magazine, January, 1970, p. 42. (Campo-Giro pistol)

Field Stripping

To field strip, remove magazine and clear chamber. Depress barrel bushing (8) flush with face of bushing lock (7), using lip of magazine floor plate. Turn bushing lock slightly so that it holds bushing depressed; grasp bushing lock firmly and rotate about ¼-turn until it unlocks from slide (9). Ease off bushing lock and bush-

Astra Model 600 in 9mm (Luger). This model has a shorter barrel and redesigned magazine release located below the grip on the left side. Grips are of checkered walnut.

Astra Model 400

EXPLODED VIEW

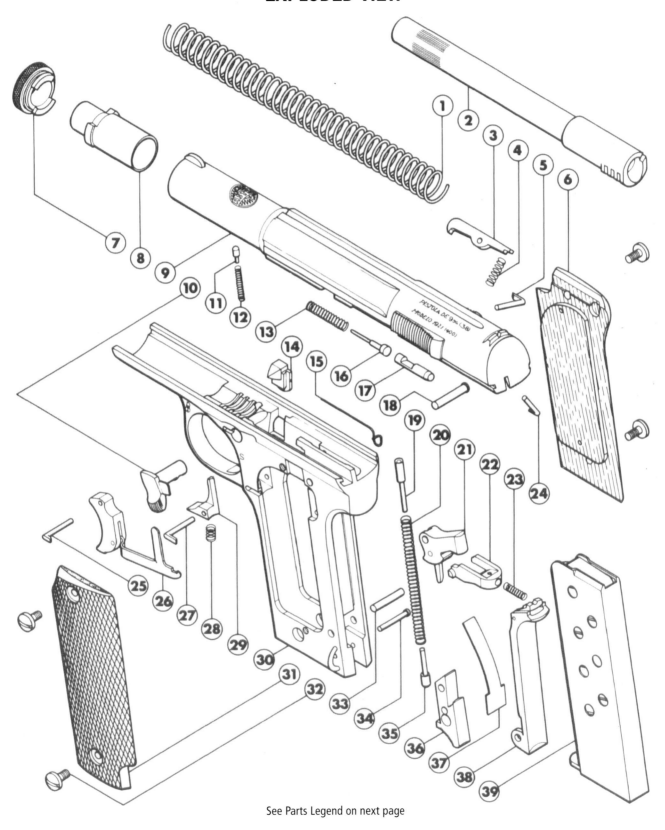

See Parts Legend on next page

ASTRA MODEL 1921 (400) Sectional View

Parts Legend

1. Recoil spring
2. Barrel
3. Extractor
4. Extractor Spring
5. Firing-Pin retainer pin
6. Right grip
7. Barrel bushing lock
8. Barrel bushing
9. Slide
10. Safety catch
11. Safety detent
12. Safety spring
13. Firing-Pin spring
14. Slide stop
15. Slide stop spring
16. Firing-Pin
17. Firing-Pin extension
18. Hammer pin
19. Hammer plunger
20. Hammer spring
21. Hammer and strut
22. Sear
23. Sear spring
24. Extractor pin
25. Trigger pin
26. Trigger and trigger bar
27. Magazine-safety pin
28. Magazine-safety spring
29. Magazine-safety
30. Frame
31. Left Grip
32. Grip Screw (4)
33. Grip-safety pin
34. Magazine-catch stop
35. Magazine-catch plunger
36. Magazine-catch
37. Grip-safety spring
38. Grip-safety
39. Magazine

Cutaway shows relationship between internal parts. Pistol is pictured cocked and with chambered round, manual and magazine safeties disengaged, sear locked by grip safety. Parts are number-keyed to the parts legend.

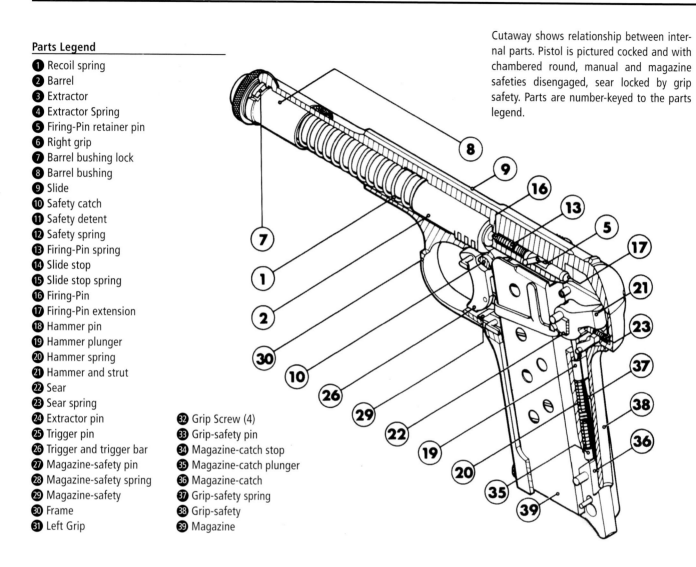

ing and remove recoil spring (1). Draw slide fully to the rear, then move slightly forward while engaging safety catch (10). Rotate barrel (2) counterclock wise to the limit of its movement, release safety and run slide and barrel forward off frame. Turn barrel lugs out of slide recess and pull barrel forward and out. In reassembly, locate barrel so that extractor notch faces downward while slide is mounted on the frame. Align lugs on barrel bushing and lock with slide channels when replacing these parts. Turn bushing lock until bushing snaps outward to retain it.

Disassembly

To strip slide, pry out extractor pin (24) with a small screwdriver inserted under its head. Remove extractor (3) and spring

(4). Firing-pin extension (17), firing pin (16), and spring (13) are released by removal of their retainer pin (5). Notch in firing-pin extension must face toward extractor on replacement.

To strip frame, unscrew grip screws (32) and remove grips (6)(31). Push out magazine-safety pin (27) and lift out magazine safety (29) and spring (28). Insert magazine-safety pin in frame hole beneath rear end of trigger bar (26), pull trigger and lower hammer (21) with thumb. Push out hammer pin (18), releasing hammer, slidestop spring (15), and slide stop (14). Depress hammer plunger (19) with punch and remove magazine-safety pin. Push out magazine-catch stop (34) and grip-safety pin (33) to free magazine catch (36) and

grip safety (38). Magazine-catch plunger (35), hammer spring (20), and hammer plunger can now be removed from bottom of frame. On replacement, the hammer plunger is identified by its concave head. With safety catch in disengaged position, push straight out of frame. Lift out safety detent (11) and spring (12). These parts must be depressed well into frame with a small punch while replacing safety. Pull downward and outward on trigger bar, while moving sear (22) and spring (23) forward into magazine well. Push out trigger pin (25). To remove and replace trigger and bar, pivot trigger forward, fully compressing the internally housed trigger-bar spring. Reassemble in reverse order.

New SIG-Sauer Pistols

by J. B. WOOD

OR THE PAST 25 years the beautiful SIG P-210 has been considered by many to be the most finely made of all automatic pistols. Now the Schweizerische Industrie Gesellschaft of Neuhausen, Switzerland, has developed two new pistols, to establish what will surely become a distinguished series. Both pistols, designated the P-220 and P-230, are so recently produced that it was not possible to obtain test samples before publication time.

We do, however, have extensive information on them, obtained by Editor John T. Amber during a visit to Neuhausen last year. Mr. Amber examined both models, and fired them on the SIG range. He says their performance was flawless. He also noted that neither was as finely finished as the P-210. Two possible good reasons for this: Intended for combat-military and personal-police use respectively, their utilitarian finish and less

> Two of them, in fact, the P-220 and the P-230, both designed for utilitarian service. Production samples functioned and shot well in Switzerland.

costly construction may help to keep the price within reason. Their old stable mate, the P-210, is expensive.

The new pistols are to be a cooperative effort, in association with the old and respected firm of J. P. Sauer & Sohn of Eckernforde, West Germany, who will actually manufacture the guns. To reflect this combination of design and production skills, the pistols will be marketed under the name "SIG-Sauer."

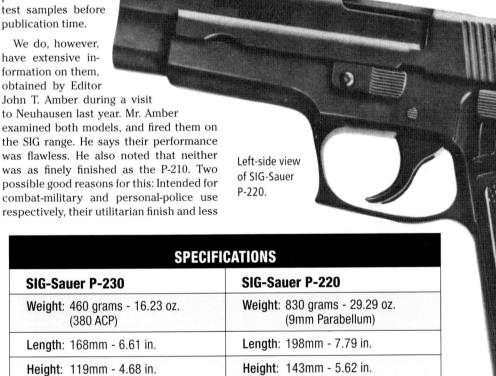

Left-side view of SIG-Sauer P-220.

SPECIFICATIONS	
SIG-Sauer P-230	**SIG-Sauer P-220**
Weight: 460 grams - 16.23 oz. (380 ACP)	Weight: 830 grams - 29.29 oz. (9mm Parabellum)
Length: 168mm - 6.61 in.	Length: 198mm - 7.79 in.
Height: 119mm - 4.68 in.	Height: 143mm - 5.62 in.
Width: 31mm - 1.22 in.	Width: 34mm - 1.34 in.
Barrel: 92mm - 3.62 in.	Barrel: 112mm - 4.40 in.

SIG-SAUER P220

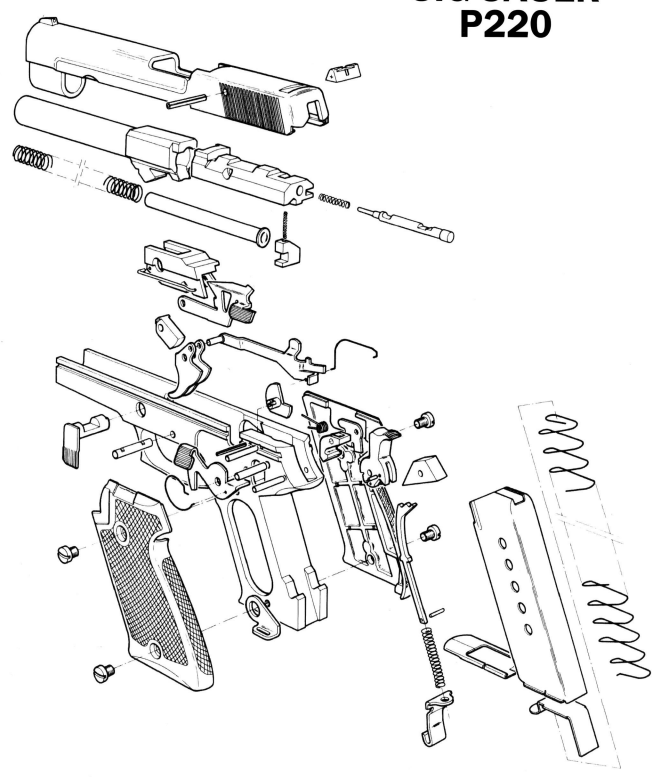

SIG P-220

The P-220 is the larger, combat-type pistol. It has an unusual feature, a de-cocking lever, located at the top forward edge of the left grip panel. This is similar to the system used on the Sauer Model 38H pistol but, unlike the Sauer, the P-220 lever is for lowering the hammer only.

The firing pin has an automatic block which is moved only by the last fraction of trigger pull. Thus, when using the de-cocking lever, there is no chance of accidental firing, even if the thumb slips. There is also a wide safety-step on the hammer at normal rest position. Between these two systems, the P-220 will be safe even if dropped on the hammer, say the SIG people. There is no manual safety, and on this point the Swiss engineers are in complete agreement with this writer. On a double action pistol with an external hammer, who needs it?

The P-220 has an aluminum-alloy grip frame and plastic grips. The magazine release is a bottom-of-handle type. The location of the slide stop, at top center of the left grip panel, is perfect. Sights are the Stavenhagen-patent "contrast" type, these said to allow quick alignment, even in low-light conditions. These consist of a white-outlined square-notch rear sight, with a white dot inlaid into the rear surface of the post front sight. The front sight is integral with the slide, and the rear is adjustable laterally by drifting in its dovetail. Vertical adjustment will also be possible by changing rear sight units — 5 sizes will be made.

The SIG P-220 will be available in 45 ACP, with optional conversion units for 38 Super, 9mm Parabellum, 7.65mm Parabellum, and 22 Long Rifle.

Magazine capacity is listed at only 7 rounds in 45 ACP, 9 rounds in the other centerfires. One wonders why they didn't use a larger capacity magazine, such as the one in their experimental SP 44/16, the forerunner of the P-210.

There is one constructional element of the new P-220 which, like the de-cocking lever, is similar to the old Sauer 38H arrangement. The breechlock is a separate part, secured in the slide shell by a heavy top lug at its forward end, and by a cross-pin. The front strap of the trigger guard is shaped to afford a good rest for a finger of the other hand when using the two-hand hold, a feature which has previously been available only on custom-made combat alterations. The unique features and cartridge options of the P-220 should make it a good competitor with the Walter P-38, Smith & Wesson M39 and M59, and Heckler & Koch P9S — the other double action pistols of comparable size.

SIG P-230

The SIG P-230 will, in the U.S., be considered a pocket pistol for personal defense. In Europe, it will have some consideration as a police pistol. Externally it bears a striking resemblance to the Beretta Model 90 pistol. Like its big brother, the P-220, it also has the de-cocking lever. The slide stop is not external, however — it is an internal automatic type, released from last-shot hold-open by a slight retraction of the slide.

The double action P-230 also has the hammer-step and firing-pin-block safety systems of the larger pistol, an external hammer, Stavenhagen sights and an alloy frame and plastic grips. Basic chambering will be for a new loading called the "9mm Police," with optional conversions to 9mm Short (380 ACP), 7.65mm Browning (32 ACP) and 22 Long Rifle. We have no dimensional data on the "9mm Police," but its muzzle velocity is listed at 1110 feet per second, which is comparable to the old 9mm Browning Long. I note, however, that a different magazine is not required for conversion to the other centerfire rounds, so perhaps it is only a slightly lengthened 380, like the Russian 9mm Makarov, which also has comparable ballistics.

To handle the increased power of the new special cartridge, the slide used with that chambering is 2.47 ounces heavier than the one on the standard 380 model. The P-230 slide is one-piece, with an integral breechblock. In its size and price range, the pistol will be compared with the Walther PPK-S, Beretta Model 90, and Mauser HSc. It should be a strong sales contender, especially in the "9mm Police" version.

Though not as costly as the celestial P-210, the new pistols are relatively expensive. The P-220 lists at 640 Swiss francs, the smaller P-230 at 580. At early 1974 exchange rates this comes to $192 and $174 respectively. Whether these are European prices or the cost in the U.S. is not known at this time. I doubt that they include the import tax. SIG-Sauer have set the approximate availability dates as follows:

P-230	7.65mm	
	(32 ACP)	Oct., 1974
	9mm kurz	
	(380 ACP)	Nov., 1974
	"9mm Police"	March, 1975

P-220 9mm Parabellum Aug., 1975

Considering their features, and the two names they bear, these two should be worth waiting for!

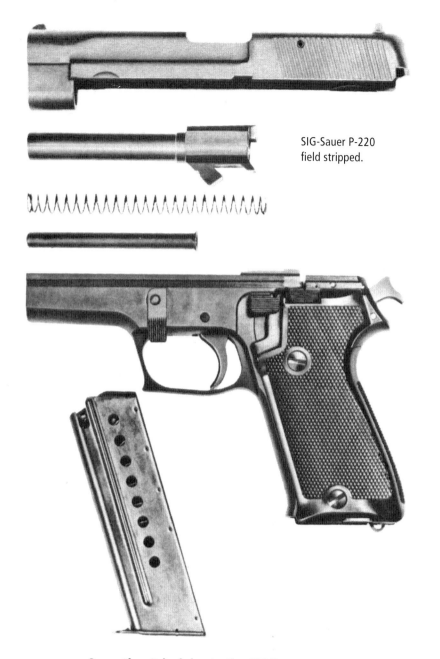

SIG-Sauer P-220
field stripped.

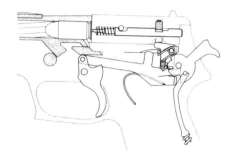

Double-Action Triggering

If the loaded pistol is not cocked, the shot can be fired by way of double-action. The trigger is squeezed, cocking the hammer via the trigger rod, and the safety lever is pressed against the lock pin. The sear is moved away from the hammer and the firing pin released by the lock pin. Further pulling of the trigger lifts the hammer out of register and fires the shot.

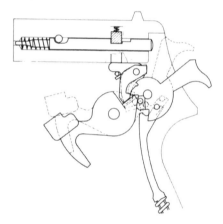

De-cocking Lever and Hammer Safety Notch

The de-cocking lever permits lowering of the hammer into the safety notch so that the loaded gun can be safely carried. The safety notch is the rest position of the hammer. The firing pin is always blocked during and after de-cocking.

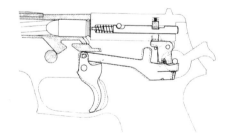

Operating Principles to the SIG/Sauer P-220

With the pistol loaded the first shot is fired by pulling the trigger double action. The trigger moves the trigger rod, which lifts the sear out of the hammer notch.

At the same time, the trigger rod moves the safety lever, which takes the lock pin out of engagement with the firing pin, releasing the firing pin just before the shot is fired. The hammer is swung forward by the hammer spring to strike the firing pin, firing the cartridge.

Recoil from the fired cartridge operates the system (comprising the slide and barrel) back against the recoil spring. After recoiling about 3mm, the lock between the barrel and slide is released, the barrel swinging down and being held in place. The slide continues its backward motion, cocks the hammer, extracts and ejects the empty case, and compresses the recoil spring. The slide recoil stroke is limited by a stop on the frame. The recoil spring now forces the slide forward, stripping a cartridge from the magazine into the chamber. Just before reaching battery position, the barrel is again locked to the slide. The trigger rod can now engage the sear and the gun is ready for single action firing (hammer cocked.)

After firing the last shot the slide is caught by the slide stop, actuated by the magazine follower. The slide stop is so-located that it can be used with the thumb of the shooting hand without shifting the gun from the line of fire as a loaded magazine is inserted.

Firing Pin Safety Catch

For maximum safety, the firing pin is locked. It is released automatically by trigger action without manipulation of any lever. The catch is not released until the shot is about to be willfully fired.

SIG-SAUER
P230

SIG-Sauer P-230
field stripped.

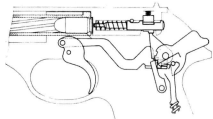

Double-Action Triggering

If the hammer is not cocked, the shot can be fired double-action. The trigger is squeezed, cocking the hammer via the trigger rod, which also presses the safety lever against the lock pin. The sear is moved away from the hammer and the firing pin is released by the lock pin. Completing the trigger pull lifts the hammer out of register and fires the shot.

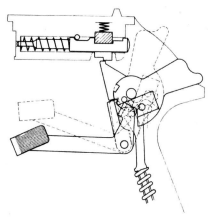

Operating Principles to the SIG/Sauer P-230

With the pistol loaded the first shot is fired by squeezing the trigger double action. The trigger moves the trigger rod, lifting the sear out of the hammer notch.

At the same time the trigger rod moves the safety lever, taking the lock pin out of engagement with the firing pin and releasing the firing pin just before the shot is fired. The hammer is swung forward by the hammer spring to strike the firing pin, firing the cartridge.

The forces of recoil push the slide back against the recoil spring, cocking the hammer, extracting and ejecting the spent case. The slide recoil stroke is limited by a stop on the frame. The compressed recoil spring now pushes the slide forward, stripping a cartridge from the magazine into the chamber. With the slide in battery position the trigger rod again engages the sear, readying the gun for firing.

After firing the last round the slide is held open by the slide stop, actuated by the magazine follower.

De-cocking Lever and Hammer Safety Catch

The de-cocking lever permits lowering of the hammer into the safety notch so the loaded pistol can be safely carried. The safety notch is the rest position for the hammer. The firing pin is always blocked during and after de-cocking.

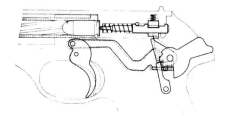

SIG/Sauer P-230 right-side view.

Firing Pin Safety Catch

Because of the automatic firing-pin safety catch, the pin is locked until just before the hammer is released. The safety catch is not released until the shot is intentionally fired. Even if dropped with the hammer cocked, the gun will not fire.

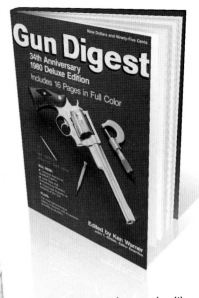

SHOOTING RUGER'S
REDHAWK

Nothing so simple as scaling up the Security Six – Ruger has come up with a whole new revolver in 44 Magnum.

by KEN WARNER

IT'S ENORMOUS. The Ruger Redhawk is here and it's big. The new double-action Ruger design in 44 Magnum offers lots to talk about, but the first impression is: It is a *very* large revolver.

The statistics bear that out. The stainless steel toolroom sample we shot weighed 52 ounces with a 7½-inch barrel. It sports the biggest double-action revolver cylinder now made, something Bill Ruger is finally convinced is a fit container for the very serious 44 Magnum round.

I once built a revolver to be bulky and heavy. I rebarreled and changed the cylinders in a Model 1917 Colt and wound up with a 53-oz. 357 Magnum, for what reason I don't remember except I thought that's what I needed. I liked the gun and I've always thought its size very impressive. It is not nearly as impressive as this new Redhawk.

The styling of the new gun is quite in line with the Security Six revolvers. The size of the cylinder dictates change, of course, since the essential dimensions at the back end remain fairly constant, designed to fit the human hand. There are differences, but Security Six shooters won't find them very distracting.

At the moment, there are two versions of the Redhawk planned. As with other models, Ruger feels that a manufacturer stands his best chance of showing a profit by providing, within his limits, something for everyone.

The gun we've shot will be the "standard" Redhawk. It has a 7½-inch forged barrel, with integral barrel rib and cylinder pin protection. It is quite handsome.

The other model will be called the round barrel model, probably because it has a round barrel. There is no rib here, nor will there be an enclosure for the cylinder pin,

but rather a stud welded to the barrel. It will be blue.

The reason for the round-barrel configuration is quite simple. With it, Ruger will be able to offer a 10-inch model for silhouette shooters and hunters, and a shorter barrel for other uses, without undue production problem. Personally, I think a 5-inch barrel would be ideal, but the betting right now is that it will be 6 inches.

Shooting the new gun is fun. It still provides all the fuss anyone could want, but experienced Magnum shooters will find it easy for repeat shots in either single-action or double-action modes. We didn't fool around "testing" a toolroom job, but you don't have to eat a whole egg to find out whether or not it tastes good. This one tasted good.

The insides of this gun fascinate William B. Ruger, Sr. He and his engineers have worked out new ways to move the power around inside, going so far in one case that they think they may get some free extra work out of the parts, notably including a spring which works in both directions.

The locking is complex on the one hand and simple on the other. There are both front end and rear end locks for the cylinder, the unlocking action up front made possible by some rather involved camming operating through the cylinder pin. It is ingenious.

In shooting, it also works like a charm. The double-action pull is remarkable; manual cocking is slick. The lockwork in at least the sample shot provides a level double-action pull weight almost all the way through to firing. There is no stackup of force, nor does it load up at the beginning and taper off. This one went straight through.

Any further discussion of these intricacies is going to require a genuine expert sitting down with gun in hand and writing the description from direct examination. It does, in fact, seem to workjust like Bill Ruger says it will.

He likes the insides; the outside fascinates me. This is a most impressive firearm. I want one.

This is a happy Bill Ruger with a good gun in his hand on a fine morning.

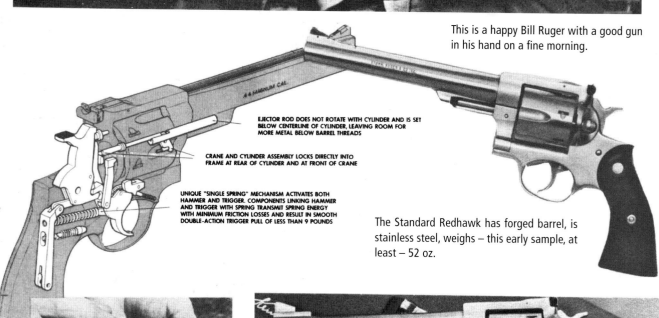

EJECTOR ROD DOES NOT ROTATE WITH CYLINDER AND IS SET BELOW CENTERLINE OF CYLINDER, LEAVING ROOM FOR MORE METAL BELOW BARREL THREADS

CRANE AND CYLINDER ASSEMBLY LOCKS DIRECTLY INTO FRAME AT REAR OF CYLINDER AND AT FRONT OF CRANE

UNIQUE "SINGLE SPRING" MECHANISM ACTIVATES BOTH HAMMER AND TRIGGER. COMPONENTS LINKING HAMMER AND TRIGGER WITH SPRING TRANSMIT SPRING ENERGY WITH MINIMUM FRICTION LOSSES AND RESULT IN SMOOTH DOUBLE-ACTION TRIGGER PULL OF LESS THAN 9 POUNDS

The Standard Redhawk has forged barrel, is stainless steel, weighs – this early sample, at least – 52 oz.

Massive revolver and massive cartridges suit' each other. Note lock stud in crane.

Toolroom sample of the other Redhawk-to-be shows round barrel, but will be blued steel. Bob Tibbets is a Ruger designer who worked on the Redhawk.

The Extraordinary
GLOCK

From no idea to radical prototype to selected service pistol in under four years? Where was the bureaucracy?

by RAYMOND CARANTA

IN OCTOBER, a Belgian magazine, over the signature of a German gun writer, reported a certain Austrian Glock 17 pistol, chambered in 9mm Luger, mostly made of plastics and stampings. The Glock 17, it was said, was considered for adoption by the Austrian army.

The gun was displayed nowhere at European shows, and was not taken very seriously until this year, when it was learnt that the Glock 17 had been officially approved as the Austrian Army service pistol. It replaces the German P-1, the light alloy descendant of World War II's P38.

In the gun business, only a few people knew the Glock Company, which was until recently mostly involved in cutlery. Headed by Gaston Glock, an independent engineer specializing in advanced plastics and metal technology for more than a quarter of a century, the firm has only 45 employees. It is located in Deutsches-Wagram in Austria.

The first significant commercial success of the Glock Company occurred in 1978 when its Field Knife 78 was adopted by the Austrian army, which placed orders for 150,000 pieces since then. About the same quantity was sold on the sporting market. Then, Gaston Glock designed, in connection with Dynamit Nobel, the German giant of chemical products, powders and ammunition, an extraordinary hand grenade made of plastics and bursting into 5,000 fragments.

In 1980, when Gaston Glock learned that the Austrian army contemplated replacing their old service pistols with a double-action model featuring a large magazine capacity, he immediately realized that the Steyr pistol could not be alone. He soon toured the competitors, asking for sub-

contracts as an industrial compensation, should a foreign product be selected.

Then, back in his facilities, he was amazed at the conventional technology on which most competitors relied and was soon analyzing the patents and consulting German-speaking experts about the requirements for a new design. He was not, himself, a firearms enthusiast, but five months later, still in 1980, he had developed a first prototype of the Glock 17 which was selected, late in 1983, as the service pistol of Austria. The Army's order is 25,000 units, 5,000 of them to be delivered in 1984.

The Glock 17 is a 9mm Luger short recoil-operated pistol on the Browning "High Power" principle as improved by SIG in their P-220, P-225 and P-226 models. Its capacity is 17 rounds. It is, regardless of operating principle, a most unusual gun.

The slide is a square-section extrusion accommodating a welded machined bolt which carries the striker and pivoted Walther-style extractor. The one-piece hammered barrel is of the linkless cam style,

The Glock 17 is very low in the hand contrary to most pistols using this style of barrel mounting. Photo courtesy Jean Jordanoglou.

Note the slender grip of the Glock 17 in spite of the unusual 17-shot magazine capacity; design allows variation in pitch. Photo courtesy Jean Jordanoglou.

The steel slide-barrel-recoil spring assembly represents 40 percent of the total weight of the pistol. Photo courtesy Jean Jordanoglou.

The trigger mechanism is entirely made of stampings; gun is striker-fired. Photo courtesy Jean Jordanoglou.

but the breech end is square and matches the inner slide square contour, which offers the centering function necessary for ensuring a high level of accuracy. This slide is 7 inches long and guided over an interrupted length of 5.19 inches by rails. The recoil spring unit is conventionally located under the barrel and the slide-barrel-recoil spring assembly weighs 16.8 ounces so as to dampen the recoil.

The receiver is an extremely light high-resistance casting of plastic material weighing only *5 ounces,* including the trigger mechanism. The receiver slide guides, insuring the sturdiness of the pistol over an expected 15,000-shot service life with NATO ammunition, are made of sheet-metal imbedded in the plastic.

The solid trigger guard is square for two-hand shooting and, as the pistol is striker fired, the trigger mechanism is entirely enclosed in the upper section of the receiver. Therefore, the grip, which only accommodates the magazine, is provided with an important hollow section at the rear and can be pitched as required, according to the customer's wishes.

The two-column staggered magazine is also a new design as it is entirely made of high resistance plastic material, with the exception of the spring and lips which are metalic. Thus it weighs only 1.43 ounces, empty, while accommodating nearly a half-pound load of service ammunition. The magazine catch is fitted at the rear of the lower branch of the trigger guard. The empty magazine lags a little and must sometimes be withdrawn by the weak hand, but this trait disappears when the gun has been broken in.

While not new at all, as its principle was already used in the Austrian cavalry pistol model of 1907 (popularly known as the 8mm Roth-Steyr), the Glock's firing mechanism is the only "pre-cocked" design made today. Single-action pistols must be hand cocked for the first shot; those shooting only double-action require a long pull each shot; and those fitted with selective lockwork require two trigger-finger positions between the first and following shots. The Glock 17 firing mechanism requires a single trigger-finger position as all the shots are fired in a "semi-double-action" mode; the trigger pull equals that of a good service pistol. The trigger travel, while shorter than that of a typical double-action gun, is longer than that of a single-action pistol.

With the Glock 17, when chambering the first round, the striker is "precocked", i.e. it is retained at about half travel and the firing pin is partially compressed. The

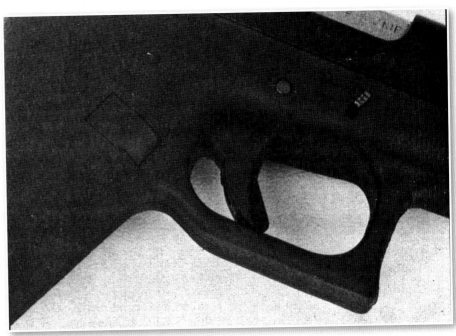

The automatic trigger safety of the Glock 17 is most efficient; it is also very simple. Photo courtesy Jean Jordanoglou.

effort necessary for firing the chambered round is set at about five pounds instead of ten, as usually required in a genuine double action mechanism. The trigger travel is limited to .40-inch.

This facilitates the basic training, avoids the "breaking the glass" climax of single-action handguns and makes the pistol with a chambered round instantly available for action. In case of misfire, the slide must be withdrawn with the weak hand only .40-inch to get another striker blow.

Beside the "semi-double-action" firing mode for all shots, the Glock 17 pistol is

Thirty rounds offhand at 25 meters under I.S.U. slow fire conditions scored 249 out of 300; the 10-ring is two inches (5cm) wide. Photo courtesy Jean Jordanoglou.

Not many problems for Austrian GIs here. Herr Glock knows simple when he sees it.
Photo courtesy Jean Jordanoglou.

The gun has Patridge-type sights and they are just 1.34-inch above the shooting hand. The rear sight notch contour is underlined in white while the ramp front sight features a 1/10-inch white dot. They are better than the average for combat shooting and still good for slow fire.

A seasoned shooter using the Glock 17 for the first time will need some dry-firing to get used to the peculiar trigger pull. Nevertheless, the shooting technique is very simple; while raising the pistol and controlling your breathing, *briskly pull* the trigger over the first ⅞-in. until you feel a definitely stronger resistance and, then, carefully aim while pressing the last ⅛-in. of pull. Tyros will find this quite natural, as will double-action revolver shooters, but people used to conventional automatics may suffer at the beginning.

Computation shows a respectable recoil velocity (defining the pressure on the hand) of 10.55 feet per second, but the recoil actually felt seems lower and just a little more than that of a conventional 9mm Luger service pistol such as our old Beretta Brigadier.

In 25-meter slow fire, offhand, our scores were in the 250 out of 300 range at the I.S.U. big bore target featuring a 2-inch ten, which is standard performance for a service pistol, the best scoring slightly above 260 of 300 and the worst under 240 of 300. On a combat shooting course involving a long run over the 17-shot magazine string with stopping, turning and shooting on command, the Glock 17 was rated by this writer as very good, but his two partners, who normally shoot Star and Colt automatics, missed several times and were slower than usual.

In our sample, bearing a serial number in the 200's, we shot 364 rounds without cleaning that included 100 rounds of French service ammunition made in 1982; 64 very old French submachine gun rounds with hard primers; 50 new German Geco half-jacketed rounds; 50 commercial full jacketed Geco rounds; 50 commercial full jacketed Remington rounds; 50 reloads with jacketed bullets and French powder. The only malfunction was a misfire with the old submachine gun ammunition and some slide hesitation when chambering the first half-jacketed truncated Geco round from the magazine.

The Glock 17 is an original, inexpensive, compact, accurate and reliable service pistol featuring a clever but controversial construction leading one to think of it as the "Tokarev" of this turn of century.

fitted with a very clever automatic trigger safety lever consisting of a spring-loaded thin metal plate fitted along the vertical center line of the .27-inch thick plastic trigger. At rest, the safety lever protrudes in front and behind the trigger, its heel preventing any trigger motion until it is depressed. This is automatic when the finger pulls the trigger. Under this action, the front end of the safety lever swings backwards, retracting the upper rear section which normally bears against the receiver, jamming the trigger. The pressure required is very low and the operation seems highly reliable.

With its low and square slide fitted over its slim plastic receiver, the Glock 17 looks quite strange at first glance. The highly pitched grip is attractive. At first handling, one is astonished at its unusually low weight of 23.2 ounces. However, when the gun is loaded with 17 service rounds, its 31-oz. weight, while still very low, enables an excellent control in practical shooting.

The grip of the Glock 17 is perhaps the best of the market as it is suitable for every size of male or female hand, which is an exception to usual large capacity double-action pistols chambered for such a powerful ammunition. Moreover, the high pitch of this grip, combined with the "semi-double-action" feature, is excellent for instinctive shooting.

This grip is exceptionally flat despite the 17-shot magazine capacity (1.18-inch thick) and its sanded temperature-proof plastic surfaces afford a very pleasant contact to the shooting hand and are not slippery. Empty, the Glock is balanced above the front area of the trigger, but this point moves about half an inch backward when loaded with 17 rounds.

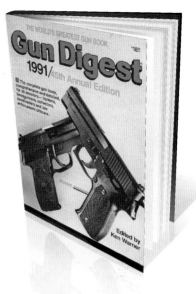

The First
MAGNUM

by KEITH R. SCHMIDT

THE Smith & Wesson factory presented the first 357 Magnum revolver to J. Edgar Hoover, beginning a 50-year marriage between knowledgeable handgun enthusiasts and the large frame Smith & Wesson revolver that lasts today. Hoover's handgun was serial number 45768 but inside the cylinder yoke of this 8¾-inch barreled revolver was stamped No. 1. Each prewar Magnum carried individual registrations. Magnum number two went to Philip B. Sharpe, gunwriter and reloading expert, who worked with Winchester to develop the zippy original Magnum load. And, ZIP it did. Ads claimed 1515 feet per second under test conditions.

During those innocent days before it became fashionable to chamber rifle cartridges in long-barreled handguns, the 357 Magnum held first place for lots of leftover down-range foot pounds of energy. Even the name was new. Previously, the term magnum referred to a large wine bottle holding about two-fifths of a gallon.

Also creative were company advertisements barking: "THE MOST POWERFUL HANDGUN EVER MADE. The S&W Magnum has far greater shocking power than any .38, .44, or .45, ever tested." The new Magnum cost 60 Depression-era dollars which was about $15 above the price of any other S&W handgun made before World War II. Rich and famous handgun enthusiasts quickly filled out orders for the new revolver. Not so rich and famous shooters begged, borrowed or tried to steal one when they weren't busy dreaming about the Magnum and its previously unheard-of handheld power. This first Magnum started American handgunners on a continual search for

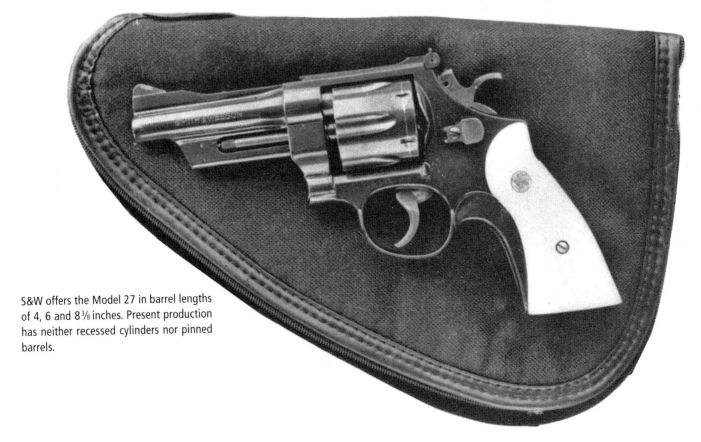

S&W offers the Model 27 in barrel lengths of 4, 6 and 8⅜ inches. Present production has neither recessed cylinders nor pinned barrels.

The Practical Pistol Course (PPC) was designed by agency instructors during the 1940s and the large-frame Smith & Wesson Magnum was a familiar sight on ranges. (National Archives photo)

more powerful sidearms to reach farther and hit harder.

In part, the early Magnum's success came because it was a quality product presented to a shooting public beginning to emerge from dollar-scarce Depression days. Offered in any barrel length from 3½ inches to 8¾ inches with personalized registration, the Magnum owner bought power and prestige in his 40-odd ounces of richly blued and specially heat-treated nickel steel. Customers wanted steak for their money and S&W added the sizzle.

Also, the large frame 357 Magnum's development coincided with law enforcement needs. Officers faced well-armed gangs during the 1920s and '30s. Lawmen needed more pistol power to penetrate automobiles. Also, they wanted enough bullet *oomph* left over to perforate bottles of bootleg gin along with the bad guy behind the wheel. To meet this need, S&W first offered the 38/44 Heavy Duty revolver to handle a hot factory-loaded 38 Special cartridge. Also, Colt sold large numbers of the 38 Super Government Model autoloader that gained fame as a hot high-velocity round. However, both fell short of the new Magnum's ballistics.

Possessing the same frame size and other similarities to the 38/44 Heavy Duty revolver, the Magnum sported a distinctive new look. S&W engineers used stronger steel

and recessed the cylinder for the powerful Magnum cartridge. A machined topstrap and ribbed barrel improved sighting under harsh light conditions. With the 3½-inch barrel, the Magnum often wore a fast draw ramp front sight developed by Capt. Frank Baughmann of the FBI. Baughmann later became head of the FBI's firearms training program where his pupils became intimately familiar with the large Magnum and other handguns. The Quantico, Virginia, FBI gun vault still retains early large frame Magnums with both 3½- and 5-inch barrel lengths.

Legendary law enforcement Magnum stories impressed. The bullet could rip through the trunk of an escaping felon's car; perforate the driver; then, destroy the engine's cylinder block bringing the auto to a slow clanking halt, they said. More a product of wishful thinking than fact, the new Magnum round did possess power and filled a need for lawmen.

Ed McGivern, the double-action revolver shooting wizard, who could accurately empty a double-action revolver faster than a heartbeat, called the large frame 357 Magnum the perfect lawman's handgun. McGivern owned several. He considered this revolver with Magnum loads effective to a range of 600 yards. Photos from McGivern's *Fast and Fancy Revolver Shooting*, published in 1935, proved a man-sized target at

this distance wasn't safe from the Magnum … at least with someone like McGivern on the trigger.

"The large frame 357 Magnum that later became the Model 27 revolver in 357 Magnum was the company's top-of-the-line custom-ordered handgun of the 1930s," explains Roy Jinks, S&W historian. "Those early handguns cost a lot for the times, but received a great deal of attention and extra workmanship at the factory."

Early shooters of the Magnum included Major Douglas Wesson who hunted a variety of Wyoming's big critters during the 1930s to prove this handgun had the right stuff. The Magnum soon became a status symbol for the well-heeled sportsman, soldier and adventurer. Ernest Hemingway surreptitiously carried one to Spain when covering that country's Civil War during 1937.

A Magnum with ivory grips initialed GSP with a S&W grip adapter accompanied General George Patton through North Africa and Europe during World War II. Patton called the blued S&W with the 3½-inch barrel his "killing gun." An avid shooting enthusiast, Patton followed the Magnum's development and ordered one of the earliest. The factory shipped a Magnum with registration number 506 on October 18, 1935 to Patton's Fort Shafter duty station in Hawaii. Today, this revolver with its

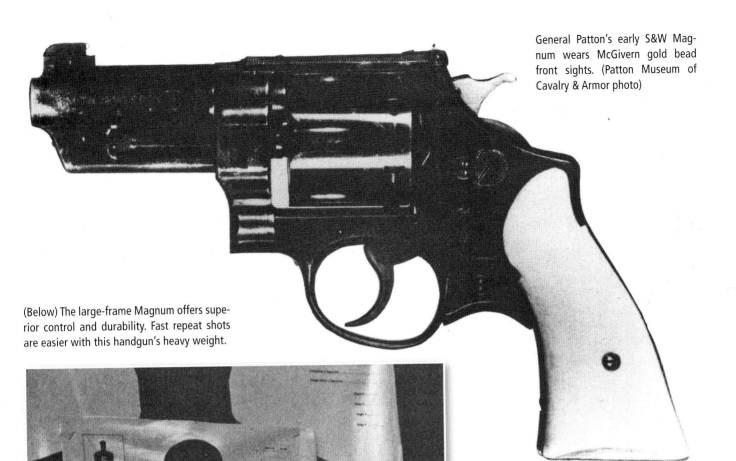

General Patton's early S&W Magnum wears McGivern gold bead front sights. (Patton Museum of Cavalry & Armor photo)

(Below) The large-frame Magnum offers superior control and durability. Fast repeat shots are easier with this handgun's heavy weight.

McGivern-style front sight of a large gold bead, assuring fast and accurate night shooting, rests on display at the Fort Knox Museum of Cavalry and Armor in Louisville, Kentucky. The revolver shows extensive holster wear on the forward portion of cylinder and barrel. Present condition reveals extensive use, but that the Magnum received loving care.

Prior to World War II, S&W stopped using individual registration numbers, and the war soon halted Magnum production. Many handgun enthusiasts believe this prewar Magnum takes first place as the finest double-action revolver ever made.

After the war, a gun-hungry public happily saw the Magnum's reintroduction. Charlie Askins promoted the handgun and cartridge in a 1950 GUN DIGEST article comparing the Magnum to other handguns by shooting pine boards, paraffin blocks, sandbags, water-filled grapefruit cans, ice blocks and jackrabbits. "Here was truly power," wrote an ecstatic Askins while comparing this handgun's performance to a rifle.

The big Magnum became known as the Model 27 during the 1950s and barrel lengths standardized. This six-gun filled police holsters regularly. Western states in particular armed highway patrols with the Magnum.

The S&W Magnum often had the 3½-inch barrel, a particular favorite of the FBI and other law enforcement agencies.

(Right and below) The Model 27 with a 5-inch barrel has been very popular with western and rural lawmen who appreciate a longer sighting radius, yet find a 6-inch barrel too cumbersome for the patrol car. They can hit with them too.

The large-frame Magnum's big cylinder makes speed loading a snap; its action helps double action use.

An older Model 27 357 Magnum with the 3½-inch barrel remains among my all-time favorite revolvers. From camping trips to my duties with a Texas Sheriff's department, the Magnum remains a proven performer. With many police departments emphasizing training and qualification with full-power Magnum loads, the Model 27 with its recoil soaking weight may find again an increased law enforcement following.

Times change. World wars, small wars, inflation, stock crashes and terrorism. But the 357 cartridge remains with us as an outstanding handgun development and the large Magnum, represented by the Model 27, still comes off the S&W assembly line.

"This handgun remains the 'glamour handgun' of the company," explains historian Jinks. "These days, a typical purchaser of the large frame 357 Magnum has a sense of the past and views a handgun as something much more than utilitarian."

(Left and below) Author and his large-frame S&W Magnum with Ajax stocks and an El Paso Saddlery holster and belt with floral carving — owners like to dress up Model 27s.

"During the late 1950s, law enforcement sales of the large magnum slowed," explains Roy Jinks, S&W historian. "In 1954, the Highway Patrolman revolver went into production which offered the same size and action but with a less expensive finish. A year later, the factory produced the Combat Magnum Model 19. With more competition, the more expensive large frame magnum became less popular."

A big handgun, the Model 27 weighs 42 ounces. The smaller Model 19 Combat Magnum weighs 6 ounces less. The weight difference is negligible except for a person who carries it on his hip all day. For the average police officer, carrying a lighter handgun with as much punch made sense.

Present sales figures for the large frame Model 27 357 Magnum rank distant third behind the popular Combat Magnum and more recently introduced L-frame. However, the large frame Magnum remains part of the S&W line due to its combination of handling characteristics, sturdiness with hot loads and its heavy weight. No other presently produced S&W handgun has a more interesting history than the Model 27 Magnum.

During 1986, S&W produced two special commemoratives of the Model 27 Magnum. One special issue celebrated the 50th anniversary of the first 357 Magnum. The other Model 27 honored the F.B.I. Five-inch barrels were standard on both. Presently, S&W offers the Model 27 Magnum as a standard part of their revolver line with barrel length choices of 4, 6 and 8⅜ inches. The company no longer offers the multitude of options available on the Magnum in years past.

The CZ-75 and its Early Clones

The Beginning of a Very Long Story

by JIM THOMPSON

FIREARMS STORIES ARE generally pretty straightforward — test an item, report on the results. Not so the '70s *Wunderkind*, the 9mm that turned so many heads eastward, the CZ-75. The Iron Curtain and the trade barriers which protected us from it or it from us have almost disappeared; factories marketing copies and clones have arisen, prospered, and also disappeared; and while the form and function of the original pistol have become supremely well-known in the United States, this only happened because the duplicates got very good, and because reporters and analysts simply refused to give up. It usually takes about a half-century for a firearms tale to become so tangled and ebullient; but the CZ-75 is not yet twenty years old, boasts almost as many progeny as a hyperhormonal rabbit, and still isn't common here, but it's getting that way.

The almost-mythical Czech CZ-75 spawned copies and near copies, which makes it the first Super-Nine.

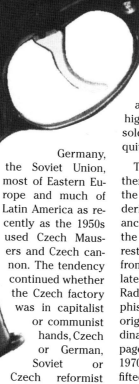

If the history of the CZ-75 and its brethren seems odd and tangled, so are its roots in the Czech arms industry. For seventy years or so, Brno-marked arms produced at *Ceska Zbrojovka* at Strakonica have been universally recognized as high-quality bargains. Many of their designs have been adopted by well-established arms industries elsewhere. The British Bren began life in Czechoslovakia; likewise the British Besa.

Germany, the Soviet Union, most of Eastern Europe and much of Latin America as recently as the 1950s used Czech Mausers and Czech cannon. The tendency continued whether the Czech factory was in capitalist or communist hands, Czech or German, Soviet or Czech reformist control. From time to time, authorities in Europe and elsewhere have complained it was very difficult to sell their nationally produced firearms output when a better-made Czech product was available, despite tariffs and barriers, for about half the price. In France and Germany, from the '30s until quite recently, Czech shotguns and hunting rifles accounted for a very high percentage of products available and sold. Even now, the CZ-75 is sold in Europe quite cheaply.

This preamble is necessary because there are still some in the U.S. who describe the CZ-75 as what it is not. It has elements derived from evolved components of more ancient and/or far inferior handguns, but the slide/frame interface and most of the rest of the pistol's functional details come from the Petter-Neuhausen patents of the late 1930s. The trigger combines beefed-up Radom geometry with a much more sophisticated base hinge spun off a Walther original. If anything in the CZ-75 seems ordinary in the 1990s, the observer should page through a GUN DIGEST from the early 1970s looking for an all-steel, double-action fifteen-shot handgun. For the CZ-75 was and remains the original "Super-Nine," and European pistolsmiths who've been working with the gun for more than fifteen years still believe it's the one with the most potential for truly precise shooting in the real or simulated combat arenas.

All of which is amazing, after all this time and after the fact that nearly every firearms firm in the world with the capacity to do so has produced and sold at least one gun either inspired by or is a direct copy of the Czech original. This kind of market impact is precisely what was intended by the gun's designers; for the CZ-75 was conceived, designed and sold with virtually no domestic civilian or military market. The guns have seen military use worldwide, but virtually always as an individual's private purchase. And they sell to this day in that most personal and competitive market.

I said the real market history of the pistol was tangled and confused. It is, in fact, so tangled that, by the time this sees ink, much will have changed. This is only the story of the earliest days of CZ-75, and its early clones and stepchildren.

I had to wait only ten days to get my first CZ-75 from P.I.M.C. back in 1986, but I was terribly impatient anyway because I had been waiting, in real terms, eleven long years. Tariffs, import restrictions on "Communist Bloc" products, a crazy quilt of erratic importers and undelivered product, and lots of promises had preceded my order and kept the pistol from me. Enticing ads for the gun in *Deutsches Waffen Journal* and the Swiss *Waffen Digest* — for less than half the wholesale price I paid, mind you — had held my attention. At one point, I had even made elaborate arrangements with a German firm to acquire a Peter F. Stahl-modified custom gun, a deal which fell apart, congealed again, fell apart again, and finally, became real in early 1991, when I took delivery of the gun and owned it for two days, total. A fellow shooter decided

In 1988, the TZ-75 from Tanfoglio in hard chrome had a lot of advantages.

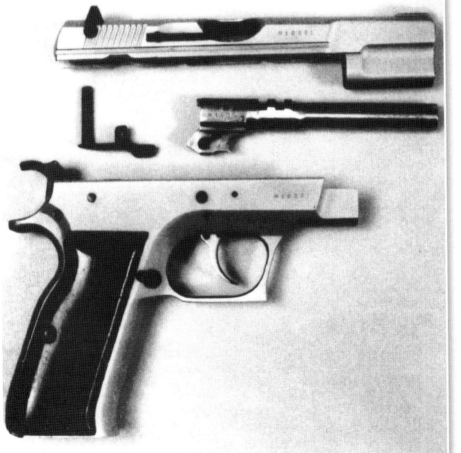

(Left) The CZ-75 and/or TZ-75 are stripped according to the time-honored Browning method, *a la* Hi-Power.

he couldn't live without it and, like many who wind up with CZ-75s, gobbled it up with a few too many dollars before I even got a chance to properly photograph it. By then, of course, I had too much time and money in the pistol, and no matter what it did for me, it couldn't possibly have satisfied me.

The same was essentially true of that first 1986 baked-enamel gun. By the time it actually showed up, praise and promises had me anticipating some sort of model of perfection which would do more or less everything, including assist me in leaping tall buildings in a single bound. I'd heard the double-action pull was smooth, slick, and truly useful; and it was, at what my weights told me was about 14 pounds, through it felt lighter. Butter smooth and predictable, I eventually slicked it a bit more with careful stone and fitting work, once the gun was broken in. I had heard the CZ-75 was beautifully made. This was mostly true, though the barrel fit was very average. To say, however, I hate paint finishes on handguns is something of an understatement; phosphated underneath, the baked-on look is my least favorite finish, ranking somewhere *after* rust. The magazines were crudely scratched with the pistol's serial number. Sights were decent, but nothing special.

That pistol was one of a batch imported by and marked "Bauska." The finish is sometimes referred to as "military gloss"… and if I'd had a surefire way to cleanly strip it off without damaging anything, I'd have been down to the phosphate more or less instantly. It's too hard, therefore brittle, and chips badly. The single-action trigger broke neatly at 4½ pounds, preceded by the gentle "takeup" — calling it "creep" suggests more tension than there really is — so common on today's semi-autos. Despite excellent overall conformance to the gun's specifications, the long wait and the opportunity to handle so many slick and graceful 9mm guns since the mid-'70s had me in a mindset to be at least slightly dissatisfied no matter what.

I sat down with the instructions and test target to do some studying. Part of the reason European guns function so well is their detailed testing and proofing. One of the tougher requirements in the Czech factory is the final approval, which requires a signature and the test target, also requiring a signature. Comrade Bobcik did mine. What I, for a long time, thought was six rounds on paper was in fact ten. Very disturbing, however, was the fact that there were two very tight groups — one dead-center and tiny, another 2½ inches away, tight, at about 1 o'clock — and a single bullet hole, fully 5¼ inches from center at 4 o'clock, completely out of the black on the 25-meter test target. Two groups and a flyer. Ah, well, I thought, probably strange ammo or bad shooting. At the time, I hadn't even a single inkle that the pistol would replicate that pattern as long as the original barrel remained in place. Later fiddling with a Tanfoglio barrel partially exorcised the demon, but fitting a tight match barrel eventually did the job. But it was aggravating.

Detailed study of the gun's innards and bore with high magnification equipment showed a lot of very atypical attention to detail and some unusual processes used in the gun's fabrication, part of which I'm still pondering. The bore was exceptionally bright, its finish approximating a #8 R.M.S. finish. The slide and frame appear to be extremely high-quality investment casting, though the exporter, Merkuria, claims all parts are forged. Some of the internal machining of the slide and especially the frame left no "tracks" even un-

der very high magnification, and so the amount of machine-induced stress in the metal's crystalline structure proved to be very low. Some extremely gentle process or treatment is used on these parts, which may be worked hot or cold, or manipulated electronically or robotically; none of the machinists I talked to could really provide much insight, though the one who said, half jokingly, "maybe it's a laser" may have been closer than he knew.

I did some measuring and checking on the barrel, and at least in this gun, it's configured more like an American tube than a typical European unit. Six grooves, right twist, roughly one turn in 10 inches (probably four per meter). But the hood and muzzle fit were well-executed, clean, loose. This is done on many semi-automatics today because manufacturers know that nothing irritates consumers more than unreliable equipment, and nothing causes more fouling/dirt malfunctions than excessively tight fit on a semi-auto. But I keep my guns well-lubricated with MDS/graphite greases and cleaner than my plates or silverware, I do not shoot in pigpens, and I demand accuracy, even at the cost of some reliability. The barrel leade cut ahead of the smooth chamber appeared to have a sharper step than I am accustomed to seeing in European semi-automatics, and I suspected this could cause problems with some fatter-nosed hollowpoints.

Determined to leave the gun in a factory-stock condition for initial testing, I still went ahead with some steps I execute with all semi-automatics. My good friend and pistol-smith John Student taught me to check everything, prevent "unexplained" problems as I work, gently polishing and closely studying parts. I merely detail polished the mainspring, recoil spring, firing pin and firing pin spring with gentle touches of 600-grit emery cloth and, afterward, pumice and oil and a silicone cloth. One removes virtually no functioning metal in these processes. I then packed the mainspring and firing pin with heavy grease and reassembled. Contrary to advice from some smiths, modern MDS greases remain viable at very low temperatures and do not migrate all over your pistol, holster and clothing, as oil does; and the lubricity of modern greases is superb, preventing corrosion in areas one cannot reach without tearing the gun apart.

The general takedown procedure is simple, and the trigger assembly is much easier to deal with than the Hi-Power or Model 1911 because it's semi-modular. There is no magazine disconnector/safety. There is nothing in this pistol of fragile de-

sign, and there are *no* sheet metal stirrups in the trigger mechanism.

The safety and slide stop on the CZ-75 and most of the current generation of clones are located on the same plane at the pistol's left. The newer CZ-85 is ambidextrous, and I've seen a European 30-caliber (7.65mm) pistol equipped with smooth, handsome wood grips and gracefully extended controls. Who knows what the future might hold?

In several thousand rounds of firing, no "regular" jams of any sort have been encountered with the CZ-75. With the original barrel, some failures to fully chamber were encountered with jacketed hollow-points conflicting slightly with the leade.

Also digested by the CZ-75 were vast quantities of surplus ammunition. And herein lies a wonderful tale. Most European ammo for 9mm is at or slightly above the old SAAMI 9mm specification, and virtually all American ammo well below the so-called "redline." NATO specifications for the cartridge are very hot by U.S. civilian standards, normal to soft by European specifications, so I hoard Greco, Norma, Lapua and Fiocchi 9mm loads. When I could still afford Lugers, I was pleased to take a superb Artillery Model for minimal money from an owner who, though advised properly, refused to shoot either European ammo or "warmish" handloads, and who was therefore convinced his gun just didn't work. Didn't work? I put 5000 rounds through it without a single malfunction. The CZ-75, especially with the Geco and Fiocchi loads, was more than accurate enough to save anyone's life; the groups thus made were essentially miniatures of Comrade Bobcik's work.

Later, with the match barrel fitted, the flyers totally disappeared. And the pistol, across a padded rest or from a Ransom rest, began to perform brilliantly. Groups of just 1 inch at 25 yards were about maximum, and with carefully controlled handloads, Geco, Fiocchi, Norma, and Federal Match, groups became ragged bullet holes. The key to this is simple, and it was about what I had expected thousands of rounds earlier: slide/frame interface on my specimen — and on all the Czech 75s I've examined — is near perfect. Only "service" barrel fit retards performance.

The "Bobcik Syndrome" was solved by the installation of $160 worth of barrel. But I'd rather it hadn't been necessary. Proof that it would be was early on, for installing the Tanfoglio-produced barrel from my TZ-75 alleviated the flyers. And the Stahl-prepared match pistol shot about the same from day one.

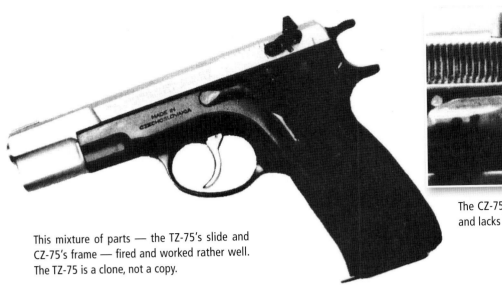

This mixture of parts — the TZ-75's slide and CZ-75's frame — fired and worked rather well. The TZ-75 is a clone, not a copy.

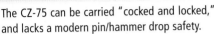

The CZ-75 can be carried "cocked and locked," and lacks a modern pin/hammer drop safety.

Looking back, I was displeased with the CZ-75 early on mainly because, in the 1980s, I had handled and tested the big-magazine Astras and Stars, Steyrs and Llamas, Bernardellis, Berettas, the Walther P-88, every one of which either aped the Czech gun or was inspired by it. And, of course, I paid over twice what the CZ sells for in Europe.

It has proven durable and, at long last, accurate. The CZ-75 contains not a single part or system not adapted from another firearm, but it's not really a copy of anything.

Known in the '50s and '60s for a set of competent but rather boring pocket semi-automatics, Fratelli Tanfoglio then made new inroads in manufacturing firearms clones and have found the horses to market their output. From F.I.E. and ExCam's early efforts to current output from a half-dozen firms, virtually all the CZ-75 clones use Tanfoglio-produced parts and are often Tanfoglio-produced and finished guns.

I've done most of my testing of CZ-75 clones with guns from the defunct F.I.E. line. European American Armory of Florida marketed many of the same models under the Witness name, and their literature showed guns in 9mm, 41 AE, 40 S&W and 45. Springfield's P9 came in many versions; it, too, had Tanfoglio parts, though in an American-finished and assembled configuration. The Action Arms AT-84 and AT-88 employ Tanfoglio parts, but were Swiss-assembled and finished. It's all part of the CZ-75 story.

Why clone guns? Historically, there have always been several reasons. Often, the original is too expensive. Sometimes — especially so in the CZ-75's case — the original is hard to get for political/com-

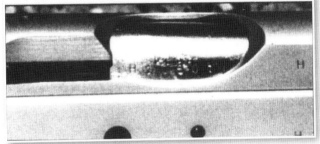

Ejection ports on TZ-75 and CZ-75 are very similar, as are the extractors. The CZ-75 is shown on top here.

petitive reasons. Sometimes, desirable options aren't available on the original. Tanfoglio got into this market smart and early. Some of those early blued guns were misfitted and displayed odd metallurgical anomalies which led to early failures. The hard-chromed pistols, however, quickly established an excellent reputation, for the hard, flexible "crust" of their finish concealed mediocre materials. By late '86, the guns were vastly improved, and by '88, the high-mounted firing pin safety had been replaced by a unit similar to the Czech original, target and compensated versions were on the market and, as nearly as anyone could tell, the F.I.E. TZ series and ExCam's TA pistols were prospering and proliferating.

All the Tanfoglio guns sport better sights than the Czech originals. Prices were much lower. Finish options and combina-

Here is the Bobcik Syndrome — two groups and a flier — out of the box.

tions could teach anybody a lesson. The Millett-style sights on the match gun are, simply put, wonderful. And the internal manufacturing techniques are as sophisticated as the Czech guns. The externals are at least as well done. Slide/frame interface is not quite as good, but is easily adjusted in a press.

In shooting all the variants, including a couple of custom guns, some interesting information developed. A TA90C purchased after ExCam ceased to exist shot better than any of the other stock pistols, including the big match gun. It was largely a case of better-than-average frame/slide fit and a barrel that happened to be very tight. Another gun of the same model wouldn't shoot close to that particular example. Most stock guns delivered 3- to 3½-inch groups with most factory loads at 25 yards, but the little TA90C, carefully rested and shot with Federal Match or careful handloads, cut group size in half. All the Czech-built and Czech-inspired pistols handle and balance well, owing to the dished out tang area of the back-strap, but the Tanfoglios run a little deeper and feel a bit better. Among all the Italian and Czech pistols — and for that matter, later with the AT-84 — there were no malfunctions at all.

I preferred the high-set firing pin safety, mostly because I'm accustomed to the Walther P-38, but I seem to be the only person on the planet who does. That may account

The trim AT-84 — and all the rest — fit a Beretta Model 92 holster just fine.

Variations on a selling theme included both bigger and smaller TZ-75s.

for the fact that all the recent pistols have returned to the original's frame-mounted conventional safety.

Double action on most guns evinced a 17- to 20-pound pull, which I was able to modify gradually to a smooth 9 to 12 pounds on two specimens which particularly irritated me. I am finally beginning to use the double action properly, by the way, and now that I'm accustomed to the varying pulls, the "grip readjustment" which is supposed to cause round one and two to land in different places just doesn't happen. The recurved combat trigger guard is one of those which can actually be used without drawing blood, unlike many that are beautifully covered with razor-sharp checkering. Single action on all guns was very like the CZ-75.

Almost all Tanfoglio guns use a recoil guide rod similar to those used by custom pistolsmiths, projecting through a hole in the slide. Whether these actually do much of anything is moot, but they generally make operations smooth and are easy to strip. Unfortunately, it is not easy

The TZ-75 Special Match had a six-inch barrel, four-port compensator and a long slide.

to replace grips on any of the guns in this whole family from standard items.

All the Tanfoglio-produced and finished guns have netted me good performance at very reasonable prices. And the eight years of continuous improvement is indeed an impressive record.

Tanfoglio is, of course, neither the beginning nor the end of the CZ-75 story. Even the Chinese are producing a CZ-75 clone, Norinco's China Sports NZ-75. John Slough Armorers in England produce a pistol called the SpitFire which appears from photos to be a clone or near clone. But the best CZ-75 clone I've handled and tested so far came from Action Arms, the late, lamented AT-84.

Just the words "made in Switzerland" can pole-vault the price of almost anything into the low stratosphere. SIG knows this, which is why their recent service pistols are actually built by Sauer in Germany. But the Swiss also have high internal industrial standards, and they fancy their machine-tool quality.

Swiss firearms have been rather strange for a long time. The Schmidt-Rubin straight-pull rifles, even the recent StG-57, are oddly configured and unusually built, but incredibly accurate. The SIG-Neuhausen P-210s specifications don't outdazzle any 9mms of the '30s or '40s, let alone the '90s, but none will outshoot it. Their guns seem to be designed for a system where cleaning weapons is almost an obsession and where everyone is essentially a well-informed

technocrat. My pistol sold for a little more than the CZ-75. It was money well spent.

General fit, finish and machine work were exceptional. I began to get the feeling that AT-84 was a seriously excellent pistol, or that mine was a specially prepared ringer, so I ran up to Mandall's in Scottsdale, Arizona, the only store I know that stocks several of most anything, and was able to confirm by measurement and eyeball that they're all beautifully made. I tested for roundness, uniformity of fit, left-right symmetry, and parallelism of major surfaces on slide and frame and their relationship to each other. Everything was close to perfect. In fact, I did not adjust the trigger or polish the springs on this gun, as I am inclined to do on others; that work was pretty much already done. It was so well-fitted I began to wonder if it might malfunction without dirt or heat.

I needn't have worried. There were no malfunctions of any kind in 2500 rounds. After my most recent tear-down, even my 20x viewing glass could find no galling or abrasion in the slide/frame interface. Barrel fit was the tightest of all these pistols, which may account for the tiny down-range groups. The first ammo shot was RIO-CBC and cheap Egyptian surplus, and both gave tiny groups shooting very casually. So the theory of good fit equalling good accuracy is borne out.

My nephew greatly admired this pistol, and he wound up with it. Otherwise, I'd probably never have found out that

all these pistols fit easily into leather for the Government Model and/or Beretta 92, for Bob immediately ordered an expensive Lawrence (G&G) shoulder holster, and what arrived, from the imprinted codes, was a very nice rig set up for the 92F. And it worked and fit well, though as I advised my nephew only phoney-baloney movie detectives actually ever really use shoulder holsters, especially under their clothes. However, after only a few months' instruction, he figured out how to get it on, after which he, too, used only the companion belt holster, also from Lawrence.

For a while, and almost by default, Springfield Armory was in a position to ship more CZ-75 clones and variants than anyone else. However, the General Agreement on Tariffs and Trade allows the government to lift politically motivated trade barriers and/or to extend to any nation the MFN (most favored nation) status which largely eliminates tariffs and duties on products from the country specified. Which is another way of saying that the CZ-75 in its original Czech form is here and so is the CZ-85.

There are so many CZ-75 guns and clones that J.M. Ramos has written a genealogy of the pistols called *The CZ-75 Family*, from Paladin Press. That book may require lengthy addenda tomorrow...or next week...*surely* by next month! The story is a long way from over for the world's first and arguably most sensible Super-Nine.

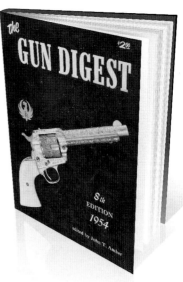

COLLECTING OLD WINCHESTERS

by BILL DEPPERMAN

NE DAY in 1937 James R. Smith was searching through a pile of "junk" rifles in a Seattle second-hand store. He picked out one that took his fancy. He paid $4.50 for it. It seemed a fair price to pay for a rifle that looked to him like thousands of nondescript old guns. But what neither he nor the dealer recognized was the significance of the words "One of One Thousand" engraved on the top of the barrel.

Today the "One of One Thousand" variety of the old Winchester Model 1873 lever-action repeating rifle is firmly established as the rifle most sought after by collectors, and among the 33 that have come to light are some valued by their owners at from $500 to $5,000. The lure of finding one of these rare rifles, which since May 1950 have leaped from obscurity, to high value, has spurred renewed interest in the collecting of long guns.

Almost everyone interested in guns has played with the notion of starting a collection. Many who take the trouble to investigate have been discouraged by high prices. If they had explored a little farther, they would have learned that it is still possible to form a rewarding and comprehensive collection of old guns at reasonable cost — if they confine themselves to old sporting shoulder guns and not to handguns. Most gun collections are based on handguns. As the backbone of most collections, the wide interest in pistols and revolvers has created a demand which has shot up prices. This is not true with the majority of shoulder guns: rifles and shotguns.

Long guns — particularly sporting rifles — are the neglected field of gun collecting and

right now is the time to get in on what in years to come will be regarded as the ground floor. Because long arms have been passed by, there are probably many millions of them now waiting discovery by collectors. This neglect finds many collectors, as well as dealers, with little basis for establishing prices. Indeed it is the author's guess that there are dozens of varieties of long guns about which little if anything is known.

The remarkable rise in price of "One of One Thousand" Model 1873 rifles is a sample of what can be expected. Finding a

"One of One Thousand" means a lot on this Winchester rifle. It belongs to a collector who knows
that he has unearthed one of the really rare finds in today's market.

"sleeper" or windfall rifle is not the basic reason for collecting rifles — but it certainly adds spice to it.

No one knows how many old rifles are still in existence but there is a clue in the fact that Winchester produced almost 6 million in models which are now obsolete and are therefore rated as collectible. Combine with this the output of all other American gunmakers in the past century and the productions must have been prodigious and the number still available large enough to sustain a very large new crop of gun collectors. This article concerns only old Winchesters.

Out of the 720,610 Model 1873s produced from 1873 to 1924, there were only 135 of the historic "One of One Thousand" variety. These were manufactured only from 1874 through 1881 except for three rifles. The manufacturing dates of the three are unknown but two were shipped from New Haven in 1893 and one in 1900. The three bear serial numbers in the 450,000 series, whereas all of the other 132 rifles of which there is record have serial numbers many hundred thousand lower. Three movie-prop rifles made up as "One of One Thousand" Model 1873s for the movie "Winchester 73" are not genuine. They are serially numbered 551,816, 703,161 and 706,716.

Each of the "One of One Thousand" variety was the most accurate of every 1,000 Model 1873s made, or was in that accuracy grade, and was sold for $100, a substantial advance in price over the ordinary '73. The "One of One Thousand" variety usually had set triggers and were engraved on top of the barrel, just ahead of the receiver, with the magic words "One of One Thousand" or in some instances with the equally potent figures "1 of 1,000." Some of the rifles were elaborately carved by such old-time masters as Conrad and John Ulrich — or they were quite simple. In some cases the mere figures "1 of 1,000☒ appear on these rifles without decoration of any kind. You could pay $5 to $100 extra for additional engraving.

During the late 70s and 80s "One of One Thousand" were among the most prized rifles a man could own. The movie "Winchester 73" was supposed to be based on a true story about one of them.

In the past 75 years the rifle drifted into almost complete obscurity. Few of even the most astute dealers in old guns had ever heard of it. Except possibly for F. P. L. Mills of Deerfield, Massachusetts, or Lloyd Bender of Galion, Ohio, who owns one of the country's great collections of Winchesters, it is safe to say that few of the individuals who owned an authentic "One of One Thousand" had any idea what they owned.

They were mystery rifles.

Then the search began.

The *American Rifleman*, in May, 1950, started it off with an article in that issue which was followed by accounts in hundreds of newspapers. It's a fair guess that a sizable percentage of the country's old lever-action rifles got a close going-over because a free Model 1894 rifle was offered by a movie company to the owners of the first 20 "One of One Thousand" rifles reported.

However, little did the owners of these rare guns realize that a free Model 94 was the least of these inducements. Ownership of a "One of One Thousand" was a far bigger prize.

What basis of value could the owners have? Sam G. Bach-elder of Santa Cruz, California, had picked up his "One of One Thousand" for $5, just 50 cents more than James R. Smith had paid for his.

F. P. L. Mills of Deerfield, Massachusetts, bought his in 1935 for $10 from the Iver Johnson Sporting Goods Store in Boston.

Phil M. Brown of Watseka, Illinois, acquired his free from a friend who "didn't want it around."

William W. Kessler of Whitmore, California, picked his out of a collection of "junk" guns in a Redding, California, second-hand store.

A few folks felt their guns had historic interest. John D. Morley of Lodi, California, inherited his from his grandfather, who has been a freight and stage operator. Granville Stuart Abbott of Lewistown, Montana, came by his via the same route. His grandfather, Granville Stuart, discovered gold in

Drawings by H. C. McBarron

Montana, was a rancher and later U.S. Ambassador to Uruguay and Paraguay. It is Mr. Abbott who values his rifle at $5,000. This was certainly one heirloom that was worth keeping.

A stagecoach driver was the donor of the rifle now owned by Thomas H. Oster of Cloverdale, California. Another gift rifle is owned by D. W. Peckham of Middlefield, Connecticut. William Lyman, inventor of the gun sight, was the donor.

Although the history of the majority of the rifles has been completely lost, two

told to the writer by the grandson of the owner. After you have read it. you will see why the grandson prefers to hide his identity. Otherwise every adventurous treasure hunter in the country would be after him for clues. Don't write me about it. either. Mum is the word.

George F. Lewis was born in Kansas in 1858 and came to Washington in 1880. Then, while engaged in the cattle business in Ferry County, he acquired his "One of One Thousand," of unknown serial number. He was proud of it and shot everything from rattlers to Alaskan brownies with it —

Do you blame Mr. Lewis's grandson for not wanting his identity known? But don't envy him. His grandfather left no map or directions to reach the lost mine and the equally well-lost "One of One Thousand."

It's no wonder that "One of One Thousand" rifles have spurred on gun collectors with renewed zeal.

Mr. Peckham refused $500 for his rifle. In a recent advertisement in the *Shotgun News* another owner offered his rifle for sale with the pointed hint: "Best offer over $1,150."

This is a famous Winchester Schuetzen "high wall" variety of the single-shot rifle. Model 1885. Good collector's items may still be found cheaply today.

have stories which are very likely typical of most of them.

The rifle owned by D. J. Harrill of Falls Church, Virginia, is an example. It was shipped from New Haven on June 30, 1876 and next showed up in Utah in the hands of immigrants. Stolen by a horse thief, it drifted into Montana with Teton Jackson, a bandit, who killed two sheriffs with it.

Another sheriff, named Frank Canton, killed Jackson in Buffalo, Wyoming, and sold the rifle to Sheriff Red Augers, who in turn sold it to a sheepman named Kingsbury. The rifle was then traded for a saddle gun by Dr. W. A. "Montana" Allen of Billings, Montana. Later "Montana" Allen gave it to Frederick G. Renner of the U. S. Soil Conservation Service. Mr. Renner sold it to its present owner, Mr. Harrill.

The "Lost Mine Rifle" is the real mystery "One of One Thousand." Here is the story

in temperatures ranging from 120 degrees above to 60 degrees below zero and in dust, sandstorms, snow, and blizzards.

One winter his rifle earned him a new car by killing 35 cougars at $20 per head. (It would take more than 35 cougars to buy a new car today!)

The lure of prospecting took Mr. Lewis to Alaska where he discovered a valuable copper mine about 60 miles north of Juneau. Lack of transportation for his ore, plus ill health, induced him very regretfully to abandon his claim. He doused his "One of One Thousand" in heavy grease, stored it in the mine shaft and then sealed off the entrance with a charge of dynamite.

Unless someone else has discovered the mine, it is still hidden some 60 miles north of Juneau — and the man who finds the mine will find a coveted rifle to boot.

I know of another that sold for $500 and won't be surprised to see "One of One Thousand" leap into the Colt Paterson $2,000 class.

And with only about 25 percent of the original rifles located, there is a good chance that many more are still gathering dust in out-of-the-way spots awaiting the sharp eye of some energetic collector.

But since we're more concerned with the kind of rifles that the average collector is more likely to acquire, let's glance over a list of old Winchesters.

While most novice collectors start by collecting anything and everything, they quickly realize that the field is so vast that they can reasonably expect to start a comprehensive collection only if they specialize.

Lever-action rifles offer one of the most rewarding specialties. (The history of the

Shown above is the Winchester Model 1886 lever-action rifle — gold inlaid, engraved, and extra-fancy wood.

lever action was told in the September 1949 issue of *Sports Afield*.)

To get down to more practical limitations, you can confine yourself to all calibers and variations of, say, the Model 1873 — better known as "the gun that won the West." There are four calibers of which the last is the least known: 44-40 (44 W.C.F.); 38–40 (38 W.C.F.); 32-20 (32 W.C.F.); and the 22.

The Model 1873 in 22 caliber is one of the most tempting varieties. It was produced for 22 long or 22 short cartridges, and some were chambered for only the 22 extra long.

It has been generally believed that Winchester produced only a handful of 73s in 22 caliber but as a result of extensive research in old records by Tom Hall, Winchester Gun Museum curator, the writer is able to reveal for the first time that a total of 19,552 of these rifles was produced.

In addition to difference in caliber, the Model 73 was made as a sporting rifle with 24-inch round, octagon, and half-octagon barrels as well as in 20-inch octagon barrels. It was made as a carbine with a 20-inch barrel and as a musket in 30-inch round barrels. For longer than standard-length barrels a customer paid a dollar an inch, with 36 inches the maximum. Rounding up a collection of these varieties is a worthwhile goal.

As a curiosity, the model was also made in shorter barrels in round and octagon in 20-inch, 18-inch, 16-inch, and 14-inch

rifles and carbines, principally for South America.

Collectors should note that a 16-inch or 14-inch barrel rifle is illegal in the United States under the National Firearms Act passed in 1934, which makes it illegal to own a rifle or shotgun with a barrel less than 18 inches unless registered as prescribed in that act.

And if you want to find a real treasure, just look around for the rifle serially numbered 19,005 that was made in 1876 for Alfonso XII, King of Spain. Yes, it was a "One of One Thousand."

The above is just a skimming of the varieties of the Model 1873 but it will give a good idea why one model alone will keep you busy for a long time. Collecting only one example of each model is another challenging goal.

Stick your toe in the water — and soon you'll be swimming!

Many other intriguing as well as important rifles and — yes, shotguns — are included in the Winchester models that have become obsolete since the first was introduced in 1866. Many of them were made in a profusion of calibers as well as styles, and in many cases there are specially engraved presentation models. In many instances, since a great many Winchesters were used to maintain law and order in the old West, you'll acquire rifles that have colorful and romantic histories.

From the standpoint of profusion of calibers, it is probable that no rifle was

ever made in America that rivaled the still-famous "single-shot" Winchester. It was made in every caliber of its time from 22 to 50, in two varieties of sporting rifle, as a target rifle, a "Schuetzen" rifle, a light carbine, a shotgun, and a musket with five different kinds of barrel and nine kinds of stock. Additionally, the receivers were either "high" or "low" wall. The "high wall" was a favorite of H. M. Pope, the great barrel maker.

Then there is the still widely used Model 1895. Where the Model 73 is frequently called the "Buffalo Bill Rifle," the Model 1895 is sometimes known as the "Teddy Roosevelt" because it was one of Teddy's favorites that also went along with him on his famous African hunting trip. Only a few years ago Bob Reeves of Anchorage, Alaska, shot the world's record brown bear with his Model 95. This rifle was produced in many calibers and during 1915–1916 was chambered for the 7.62-mm Russian cartridges for the Russian Imperial Government.

What may be one of the most difficult of all oddities to find is the so-called "Thumb Trigger" Model 99. This unique three-pound 22-caliber rifle was introduced in 1904 to compete with low-priced foreign rifles but enjoyed its greatest popularity as a rabbit rifle in Australia. Instead of having a conventional trigger on the underside of the stock, this novel rifle had a trigger directly under the head of the bolt just *above* the small of the stock and was fired by pressing the trigger with thumb.

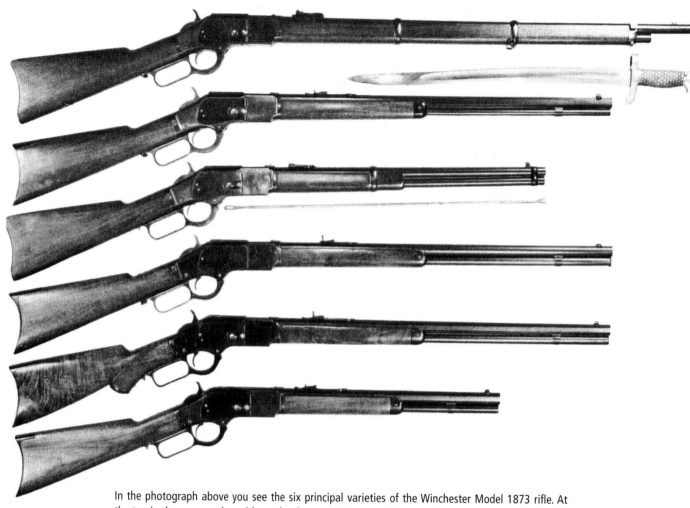

In the photograph above you see the six principal varieties of the Winchester Model 1873 rifle. At the top is shown a musket with a saber bayonet. Next to this, below, is a sporting rifle. Then comes a carbine (jointed cleaning rod carried in a butt recess). The fourth is a 22-caliber sporting rifle. The fifth is the sporting rifle with a pistol-grip stock. Last is one with a 14-inch barrel. A 16-inch or 14-inch barrel is illegal in this country under 1934 National Firearms Act which makes it illegal to own a rifle with a barrel less than 18 inches unless registered — as prescribed in that act.

The designation of Model 99 for the Thumb Trigger rifle, which was produced in 1904, will puzzle many who remember that many Winchester models bear numbers of the year in which they were introduced. The model number designated the year of introduction only with older models. More recent models frequently have arbitrary model numbers.

Another oddity by present standards is the double-barrel breech-loading Winchester shotgun, first introduced in 1879.

These guns, with Damascus barrels, were made in England by three different English makers and discontinued in 1884. They were followed by the first Winchester-manufactured shotgun, the famous 1887 lever action.

One of Winchester's few military rifles was the Lee Navy or Lee Straight Pull. Described as the first American rifle for clip loading, it had a 28-inch nickel-steel barrel with a wood stock running nearly to the muzzle, and it was used during the

Spanish-American War. Made for only five years, from 1895 to 1900, it is a rarity since only 20,000 were produced. Winchester disposed of all Lee Navy parts in 1916.

If you want a really complete Winchester collection, you'll have to start with the firearms that were direct ancestors of the Winchester. The original, the Walter Hunt "Volition Repeater," exists only as a patent model. It was followed by the Jennings, also a lever-action repeater, by Smith and Wesson pistols, by Volcanic rifles and pis-

The Winchester Lee Straight-Pull rifle, 1895. There are many types of obsolete rifles and shotguns that are available — and should increase in value.

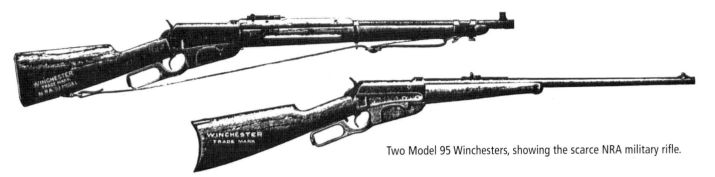

Two Model 95 Winchesters, showing the scarce NRA military rifle.

tols, and by the Henry rifle. The historic first rifle to bear the name Winchester appeared in 1866.

As you will see from this brief roundup, collecting old Winchesters can become a big job and, like the author, you will be amazed that a field as large as this has been so thoroughly overlooked in the race by collectors to acquire only handguns.

Dealers will help you acquire old Winchesters, or you can secure them independently by going out on your own collecting expeditions.

Here's a method adopted by the author many years ago when he assembled what he believes to be one of the country's largest collections of old telegrams. Place small classified advertisements stating your wants in magazines read by people who are likely to own old guns.

You'll find that answering the mail you receive from a little four- or five-line advertisement will afford a stimulating interest all by itself — and will open up many pleasant friendships for you.

In this way, before you actually realize it, you'll have a collection started as well as having opened up a wide field for possible finds of desirable items. But get started — that's the main part of the whole business. After that the whole thing will keep going on its own momentum.

Here's another important step for you to take.

Buy old catalogs of old firearms that are issued by Robert Abels of 860 Lexington Avenue, New York City, or Martin B. Retting of West Hurley, New York.

Abels has been a Winchester specialist for many years. As a matter of fact, it was just a few months ago that he became the first dealer to acquire one of the prized "One of One Thousand" items

Phil Sharpe's *The Rifle in America* is one of the best sources of information on old Winchesters. Here are some prices that will give you some idea of what may be paid for obsolete Winchester firearms in today's market. For example, you may secure a Model 02, in fair condition — if you are lucky — for as little as $5. On the other hand, a Model 1873 "One of One Thousand" might cost you $1,583. There are many that can be bought, with reasonable luck, for quite low prices.

A Model 99 Thumb Trigger has recently been purchased for only $6. A Model 00 Single Shot for $8. These, of course, when bought, were in just fair condition. But even those in good condition might cost only a few dollars more!

A Model 1876 "One of One Thousand" brought $485 in fair condition. In good condition," this same rifle was sold for $1,906. While it is naturally desirable to get a rifle in the best possible condition — for your own personal satisfaction — the "fair" condition ones may still be very much worth having.

Here are some other prices to give you art idea of the market today.

A Model 1866 Winchester, in fair condition, will bring about $21. When in good condition, the same rifle will cost about twice as much.

A Lee Navy rifle in fair condition has lately been sold for $16. The same rifle, in a really good condition, brought $31.

The pre-Winchester Volcanic lately sold for $51 in a fair condition, $99 in good condition.

Let us look over some of the other current prices of obsolete Winchesters. The pre-Winchester Henry rifle, in fair condition, brought $40. The same rifle, in good condition, sold for $79. The Hotchkiss, in fair shape, sold for $15 and in good, $32.

The big thing to keep in mind is that you are now actually in on the ground floor. This means that it is well within reason that you may unearth a really valuable rifle at a small price.

The whole collecting field has had such a history. The collectors who looked ahead, and got the jump on the other fellow, invariably made such finds as were seldom — if ever — discovered again.

Get started on your collection now.

(Reprinted by courtesy of *Sports Afield*.)

WORLD'S MOST POWERFUL RIFLE!

Weatherby

by JAC WELLER

A SHOT RANG out. The bull elephant in full charge died instantly, his five tons of inert bulk sliding to a stop over jungle bush. Rhinos and even the terrible and powerful Cape buffalo have been stopped in their tracks by a single bullet. The new 460 Weatherby rifle packs more power than any other shoulder weapon.

Roy Weatherby has always been a worshipper of bullet speed. His small bore rifles have been in a class by themselves. They would shoot through armor plate which other factory rifles of their bore diameter wouldn't dent. They kill well at all ranges. I have used a 257 WM for years on suitable game and once killed a Scottish stag at 281 yards dead in its tracks with

---

Several unfeeling friends helped the author test-fire a 14-lb. 460 Weatherby Magnum and other big bores — despite the 460's over-normal weight, some of the shooters passed up the chance for a broken clavicle in the prone position.

---

it. The little 87-grain bullet blew up in the beast's lungs. This is the flattest shooting commercial rifle available over the longer hunting ranges.

I have also used a 375 Weatherby for larger game and for some type of target work. This particular rifle happens to be the very best that I know of for shooting a prone position match at a one-third sized Rocky Mountain sheep silhouette-target at 100 yards. It's deadly on the largest varieties of American game, too. A 300-grain soft-point bullet will blow up in an animal the size of a caribou or larger and not make an exit wound. All this energy expended inside an animal kills quickly.

Weatherby and his California rifle-making firm had until recently no weapon that could top the British big double rifles in muzzle energy. Even his 378 Weatherby Magnum couldn't match the 600 Nitro-Express at close range. In the African game field, the

ultimate in stopping power is sometimes required.

This situation, however, was changed with the appearance of the 460 Weatherby Magnum; it's more powerful than any other standard shoulder arm. The Holland and Holland belted case has been used for most of the "Magnums" designed in the past 25 years, Winchester using it for their latest 264, the 338 and 458. The 460 WM case, however, is considerably larger, and has about 50 per cent more volume. Actually, the 460 and 378 WM cases are the same, save for the neck. That "460" is a misnomer, really; bullet and groove diameter of the barrel are the same as the 458 Winchester, or .458". However, the same 500-gr. bullet can be driven at better than 2,700 foot seconds in the Weatherby case, but at only about 2,150 in the Winchester adaptation of the old H&H design.

When I ordered my 460 Weatherby, I specified a heavy rifle. I didn't want a weapon that could be shot only a few times at game because of its heavy recoil. I wanted to test it thoroughly on paper targets and at simulated game targets. I wanted something that others could shoot also, and without extreme discomfort. A heavier-weight rifle was the answer.

A package finally arrived from Weatherby, in it my new rifle and the ammunition for it. I liked both immediately. The barrel was 26 inches long and straight, 1⅛ inches in diameter from action to muzzle. The rifle weighs 14.1 pounds with a Lyman 4x Ail-American scope in a Buehler one-piece mount. Fred Jennie of the Weatherby firm felt that their new Mark V action and most recent means of anchoring the 460 barrel in the stock would make for even greater ac-

curacy than I get from my favorite 375 WM of about the same weight.

The weapon was beautifully finished, the California mesquite stock showy and graceful. My wishes had been followed everywhere, except that the pistol grip was a little on the slender side, a characteristic of Weatherby rifles that they have trouble avoiding even on a special order. My pistol grip was considerably heavier than their standard, but still wasn't large enough. I like a handful of rifle.

I didn't have time to fire the new 460 for a week or so. I did examine, however, the new Mark V action, a radically new variation of the original Mauser idea. Instead of the conventional two locking lugs at the head of the bolt, there are a total of 9 much smaller lugs arranged in three rows of three, on the interrupted-thread system used in artillery breechblocks. The new action design was almost a necessity if a standard-size rifle was to fire the 460 cartridge. Two conventional locking lugs, designed to stand the enormous thrust of the 460 ammunition, would have required an action unpleasantly bulky. However, the Mark V action has all the strength required without an increase in over-all diameter.

A somewhat debatable additional advantage of the Mark V design is the lessened bolt lift, reduced from about 90 degrees to

Jac Weller's new 460 WM.

Pete McCrohan, 230 lbs., blinks under the recoil of the heavy 460 Weatherby Magnum.

Tests With Average Riflemen

I had been planning for some time a series of tests in which American riflemen of various sizes, ages, and abilities would shoot their favorite sporting rifles and four big rifles at simulated game targets. The original four heavy rifles were two Winchester Model 70's in 375 and 458, my 375 WM, and the double 470 Rigby. The 460 arrived in time to be included as an additional heavy rifle.

The targets were those used at the Camp Fire Club Outings. The Rocky Mountain sheep event has already been described. The "rising bear" is a silhouette of a full-sized grizzly seen from the side at 100 yards for a period of three seconds only. The "running deer" is also a silhouette which travels on the truck of a narrow gauge railway backwards and forwards between two bullet proof walls. All three targets are divided into sections, each section having a different count value. However, the dividing lines are not visible from the 100-yard firing point, even with 4x scopes, the highest power allowed.

Ten men finally took part in these tests. The pertinent results, as far as the 460 was concerned, is that only four men completed their sighting-in shots and their 15 rounds for record with this rifle. I made no effort to persuade anyone to fire one shot more than he wanted to. If the 460 was too much rifle, I wanted to know just that. Of the six men who did not complete their firing, however, five noticed no particular discomfort firing offhand. It was the prone position at the sheep target that hurt.

An experienced African big game hunter watched our tests. He has used the 460 Weatherby to kill two African game animals with two shots, but did not notice the recoil doing it. In the excitement of actual game hunting, you don't notice heavy recoil. He refused, however, to fire at paper targets from the prone position. He felt that firing a rifle like the 460 on targets might cause him to pick up a flinch that would be hard to cure. The less experienced shooters in our group certainly started to flinch a bit after a few shots.

The four men who did fire the full course with the 460 shot astonishingly well with it.

approximately 60. This means easier operation for someone just learning to handle a rifle, but I still haven't become used to it.

The Mark V bolt is of the new completely enclosed head type, following the lead of Remington several years ago in their 721–722 series. In this arrangement, the head of the bolt actually encloses the rear of the cartridge completely. Even if a cartridge case head cracks or breaks off with pressure, the gas does not drive parts of it back into the shooter's face.

First Firings and Recoil

I waited until I had an entire day for careful, leisurely shooting. I bore sighted and roughly adjusted the scope. My first shot was offhand at 25 yards. I was pleasantly surprised; the big rifle had recoil, lots of it, but its own weight made it bearable. The rifle came back with a sudden, but not vicious kick. The muzzle blast *was* severe. The shot was just out at six o'clock.

Since I had all day, I fired several other rifles of heavy recoil. The first of these was a double 470 Rigby which weighs 11 pounds and has 5,400 foot-pounds of muzzle energy, a lot less than the 460. The relatively greater drop of the Rigby stock and the lighter weight causes it to recoil almost as noticeably as the Weatherby. I then tried my 458 Winchester; the recoil was bruising because of the rifle's light weight (8.8 pounds), but in general considerably less.

I fired the 460 some more, this time prone with a tight sling. The rifle is pleasant for me to fire, even for 40 rounds. The stock fits nicely and has little drop. The only danger is that someone may fire the rifle carelessly, with his forehead too close to the telescope. At the instant of firing, since the shoulder supports even this rifle along

a line below the bore, there is a turning moment which causes the muzzle to kick up and send the sharp edge of the telescope back in a short arc that can cut the forehead. I realized this possibility initially and fired more than 100 rounds before I became careless and opened my eyebrow almost to the bone.

Accuracy

Weatherby sent me a 3-shot target fired at the factory at 100 yards. All three bullets were in the same irregular hole. I was pleased; however, a 3-shot group is not necessarily indicative of the average accuracy of a rifle. Further, it was fired bench- or machine rest; I want my rifles to shoot well from a prone position.

I tightened up my sling, took a firm low position and fired a 5-shot group every half-hour until I had six targets, using Weatherby's full velocity factory ammo. Not one group was as large as two inches, center to center. The average was about 1.62 inches. This accuracy is almost as good as I can do with any rifle and in a class with a good 30-06 or 300 H&H Model 70 Winchester heavy-barreled target rifle. It's far beyond the capacity of most sporting rifles. In spite of the considerable recoil in a prone position, I was truly pleased with the weapon.

TABLE 1: Comparative Ballistics

Cartridge	Bullet weight in grains	Muzzle velocity in ft. sec.	Muzzle energy in ft. lbs.	Type of rifle
375 Weatherby	300	2,800	5,220	Bolt
378 Weatherby	300	3,020	6,060	Bolt
458 Winchester	500	2,125	5,010	Bolt
470 Rigby	500	2,160	5,400	Double
577 Nitro-Express	750	1,950	5,500	Double
*600 Nitro-Express	900	1,950	7,600	Double
8-bore (.840")	1,000	1,800	7,200	Double
460 Weatherby	500	2,640	7,750	Bolt

*Not actually tested; no rifle available.

In spite of its weight and recoil, it handles very nicely indeed. Three of the four men shot it better than they did their favorite sporting rifle. A 14-pound rifle is no disadvantage on the bear and deer targets, at least if you don't have to carry it all day first. The heavy barrel, once in motion tracing the "running deer," or coming to rest on the "rising bear," tends to be stable because of its weight. The 460 Weatherby trigger pull is extremely good.

Reduced Loads

In the course of the ten-man firing experiment, and during some other firing with full velocity ammunition, we began to wonder about reducing the velocity. We didn't shoot any really small groups, and Frank Jury suggested that perhaps the recoil was just a little too much for accurate prone position shooting. He and I decided to load up some 460 cases with standard 500-gr. open point bullets and a moderate charge of 50-caliber machine gun powder. This powder certainly should burn well in a case of this capacity. I didn't even set the measure by weight, but adjusted the charge to just fill the case to the beginning of the neck. There would be, even with the bullet seated all the way home, an appreciable air space remaining. After adjusting the charger to give this amount of powder, I found it to weigh 107 to 108 grains. I increased the setting to give an even 110 grains. We used, of course, the Federal No. 215 primers, especially formulated for large-capacity cases of this order.

With a number of reloads of this type, Jury and I fired several five-shot groups at 100 yards, all prone position with a tight sling. The recoil from these was perceptibly less, but it wasn't a squib load. We had seven consecutive groups under 1.75 inches with one group of 1.050 inches. I fired a few rounds of this type over three separate week ends under different weather conditions; only one of a total of 14 groups measured more than two inches. Actual velocity was measured at between 1,672 and 1,716 fps. Here is a rifle that fires even definitely reduced loads accurately.

We suspect that full factory loads would be a bit more accurate from a machine rest, or even from a bench rest, if the firer had a good hefty bag of sand or something of this nature between the butt of the gun and

his shoulder. However, for prone position shooting, the lower velocity is better. The 50-caliber machine gun powder with its larger granulations seems to burn just as well in the big 460 case as the IMR 4350 used in the Weatherby factory loaded ammunition.

Power

Roy Weatherby claims that his new 460 is the most powerful rifle in the world. We didn't take for granted anyone's claims for ballistics, but actually measured actual velocity of several powerful rifles and weighed the bullets. The velocity tests were conducted through the courtesy of the Hercules Powder Company in my presence at their Kenvil, New Jersey, plant. The results of these tests are given in Table I, The 460 Weatherby outclasses the 458 Winchester, the 470 Rigby, even the 577 Nitro Express. My 577 Holland and Holland double rifle is not, however, of the most modern type. We didn't have a 600 Nitro Express for test, but the indications are that even this very powerful short range weapon would be at a disadvantage compared to the 460.

A word about muzzle velocity figures for the 460 WM. We found it to be between 2,631 and 2,644 fps with the only lot of factory ammunition available. The Weatherby catalog gives muzzle velocity as 2,725. I'm sure this velocity is possible, but to actually get it from my rifle would give considerable extra recoil. Perhaps the 600 Nitro Express, a rifle we didn't have, doesn't deliver quite its listed ballistics; our 577 didn't. The 470 Rigby, on the other hand, gave by actual test about 100 footpounds more muzzle energy, with today's British factory loadings, than the figures listed in the latest ICI catalog.

I included in the velocity tests a British double hammerless nitro-proved 8-bore rifle. This is not a Paradox or Explora shotgun-rifle combination, but carries full-length rifling in its 24-inch Whitworth steel barrels; it weighs 16½ pounds. It was made by Evans, a well-known riflemaker between 1900 and World War I, who had been Purdey's factory superintendent before going into business for himself.

This rifle labored under the disadvantage of improper ammunition. The 8-bore loaded brass cartridges which came with it were actually for an 8-bore H&H Paradox gun,

Roy Weatherby and frined in Africa — the rifle is the 460 WM.

these having only a few inches of the barrels rifled, at the muzzles. Their 1,000-grain bullets are driven at only about 1,600 fps, which gives 5,700 foot-pounds of muzzle energy. I wanted a real modern load worthy of this superb weapon.

I talked at length to Dr. Leonard Farmer of Hercules. I had some turned-aluminum cartridge cases made of a strong heat-treated alloy, and using them we worked up a real load using Sharpshooter, a Hercules 30 per cent nitroglycerine double-base powder.

Some trouble was had in working up this handload for the 8-bore Evans. Early trials with Bullseye or Red Dot as a priming charge behind either 50-cal. MG powder or 4350 gave erratic, incomplete burning behind my .858"-sized "round" ball-round except for the cylindrical band left by the swaging.

Dr. Farmer suggested a 15 gr. load of Red Dot as a primer plus 50 grains of Sharpshooter, and this worked much better. Later the Red Dot was discarded, and a straight charge of 96 grains of Sharpshooter was used in the tests, topped by six ½-inch wads and the sized spherical ball.

Groove diameter of the Evans 8-bore runs .840", so the ball is still being bore-sized a fair amount.

In these tests I found no appreciable advantage in the conical bullet — it and the round balls weigh about 1,000 grains each, and accuracy, in my hands, was as good

TABLE II: Rifle Details and Handling Times

Caliber	Type of rifle	Make & model	Weight of rifle	Length of bbl.	Length of rifle	Drop of stock	Sights	Average time for one shot	Average time for two shots	Average time for four shots
458 Win.	Bolt	Win. M70	8.8 lbs.	25″	46″	2⅝″	peep & bead	1.9 sec.	6.1 sec.	12.5 sec.
460 Wea.	Bolt	Mark V	14.1 "	26″	47″	2⅞″	4x scope	2.6 "	7.7 "	14.5 "
470 Rigby	Double	Rigby	11.0 "	26″	43″	3″	peep & bead	1.8 "	3.4 "	15.0 "
8-bore	Double	Evans	16.5 "	24″	41″	3¼″	open & bead	2.0 "	3.6 "	Impractical

TABLE III: Riflemen Details and Comments

Name	Age	Height	Weight	Experience	Comment
Johnny Boren	39	5′9½″	160	Moderate	They're all fun to shoot!
Sandy Dillon	42	6′2½″	230	Moderate with rifles	I like those double rifles!
Red George	41	6′2″	200	Great	The 460 Weatherby in a walk.
Frank Jury	55	6′2″	215	Great	I ought to have my head examined. These things kick!
Pete McCrohan	47	6′3″	230	Moderate	That Rigby hurts me most, particularly the second shot.
Jac Weller	47	6′1″	230	Great	For dangerous game at all ranges, I'll take the 460 Weatherby.

with the spherical as with the pointed bullet. There was no indication of excessive pressure, but so much recoil that most men firing it were pushed back a full step. Bullets of two different types were used which weighed 990 and 1,045 grains. The 96-gr. Sharpshooter charge gave a velocity of between 1,785 and 1,810 fps and a muzzle energy of 7,200 foot-pounds. Even though the computed energy of this rifle is less than the 460 WM, some experienced big game hunters believe that the approximately 1,000-grain, .840-inch lead slugs give an even greater shock to living game.

Final Tests

The 460 Weatherby Magnum and other powerful rifles are only really necessary when facing dangerous game at close range. The white hunters in Africa for years have preferred double rifles, mainly because of their facility for getting in a quick second shot. We decided to test actual shooting time, using a target of opportunity such as the Camp Fire Club's "rising bear" and a stop watch. Six men of varying experience fired two pairs of shots, two single rounds, and then a string of four rounds with full power ammunition from the 460, the 458, the 470, and the Evans 8-bore. Because the 8-bore ammunition was not full-length resized we dispensed with the four-shot string with this weapon. The idea was to take sufficient time to be sure that the shots were in the fatal area, but get reasonably quick shooting comparable to actual hunting conditions. Any firing in which the target was missed completely was done over.

The results of our tests are shown in Table II. You *can* get off a second shot quicker with a double, and a scope sight is a slight disadvantage in quick shooting. Throughout the entire tests, no one of the six firers ever failed to score on the simulated bear at least one mortal shot from a two-shot string, nor less than three out of four shots.

The Weatherby was at some disadvantage, in one way or another, compared to all three of the other rifles. However, I consider that these are more than counterbalanced by the greater range, sustained power, and accuracy of the 460. The 8-bore Evans, for instance, is estimated to have lost more than half its power beyond 150 yards, while the 460 Weatherby still has about 78 per cent of its energy remaining. A scope sight slightly delays shooting, but it decreases misses. The iron sighted weapons have a top useful range of about 100 yards; the scope sighted Weatherby would be good for 300 yards or even more. Even though a double rifle can get off its first two shots quicker than a bolt action, the 460 can get off *four* shots as quickly as the 470 Rigby, despite the latter's automatic ejectors and two cartridges held in the left hand.

Cost, Ruggedness, and Repair

The 460 Weatherby Magnum, with a good telescope sight, costs over $500. This is a lot of money, but scarcely a fifth of what you'd have to pay today for a 600 Nitro Express double. The even heavier Evans 8-bore double isn't available at all. There probably aren't half a dozen of the modern type in existence. The big British double rifles are about as rugged as they can be, and they're made with top materials and workmanship. Their design, however, is such that troubles do occur. Extreme carefulness in cleaning is a must for these pieces. Most white hunters carry along with them a number of spare small parts, which they occasionally need. A double rifle, though, is two rifles in one. A broken part on one side doesn't effect the other side. However, breakdowns do occur.

The Weatherby Mark V action is probably even more rugged, and certainly requires less attention than any double rifle. The one possible disadvantage is the short bolt throw; extraction is not quite so positive as in the conventional Mauser-type bolt actions. A sticking case does sometimes occur. This is unlikely with factory ammunition, but can happen with even full-length resized reloads.

Conclusions

The 460 isn't necessary for any American game and may not be required even for African game. It's better to have the extra energy, however, and not need it, than need more punch and not have it. The 460 is the most powerful practical rifle available. Its knockdown ability and accuracy gives you the very best insurance of getting your game and coming back yourself. It will be interesting to see what the white hunters do as their old, heavy double rifles need replacing. These men may be shooting 460 Weatherby's soon. They're lighter, cheaper, just as trouble free, and easier to maintain in the jungle. But they can't get off that second shot quite so fast.

160-lb. John Boren, who participated in the big-bore test firing, is thrown well out of the plumb by the 8-bore Evans.

The Ruger 10/22 Carbine

An introduction to the new and exciting autoloading 22 carbine from the great gun works at Southport, Conn.

by T. R. RUSFEL

EARLY IN 1963, Sturm, Ruger & Co., Inc., began working on the design of a 22 self-loading rifle. From this effort has emerged the recently announced Model 10/22 carbine and its unique 10-shot rotary magazine. The Company's objective was to construct a 22 autoloader which would be a companion piece to their 44 Magnum carbine. With that basic specification in mind, they've come up with a light, well-balanced arm that holds many imaginative, but practical features. To save weight and for reasons of production efficiency, aluminum was adopted as the logical material for the receiver and trigger guard frame. Both components were carefully designed with durability and ruggedness in mind. Thin shapes were avoided in designing these parts and there's an ample mass of material in areas where stresses are concentrated.

The method of attaching the barrel is completely new, and the usual threads at the breech end of the barrel are eliminated. Instead, the barrel is pulled tightly against the usual tightening shoulder by two long screws, which

lie beneath the barrel, through the medium of a V- block clamp.

The self-loading breech mechanism is based on the blow-back principle, a general design not unusual in firearms. However, the Ruger designers were able to make room for a breechblock of ample size to insure adequate inertia, consequently the 10/22 shows no cartridge case deformation arising from premature opening of the breech. Support of the cartridge during firing is further aided by the swinging type hammer actuated by a coil spring and strut. The strut is pivoted to the hammer in such a way that the spring exerts its force most effectively as the hammer strikes the firing pin and rear end of the breechblock, but as the breechblock retracts after barrel pressure is diminished or disappeared, the pressure of the hammer against the breechblock is reduced. This type of hammer not only helps achieve very smooth breechblock motion, but also provides ultra-short lock time. The designers also were particular that trigger and sear proportions would insure crisp trigger pulls, with a minimum amount of fitting and finishing at final assembly.

A nice feature of the design which will be appreciated by shooters who like fine

guns is that the trigger guard is integral with the internal frame work of the mechanism. This certainly makes for a more "engineered" look than the usual cheap metal bent into the form of a trigger guard bow.

However, the most distinguishing feature of the 10/22 is its 10-shot rotary box magazine. This design has the obvious merit of compactness — the magazine fits flush with the bottom of the gun, which isn't true of any other detachable magazine we know of having this capacity. The construction of the magazine itself involved a great deal of design time and experimentation; it went through several stages of development before the production form was evolved.

The important characteristic of the magazine is the solid steel portion through which the magazine is loaded and from which the cartridges are fed into the chamber. This component, which the factory refers to as the magazine throat, has the usual retaining lips and ramps to control the movement of the cartridge, but being of solid steel, this is one magazine which can be relied upon not to get out of adjustment. Development of this throat design alone was a big problem, because of its complex configuration, but it was solved by Bill Ruger's new subsidiary operation, the Pine Tree Castings Corp. in Newport, N. H. Although the magazine has the external appearance of a sort of "little black box," internally it is cylindrical. The spring-loaded rotor, which functions as an ordinary magazine follower, mounts on a central pivot pin, somewhat on the order of the Savage 99 or Mannlicher-Schoenauer. A lot of thought and armsmaking experience went into the design of this magazine, which ought to be extremely rugged and reliable in actual service.

All in all, this new 10/22 shows a refinement and advanced — yet rugged — design that is particularly impressive in view of the attractive moderate price.

Our test shooting of the Ruger 10–22 was hasty and brief, regrettably, for it was a pleasant gun to shoot, and it performed very well despite the fact that it was an early, semi-production piece, and not quite up to par in a couple of things — which we'll get to later. Because the new 22 carbine was in our hands for only a day, we didn't have time to mount a scope properly. We got good groups nevertheless, using CCI HySpeed 22 LR ammo. That brand and lot performed best of several — Federal Monark, Winchester-Western Super-X and Winchester Leader. We used the new Savage bases and a 4X Savage scope, and groups at 100 yards ran 2⅛"–2½" slow fire for 5 shots. The day was virtually windless, happily, but even so that's good performance for a light autoloader — or most any other 22 rim-fire, for that matter.

Our first test of the Ruger 10–22 was a trial — Bob Steindler of GUNS came out to Creedmoor Farm (the GUN DIGEST ballistic range) to join in shooting the new rifle, among others, because the sample 10–22 would be here for so brief a time. Bob quickly expended 225 rounds (mixed brands) at slow speed and rapid without getting a hangup of any kind except a few when the breechbolt was hand-released.

During this function firing, open sight groups at 100 yards went into just over 4 inches, for an average, not bad for these old eyes (Bob can't do too well with metallics, either), and considering that the barrel got fairly hot with pretty rapid-fire shooting.

Chief annoyance was the heavy, nonsmooth trigger pull — which Ruger's Ed Nolan says will be OK in production rifles.

The 10-shot rotary magazine is a little jewel. Despite ours carboning up pretty thickly, it worked without a single hitch. Made of steel and Cekon, a really tough

plastic, this big-capacity small device has been brilliantly engineered — you'll agree on that as soon as you see it, I think.

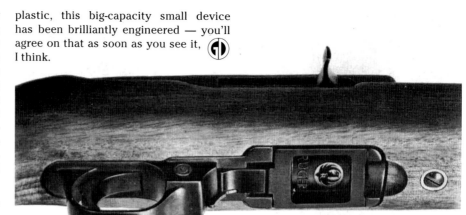

Above: Trigger assembly of 10/22 showing 10-shot rotary magazine in place.

Left: Field-stripped parts of Ruger's new rimfire.

Below: Exploded view shows component parts of the rotary magazine.

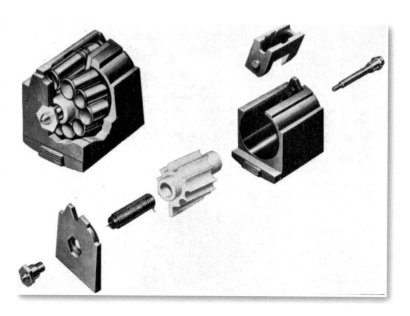

RUGER'S REACTIONARY RIFLE

Yes, reactionary, in the sense that the genius of Southport has brought forth the Victorian, a superb new single shot rifle that is indeed a throwback. Craftsmanship, elegance and assured performance were respected watchwords of that period, and the new Ruger exemplifies them all.

by ROGER BARLOW

NTERESTING, is it not, that the most exciting gun news of recent months, if not years, was the announcement and introduction of a new high grade rifle by Sturm, Ruger & Co. — a rifle without a magazine or clip, without a bolt, slide or automatic action; requiring each cartridge to be manually inserted in the breech. In plain words, *a single shot*! The gun world has come pretty near full circle in just 80 years to get us back to a type which was once considered to be the finest sporting rifle of all. In fact, a good many American gun enthusiasts still consider those late 19th century single shots to be the most desirable firearms ever made.

Indeed, what knowledgeable gun bug can resist making tracks to Abercrombie & Fitch or Joe's Gun Shop when he hears that there is a mint condition Peabody-Martini Creedmoor, a Mid-Range Ballard, Alexander Henry or Sharps-Borchardt for sale or just on display?

This is the same sort of honey that brings all the automobile bugs in full flight to the local Sports Car Center when the news

spreads (like wildfire, of course) that there is a Bugatti Type 55, an SSK Mercedes, a Lancia Dilambda or a 32-valve Stutz Black Hawk in the shop. Who has eyes for even an E Type Jag or a hot Corvette, much less a Pontiac Grand Prix (!), when such noble iron is on display.

And who has eyes for any of the myriad current examples of mass produced Mauser derivatives (complete with die stamped checkering) when there is a Gibbs Farquharson to fondle, admire and dream of owning!

The appeal which these fine old single shot breechloaders have for present day shooters is a delicate blend of appreciation of superb workmanship, admiration for good engineering and design, and reverence for a great name whose fame was justly earned. Those were rifles for sportsmen and shooters of discrimination, to be owned with pride and passed on from father to son; not mere shooting iron to be sold at the cheapest possible price; soon to be allowed to degenerate into rust and splintered wood. These magnificent single shots were the Pierce Arrows and Rolls-

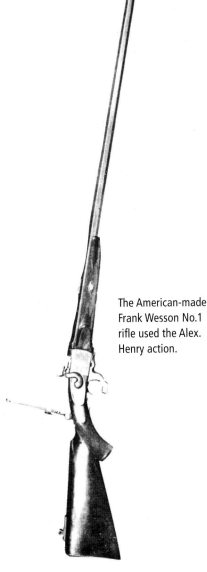

The American-made Frank Wesson No.1 rifle used the Alex. Henry action.

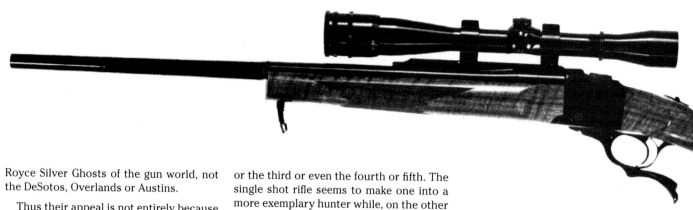

Royce Silver Ghosts of the gun world, not the DeSotos, Overlands or Austins.

Thus their appeal is not entirely because they are single shot rifles but is, to a very considerable extent, based upon their excellence as rifles. Yet the mere fact that these firearms provide the hunter with but a single chambered cartridge, not backed up by anywhere from three to a dozen more in a convenient magazine, somehow elevates the act of taking game with such a rifle to a rather special plane of achievement.

The Single Shot Afield

The man with a single shot rifle, stalking his game skillfully, thoughtfully calculating his range, not just shooting at his quarry but selecting the most effective spot to place that bullet, then carefully aiming and making that one shot count — that man surely is more of a hunter than is the fellow having half a dozen shots available in his repeater. The latter ignores many of the subtleties practiced by the man with the single shot, he often casually blasts away, knowing that he can fire again quickly if he misses the first time, or the second time,

or the third or even the fourth or fifth. The single shot rifle seems to make one into a more exemplary hunter while, on the other hand, the repeater or autoloader all too often seems to lure one into careless hunting and shooting habits, whether with rifle or shotgun.

Certainly many hunters using magazine rifles do practice all the hunting skills and do indeed make that first shot really count — just as though there was only one shot available. All too many of us shooters using "repeaters" seem disappointed if we don't actually have an opportunity of getting off a burst of three or four shots. Like small boys, it seems we aren't having as much fun as we anticipated unless there is plenty of noise.

I'm sure we've all been in the woods with an old and really experienced deer hunter who, upon hearing a shot in the distance, will pause and listen attentively for a moment and then say with quiet satisfaction. "Meat on the table for someone." Let that one shot be followed up by three or four in rapid succession and his reaction will probably be to spit with silent disgust and walk on. He knows from years of practical

experience that a volley like that more often than not means inept shooting or shooting when there was no real chance of scoring a hit in the first place.

As a hunter who regularly goes afield with bolt action magazine rifles as well as with single shots, I can certainly testify that I personally derive appreciably more satisfaction from my hunting when taking game with one of the latter. (Incidentally, I have found that a second *considered* shot can be gotten off in surprisingly quick time, when using a single shot, if a spare cartridge is held between the fingers of the left hand.) Using a single shot most certainly doesn't guarantee one a clean kill with the first shot everytime but, like the man says, we try harder.

That a sizeable segment of the American shooting public has a continuing high regard for good single shot rifles, especially those of the falling or dropping block type pioneered over a hundred years ago by Sharps, can be seen in the steady demand for usable actions of this type which can be used as the basis for handsome and accurate varmint rifles, barreled and chambered for modern cartridges. Wilbur Hauck has had a substantial backlog of orders ever since he started building complete rifles based upon his own modern design of falling block action about 10 years ago. My own Hauck, a 219 Donaldson Wasp, has to date been the best rifle I've ever owned and it is always the center of interest at a rifle range.

So it was only natural that, as soon as Bill Ruger had a prototype of his new rifle to show and some actions in production to study, I wended my way to Southport, Conn., for a visit. Now, without further delay let me tell you that this new Ruger single shot is a gun lover's gun. Handsome it is on the outside, but it is fascinating on

Queen Victoria at Wimbledon. Her Majesty opened first meeting of the National Rifle Association on Wimbledon Common, July 1, 1860.

RUGER'S REACTIONARY RIFLE

the inside, for the action is something of a design and engineering achievement.

Ruger Rifle Elegant

This is a beautiful and elegant rifle because Bill Ruger himself knows and appreciates this quality in a firearm. He owns and uses an enviable collection of fine single shots — Sharps, Alexander Henrys, Gibbs Farquharsons, Westley-Richards, Frasers, etc., as well as many magnificent English double rifles. He intends that his own single shot rifle will be at home and acceptable as an equal in such distinguished company.

Sharps pioneered the falling block, breech-loading action with external hammer in 1848, not long before the introduction of metallic cartridges, but Scotsman Alexander Henry refined the original concept and built rifles which had greater grace and beauty of line as well as better balance, guns which come up to the shoulder with the natural speed and ease of a good shotgun. Bill Ruger pointed out his appreciation of these virtues in a rifle, and freely acknowledged the influence of Alexander Henry's work upon the appearance of his own rifle. The Farquharson exerted less influence largely because the action is less graceful, appearing with the lever, in profile, rather deep and clumsy — also the esthetic flaw of most Martini pivoting block actions which are, additionally, much too long to look right. However, the lever of the Ruger has the distinguishing Farquharson look about it but it appears more graceful because it seems to lie closer, and in better relation to the receiver.

While it is clear that this Ruger single shot owes much of its light, sleek appearance to the good taste of Alexander Henry

and to Bill Ruger's appreciation for the elegance and dignity of the Victorian period, the engineering is strictly 20th century, with no bows to the past other than the retention of the basic concept of the long-established dropping block action.

I was amused and pleased to discover that Bill Ruger shares my sense of revulsion to the sloppy feel of most Mauser type actions when the bolt is opened — it simply rattles around with all the sound and feel of mechanical precision displayed by a piece of scrap iron being shaken around in the bottom of a tin bucket! Sure, such an action is snug and tight when the bolt is closed and ready to fire and, most assuredly, it shoots with enviable accuracy; nevertheless, it doesn't give one the satisfying feeling of handling a piece of precision equipment — which a good single shot does!

The new Ruger is what is known as a

hammerless action (which type came into being on both sides of the Atlantic about 1872), although unseen within that quite small breechblock lives a real hammer. The Ruger breechblock could be held to such compact dimensions because no effort was made to place a mainspring within its confines. The hammerless Sharps-Borchardt required a breechblock of considerable length to contain its spiral mainspring, as did other somewhat similar actions. The Ruger mainspring is located just forward of the receiver, covered by the fore-end. Actually, one of the early guide lines laid down by Bill Ruger for his design staff to follow set the maximum depth of the action at its present pleasingly slim dimension. However, this edict set a whole series of interlocking problems for Harry Se-fried and Larry Larson, the two Ruger engineers involved in the development of this gun. Both were faced with a situation not far removed from

In answer to Barlow's question about the difficulty of pleasing everyone with ideas as to how a gun should look, Bill Ruger had this to say: "Whenever anything great is created, it is the outcome of someone's convictions. The corollary of this would be that an attempt to please the majority can produce only an Edsel." Barlow's opinion is that the Ruger factory is more likely to turn out a rifleman's Bentley than an Edsel!

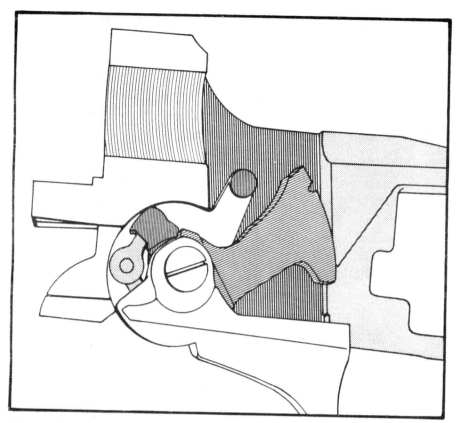

This view of the sectioned Ruger receiver shows the hammer in *fired* position, lever closed. The breechblock (not seen here to permit the hammer to be shown) would also be in the upward, closed position. The first 6° movement of the lever starts cocking the hammer, thus allowing the firing pin to retract before the breechblock starts to move downward (with also a 3° slant to the rear).

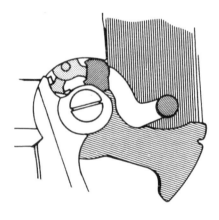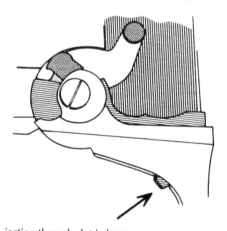

Left: lever open, hammer cocked, breechblock down, toggle buckled into its recess in receiver wall.
Right: lever closed, breechblock raised, hammer cocked. Tip of hammer (cocking indicator) pro-

jecting through slot in lever.
Far Right: cam surface (left side of breechblock) moves sideways fast, disengaging it from cartridge extractor groove at end of ejection stroke, permitting fired case to be kicked clear.

Improved Extraction-Ejection

Most important of these improvements had to do with extraction and ejection. Earlier single shot rifles used only rimmed cases, upon which a simple extractor of robust size could get a good bite. Yet most classic single shots seemed prone to some extraction difficulties even with

the classic example of impossibility, the Blivet — trying to put 5 pounds into a 2-pound bag! Their goal was not merely to meet Bill Ruger's esthetic requirements of a clean and well-proportioned shape for the receiver and breechblock but, additionally, to provide mechanical refinements not found in earlier falling block actions.

black powder cartridges, then getting into even more trouble as pressures rose with the advent of smokeless powders. The English ammunition makers, Kynoch, marketed a number of rimmed versions of popular rimless big game cartridges, specifically intended for single and double rifles, loading them down to lower velocities and pressures. Most people have assumed that this was done only to ease the strain upon a break action double rifle, but extraction difficulties may well have influenced this decision to an even greater extent. It seems odd that it was deemed necessary to have a rimmed, low pressure version of the 375 H&H when the same rifle makers were building similar actions able to stand the bending strain imposed by such horrendous cartridges as the 577 and 600.

As far as the single shot, falling block action is concerned, it is quite as strong as a bolt action and 60 years ago it was probably appreciably *stronger* than the two-lug bolts of that day. But a bolt action provides powerful initial camming movement capable of extracting all but the most outrageous overloads, while none of the single shot designers of the last century ever arrived at a really good solution to all the problems of getting that fired case out of the chamber.

Even my 240 Apex Holland & Holland falling block (Woodward & Holland Patents), one of the latest designs of the great period of single shot rifles, is a bit lacking in initial extraction power. It functions well with factory cartridges, these a "loaded down" version of the rimless 240 Magnum, but a reloaded cartridge, brought up to 243 velocity with 4350 powder, tends to require so much pushing on the lever that one has a sense of straining the extractor mechanism. Obviously the makers chambered this gun for the 240 Flanged, rather than for the more useful 240 Magnum, for this very reason.

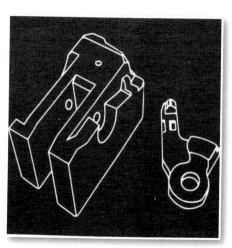

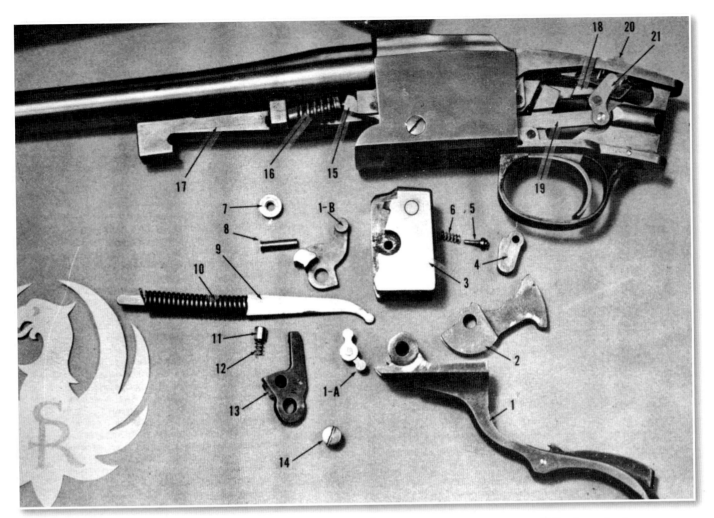

Parts List

1. Lever. (1-A) Toggle. (1-B) Lever Arm
2. Hammer
3. Breechblock
4. Striker
5. Firing pin
6. Firing pin spring
7. Ejector roller
8. Ejector roller pin
9. Hammer strut
10. Hammer strut spring
11. Ejector plunger
12. Ejector plunger spring
13. Ejector
14. Lever pivot pin
15. Ejector cam
16. Ejector spring
17. Receiver extension
18. Sear
19. Safety bar
20. Safety
21. Safety arm

The toggle (1-a) serves two functions. First, as a connecting piece between the lip of the lever and the lever arm (1-b) which actuates the breechblock; secondly, as a sort of "motion absorber" by folding or buckling in the middle and moving its center section into a recess in the receiver wall, thus arresting the downward movement of the breechblock while allowing the lever to move further downward to provide additional movement of the extractor-ejector.

The striker (4) is interposed between the hammer (2), and firing pin (5) to permit a shorter hammer to be utilized and to keep the breechblock as small as possible. The firing pin inclines upward at a 5° angle. The striker pin is inserted in a hole in the right side of this breechblock but production models will be fitted from the left side.

The ejector roller (7) imparts a very rapid closing or return movement to the ejector when the breechblock is being closed, but with a minimal amount of friction as it contacts the rear of the ejector.

The hammer strut (9) transmits the thrust of the main spring (10) directly to the lower leg of the hammer, moving only about 0.2" in the process. Re-cocking the main spring is spread over 45°–50° of movement of the lever, so the effort required is small. The end of the strut fits into a slot and recess in the lower leg of the hammer.

The ejector plunger and spring (11 & 12) force the ejector inward (laterally) toward the cartridge head.

The ejector cam (15) is pivoted just forward of the receiver, interposed between the end of the lever and the ejector itself. After the breechblock has moved downward some distance, the lip on the end of the lever impinges on the ejector cam, exerting powerful leverage on the ejector for initial extraction (about 1/32"); then this movement is speeded up and, as the ejector cam goes over "dead center," the spring (16) imparts a powerful and rapid kick to the ejector, through the cam, throwing the cartridge right out of the breech. The movement of the ejector cam after it goes over dead center out-runs the lip of the lever, but if the spring is removed the final movement of the cam and ejector is provided by the final movement of the lever — with the result that the cartridge is merely extracted, not ejected.

The receiver extension or fore-end hanger (17) will be of slightly different shape in production rifles. It carries both the ejector spring (as seen here) and the mainspring and hammer strut along its underside. The adjustment screw for varying the pressure on the barrel is fitted at the forward end.

The sear (18) is blocked by the safety when it is in the "on" position, while the safety bar (19) blocks hammer. The safety (20) is a sliding shotgun type, located on the tang.

Ruger's design and development team was determined to provide not only easy and positive *extraction* for all modern cartridges, including such popular magnums as the 7mm Remington and 458 Winchester, but to also provide automatic *ejection* of the fired case as well. To this end they have engineered into the Ruger action exceptionally powerful leverage, both for the initial downward movement of the breechblock and for the first movement of the extractor. When the breechblock has moved down far enough to clear the path of the cartridge the extractor action is speeded up; then, when the case has been withdrawn sufficiently to be moving freely, the force of a small but powerful spring is used to impart a sharp "kick" to the extractor, throwing the empty case clear of the action. This special ejector spring also resides forward of the receiver (and is exposed to view by removing the fore-end) and can be easily disconnected, thus letting those shooters who want to save their brass simply pick the partially extracted case out of the breech rather than off the ground. It took some clever engineering to arrive at a simple and reliable way to move the extractor sideways at the end of its travel, to quickly clear the extractor groove of the case head so as not to interrupt its rearward momentum after imparting the final ejection "kick" to the case.

New Action Simple and Strong

Not only did Sefried and Larson keep all the mechanism neatly contained within the action and fore-end but they finally worked a minor miracle by pivoting all main components upon *one* pin — upon which the under lever also pivots! Most falling block actions have two or three pins going through the receiver walls, which neither contributes to the appearance of the rifle nor to the ease of disassembly. Actually, there are two more pins

in the action but they're both in the breechblock itself, thus never seen unless the action is dismantled. Even upon maximum downward movement of the lever the Ruger presents an unusually clean and uncluttered appearance, for there are no connecting bars or levers to the internal mechanism. However, when at full cock, the hammer is partly exposed until the lever is closed.

The first 6-degree movement of the lever retracts the firing pin, before movement of the breechblock commences; the latter then travels downward but with a 3-degree backward slant to quickly reduce rubbing pressure on the cartridge head. This makes the action easier to open than might otherwise be the case. This 3-degree slant also provides some slight camming action as a new cartridge is seated during the final movement of closing the action.

The gratifying minimum of cocking levers, connecting rods and links of various types in the Ruger springs from the basic simplicity of the action design, largely made possible by an ingenious use of multi-purpose shoulders, projections and abutments on the various internal elements of the action, including some formed on the inner walls of the breechblock itself. Such simplicity of design, note well, is often far more difficult to achieve than is a more complex solution to the problems involved. A look at the photographs of the details of a cut-away action will make the operation of the Ruger easier to comprehend.

Much care has gone into the trigger and safety design. No set trigger will be available (which I regret) but easy adjustment of the conventional trigger is provided for *weight of pull* and for *over-travel*. The best possible type of safety is provided — the highly convenient thumb-operated "shotgun" design, mounted on the upper tang, and it blocks

both sear and hammer. To learn if the hammer is cocked a shooter need only slide his trigger finger just forward of the guard, along the underside of the lever; there a small projection on the cocked hammer protrudes through a narrow slot in the lever for about ⅛-inch, thus can be easily felt or seen.

26-Inch Barrels

The button-rifled barrels for this single shot rifle are being made to Ruger's specifications by an outside supplier, and Bill says these will be available in different weights. The barrel is free floated — there is no contact with the wood of the fore-end, which is carried on a steel hanger welded to the receiver. There is a screw adjustment near the end of this hanger to enable a shooter to apply varying degrees of pressure to the barrel, if desired, when tuning an individual rifle and load. This steel hanger also carries and provides the abutments for the mainspring and the ejector spring.

Bill Ruger, Larry Larson and Harry Sefried talked at some length on the matter of this rifle being able to provide a hunter with the maximum velocity a magnum cartridge usually delivers, which usually requires a 26-inch barrel, while still keeping the overall length of the Ruger to a convenient and handy dimension. The short length of the receiver of a falling block rifle renders this possible. In contrast, a bolt action receiver will usually be almost 3 inches longer — to compensate for which many manufacturers are now fitting 22-inch (and even shorter) barrels. This may make for a bolt action rifle of a more desirable total length, but if you want all the greater performance your modern cartridge is capable of delivering, this is not the way to get it.

The Ruger will have as standard a 26-inch barrel, delivering the full, advertised velocity of such cartridges as the 264 Win. Mag., the 7mm Rem. Mag. or the 300 Win. Mag., yet will still be handy enough to carry into the mountains on a sheep hunt or after mule deer, anywhere you want the flattest possibly trajectory, the least wind drift and most bullet energy.

Long range big game hunting (as with varminting) demands a scope sight and so this rifle will be without iron sights except perhaps on the really big calibers, or as an option) but will have a gracefully contoured dovetailed ramp atop the breech-end of the barrel to take a strong, simple and inexpensive scope mount.

Now that we already seem to be out West hunting mulies with the Ruger, I'm reminded that a rather famous Westerner is also associated with this single shot project at Ruger's. Len Brownell, renowned as a stock-maker, has come East to take charge

Barlow tries out an incomplete work-horse test gun, finds it comfortable to shoot with 7mm Rem. Magnum factory loads. Note the main spring carried by the steel fore-end hanger.

of making the stocks for these rifles. He was at Ruger's New Hampshire plant for some months prior to the commencement of actual production, training women in the art of checkering (and the way Len does it, it *is* an art) while carving out the prototype stocks himself. Actually, the single shot rifles will be manufactured in their entirety at the New Hampshire factory under Len Brownell's supervision, no rifle to leave the plant until and unless he is satisfied with it in every detail. When I had this meeting at Ruger's Southport factory, production of the single shot had not yet started. The first rifle to the final design, which was for showing to the press at the NRA convention in April, was being constructed in the tool room just outside Bill Ruger's office door. The only model I had an opportunity to shoot was one without sights or fore-end, which was being used on a short indoor range at that time merely to check extraction with normal and proof loads. A few 7mm Rem. Mag. loads fired in this lighter-than-normal, incomplete gun sold me on its comfortable shooting characteristics and the Tightness of the stock design. Bill Ruger ruefully commented that all of his friends and acquaintances wanted to help him design that stock and that he could hardly visit one or another of his shops without being besieged by a gaggle of would-be woodmen, with or without skill! My own opinion of the prototype was that it was perfect for my taste.

Lost Wax Castings Used

There may be considerable controversy over Ruger's extensive use of "investment" castings in the manufacture of this action, but such criticism will be based largely on the misconception that casting still means the use of cast iron or other materials inferior to modern chrome steels, and that forging (hammering heated metal into the desired shape) produces parts in which the metal is clearly superior in grain structure as well as strength. In actual fact many forgings, including some used in firearms manufacture, end up with the "grain" formation aligned (as it should *not* be) in the same direction as shear loads will be applied.

The casting techniques employed by Ruger's (in their own New Hampshire foundry) produce precision castings of *chrome steel* with a desirable homogenous grain structure providing admirable strength and wear characteristics. Both the receiver and the breechblock benefit from being made by this investment casting process. If the former had been machined from a forging, considerable metal would have been removed from its rear wall simply to make the necessary cuts elsewhere and so the finished receiver would have been structurally inferior. The breechblock also benefited from being

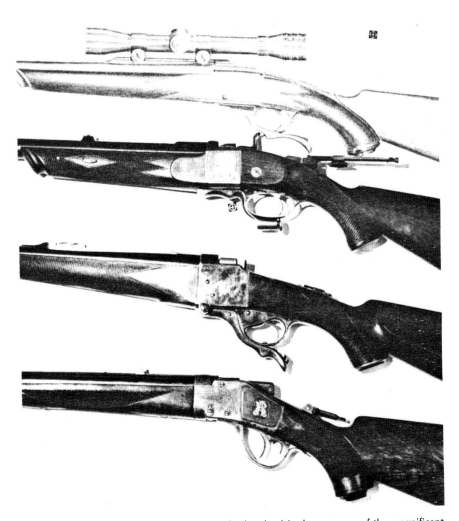

A drawing of the final design of the Ruger single shot (top) in the company of the magnificent rifles of the last century which were its inspiration — an Alexander Henry, a Farquharson and a Sharps-Borchardt.

cast, for necessary shoulders, guides, complex cam contours, etc., are accurately cast as integral parts of the internal walls. Most of the moving parts — hammer, lever arm, extractor, etc. — are also beautiful examples of the art of investment casting.

Castings are not used in this gun primarily for economy of production (Bill surmised that many parts could actually be made more cheaply on machine tools) but because it is the best way to do the job in the light of 20th century technology.

Obviously, Ruger's *had* to consider some economies; for if a gun is to sell for under $300 it cannot carry engraving like a $3,000 Purdey nor can each internal part be jeweled or "exhibition finished." These are niceties which a customer with plenty of money to lavish upon a gun could deal with to his own satisfaction and taste after buying a standard grade rifle. No doubt some single shot enthusiasts will spend considerable extra money to bring their own Rugers up to the standards of detail finishing found only in expensive English "first" grade guns.

Even produced to sell for only $280, this new Ruger may very well be the best single shot rifle ever made — it's as elegant and graceful as an Alexander Henry, has a better action than even the famed Farquharson, has a more accurate barrel than could be bored at the time the "classic" falling block rifles were made, has the advantage of the most modern metals and technology in its manufacture and, perhaps equally important, it is being built in the factory of a man who holds the artistry, engineering and painstaking craftsmanship of the Victorian period in such esteem that this finest product of Sturm, Ruger & Co. will probably be called *The Victorian*. What a bold and yet comforting conceit in this day of nuclear science and moon rocketry! It will help to keep us from getting further out of touch with that Golden Age of guns and hunting. Of course, the era also produced a large variety of remarkable men ... I think time quite possibly slipped a cog somewhere, to our advantage, putting an Eminent Victorian — Bill Ruger — into this computer age!

REMINGTON'S 40-XB

by JIM HORTON

UCH OF MY shooting in recent times has been with the shotgun, more particularly the trap gun — one year I spent 50 Sundays shooting the clays and only lousy weather prevented my going out the other two days.

One day not long ago, though, I read with renewed interest an article in a recent Gun Digest by *Field & Stream's* gunscribe, Warren Page, called "Half-Minute Rifles." In it I learned that Remington had a centerfire rifle available, *guaranteed as to accuracy*. My ears perked up, my interest increased, and I knew I'd have to have one of 'em! After much hard thought on caliber choice I ordered a 40-XB heavy barrel model in standard 6mm Remington caliber, with a twist of 1–10".

I was, of course, impatient to have the rifle in my hands as soon as possible, but because the 40-XB is a special order rifle it takes time — in my case it was close to 8 weeks.

Specifications

The 40-XB can also be had with a light or "standard" barrel. The heavy barrel model weighs in at 11¼ lbs., less sights, the standard is 1½ lbs. lighter. Both barrels are about 27¼", and for some $20 extra, stainless steel barrels can be had. They're recommended, by Remington, for such hotter cartridges as the 7mm Rem., 30–338, etc., and they will also give increased barrel life for the 6mm Rem. and 22–250. This is something for the varmint hunter to consider.

Most 40-XBs supplied are single shot; repeaters can be had, again for an extra $20, in cartridges up to the 7.62 NATO, better known as the 308 Winchester. The SS style has a slight edge in accuracy usually, the action being stiffer because there is no weakening cut-out through the bottom of the action and stock.

> Accuracy, particularly with over-the-counter rifles, often is worse than the buyer expects, or hopes it will be. Remington, however makes a gun with a guaranteed level of performance– less than one-half MOA in some calibers! Here's a full report on a workout of their hot 40-XB

One other option is a $40-extra trigger with a 2-oz pull, for bench-rest and target shooting. It is generally considered too light for field use. However, the trigger on my 40-XB can be adjusted down to about 8 ounces, with safety, and it's a joy to use.

Every Remington 40-XB, before it leaves the factory, must fire three 5-shot groups at 100 yards, these not to exceed a certain accuracy standard for the cartridge being fired:

Cartridge	Group Size	Twist
222, 222 Mag., 223	.45"	14"
22-250	.55"	14"
6x47 (6mm-222 Mag.)	.55"	12"
6mm Rem. (244 chamber)	.60"	10" or 12"
6mm Int. (6mm-250)	.60"	12"
6.5x55	.70"	9"
7mm Rem. Mag.	.75"	9"
7.62 NATO (308 Win.)	.75"	10"
30-06	1.00"	10"
30-338 (30-7mm Mag.)	1.00"	10"

Test groups and loading data are furnished with each rifle, the targets with my rifle averaging .47", well under the .60" maximum average allowed. Interestingly, these groups were fired with custom made bullets, not factory! Whether this will continue now that Remington offers match grade bullets in 22 and 6mm (the Power-Lokt

stuff) is moot. Note that Remington doesn't guarantee that the user of their 40-XB rifles will obtain the same accuracy shown by their test targets, and in watching some reloaders at work I can well see why.

All 40-XBs have scope blocks attached, but some short target type scopes, at least, are too short to reach the bases. My 10x Unertl Varmint scope wouldn't fit. The base separation is 10.6" instead of the older 6.8" or 7.2" dimension, with one base on the barrel and the other on the receiver bridge. The receiver ring, also tapped, comes sans base, and would allow a 7.2" separation. The longer target scopes present no problem, of course. The 10.6" separation has an advantage; it takes 6 clicks instead of 4 to equal 1 MOA (1" at 100 yards), giving more precise impact adjustment.

The walnut stock is of target type, the wood plain and straight grained for strength. Barrel and action are hand-bedded, with the barrel free-floating. A barrel bedding device at the front end of the stock controls tension between barrel and fore-end, and can also be used with electrical bedding devices. The underside of the stock has a rail inletted flush with the wood, permitting adjustment of the attached front swivel and handstop, designed for target shooters. The handstop is easily removed for field or bench shooting.

The Cartridge

The 6mm Rem. is nothing more than the 244 Rem., given a new name, different bullet weight and a change in barrel twist. To go a little farther back, the 244 came from the 257 Roberts, which first saw the light of day using the old tried-and-true 7×57mm Mauser case. The bullet diameter is hardly new either, as it dates back many years, both here and abroad. You never heard of the 6mm Lee Straight Pull rifle?

The 244 Rem. and the 243 Win. came out about the same time, but the 244 lost the race rather early when it was found that the twist used, 1–12", wouldn't stabilize bullets of 100 grains or heavier if spitzer pointed. The 244 was first loaded with 75- and 90-gr. bullets while the 243 was available with 80- and 100-grainers. With the 243's 1–10" twist no troubles were had with 100-gr. sharp pointed bullets. Remington had looked on the 244 as mainly a varmint cartridge, but the public found the 243 a pretty good deer cartridge, so much so that 250–3000 and 257 Roberts sales hit rock bottom as a result. Regrettable, too, for both loads make darned fine cart ridges when reloaded.

Remington finally saw the light and changed the twist of the 244 to 1–10", but for some reason they never did say much when this was done. Probably too late to do much good anyway. With the introduction of the Remington 700 rifles a "new" cartridge, the 6mm Remington, also made its appearance. There are no specification differences between the 244 and the 6mm Rem., but reloaders should reduce the 244 charges a bit before using them in the 6mm Rem., if only because of the faster twist of the latter.

6mm cartridges were originally loaded only with 100-gr. bullets, but late in 1965 an 80-gr. loading was announced. Pleasing news to the non-reloading varmint hunters.

Sighting Equipment

Because my Unertl wouldn't work. I snapped up a B&L 6–24x scope when it was offered at an attractive price. It does add to the weight and bulk of the rifle no little bit, but then this isn't a rifle anyone would want to carry in the field for any great distance.

This B&L variable is a great work of art, and optically won't take a backseat to anything, but there is room for improvement, mainly in the method of adjusting parallax. The Parallax Adjustment Selector Ring, as B&L calls it, moves the objective (front) lens elements back and forth. The higher the power setting the more precise this adjustment must be. If one makes an adjustment at low power and the scope is then zoomed to high power it will be out of focus, so always adjust for parallax at the maximum power setting you intend using.

The variable-power aspects of this B&L scope give it advantages over fixed power scopes. You can, for example, seemingly dial away mirage by lowering the power setting. The mirage is still there but it isn't as noticeable. The glass can also be used as a spotting scope.

Author's Remington 40-XB, ready for testing. Hollywood tool, set up on bench, allowed reloading at range. Rifle delivered excellent groups, favorite loads beating the factory guarantee. Scope is Bausch & Lomb 6x–24x.

Reloading

Before the rifle arrived several different makes and weights of 6mm bullets were ordered, along with 100 unprimed cases, 40 factory loads with 100-gr. bullets, and a set of RCBS neck sizing dies. In a rifle mainly to be used for target work there isn't much sense in getting a full length sizing die. Resizing is also easier, as only the neck is worked. As of now some cases have been reloaded 20 times and still slip easily into the chamber.

The unprimed cases were first trimmed lightly on a Forster trimmer to make the mouths smooth and even — most looked as if they had been factory trimmed with a dull hacksaw, one with several teeth missing! This seems to be a common situation with all makes of primed and unprimed brass, not an exception. All cases were chamfered, then primed with Remington large rifle primers. Alcan primers were also used later, but my shooting could detect no difference between the two, which speaks rather highly for a newcomer to the rifle and pistol primer field.

All loads were assembled on a Hollywood Senior Turret Tool, a product I can't praise enough. Workmanship is top notch, as it is on all Hollywood tools, something that seems to be disappearing from the American scene. A Hollywood micrometer powder

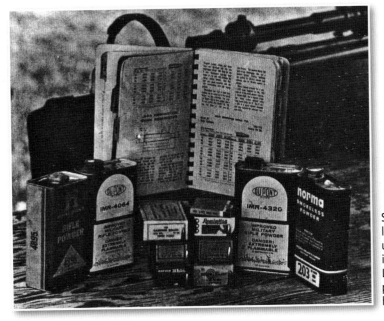

Some of the bullets and powders used by Horton in testing. Speer's Loading Manual provided basic handload data.

measure was also used throughout, and it performed without a hitch. No loads were weighed, though the measure was first set using the big Ohaus scales, a fine machine but rather too large and bulky to take afield.

Bullets

6mm bullets are available in a large array of types and weights. 60, 70, 75, 80, 85, 90, 100 and 105 grain sizes, and hollow point, spitzer, semi-pointed and round-nosed, in flat and boat-tail design, are offered. All point and base types aren't available in every weight, of course.

Aside from the new Remington Power-Lokt bullets, there are no factory 6mm match grade bullets on sale. Gardiner of Rockford, Ill., now specializes in 6mm bullets, match and hunting types, and Col. Hollidge is well known for his match bullets, 6mm as well as 224, etc.

My 40-XB was factory tested with Crawford Hollidge (Marstons Mills, Mass.) bullets, so a supply of these was ordered. These are soft swaged, hollow pointed and run about 70 grains. Later on some heavier Hollidge bullets were also purchased.

The Remington 40-XB centerfire rifle as factory delivered. It is made in two barrel weights and twelve calibers, from 222 to 30–338, all with guaranteed accuracy levels. Trigger pull is easily adjusted on the 40-XB by means of an Allen wrench, making removal of barreled action from stock unnecessary. Standard trigger was set at 8 ozs. for test shooting. A 2-oz. trigger is available at extra cost.

Shooting

My first groups were fired, after sighting in, with factory 100-grain ammunition. It would be a gross understatement to say that accuracy left something to be desired, for the last three 5-shot groups averaged about 1½". However, as it was about 15 months since I had done any serious rifle shooting I laid part of the blame on being out of practice. Such didn't prove to be the whole case though, because after I had become used to the rifle and shooting from a bench again, groups with the other box of factory loads didn't improve much, going about 1⅜" average for four groups.

After all cases had been fire-formed I began loading and shooting in earnest.

Without a doubt the best shooting load was the one used at the factory for testing accuracy, i.e., 40.5 grains 4064 and the 70-gr. Hollidge soft swaged bullets. This load averaged .380" for a series of groups.

It became apparent that the lighter weight bullets were the shooters, because for the most part anything over 75 grains didn't perform well. Also that 4064, combined with light bullets, gave the best accuracy. Here is a table of my results, the group sizes being the average of about 5–6 strings of 5 shots:

Bullet	Powder	Group
Gardiner 70-HP	40.5/4064	.625"
Hollidge 70-HP	40.5/4064	.380"
Sierra 60-SP	41.0/4064	.625"
Sierra 75-HP	39.0/4895H	.625"
Speer 90-SP	35.0/3031	.800"
Speer 105-RN	35.0/4320	.750"

I like boat-tail bullets, but the Sierra 85-gr. BT just won't shoot in this 40-XB, groups running around 1"-1¼".

Remington has two new 6mm bullets on the market — on the market if you can find them, that is! One is a hunting type, the other target style, both 80 grains. So far the only one that I have had a chance to shoot has been the hunting bullet. This is rather odd looking in that it could, in all truthfulness, be called a full metal-jacketed hollow point, with a dimpled bottom! How does that grab you? The nose of the jacket is folded over and in and, looking closely, you'll see 5 cuts in the nose for quick expansion. Do they shoot? You're darned right they do. The first load, using 40 grains of 4320, gave a ½" group.

Going up and down (very little up, though) in ½-gr. jumps neither hurt nor helped group diameter. With its small diameter hollow point, this should be a flat-shooting bullet.

The Norma 75-gr. HP bullet shoots well too, though not quite as good as the Remington. 40 grains of Norma's No. 203 gave an average of about ¾", and I finally settled on the Norma recommendation of 42.3 grains of 203, with groups wavering between ⅝" and 11⁄16".

I have a chronograph, and the following velocity tests were run.

Remington 6mm Velocity Data

Bullet	Load	Velo.
70-gr. Gardiner	40.5/4064	3404
80-gr. Speer Spitzer	35/3031	3121
70.5-gr. Hollidge	40.5/4064	3401
105-gr. RN Speer	35/4320	2834
60-gr. Sierra HP	41/4064	3541
75-gr. Sirra HP	39/4895	3434
75-gr. Norma HP	42.3/203	3530
80-gr. Rem. HP	40/4320	3229
90-gr. Rem. 244	factory	3162

Of interest to me was the velocity consistency of the various loads. Some were markedly better than others. Lowest variation came with the 80-gr. Remington bullet ahead of 40 grains of 4320 — a mere 11 fs. 35 grains of 3031 with the 80-gr. Speer was almost as good, 19 fs. Least consistent was the load using the lightweight 60-gr. Sierra — 89 fs. Remington's factory load varied only 30 fs, good results with machine-loaded ammo.

Odds & Ends

I could have decreased the 40-XB groups, I imagine, by sorting cases for uniform capacity, checking bullets to see that they weren't out of round, and other tricks of the trade that the serious benchrest shooter has up his sleeve. However, I was more concerned with doing things as the average reloader would — loading good ammunition without being a perfectionist about it. As far as the results are concerned I'm more than happy with the outcome.

One thing I did do that helped maintain bore condition was to clean the barrel with Jim Brobst's J-B Compound after every shooting session. This is a paste-like very mild abrasive which rids the bore of any fouling. A little bit really makes the bore smooth and shiny, but it isn't at all damaging to the bore. All traces of it, of course, must be re moved before shooting.

The
444 MARLIN
and its Big Bore Brothers

by CHRISTIAN H. HELBIG

ARLIN'S Tom Robinson and Art Burns engineered the new 444 — not without a lot of testing and research — and a couple of years ago during a visit to Marlin they showed me the new round as well as some penetration tests on steel plates. The results were quite impressive from this revival of the big-bore straight case of yesteryear. Now, though, one can get this cartridge style in a strong, modern Lever action, with scope-mounting potential! How would this new powerhouse compare, I wondered, with such past greats as the 45–70, that old favorite of mine, the 38–55, and the 405 WCF, all of the same basic case type? Such a comparison, it seemed to me, was more valid than lining the 444 up against modern high velocity, long range, bolt action cartridges. After all, to be fair about these things we must compare apples with apples, no? However, as you'll see, the 444 stacks up well against some modern cartridges, too. The 444 is meant to be a medium-range powerhouse, for timber and brush hunting where the range is 100 to 175 yards; beyond that, use an '06, a 270, etc. I have taken many deer and bear (also a wolf) all *under* 150 yards in Canada and the eastern U.S., with never a chance for a shot beyond that distance.

The 444 has many attributes — power, accuracy, good velocity and good bullet diameter — but it has some faults also, like too light a bullet and too light a jacket for much of the game it will be used on.

A big plus factor is the strong and reliable action of this 444. Of all lever guns, the 336 is the least complex, the easiest to take apart or clean (I dislike very much to clean from the muzzle, because this practice *will* damage the crown no matter how careful one is). A screwdriver takes the 336 apart for cleaning or inspection. The side ejec-

> Marlin's 444 is the latest of a long line of large-caliber lever actions to come down the pike. Here an aficionado of the type compares this new shooting iron with some of its predecessors.

Marlin M336 chambered for the 444 cartridge is shown here with Micro-Power 4x scope and detachable sling.

tion and central scope mounting advantages have been mentioned thousands of times but are still darn important.

Factory ballistics for the 444 — 240-gr. bullet at 2400 fps, with 3069 foot pounds at the muzzle — are very respectable! My chronographing of 444 factory ammo gave a remarkably close 2345 fps, at 47° F, so it really is the most powerful lever action rifle we have today, at the muzzle! However, I rarely shoot game at this short range, so let's compare ballistics in the 100 yard column. That's where a lot of game is taken — or nearer — and there is the place to look at any cartridge, not at the muzzle.

The factory 240-gr. bullet has been criticized as being too lightly constructed, as well as being too light in weight. These points are quite true if the 444 is to be used on bear, elk or moose, but for the average white-tailed deer it is near-perfect, even with its very thin (.015") jacket. I'm sure it is the same jacket used in the 44 Magnum.

Blood Trail Wanted

Hit a deer anywhere in the chest cavity with the 444 and you will have your venison, but if you smack it in the shoulder you'll have the front half ruined and worthless. I like heavy bullets that penetrate clear through, assuring a good blood trail that is easy to follow, even in dry leaves. Now I can hear a chorus of readers saying, "Well, my deer dropped in its tracks." Sure, this sometimes happens, but often the deer goes off like a shot. It is amazing the distance they can travel with lungs completely blown up. I've had deer go as far as 200 yards without lungs, liver or heart. The 444 will assure more hunter-success simply because it will ordinarily provide a good trail to follow. Deer and bear can hide so easily that one can walk right past them. A few years ago I shot a good black bear in Canada, but because there was no exit hole, and no trail, it took three of us 30 minutes of very unpleasant searching to find him under a clump of spruces, a mere 35 yards away! Not knowing just where he was or how active he could become, I was, to say the least, damn nervous. In that situation the 444 would have given a blood trail, I'm fairly sure.

Remington lists mid-range rise at only .6", when zeroed at 100. This is very close to 30-30 and 35 Rem. figures, and gives a drop of 10" at 200 yards. This should give nobody any problems; just sight-in 1" high at 100 and it will print only 8" low at 200 with iron sights, 6" to 7" with scope. So, in the general woods hunting conditions one need not hold over if the 444 is sighted-in for an inch high at 100 yards. This natter trajectory is the second advantage the 444 has, especially over the older 38–55 and 45–70. Their range is limited to 150 yards *maximum*. Despite the short slug of the 444 and its rapid velocity loss, it still packs 1814 fp at 100 yards, about what the milder 44 Magnum rifle load does at the muzzle. So one in effect has in the Marlin 444 an extention of 100 yards over the 44 Mag. This 1814 fp also equals, beats or near-equals commercial loadings of the 250–3000, 30-30, 32 Spl., 35 Rem., 7mm Mauser and 8mm Mauser rounds at 100 yards. Not bad, and that .43" diameter bullet does have a lot of tissue-destruction properties. Therefore we can rate the 444 as a topflight deer load in its factory persuasion, with a promise of extra potency over the standard 30-30, 35 Rem. and 32 Spl.

Now let's look critically at the 444 for such larger game as black bear, elk, moose and the like. For blacks it will be OK, but even on them it is still marginal as factory loaded. Other hunters may not agree with that, but I stress the ability of a cartridge to anchor this class of game, and anchor it quickly. Too many fine specimens are lost, only to die later. A Canadian outfitter told me that two out of 5 bears hit get away, never to be recovered — an appalling state of affairs. Naturally some escape because of lousy shooting which no cartridge can overcome, but a more powerful load would certainly cut down the losses.

On such game the bullet will, at times, need to penetrate tough muscle, heavy bones and fat to reach the vital chest cavity. The 240-gr. 444 bullet with its poor sectional density and thin jacket is just not up to the task. Needed is a slug with SD and jacket thickness far greater than those

loaded now. The 240-gr. bullet has an SD of .186, the same as an 85-gr. 257 or a 125-gr. 308, but it has a far worse ballistic coefficient than either because of that flat point. Heavy game needs an SD of .215 to .235, hence a 275-gr. and 300-gr. bullet respectively. With a 300-gr. bullet having proper jacket thickness the 444 could be loaded to 2100 fps, yet stay with factory pressures. That's within 100 fps of the old 405 WCF, so much used and admired by Teddy Roosevelt and other noted sportsmen of that era.

Thoughts on Bullets

Considered adequate for most heavy game, including some African species, many lamented the 405's passing. Now we have its equal — in a better action — if the bullet makers will give us the right projectile. With an .030" jacket such a bullet should hold its own with anything but the 458, up to 200 yards. Naturally it should have less lead exposed and not be so square nosed as the factory 240-gr. (I use an .030" jacket only as an example, the correct thickness can be best determined by such makers as Speer, Hornady, *et al.* To show how thin the factory 240-gr. jacket is, some bullets recovered from the backstop had rifling marks *ahead* of the cannelure, which area before firing is quite a bit below bore diameter. High acceleration accounts for this upsetting or slugging-up, a rate of speed gain this jacket was not designed for.

Handloading cast bullets in the 444 can be rewarding in more ways than one — shooting $6.05 for 100 jacketed bullets gets costly. Many good moulds are on the market, the gas-check designs being best. With a moderately hard alloy one can drive a gas-check bullet at adequate deer load speeds if desired. Most cast loads, though, will be for fun and practice. 44 moulds are easy to use, getting perfect slugs being no problem usually with any mould of 35 caliber and up. It has been said that Marlin's Micro-Groove rifling doesn't perform well with lead bullets, but I've had no problem. Don't fret whether a 300-gr. bullet will stabilize in Marlin's 38" twist — they do, and

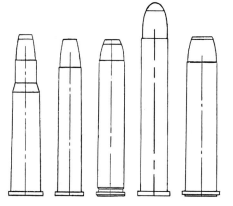

Cartridge drawings of, from left, the 348, 38–55, 444, 405 and 45–70.

even 320-gr. bullets show no instability.

The best powder for the 444 is 4198; nothing else gives top velocities. Even this powder is not the perfect feed when using such heavy bullets as Shooting Associates 290- and 320-gr. numbers. With these start out by trying Hercules Reloder 7, which is actually slower than 4198 in a straight sided case. Watch it in a bottleneck, though.

We have compared the 444 to the old 405 only briefly, because 405s are rather scarce, ammo is not being loaded and cases are just about extinct. Now let's stack the 444 up against the most popular old-timer of all, the 45–70. This may come as a shock, but this 45 will do almost anything the 444 will do, and do some things better! We will compare only handloaded ballistics of the 45–70. Bear in mind these loads are for Winchester 86 rifles only. Single shots or low-strength repeaters are *not* included.

Why make this comparison — and cite 45–70 loads — for the obsolete 86? Admittedly, the 86 is heavy, its stock design isn't the best, it is limited to iron sights and the cost of one in good condition is high. Nevertheless, many hunters have them and want to use them on game. Many of these are used only with factory ammo, which has to be underloaded to be safe in the weaker models, thus are not performing at their top capabilities.

Properly handloaded, the 45–70 will give 16% more energy at 100 yards than the 444. I'm thinking here of Elmer Keith's famous load, which I've shot often. With some discomfort, too, I might add, since it separates the men from the boys. As checked in the NRA *Reloading Handbook* this 53/3031 load gives 1871 fps with a 405-gr. bullet. Out at 100 yards it still goes along at 1530 fps with 2100 fp of energy. The 300-gr. bullet can be loaded to 2150.

The 45–70 is just about the oldest centerfire cartridge still extant in the U.S., dating back to 1873, but today the factory load is tamed way down so as not to maim those idiots who can't — or won't — read the warning labels on the boxes about using high velocity loads in the old klunkers. Still, the current load — 405-gr. at 1320 — is quite potent up to 100 yards on deer and blacks, and I wouldn't feel at all helpless if I were so armed. While the old high-velocity, shock-power versus heavy bullet, deep-penetration argument will go on forever, both sides have their points, and I'm a middle-of-the-roader. I believe in the heavy bullet and penetration for large and dangerous game, and in the high-speed jobs for long-range light game. This boils down to nothing more than the proper cartridge for the game hunted, and that's why I say the 444

Winchester M71 was made only in 348 caliber, though its predecessor, the M86, was chambered for many loads, including the 45–70, discussed in text.

is fine for deer as loaded but should deliver a 300-gr. punch for heavy stuff. Frankly, I think this ultra-high-velocity stuff is a bit overdone; game certainly can't be all that tougher to kill today than it was 50 years ago. The truth is, our present "hunters" can't always shoot as well as they should.

An Old-Time Favorite

Last is my favorite old-timer, the 38–55, once considered the most accurate of the lever action cartridges. Give this round a transfusion with modern handloads and it turns out to be a real gem. *This is the least powerful of the straight sided cases and the author recommends it only for deer and (in the hands of a good shooter) black bear. My pet lever gun is a 336 Marlin with a mint 38–55 barrel, made for the old Model 93, but the threads are the same, and I've even got tight headspace. 20 inches is all I wanted, so out came the hacksaw. These straight cases have such good expansion ratios that a 20" tube gives very little velocity loss. Cast and factory bullets all do well, staying in 2" almost all the time (with scope).

Again I found the same slugging-up of the factory 255-gr. bullet when driven at 1900 fps, but I won't name the load — too hot. Lyman's 375296, a gas-check hollow point 275-gr. bullet, does well with 4198, 3031 or Hi-Vel 2, all loads checking out on the chrono between 1800 and 1870 fps. (Just watch that 4198, though; no more than 28 grains or you get sticky cases. With the other two powders you just cannot get enough into the case to get over 35,000 psi.) This 336 of mine goes 7 pounds even with scope, fully loaded, and is a joy to tote around the woods. It will one day account for a bear. It's a challenge to me to collect a head of game with all of my rifles, even though I could use my 30-06 for all hunting. I enjoy bagging a trophy with a rifle I've built up, using a handload tailored to that gun.

Mid-range trajectory of my 38–55 loads over 100 yards is about 1.7", so as usual I sight 1" high at 100 yards and forget the drop; I wouldn't attempt a shot over 150 yards anyway.

*These loads should be used in Winchester 94s and Marlin 93s only.

One may wonder why the 38–55 was compared to the 444, since the former is quite a bit less potent. It was used because it further illustrates how a straight case will give greater energy than a bottleneck type, capacity being equal. Example: the 444 Marlin, with a capacity of 51 grains of water, gives 3069 fp at the muzzle with only 40,000 psi. Load the 358 Win. to 50,000 psi and with the 200-gr. bullet you get only 2840 fp, the 358 having the same 51-gr. capacity. Go down in bore size another step to the 308 Win. and again at 50,000 psi you realize only 2670 fp with the 200-gr. bullet. Naturally velocity goes way up as bore decreases and we benefit by flatter trajectories, but sheer energy goes down. This attests to the shrewdness of the boys at Marlin; they know this fact well and used it effectively. I believe the 444 could be the greatest thing in woods hunting ever, if only the factories would load better and heavier bullets.

Two other lever cartridges are worth mentioning — the 33 WCF and its successor, the 348. Both were good, up to a point, but both are bottlenecks, giving velocity but losing the important foot pounds of brute power that I like on heavy, tough game. Even the 348, with its 2840 fp muzzle energy (the now-obsolete 250-gr. load had 3060 fp) doesn't beat the 44 — which comes in a lighter and more versatile action.

Good Results with 444

The Marlin I shot in this testing functioned perfectly; in fact, it seemed a bit smoother than a run of the mill 336. My groups with Remington factory ammo ran 2" on average. The 444 is certainly not a varmint rifle, so these groups from a straight factory rifle are darn good. If you will tinker with your loads, groups will shrink a bit, I'm sure.

Recoil is definitely *not* a problem, what with the recoil pad and Monte Carlo stock on the Marlin. I could shoot a 444 all day without discomfort, something you can't do with the older Winchester 86 stock design. However, I feel that the rifle is decidedly muzzle heavy, and, while I'm not suggesting you hack off your barrel, a 2" reduction would be nice and wouldn't hurt velocity much. What I would prefer on a rifle of this power is a pistol grip stock, in order to hold the butt more solidly into the shoulder. This alone would add some ounces towards the rear for better balance.

Very noticeable in the 444, as with other straight cases, is the easy lever opening and the non-necessity of full length sizing. The case has no shoulder to stretch and cause tight closing. Barrel bands on this powerhouse *must* be kept tight, otherwise they start to move and gum things up. For this much recoil it would have been better to thread the magazine tube into the action, a la the Model 86, then tie it all down with one band instead of those unsightly two on the 444.

Shooting Assc. were to have sent me some of their 290-gr. and 320-gr. 44 bullets, these called the Nuro-Shok, but as of now none were delivered for testing. These look, at least, like an elongated home-swaged, half-jacket job of standard form. My own idea of the correct bullet is a 300-gr. one with a nose a little more rounded than the factory bullet, and having a smaller flat spot. The sharp shoulder of many home-swaged bullets will, at times, jam in the end of the chamber, and even the semi-wadcutter Lyman 429244 caught in the Marlin I tested. This is no problem on the range, but you don't want it to happen when hunting. A 300-gr. bullet is about maximum in this 444 case, since anything heavier will leave too little powder space. One has a short limit in the 336 as to over-all cartridge length, and a bullet that gets much over 300 grains defeats the purpose, and you're right back to 45–70 trajectories.

To sum it up, the 444 Marlin is an excellent deer rifle as issued and could become really a great rifle for heavy and dangerous game with the proper heavy bullets. Let's start wishing our makers give us this load. 🜨

Lever Action Ballistics

Cartridge	Bullet, grs.	M.V.	M.E.	V, 100 yds.	E, 100 yds.	Remarks
444 Marlin	240 SP	2400*	3069	1845	1814	Rem. factory load
45-70	405 SP	1871	3140	1530	2100	53/3031/405 SPT†
45-70	405 Gr.	1320	1570	1160	1210	Factory load
405 WCF	300 SP	2220	3280	1940	2500	Factory load (disc.)
38-55	280 SP	1854	2130	1475	1350	32/HiVel-2/280 SP
38-55	255 SP	1320	985	1160	760	Factory load
348 WCF	200 SP	2530	2840	2220	2190	Factory load

* Actual 2345 on Chronograph. † Chronograph, figures from the NRA Reloading Handbook.

GREAT GUNS!
Winchester's Model 9422s

Speak of Winchester and the average listener thinks of lever action rifles, more particularly the Model 94 nowdays. Combine that worldwide recognition with 22 rimfire cartridges and you've got the new 9422 — in both regular and magnum chambering. Handsomely styled, well made in the old fashioned way, flawlessly functioning and accurate, the new Winchesters are, indeed, great guns.

by JON R. SUNDRA

ERTAINLY NO NAME is more synonymous with lever action rifles than Winchester. Equally certain is the fact that the Model 94, now in its 78th year of production, is among the best loved rifles ever made. Team these two factors with the world's most popular cartridge, the 22 rimfire, and you should have all the requisites of a great gun.

It was precisely this kind of reasoning, me thinks that prompted Winchester to introduce its new Models 9422 and 9422 Magnum (WMR). Previewed at the recent NSGA Show, these new lever – actions caused quite a stir — and well they should have. These new rifles are impressive by any standards — especially when one considers that "It's a Winchester" has carried the weight it once did.

Spit and Image

As the name implies, the 9422 is patterned after the perennial 94, and a striking facsimile it is, too. Except for its slightly thinner grip, physical size, weight and silhouette of the two guns are almost identical. Tipping the scale at 6½ pounds, this 22 is a man – sized carbine in every respect.

The pleasant heft and feel of the rifle no doubt result from its "old – fashioned" construction. If my test rifle, one of standard 22 caliber, had any non – ferrous alloys or plastic parts on it, I certainly couldn't find 'em. The 9422 is a genuine, all – walnut/ steel rifle; a rare breed these days!

Looking at the gun's exterior, the wood – to – metal fit of buttstock and fore – end is quite good. At the fore – end, for example, instead of the usual practice of putting a U – shaped notch in the bottom of the barrel channel to accommodate the tubular magazine, a separate hole is used

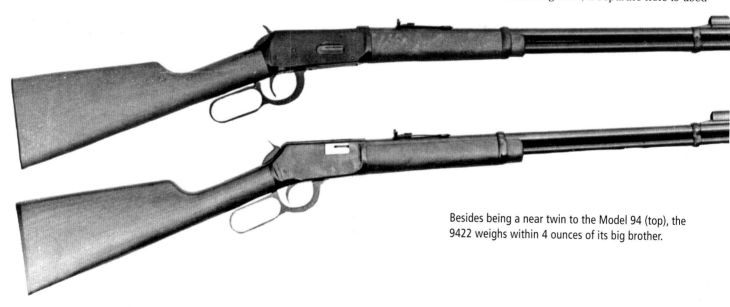

Besides being a near twin to the Model 94 (top), the 9422 weighs within 4 ounces of its big brother.

— even though there's less than 1/16" between barrel and magazine tube. The fit of the butt – stock to the tang is equally good; however, because the wood stands a little above the metal all the way around, there's an initial impression of ill fit. On closer inspection though, the uniformity of overlap and the glove – like fit throughout are evidence to the contrary.

Mechanism Details

Unlike its big brother, the 9422 has side rather than top ejection, and a solid – top receiver. The bolt is a two – piece affair, and lock – up is achieved by using a single lug, which engages a recessed shoulder milled into the inside top of the receiver. This ingenious old Browning design is still used in many areas; Model 12 Winchesters and Ithaca 37 scatterguns, to name a couple, though both are slide – operated rather than lever – actuated. Nevertheless, the lock – up principle is the same. As the bolt all but completes its forward travel it is cammed upward, allowing the locking lug to engage the recessed shoulder. The pivotal point for this vertical movement is provided by two lips at the front of the bolt, these resting on a sill at the front of the receiver, just beneath the barrel.

Bolt movement on the 9422 is through direct action of the lever, with no linkage or cams for mechanical advantage. Lever throw on the test carbine is 64°. The trigger engages the hammer directly, which has a half – cock or safety position.

Take — down of Model 9422 requires only a few seconds. Because Barrel and receiver remain mated, scope settings are unaffected.

In addition to relying on magazine tube spring pressure to feed cartridges onto the carrier, this gun also *pulls* cartridges from the magazine. When the action is fully open, the rim of the cartridge sits within a vertical raceway machined into the front of the flat bolt face. As the lever is closed, a cam — actuated finger pushes the cartridge (sliding it upward within the raceway) up to hamber level, where it is then pushed home by the closing bolt. It's not a new design by any means but it is ingenious — and positive. During the test – firing of 150 rounds the feeding, extraction and ejection were smooth and faultless.

Speaking of ejection, rather than having a slender, finger – like spring fixed inside of the receiver wall as do some designs, the 9422 uses an ejector rod that slides within a groove on the bolt itself. It's a system which should prove to be positive as well as durable. Even a deliberately sluggish working of the lever easily tossed empties clear of the port.

Magazine capacity of the 9422 is 21 Shorts, 17 Longs or 15 Long Rifle; the 9422M holds 11 of Winchester's 22 Magnum Rimfire cartridges.

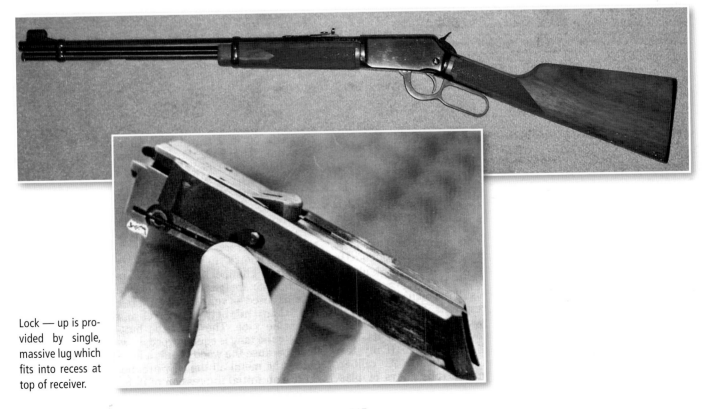

Lock — up is provided by single, massive lug which fits into recess at top of receiver.

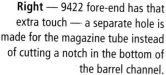

Right — 9422 fore-end has that extra touch — a separate hole is made for the magazine tube instead of cutting a notch in the bottom of the barrel channel.

Right — Semi-buckhorn rear sight provided on 9422 is better than average.

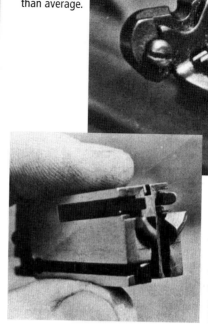

Left — Wood-to-metal fit on 9422 was very good. Take-down screw to gun's 4 main component parts takes only the twist of a coin and a few seconds.

Left — Protruding lips on bolt face provide pivot for vertical lock – up movement. Note vertical raceway for feeding cartridges up from magazine level.

Acceptable Accuracy

Getting back to the outside of the gun, sitting atop the 20" barrel is a hooded ramp front sight with bead and a semi – buckhorn rear. As iron sights go, they are quite good and a refreshing change from the stamped, sheet metal variety. Groups fired from bench rest at 50 yards average around 1½". Most shooting, however, was done with the excellent little 4x Bushnell Scope — chief XXII clamped onto the receiver, which is grooved for standard tip – off mounts. Using it, 5 – shot groups shrank to an average 1⅛" with Remington and CCI hollow points. Another ⅛" was cut from that with Eley Tenex match ammo, run through for comparison. I felt no need to use shorts or longs in a hunting rifle such as this, but I'm sure they'll at least function as well as the long rifles.

Although not advertised as being take – down rifles, the 9422 and 9422M are certainly that. A coin to turn the single as-sembly screw and all of 30 seconds are required to dismantle the rifle into its four major components, for easy carrying or thorough cleaning. Because the barrel and receiver remain mated, scope settings are unaffected by disassembly.

All in all, these new Winchesters should capture the fancy of lever lovers everywhere. As critical as I tried to be I could find nothing to criticize! Basic design and execution of the Model 9422 are truly superb, and they're well worth the retail price of $100. All I suggest is that Winchester furnish a hammer extension, as does Marlin on its Model 39, so the hammer can be thumb – operated with a scope mounted. 🔵

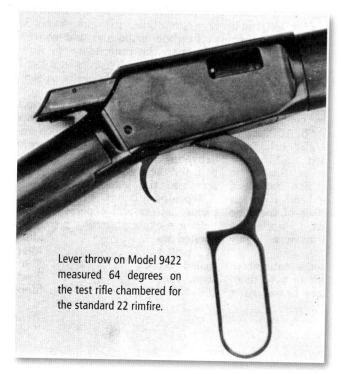

Lever throw on Model 9422 measured 64 degrees on the test rifle chambered for the standard 22 rimfire.

The turn of a coin disassembles the M9422.

The Model 70
WINCHESTER
1936-1963
a history of its halcyon years

by KAM NASSER

To THE AVERAGE hunter the Model 70 Winchester rifle may have no special meaning. To a man who knows guns and is a hunter, the Model 70 means a truly fine bolt action rifle. To a man who collects pre-64 70s there is no production rifle around today which can match the workmanship and appearance of the Model 70 made before 1964.

I am from Iran, a great land for hunting. Before I left there, in early 1956, I had taken part in many hunting trips and I'd always listened with a keen interest to those people who knew something about rifles. My first chance of looking over various rifles came during hunting trips I made, as a youngster, with some members of my family. Since one had to be 18 to own a rifle in Iran, my rifle shooting experience was limited to those times when I was allowed to handle someone else's rifle. During the course of some of those trips I began to understand better the arguments of my elders about the operation of Winchester 70 rifles compared to others. Even so, it was not until I graduated from college in this country, and had owned several rifles, that I could really appreciate the differences between the old 70s and other rifles. At that point I got rid of several off-brand rifles and bought, in 1962, my first Model 70, a 30-06 featherweight. Since then, whenever I've had the opportunity and the money, I've invested in pre-64 Model 70s — and "investment" is the operative word!

Prices for old Model 70s have climbed steadily since 1964. Those who didn't consider this trend a few years back are today well aware of current market values. They also know that, along with several other discontinued Winchester firearms, the cash value and trading worth of their 70s are high — and getting higher! They've also learned that if one buys right that the chance of losing money on them is quite nil. The story of the Model 70 may very well follow in the footsteps of the Model 21 Winchester shotguns which, when produced, were sold for as little as $100 or less. Note that today, even though 21s are still being made, prices start at around $1,200 and go up. The old 21s have increased in value accordingly, if not more so.

The era of the old 70 goes back to 1925, with the introduction of the Winchester 54. Model 54 rifles, unfortunately, weren't very good looking and had several undesirable aspects — an awkward wing-type safety, a disliked trigger system and a non-detach-

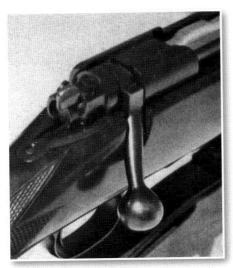

Left, a pre-war Model 70 action; middle, a transition type compared to a later production rifle at right. Note the safeties, bolt appearance, contour of the back of the actions, as well as the shapes of the breech bolt sleeves.

able floorplate, among other things. While the quality of the 54 improved considerably toward the end, Winchester discontinued it in 1935, offering in its place a new rifle — and a new action — the better-designed Model 70.

The 70s made before WW II look very much like the last of them except for the safety, which swung behind the bolt sleeve to the left, and a difference in the tang. This safety was OK with open sights but cumbersome and hard to manipulate with a scope mounted. By the way, pre-WW II 70s did not generally have the bridge tapped for scope sight screw holes. The top of the bridge was recessed, too, the recessed area showing a wavy-line matting.

As early as 1937 both Pachmayr and Tilden offered their own versions of Model 70 safeties, as did Griffin & Howe, no doubt to eliminate the awkwardness of the existing one when a scope was mounted. There is a strong possibility that Winchester adopted the plan of the Pachmayr and Tilden safeties, for one looking very like the Tilden was incorporated in their post-war models. At the same time the appearance of the bolt handle was changed to allow proper clearance for the scope rings.

First Model 70s

The first announcement of the Model 70 rifles came toward the end of the year 1936. The indications were that the rifle was going to be produced in 250–3000, 220 Swift, 300 H&H, 257 Roberts, 270, 30-06, and 7×57mm calibers. From this period on the Model 70 went through interesting changes, with 3 distinct periods covering its life span: (1) the pre-war period, from 1937 to World War II, (2) the post-war period ending with the late forties — also known as the transition period, and finally the last chapter, (3) the early 1950s through 1963.

Model 70s were not only produced in standard and feather-weight grades, but in supergrades, target models, carbines and even a few sniper rifles. Supergrades resemble the standard and featherweight 70s in every way but the stock — they have much more generous and better checkering, a capped pistol grip, a cheekpiece and a black fore-end tip. A sling strap with quick detachable swivels was also included, and the word "supergrade" was stamped on the floorplate. Usually the actions were smoother. Perhaps one reason the supergrades were not overly popular was that many potential buyers felt that the differences between them and the standard models were not great enough to warrant the extra cost.

Supergrades were not produced in all calibers. The chart below shows which calibers were produced in supergrades, in both featherweight and standard models.

The Winchester National Match rifle or the standard weight target rifle met most requirements of the big bore shooters. The N.M. rifle appeared in 30-06 caliber only, with a 24-inch floating-type barrel, a marksman stock with full pistol grip, and a weight of 9½ pounds. These came equipped with a Lyman No. 77 front sight on a forged ramp and the Lyman No. 48 receiver sight, pi as target-scope bases. Another version of this rifle was also produced, known as the heavyweight target

model, at 10½ pounds, without forged ramp. A still heavier style was also marketed, this one called the Bull Gun, its weight almost 13¼ pounds with a 28-inch barrel in 30-06 and 300 H&H calibers. A few sniper rifles in 30-06 caliber were also made, but their fate and details are not clearly known. The story goes that a few prewar 70 actions were fitted with Model 54 30-06 barrels for this purpose.

A Model 70 rifle was also developed for long-range small game shooting, called the varmint rifle. It weighed 9¾ pounds. The receiver was not only tapped for most scope mounts and a receiver sight, but the barrel was also tapped for front sight bases. Target-type scope blocks were provided in much the same way as for the target models. A feature of one Model 70 varmint rifle was a checkered Monte Carlo stock. Others came with a plain, unchecked marksman stock, these with wide, beavertail fore-ends. Over the years the target and varmint models appeared in 22 Hornet, 220 Swift, 243, 250–3000, 270, 30-06, 300 H&H and 35 Rem., almost in all instances with a 24-inch medium-weight barrel. Varmint rifles were made in 220 Swift and 243 with 26" heavyweight barrels and, in later years, with stainless steel barrels exclusively.

With the announcement of the Model 70s in 1936 it was clear that the rifle was going to be produced not only in the standard 24-inch barrel lengths but also with 20-inch barrels, then known as carbines. For some years carbines were offered in 22 Hornet, 250–3000, 270, 7×57mm, 300 Savage, 30-06, and 35 Remington. These carbines bring premium prices today, for they're unusual pieces in any collection. While the idea of a 20-inch barrel was certainly well ahead of its time, they did not sell well, and the ax fell in 1951.

Pre-War Quality

Pre-war 70s are outstanding examples of firearms craftsmanship. Their blueing is excellent, the checkering very fine, and the quality of the stock is much superior to those of a later date. The wood appears to be of a denser and darker walnut, and in some instances these stocks were very handsomely figured. Pre-war 70s also had a much smoother action, no doubt because of the time and trouble taken then in making each rifle.

There were at least two different barrel diameters available, as evidenced in the 375 Holland and Holland caliber; one reason was that the 375 was produced in a 24-inch barrel during the first year (serial numbers under 10,000), while those made later had a 25-inch barrel. In the 1960s a

Calibers	Supergrade Standards and Barrel Lengths	Supergrade Featherweights and Barrel Lengths
22 Hornet	24"	
220 Swift	26"	
243	24"	22"
250–3000	24"	
257 Roberts	24"	
270	24"	22"
7×57mm	24"	
300 Savage	24"	
308		22"
30-06	24"	22"
300 H&H	26"	
35 Remington	24"	
375 H&H	25"	
458	25"	

third variation appeared. In these the contour of the barrel was changed slightly, creating a more distinct drop a few inches away from the action. By the way, the early prewar 375 H&H Magnums had the barrel boss-sight base of the standard 70s, but later-made barrels did not.

It is my belief that more special-order factory rifles were produced during the pre-war period than in any other period in the life history of Model 70 rifles. Fig.2 shows a couple of special-order supergrades made during 1943; a 30-06 and a 375 H&H, both having 22-inch barrels. The first 22-inch barrel production rifle, however, the featherweight 308, was not marketed until 1952. The 375 H&H was never cataloged with a 22-inch barrel.

The production of pre-war Model 70s stopped somewhere in the 63,-000 serial number range. Those 70s serially numbered from about 63,-000 to approximately 100,000 are considered "transition" models. In the transition period the safety was the leaf type and the shape of the receiver tang was still of the double radius type. It was just after this period that the cataloging of many of the more important calibers — 7×57mm, 35 Remington, 250–3000 — as far as collectors are concerned, came to an end. However, it was possible to buy these or other calibers as late as the 1950s, but only on special order. Also, according to Winchester, in the past one could convert from one caliber to another, if feasible, such as changing a 270 to 7×57mm. This practice was discontinued after 1964 in order to make barrels and other parts on hand last for years to come. No, no matter how desirable you think it, you can't alter your 270 or 30-06 to a 7×57mm today! Not by New Haven, anyway.

The approximate serial numbers are quite important when it comes to knowing the pre-64 Model 70s. It is important to note that Model 70s after the war were serially indicated from 63,000 to 700,000; anything introduced after the 700,-000 serial number is classed as or called the "new Winchester Model 70," certainly a name given by the collectors to differentiate the old ones from the new.

Pre-64 70s were made in 20 different calibers, from the small "Mighty Mouse" 22 Hornet to the "Booming Bertha" 458 Winchester Magnum. The entire list of calibers follows:

Only 243, 264, 270 and 30-06 were produced in both featherweight and standard models. The 358 was introduced only in featherweight style and the 308 could be bought as a standard model on special order. Most calibers were produced in standard and supergrade form, but the 458 Winchester Magnum was the only one offered in supergrade alone. See our Model Chart for comments on the 300 Savage.

It is safe to say that the transition period ended with the beginning of the early 1950s. Many collectors considered that it was just after the transition period, and through the middle of the 1950s, that the Model 70 was at its peak. The Model 70 went through many small and major changes even after the transition period. The low-comb standard stocks of this period had a fatter and rounder fore-end. On rifles just after the transition period, the pistol cap area drops off about 3/16-inch to ¼ -inch, about the same as during the transition period. One of the common characteristics of these rifles, and of those prior to this period, was the integral front sight ramp, ground off along the sides and blued; I have seen many Model 70s, serial numbered in the 300,000 range, with this characteristic. After this period, however, or perhaps toward the latter half of the 1950s, the sight ramps were sweated on and then blued.

Calibers	Introduced	Discontinued	Standard Barrel Lengths	F'weight Barrel Lengths	Carbine Barrel Lengths	Target & Varmint Barrel Lengths **	Supergrade Barrel Lengths ***
22 Hornet	1937	1958	24"		20"	24"	24"
220 Swift	1937	1963	26"			26"	26"
243 Win.	1955	1963	24"	22"		26"	22" 24"
250-3000 Savage	1937	1949	24"		20"	24"	24"
257 Roberts	1937	1959	24"		20"	24"	24"
264 Win. Mag.	1959	1963	26"	22"			
270 Win.	1937	1963	24"	22"	20"	24"	22" 24"
7x57mm	1937	1949	24"		20"	24"	24"
7.65x53mm	1937	1937	24"				
300 Savage*	not cataloged	not cataloged	not cataloged	not cataloged	not cataloged	not cataloged	not cataloged
308 Win.	1952	1963	24"	22"			22"## 24"
30-06 Springfield	1937	1963	24"	22"	20"	24" 26" 28"	22" 24"
300 H&H Mag.	1937	1963	26"			26" 28"	26"
300 Win. Mag.	1963	1963	24"				
338 Win. Mag.	1959	1963	25"				
35 Rem.	1944	1947	24"		20"	24"	24"
358 Win.	1955	1958		22"			
9x57mm	1937	1937	24"				
375 H&H Mag.	1937	1963	24"# 25"				25"
458 Win. Mag.	1956	1963					25"

*Factory records do not indicate that the 300 caliber was cataloged; however, research of the literature shows that a good many were produced, not only in standard 24" barrel rifles but also in 20" models.

**Authorities from the factory prefer to combine the varmint and target models in this category. The differences, though, are indicated in the text of this article.

***Supergrades were not produced in 20" barrels.
#During the first year of production, 375 H&H Magnums were produced in 24" barrels, thereafter in 25" barrels.

##Standard 24" barrels in 308 calibers were available on special order.

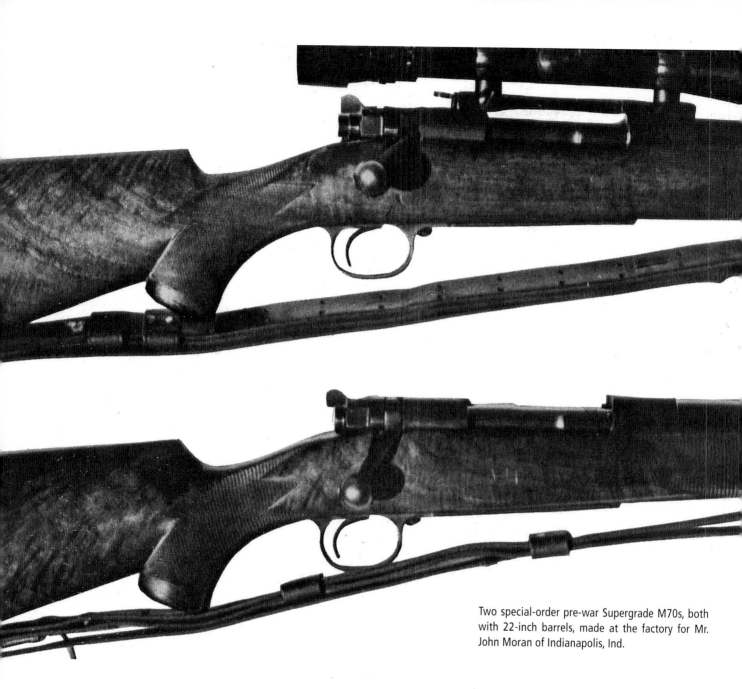

Two special-order pre-war Supergrade M70s, both with 22-inch barrels, made at the factory for Mr. John Moran of Indianapolis, Ind.

Model 70s of this post-transition period were also fairly heavy, one reason being the steel buttplate and floorplate and, in most cases, the solid bolt handles. The checkering was full and very good looking. Up to about 1953–54 one could find the year of a rifle's manufacture stamped into the bottom of the barrel, just in front of the action. However, this does not necessarily mean that the entire rifle was produced at that particular date, since the component parts could have been put together, following a request for a particular caliber, at a later date. For example, my pre-64 Model 70 in 7×57mm is of early 1950 production, but the barrel is stamped 1942. Also, Winchester barrels were not so-stamped for a time in the 1950s, and it is quite possible

to see some without *any* marks under the barrel.

Featherweight 70s

In 1952 Winchester came out with a barrel innovation, the Model 70 featherweight in 308 caliber, which was subsequently produced in 5 other calibers — 243, 264, 270, 30-06 and 358. Since many shooters thought the standard Model 70 was a bit too heavy, the featherweight was a welcome addition to the Winchester line. The major change was basically the 22-inch barrel, but Winchester also did away with that boss on the barrel which marks the standard grade rifle, and thereby eliminated as well the stud screw of the foreend. The new shorter rifle came with an

aluminum floorplate and trigger guard. All of these factors contributed to the lightness of the new featherweight model, at 6½ pounds, and with an over-all length of 42½ inches.

This was the period during which the high-comb stocks became popular. With the onset of these Monte Carlo, or high-comb stocks, Winchester eventually switched over from the Winchester 22G sporting rear sight, generally associated with low-comb stocks, to the Lyman No. 6 folding-leaf sight.

Of the 6 featherweight calibers produced the most sought after are the 243, 270 and 30-06, as far as the shooting public is concerned. The Model 70 featherweight could certainly be considered — at least by many — as one of the handsomest rifles ever factory-made in this country.

In the late 1950s an effort was made to lighten both featherweight and standard rifles even further. The steel buttplate was changed to aluminum on all models, as was the bolt handle ball, drilled to make it slightly lighter.

By the time the rifles were discontinued in 1963 many interesting changes had occurred. Because of the cost of production, and because other manufacturers had simplified their manufacturing techniques, increasing their sales by so doing, Winchester could not afford to continue with the old expensive methods. In this era no doubt everything was tried to save the life of the old 70 rifles. The checkering on both fore-end and pistol grip was reduced considerably, the steel or aluminum buttplates were replaced by plastic. On the Magnum calibers the factory solid-rubber recoil pads were changed to the see-through type. Less time was spent on staining and finishing the stocks, since some appear to be much lighter-toned, less well done than the stocks of previous years. Wood to metal fit fell off as well. The bolt sleeve, which originally had a straight vertical cut on the safety side, was left round. It is interesting that this period coincides with the boom in the Winchester short belted magnums, such as the 458, 338, 300 and 264. One can find "458" stamped under the action of 264, 300 and 338 rifles, perhaps denoting that the particular action could have been just as easily used in a 458.

In spite of its efforts, Winchester could not keep production costs down, and a complete change became inevitable. By 1964 the old Model 70 rifle had become a thing of the past in the annals of firearm history.

A few Model 70 calibers, such as the 264 and 220 Swift, were furnished with stainless steel barrels as well as in chromemoly steel. The finish on these stainless steel barrels (standard or heavyweight) is obviously different, for they were first sandblasted, then blued, giving them a sort of Parkerized appearance rather than the highly polished finish of standard barrels.

All Model 70 actions, at least in profile and at first glance, look alike. The 300 and 375 Holland and Holland long-case calibers differed from the others in that the top rear edge of the receiver ring and the front of the bridge were cut away to accept these lengthy magnums. Other than this, without a close look, one can't tell the difference between the action of a 22 Hornet and that of a 30-06, a 257, et al. In such small-case calibers as the 243, 257, 308, etc., as opposed to the 270 or 30-06, the bolt carried a little metal piece on the left-hand side of the bolt body, generally known as the bolt stop extension. The smaller-caliber magazines were fitted with partitions to decrease their inside length.

Many Model 70 parts are interchangeable from rifle to rifle because of the size or similarity of some calibers. For instance, the 308 magazine is the same as that for the 257; the 270 is the same as that of the 7×57mm and 30-06. Many small parts are the same for virtually all calibers, being usable from one rifle to another.

The Collector's Problems

Since pre-64 Model 70 actions are in great demand today by custom gunmakers, the collector is faced with a problem. Since many hundreds of these pre-64 70s were robbed of their original Winchester barrels to make room for a custom barrel, many of the old 70 barrels are floating around on the market. Some, of course, have been already fitted to other Model 70 actions, resulting in "new" 70 rifles. Yet, as far as appearance is concerned, they all look the same. It is disturbing, to say the least, to come across a Model 70 with a barrel and caliber that is not appropriate for the action. For example, I've seen a 300 Winchester Magnum with a serial number in the 200,000 range, but that caliber wasn't produced until 1963. A genuine 300 Winchester Magnum is highly unlikely

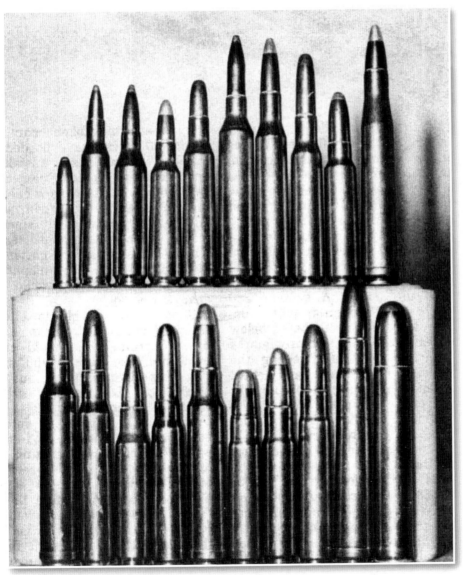

Cartridges for which the old Model 70 Winchester was chambered. Top row (from left) 22 Hornet, 220 Swift, 243, 250–3000, 257 Roberts, 264 Win. Mag., 270, 7mm, 300 Savage, 300 H&H Bottom (from left) 300 Win. Mag. 30-06, 308, 7.65mm, 338 Win. Mag., 35 Rem., 358, 9mm, 375 H8.H, 458 Win. Mag.

Outstanding examples of pre-64 Model 70 featherweights. From top: 30-06 with B&L 2½ to 8 scope, 270 with 4x Weaver in Buehler mounts, and a 243 with a B&L 2½-5x scope.

to be serial numbered below 400,000. Examining the proofmarks is another way of detecting the originality of the barrel and action. In almost all cases the proofmarks are perfectly aligned; that is, the proofmark on the barrel and that on the action are in straight line, with the exception of a brief period. During the very end of the pre-64 production years (about 1962–63), this exact alignment on 300 Winchester Magnums did not hold true. As a matter of fact, I own one of these and have seen several others showing this variation.

By the same token many old Model 70 stocks have flooded the market; it would be a mistake to use a latter-production stock, say of the 1960s, with its narrow checkering, on an early production model. All featherweight and standard stocks can be interchanged (except when the tangs differ), but in the instance just cited the inappropriate type of checkering would be a dead giveaway.

It is quite possible to alter a standard grade 70 to make it look like a carbine. One could cut 4 inches off the muzzle and sweat the front sight back on, but that won't work because the carbines were discontinued in 1951, and their front sights were integral with the barrel, not sweated on. As with other fields of collecting, real expertise doesn't come overnight; one must have looked at several hundred Model 70s before the authentic rifle can be told from the phony. Well, the situation isn't all that critical yet, but such fakers could be the collector's hangup in the future — especially the novice collector!

One of the most unusual 70s I've seen was a 300 H&H Magnum converted to appear like a 300 Winchester Magnum. The idea behind this particular trickiness goes back to the 1950s, when the 300 H&H Magnum was the only 300 Magnum around, and at times the rifles were simply stamped "300 Magnum." If the

breech end of the barrel is cut off a bit and the barrel rechambered to the 300 Winchester Magnum, the barrel would be shorter, all right, but it would look quite genuine. Nevertheless, the serial number would give it away. Here's another — restocking a standard grade 70 in 30-06 with a National Match stock would make it look like a target model, but the informed collector knows that the National Match barrel did not permit a hood or sight cover to be placed on the front sight ramp. Also the action of a National Match rifle had a clip slot cut into the bridge, whereas regular pre-64 Model 70 standard rifles in 30-06 calibers did not except for the quite early ones.

Model 70 Prices — Then and Now

Let me now discuss and analyze prices of the most sought after Model 70s — what they cost when introduced and what they're worth today.

The three types of Model 70 buttplates. From left: steel, aluminum and plastic.

In 1936, when the Model 70 was first announced, the retail price was $61.25 for the standard rifle. That, incidentally, was only a few dollars over the retail price of the Model 54. In the 26 years of Model 70 production, cataloged prices more than doubled. In 1963 the list price was $139 for featherweights and standard grades, and about $15 more for the magnums, target or varmint models. An exception was the 458 Magnum, which retailed at $310. Since the discontinuation of the old Model 70 prices have skyrocketed. Those who began collecting pre-64 Model 70s only a few years or so ago are finding out that they're not only becoming extremely hard to come by, but that their prices are also getting too rich for the average man's pocketbook. So it is important to look at today's market prices honestly and realistically and, I hope, without any bias. There are books available today which set certain prices on these rifles, but I contend that most of these "Purple Book" values are misleading, unreasonable and unrealistic. The collector should not necessarily be misled by gunshop prices, either. Obviously these stores have to

make a little profit on a rifle to meet their operating costs, and they can also afford to hang on to their merchandise for a lot longer time. Moreover, they must allow for trades.

Collector's values for pre-64 Model 70s are based on the following factors, not necessarily in this order:

1. Rarity of the caliber.

2. Type, i.e., standard, super-grade, carbine.

3. Special factory versions.

4. Originality and condition.

Generally, of the many Model 70 collectors to whom I've spoken or know, few tend to place more value on their rifles than the average going prices. On the contrary, some have got fantastic prices for theirs. So it may be pointed out that the old rule of thumb, "They are worth as much as you can get for them," still stands.

For a start, please note that any pre-64 Model 70 action in excellent condition is worth at least $100 because of their high demand by custom rifle builders.

The slow sellers of the past, such as standard grade rifles in 35 Remington, 250–3000, 300 Savage and 7×57mm calibers (which in most instances were produced for a short period of time and then discontinued) have become essential to any Model 70 collection worth the name. These calibers, in the original box or in mint condition, bring from $350 to $400. Those two rarest calibers (7.65mm and 9×57mm) that every one talks about but few have seen, would bring the very top prices; I've never seen either.

On the other hand, such very common calibers as the 243, 270, 30-06 and 308 are not very hard to find. Of these, the 243 and the 270 seem to be very good sellers, and in excellent to better shape bring $150 to $175. Even so, they are becoming scarcer. The magnum calibers are increasingly hard to find; among them the 300 and 338 Winchester Magnums and the 375 H&H Magnums are quite sought after by collectors and shooters; prices asked are around $200 to $250. Of these three calibers, since the 300 Winchester Magnum was produced only in 1963, it can be

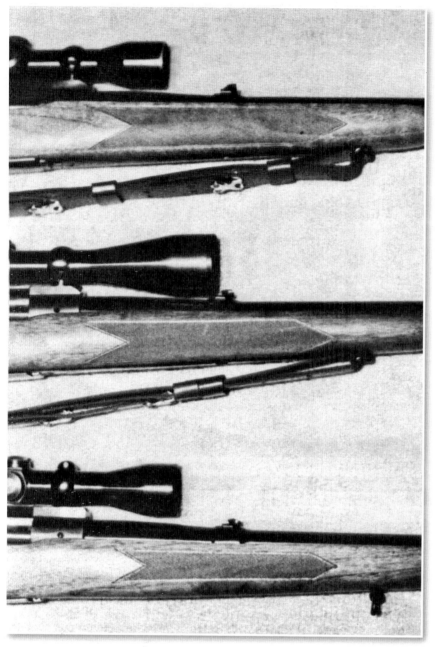

The checkering of Model 70s shown chronologically. From the top: a late 1940 257 Roberts, 22 Hornet of the middle 1950s, and a 300 Winchester Magnum of the 1960s.

hence the values. The price range depends on the condition, of course, and is in the neighborhood of $200 to $225.

I've been asked many times which I prefer — the featherweights or the standard grades. There is not much choice between them, really, for only 6 calibers (243, 264, 270, 308, 30-06 and 358) were produced as featherweights. I like all the featherweights, though some of my friends disagree with me. I'd call it a matter of personal preference because I don't think the choice has anything to do with collecting values. There is no doubt in my mind, though, that some of the other calibers — the 257 Roberts, 7×57mm, 250–3000, 22 Hornet — would have done quite well had they been introduced in featherweight models.

So far the prices I've mentioned relate only to the standard grade Model 70s. However, within that same group the transition models and the pre-war Model 70s command special attention. In excellent or better condition these would bring slightly more money over the later issues. The supergrades, undoubtedly the cream of the crop, are the top pieces for the collector. Thumbing through the first issue (1944) of the GUN DIGEST, the supergrades were shown at the unbelievable price, today, of $107.85, compared to standard models selling at $78.45. Today, on the average, supergrades would bring roughly $100-$125 more than a standard model.

Model 70 National Match prices are right up there with those supergrades in the medium price range, such as the 220 Swift and 22 Hornet. The 70 Bull Gun perhaps, is in the same category. The 20-inch barreled Model 70 carbines, in such rare calibers as 250–3000, 7×57mm or 35 Remington, would no doubt top the field in terms of collector interest and value; since not many were made in the rarer calibers, any one of them would enhance the collection.

To some collectors any variation in Model 70 rifles is important, such as those of the post-war period without sight slot and front sight ramp, or a rifle of pre-war and transition vintage. Because the transition period covered only a few years, generally any rifle of this period is more in demand; naturally the supergrade of the same period is even more desirable and interesting, since logically there could not have been too many of them made during that period. Moreover, some of these Model 70s were factory engraved and gold inlaid on special order. An example of such workmanship is found in the 23rd

expected to climb considerably over the rest of the magnum calibers in the near future. The slowest seller among the magnum calibers, besides the 264, seems to be the 300 H&H, which was pushed right out of the market by the appearance of the 300 Winchester Magnum. The market value of these last two is somewhere between $175 and $200, again if in excellent or better shape. The 264 Magnum, made with 22- and 26-inch barrels, sells best, in my experience, with the longer barrel.

Between the rare and the common calibers, a wide range of good to outstanding calibers exist which are not necessarily easy to obtain. Even though some Model 70s — 22 Hornet, 220 Swift, 257 Roberts — were continuously produced over the years, this does not make them any less valuable; as a matter of fact these 3 calibers, along with the 358, are the next biggest stumbling block in front of the collectors (the toughest calibers to find, for most collectors, are the 35 Remington, 7×57mm, 250–3000 and 300 Savage). Even though as many of these were produced as were the 270 and the 30-06, they are much more desirable for the collector,

Winchester factory photograph of an early Super Grade M70 rifle. Note Lyman 48 sight and early-type safety.

issue of the GUN Digest, page 139. Here, obviously, we are talking about a four-figure price tag.

All prices mentioned, by the way, are relative — the condition of the rifles is highly important. Chances are most of them won't be in the original box, or mint or even in excellent condition. Accordingly, the price may take a sharp dip. I've seen a good many rifles in the rare calibers with their barrels chopped off two inches or so, re-chambered, the bolt altered, with disastrous results. Naturally, if an individual has collected 18 of the 20 known calibers, the asking price for the whole collection would be higher, in spite of the condition of some of the rifles.

As far as I can tell, from information received in recent years, pre-64 Model 70 collectors are specializing. Some stick to the super-grade models, some prefer the prewar and transition periods, while others collect post-transition Model 70s with serial numbers in the 100,000 to 300,000 range. Some — perhaps after a good profit — are collecting everything in sight! Me? I'd like to have one example of each model and period.

Many people ask "Why a pre-64 Model 70?" The answer is very simple. If one is familiar with good workmanship and quality and is, as well, a collector who puts high value on any good firearm, he knows he can't go wrong by collecting these old Model 70 rifles. There is, of course, more

to Model 70 mania than this simple explanation. In these rifles one finds the wide-head, reliable, Mauser-type extractor, noted for its smooth operation. Many parts of the action were forged and machined; the checkering was done by hand; the excellent 3-position safety, inoperative unless the firing pin is cocked; the ease with which the entire action can be taken apart and reassembled.

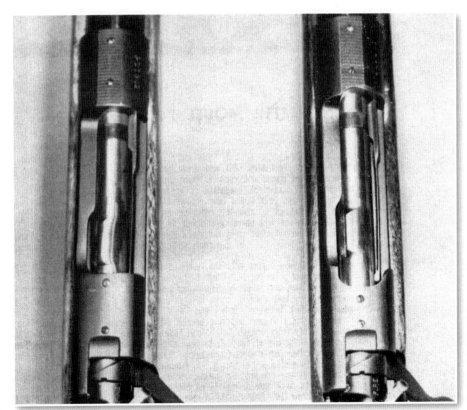

Two pre-1964 Model 70s — at left a 30-06, at right a 375 H&H Magnum, both standard grades. Note receiver ring and bridge cuts in the magnum.

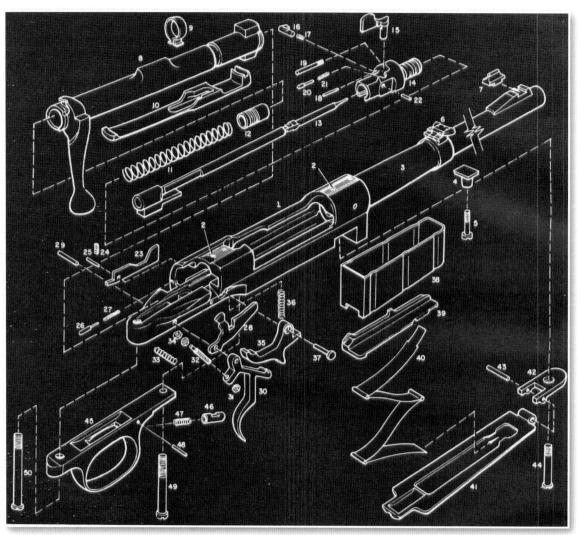

WINCHESTER MODEL 70

Disassembly — Depress bolt stop (28) and draw bolt to rear out of receiver. Remove barrel and receiver from stock by unscrewing fore-end stud screw (5), magazine cover hinge plate screw (44), and front and rear guard bow screws (49,50). Remove magazine cover assembly complete with spring (40) and follower (39). Lift receiver and barrel group out of buttstock. Guard bow (45) may be removed from buttstock. Ejector (23), bolt stop (28), trigger (30), sear (35) and their springs may all be removed from receiver by driving out their retaining pins. Bolt stop plunger (26) and spring (27) are removed from hole at rear of receiver after removing bolt stop. Extractor (10) may be turned slightly on bolt and is easily disengaged from lips of extractor ring (9). With bolt cocked, move safety lock (15) to its intermediate position between "safe" and "fire." Depress breech bolt sleeve lock (16) and unscrew breech bolt sleeve and firing pin assembly from breech bolt. Move safety lock to "fire" position. Pull firing pin sleeve (12) to rear slightly. Turn sleeve ¼-turn in either direction, disengaging sleeve from firing pin (13). Withdraw sleeve and spring (11) from firing pin, taking care not to let the compressed spring escape forcibly. Breech bolt sleeve (14) is removed from firing pin by unscrewing firing pin stop screw (19). Reassemble in reverse order.

Parts List

1. Receiver
2. Receiver Plug Screws
3. Barrel
4. Fore-end Stud
5. Fore-end Stud Screw
6. Rear Sight
7. Front Sight
8. Breech Bolt
9. Extractor Ring
10. Extractor
11. Firing Pin Spring
12. Firing Pin Sleeve
13. Firing Pin
14. Breech Bolt Sleeve
15. Safety Lock
16. Breech Bolt Sleeve Lock
17. Breech Bolt Sleeve Lock Spring
18. Breech Bolt Sleeve Lock Pin
19. Firing Pin Stop Screw
20. Safety Lock Plunger
21. Safety Lock Plunger Spring
22. Safety Lock Stop Pin
23. Ejector
24. Ejector Spring
25. Ejector Pin
26. Bolt Stop Plunger
27. Bolt Stop Plunger Spring
28. Bolt Stop
29. Trigger Pin
30. Trigger
31. Trigger Stop Screw Nut
32. Trigger Stop Screw
33. Trigger Spring
34. Trigger Spring Adj. Nuts (2)
35. Sear
36. Sear Spring
37. Sear Pin
38. Magazine
39. Magazine Follower
40. Magazine Spring
41. Magazine Cover
42. Magazine Cover Hinge Plate
43. Magazine Cover Hinge Pin
44. Magazine Cover Hinge Plate Screw
45. Guard Bow
46. Magazine Cover Catch
47. Magazine Cover Catch Spring
48. Magazine Cover Catch Pin
49. Front Guard Bow Screw
50. Rear Guard Bow Screw

Buttstock, buttplate and sling swivels are not shown in the exploded drawing.

A Model 70 National Match rifle, made about 1952.

What the future holds for the old Model 70 design is anybody's guess. There are some who feel that Winchester will ultimately capitalize on the consumer demand and start reproducing the old Model 70 rifle on a limited basis, in much the same way the Winchester Model 12 shotgun is offered. This would, for a time at least, shake up the collectors. However, if and when they are reproduced the prices are certainly not going to be any cheaper than those current for new Winchester Model 70s and chances are they'd go at top prices. Others contend that Winchester, by so doing, would downgrade their new 70s, thereby pulling the (sales) rug from underneath them.

At present there seems to be a pressing factor for Model 70 collectors. Parts easily available a few years ago are becoming depleted to a point where some of the rare calibers cannot be rebarreled to restore their original condition. Eventually, of course, all parts will be exhausted, as is the current situation facing the owners of Winchester Models 75, 72, 43, etc. Some far off day pre-64 Model 70s will find their way into showcases or museums, along with such cherished firearms of the past as the Sharps, the early Colt, the Lefever, the Parker and many others.

While I don't mean to damn with faint praise, it is quite correct that the "new" Model 70 Winchesters are as good as any rifle made today anywhere — strong, reliable, accurate and well made — but neither they, nor any other rifle, can match the superb quality and craftsmanship of the pre-64 Model 70, the rifleman's rifle. 🔄

H.I.H. Prince Abdorreza with two record-class Red sheep, collected in northern Iran. The rifle — a custom pre-64 Model 70 in 7×57mm, made by Al Biesen of Portland, Oregon.

Some Special Seventies

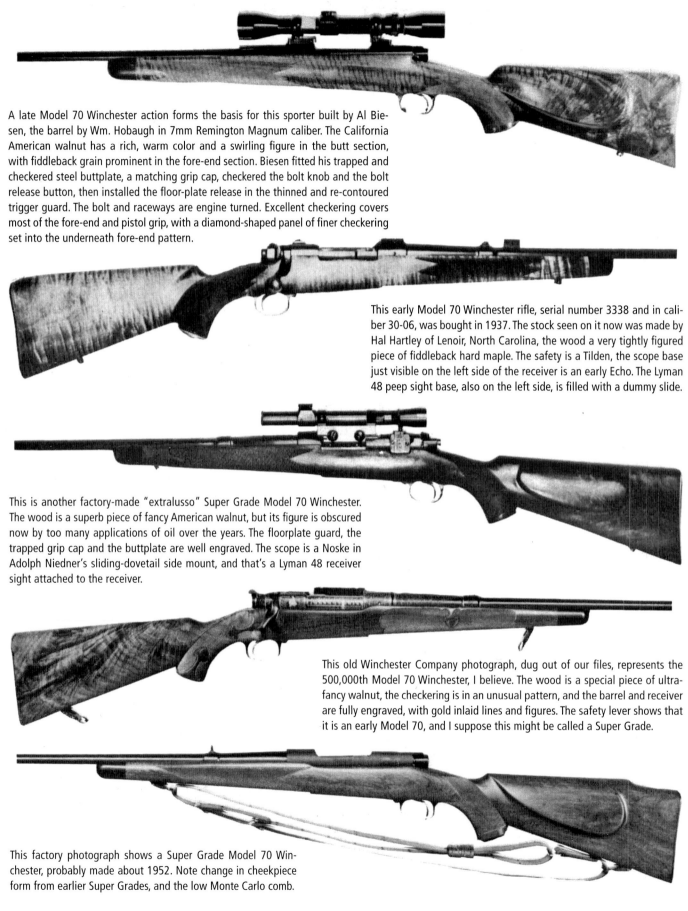

A late Model 70 Winchester action forms the basis for this sporter built by Al Biesen, the barrel by Wm. Hobaugh in 7mm Remington Magnum caliber. The California American walnut has a rich, warm color and a swirling figure in the butt section, with fiddleback grain prominent in the fore-end section. Biesen fitted his trapped and checkered steel buttplate, a matching grip cap, checkered the bolt knob and the bolt release button, then installed the floor-plate release in the thinned and re-contoured trigger guard. The bolt and raceways are engine turned. Excellent checkering covers most of the fore-end and pistol grip, with a diamond-shaped panel of finer checkering set into the underneath fore-end pattern.

This early Model 70 Winchester rifle, serial number 3338 and in caliber 30-06, was bought in 1937. The stock seen on it now was made by Hal Hartley of Lenoir, North Carolina, the wood a very tightly figured piece of fiddleback hard maple. The safety is a Tilden, the scope base just visible on the left side of the receiver is an early Echo. The Lyman 48 peep sight base, also on the left side, is filled with a dummy slide.

This is another factory-made "extralusso" Super Grade Model 70 Winchester. The wood is a superb piece of fancy American walnut, but its figure is obscured now by too many applications of oil over the years. The floorplate guard, the trapped grip cap and the buttplate are well engraved. The scope is a Noske in Adolph Niedner's sliding-dovetail side mount, and that's a Lyman 48 receiver sight attached to the receiver.

This old Winchester Company photograph, dug out of our files, represents the 500,000th Model 70 Winchester, I believe. The wood is a special piece of ultra-fancy walnut, the checkering is in an unusual pattern, and the barrel and receiver are fully engraved, with gold inlaid lines and figures. The safety lever shows that it is an early Model 70, and I suppose this might be called a Super Grade.

This factory photograph shows a Super Grade Model 70 Winchester, probably made about 1952. Note change in cheekpiece form from earlier Super Grades, and the low Monte Carlo comb.

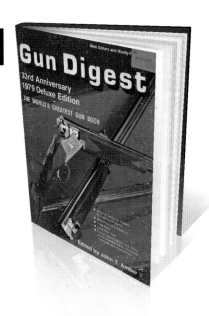

THE MODEL 77
RUGER RIFLE

It wasn't easy, deciding to buck the prevailing trend in gaudy rifles, but Bill Ruger acted with courage and boldness in styling and designing his first bolt action rifle. The dangerous gamble paid off, and the rest, as they say, is history.

by DANIEL PETERSON

N 1968 STURM, RUGER & Co. introduced a new rifle — basically on a Mauser-type turn-bolt action with two forward locking lugs. At that time it hardly seemed likely that the gun world was breathlessly awaiting yet another bolt rifle. Besides the three long-time American favorites — the Winchester M70, Remington's M700 and the Savage 110, there was a host of other commercial bolt actions available from foreign shores, plus thousands of military Mausers, Springfields and Enfields. It was obvious that a newly-hatched bolt rifle had to have a lot going for it to compete successfully. From the start, however, it was apparent to many riflemen/hunters that Ruger's new rifle had desirable design aspects that set it apart from most of the others.

Like many other young gun nuts, I was devoted to the writings of Jack O'Connor. Anytime an article appeared in *Outdoor Life* about bolt actions you could be sure it would show pictures of and carry comments on those beautifully classic rifles made by Biesen, Milliron, Brownell and others. Most anything made by these craftsmen had the typical classic looks; straight and elegant stocks without Monte Carlo combs or rollover cheekpieces, gracefully sweeping bolt handles and hand checkering in multi-point or fleur-de-lis patterns. Seeing such rifles made my head swim. I longed for the day I'd own one of them, but I might as well have wished I could fly. I feel sure that such articles by O'Connor and other writers had a certain salutary effect on many riflemen as to what the bolt-action sporter should be, what it should look like.

The Brownell Touch

As popular as the Remington and Winchester bolt actions were at this time, both had "checkered" stocks which, in fact, were not truly checkered — instead the pattern revealed diamonds pressed in *reverse*, the design sunk into the wood by a system of heat and pressure.*Frank Pachmayr, head of the Los Angeles shop that bears his name, commented to me in the 1960s that this press-in technique could just*

Author with a morning's bag of crows taken with a Ruger 77 in caliber 22–250 Rem.

as well have used dies that produced raised diamonds, thus closely simulating handcut checkering. Frank was long familiar with such die work, his factory using a wide variety of them in making Pachmayr recoil pads and handgun grips. J.TA. Such stocks were compromises, near-classics, perhaps, if one stretches a point, yet not far from the California school of design. They contained elements not really needed on a stock — Monte Carlo combs, white line spacers at butt, grip and fore-end, the latter plastic tipped, as was the butt-plate usually.

Winchester, since 1965, has produced at least 6 different Model 70 buttstocks, none very attractive to the rifleman wanting a classic handle. The old M70 had gained its reputation as the "Rifleman's Rifle" with a simple-lined, well-designed stock, especially in the years before WW II.

The Ruger stock, however, was designed by Lenard Brownell, the famed Wyoming gunmaker, which displayed the epitome of the classic style.

The Ruger Model 77 stock has nothing that isn't needed on a hunting rifle, but no more than that. It is hand checkered in a simple, borderless point pattern which looks and feels good. The finish is of a warm, semi-oil type that was welcomed by the conservative minded rifleman who had been used to seeing the hard, cold, California style supposedly "in" at that time. In addition the M77 had many features that had previously been available only on true custom rifles. Among these desirable aspects were a (hinged) floorplate-release latch inside the trigger

Ruger 77 rifle here has round top, standard barrel form. Trim, graceful lines proclaim the classicism of this outstanding Brownell design.

guard bow, a top tang safety, and a barrel — if desired — free of sights or plugged screw holes. The M77's weight, too, was a factor in its appeal. For years the more astute rifleman/hunter had been searching for a handy, lightweight rifle, hefting with scope about 8 pounds. The M77, with scope, could just wriggle under the wire in this department. In total, the M77 resembles, as closely as any production rifle can, costs considered, the style and the mechanics of those eye-appealing custom jobs.

Mauser Extractor

However, another design factor, I believe, helped increase the acceptance of the M77 when it was introduced. When Winchester designed the post-1964 M70 one of the features abandoned — which many writers criticized — was the sturdy Mauser-type wide-claw extractor. Many riflemen, myself included, believe that the broad-arc Mauser extractor is stronger and more reliable than the newer, cheaper-to-manufacture bolt-head type now in use. I know of several such extractors that failed to work. Ruger wisely retained the Mauser extractor in the M77.

All of these factors, then, were a decided plus for the new Ruger bolt rifle. However, I also think that the Ruger came along at precisely the right time to give additional impetus to its popularity.

Initially the M77 was offered in a medium length action only (2.925" magazine length), designed to handle the popular 308-length family of cartridges. The first four cartridges offered were the 22–250, 243, 6mm and 308. These were followed in 1969 by the 284 Win., the 6.5 Rem. Mag. and the 350 Rem. Mag., though these last three have been since dropped. (They're being sought out by collectors already.) I feel that the idea behind the short action was to put Ruger in something of a monopolistic position, bearing in mind that short actions have always had a dedicated following, as well as the fact that everyone made the standard-length action. However, because of demand, in late 1970 Ruger brought out the long action M77, (3.380" magazine length) calling it the M77

Magnum. It was not a true magnum action, of course, if one compares the Mauser extra-length action, but one designed for 30-06-length cartridges and the belted short magnums. This normal-length action was first offered in 30-06, 25-06, 270 and 7mm Rem. Mag. From time to time other cartridges have been offered in both action lengths, as we shall see.

One of the few things disliked aesthetically about the new M77 was its odd-shaped bolt handle. The 1917 Springfield (Enfield) had a similar one. Some writers even compared its form to a dog's hind leg. Functionally it was satisfactory. However, a new style bolt handle was offered in 1970. A marked improvement, it bore a great resemblance to the old M70's bolt style, having a similar rearward slant and a pear-shaped hollowed-out knob. This is the rarest of M77 bolt handle types. The third and current style, identical to the second type but without the hollow knob, has been used for the past 4 or 5 years. However, in checking with the factory I was told that the old crooked handle is

still in production, but I haven't seen a new rifle with this bolt handle in several years.

Varmint Type Appears

In 1971 the varmint type M77 appeared. First offered in 22–250, the M77V had a heavy barrel tapped for varmint-target scope bases. Several other popular varmint calibers appeared in subsequent years.

In 1972 Ruger began the most startling resurrection of supposedly dead cartridges ever recorded in the annals of firearms production. The gun magazines were filled with the announcements of these reintroduced cartridges. Short production runs were made of the 220 Swift, 257 Roberts, and 7×57 Mauser at various times during 1972 and '73 to test the market. These short runs were grabbed off the dealer shelves immediately. Ultimately the Swift, 257 Roberts, 250 Savage, and 7×57 became regular cataloged offerings. Not only were these all excellent, time-tested cartridges, they had all been offered in the pre-64

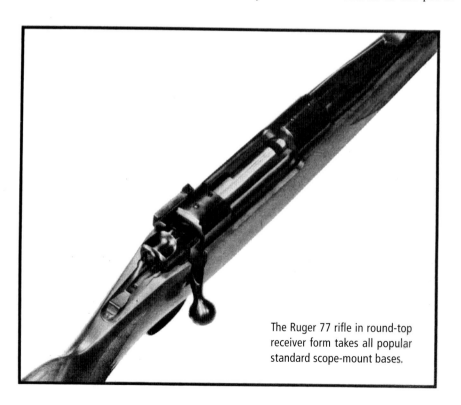

The Ruger 77 rifle in round-top receiver form takes all popular standard scope-mount bases.

This is a Ruger 77 rifle with varmint-type barrel, integral scope-mount bases and the current bolt handle.

M70s, another similarity between the two rifles. This quick success clearly demonstrated, I think, that there were many people who desired a commercial 220 Swift or 257 Roberts but were unwilling to pay the steep collector's price for an old M70. Offering the 250 Savage in the M77 was probably the most ideal mating ever made commercially, especially since the short action was used. The 257 Roberts was chambered in the long action, which allowed for shallow seating of the bullet, given adequate throating.

When the M77 first came out one could order (from Ruger) a steel floor-plate and trigger guard, but only as separate parts. These have never been offered on 77s from the factory with one exception. In 1976 Ruger offered the M77 in a 458 Win. Mag. made with a "Circassian" walnut stock — actually French walnut. This stock, somewhat fuller than the regular stock, I understand, comes with the steel floorplate and trigger guard as standard. These parts, beautifully finished and blued, enhance the beauty of the entire rifle. There is a weight difference, of course — the steel components (minus the guard screws) weigh about 7 ounces as opposed to 3 for the alloy units. As nice as it would be if these were standard items on all

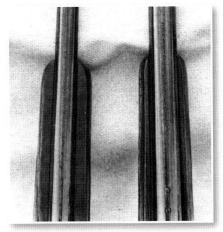

Fore-end at right is the old style with narrow top compared with new style at left. Author feels these top ledges would be more functional with less flat surface exposed.

M77s, the price would go up, as would the weight. Incidentally, these parts are available from time to time, in long action form only, at about $20 for both. However, you may have to wait quite a while since production is quite low on the rifle using them. They are *not* shown on the parts list in the M77 owner's manual.

Trigger Pulls

Perhaps the greatest complaint against the M77 concerns the trigger pull. Though nominally adjustable for weight of pull, the criticism has been that this adjustment still leaves something to be desired. For a hunting rifle I feel that no complaint whatsoever is justified. At the bench and on varmints, where optimum trigger control is necessary, it is something else. Currently my M77s have Ruger triggers, which I've worked down to 3–3½ lbs. In correspondence with Jim Carmichel he wrote that he'd talked several times with Bill (Ruger) about the quality of the triggers. Jim added, "... I must admit that with a little tinkering the triggers can be adjusted quite nicely. I have heard that some of them resist adjusting but of the three or four I own, all have been adjusted down to about a 2–2½a lb. letoff." However, for those that must have something better, Canjar makes set-type and single-stage replacement triggers.

An unusual design aspect of the original M77, and still incorporated, is the integral-base system for scope mounting. Using the pair of rings supplied by Ruger, no other bases are needed. This not only saves money but eliminates one step, that of mating mount with receiver — which often enough introduces problems. Although this system in different forms had been offered on Czech Brno actions and on the Finnish Sakos, it was a first for an American made production action. I believe it is a most excellent system. The ring bottoms clamp onto the receiver bases via grooves milled into each side. The ring tops attach to the lower rings by using two 6–40 screws on each. *Early-production scope rings were split vertically, unlike the horizontally-divided halves now in use. These original rings were criticized, too,*

hence the change. I like the older type — I think they're better looking and I've had no trouble with them. J.T.A. Two ring heights are available — the standard sets that come with the rifle (Cat. No. D71), and a set ⅛" higher (Cat. No. D71H). I would like a set even lower than standard, for use with straight-tube scopes. Even with the standard rings some scope objective housings touch the barrel, necessitating shims or the use of the higher rings.

In 1972 the M77 appeared with another receiver profile, this one called the "round top," tapped for all popular commercial mounts, but offered only in the longer action. However, I still prefer the integral-base receiver because I believe it secures the scope in the most positive way. Sales of the two receiver types reflect the same preference by the buying public.

The other important design feature of the M77 is the patented diagonal (slanted) front guard screw. This angled screw not only pulls the barrel-receiver assembly together, it also pulls the recoil lug firmly back against the recoil shoulders of the stock — assuming correct dimensioning. The M77 action is flat bottomed, and I've found the bedding of the action and barrel to be excellent, especially in the action area. In fact, some notable gun authorities feel that the M77 actions are bedded so well that it is one of the few actions that cannot be improved by glass bedding. However, it isn't unusual to find some high spots in the barrel channel, which causes some binding, especially along the sides. This can easily be corrected, though, with some light sanding. I have also found that the wood-to-metal fit along the edges of the action has, in some rifles, been rather poor. This is especially true at the rear of the tang.

The fore-end's last inch or so beds tightly against the barrel. In examining many M77s I have found their fore-ends exerting, sometimes, as much as 12–15 lbs. of pressure. I regard this as somewhat excessive, but in my experience many such rifles, though untuned, shoot quite well. Of course the accuracy seeker will certainly want to examine the barrel and action for any excessive rubbing. Of the several

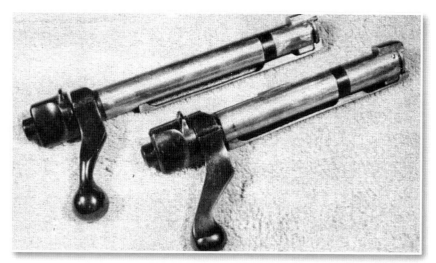

The longer bolt, from a Ruger 77 in caliber 458, has the current bolt handle style. The other bolt shows the earlier type of handle.

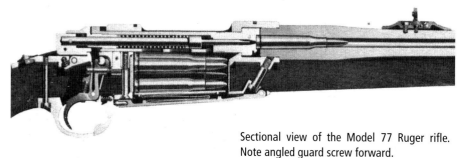

Sectional view of the Model 77 Ruger rifle. Note angled guard screw forward.

sporter weight M77s I own and use, all can be relied upon to shoot careful handloads with the right bullet into 1–1½" groups at 100 yards if I do my part.

Varmint weight M77s have achieved a high reputation for accuracy. I've read many reports of M77s in 220 Swifts giving exceptional accuracy. Although my experience has been limited to only one Ruger Swift, it certainly lives up to those findings. My Ruger 22–250 consistently delivers 5 shots at 100 yards into groups of ½- to ¾-MOA. Interestingly, perhaps, my most temperamental M77 is a late model 257 Roberts. After trying nearly every usable powder/bullet combination, this rifle seems to prefer IMR 4350 teamed with 100-gr. Hornadys.

As in any rifle, we now know, much can be done to maintain high accuracy by judiciously cleaning the barrel regularly and frequently, and by not shooting so fast as to heat the barrel excessively.

In my long-time association with the M77 I have examined and shot many of them. They generally are found with quite straight-grained walnut, but it's quite common to find some nice figure in at least part of the stock. I have, in fact, seen quite a few M77 stocks with rather exceptional wood

figure. One of mine, a 25-06, shows a handsome figure in the butt-stock. Checkering is generally very good, with few runovers, the

diamonds sharp and well formed. However, from time to time I've seen checkering that looks as though the checkering tool had dulled, causing the diamonds to be less than sharp and the grooves somewhat cluttered with wood shavings. Blueing has been very good, the polishing really excellent; in fact the metal finish has been as good as that on many much more expensive rifles. The bolts sometimes operate a bit roughly as they come out of the box, but usually they slick up quickly with use. Several of mine were improved by hand stoning until now they snick in and out delightfully, as well as feeding and ejecting more smoothly.

The M77 has been offered in 3 different barrel weights and lengths. The 22" lightweight or sporter weight is standard except for those calibers needing longer barrels for ballistic reasons. Those cartridges with 24" barrels, other than the varmint models, include the 25-06, 7mm Mag., 300 Mag., 338 Mag. and the 458 Mag. The original short run of 257 Roberts rifles had a 24" tube. I would call the 24" barrel a "medium" weight, since it is far more husky, especially back toward the receiver, than the 22". The varmint weight barrels have all been 24" except for the 26" Swift. Recently Ruger offered a "sporter weight" Swift, with the 24" medium-weight barrel.

One caliber, the 308, was originally offered in sporter weight, then reintroduced in 1976 in the varmint version for silhouette shooting. It is now being made again (1977) in the 22" sporter weight.

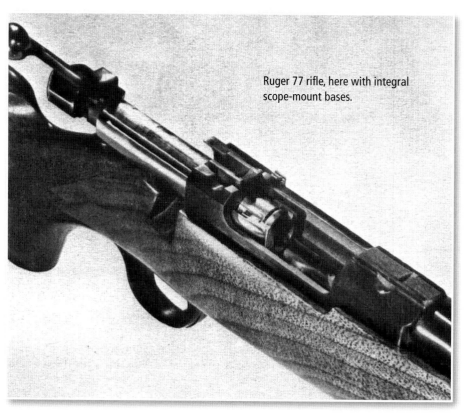

Ruger 77 rifle, here with integral scope-mount bases.

Changes Desired

If I could change the M77 there are several things I'd. do. Though there is little fault with the stock, I feel it could be slimmed or narrowed down in the action section and in the fore-end. Older M77 fore-ends were narrower at the top, a treatment that was superior, in my judgment, to the present style. I would also like to see, regardless of cost, the steel floorplate and trigger guard offered on the complete rifle in any caliber and on short and long actions. Finally, I am sure that if Super Grade M77s were offered there'd be many buyers standing in line, money in hand. Perhaps these could have a larger and fancier checkering pattern, steel floorplates and trigger guards, a steel grip cap replacing the plastic one, and some time spent on slicking up the action. In talking with the Ruger people in New Hampshire, where the M77 is made, they say there has always been difficulty in keeping up production on the M77 as it is now, that being one of the main reasons why a Super Grade has never been offered.

Variations

A few minor variations in M77s, through the years, have not been design changes. For example, during the early life of the rifle, the rubber butt pads used had rounded edges; the square-cornered type has been used since then. The dimensions of the checkering pattern have varied slightly, although the pattern itself has not changed. The Ruger people tell me that the size changes minutely when bad runovers occur, a few additional lines being put in to eliminate these errors. The easiest variation to spot is on the fore-ends, as previously mentioned. Originally the top of the fore-end was about 3/16" wide on each side, whereas the newer style is wider, some 5/16" wide. This wider type suffers, to my way of thinking, in appearance and in practical terms. This wide platform allows snow and rain to accumulate, to run perhaps into the barrel channel. A better treatment would be to show an outside downward curve, letting water/snow run down the stock exterior.

There have also been slight differences in the circumference of the pistol grip; not noticeable to the eye but obvious to the feel and the tape. I have also noticed that earlier M77 extractors were drilled to match up with the hole in the right side of the receiver ring, meant to vent escaping powder gases in the event of a case failure. These holed extractors have not been seen for several years.

Finally, there have been differences in what I call the "ribbing" or the grooves that

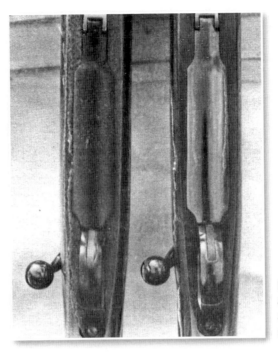

Ruger 77 at right has steel trigger guard and floorplate (sometimes factory available at extra cost), the rifle at left has standard alloy types.

At left, the original Ruger telescope ring; the other is the current style.

run lengthwise on receivers with integral scope bases. Sometimes this ribbing is larger and coarser, a result of different mould dimensions, I've heard. A small thing, of course, but interesting for the Ruger collector.

Collecting Ruger 77s? Don't laugh. Some discontinued calibers are skyrocketing in price, notably the 358 Win., a non-cataloged caliber. A recent issue of *Shotgun News* advertised one "as new" for $350. I expect that now, with the 257 Roberts and 250 Savage out of production, their prices will quickly increase as well.

Conclusions

Since the Ruger M77 was introduced in 1968, it has offered the rifleman much that is good. It is, in my opinion, the finest-stocked commercial production rifle ever offered. It gave the conservative, classic-minded rifleman something to cheer about. It combined the proven old with the proven new — plunger ejector and recessed bolt face. It was, I feel, at least partly responsible for the move from pressed checkering to cut checkering on some rifles. Ruger proved that well done hand checkering could be offered on a rifle that was competitively priced. It became a rifle that offered new-generation riflemen calibers, some with superior ballistics, considered dead by the larger companies. Most of all, Bill Ruger had the courage to bring out a rifle that was, many felt, behind the times. It was without white-line spacers, had no Monte Carlo combs, no "plastic finish." One of Ruger's old M77 advertisements noted that "not a penny is spent on meaningless ornamentation." I heartily agree.

Perhaps you wonder what we conservative-minded shooters mean when we refer to a "classic" rifle? According to Mr. Webster "classic" means "of the highest order, correct, refined." As far as bolt-action rifles are concerned, that definition fits the Ruger M77 perfectly. 🔘

(Late in 1977, at Remington's seminar for writers and editors, a variant of their M700 centerfire rifle was introduced — the Classic. Simply and functionally designed, the new rifle has no cheekpiece, no Monte Carlo comb, no white spacers, no fore-end tip. There's no grip cap, either, and the bottom of the pistol grip lies close to the stock's toe line, as it should. I don't know what prompted this step, but the Classic 700 is a handsome sport-er — and welcome. J.T.A.)

Notes on Ruger M77 Bolt Action Rifles

The following calibers were once offered in the M77 (some were reintroductions), but all have now been discontinued except the 220 Swift and the 280 Remington.

220 Swift	280 Remington
250–3000 Savage	284 Winchester
257 Roberts	350 Remington Magnum
6.5 Remington Magnum	

The three barrel weights offered in M77s. From left — medium, varmint and lightweight.

This list shows the calibers that have been or were commercially offered in M77s. Barrel lengths are in inches.

Calibers	77R	77RS	77V	77ST
22–250 Rem.	22	22	24	
220 Swift	24		26	
243 Win.	22	22	24	
6mm Rem.	22	22	24	
250 Sav.	22	22		
257 Rcb.	22&24	22&24		24
25-06 Rem.	24	24	24	24
6.5 Rem.	22	22		
270 Win.	22	22		22
7.57	24&24	22&24		24
280 Rem.	22	22		
7mm Rem. Mag.	24	24		24
284 Win.	22	22		
308 Win.	22	22	24	
30-06 Spfg.	22	22		22
300 Win. Mag.	24	24		24
338 Win. Mag.	24	24		24
350 Rem. Mag.	22	22		
358 Win.*	22			
458 Win. Mag.		24		

*non-cataloged. Ruger factory officials said that one short run of nearly 1000 rifles were assembled in 358 Win.

The Winchester
MODEL 94

A hunter's history of the most popular sporting rifle in the world–and still going strong after some 85 years. An enviable, unprecedented record

by H. V. STENT

ILLICIT THOUGH IT MAY BE, the American hunter's long love affair with the Winchester 94 seems to be steaming along as torridly as ever.

It started when the 30-30, termed "a truly epoch-making cartridge" in the *Speer Reloading Manual*,* (7th ed., 1966, p. 213.) became the first sporting rifle cartridge in America to be loaded with smokeless powder.

As such, it staggered the shooting world. Until 1895 all sporting cartridges shot thumb-sized bullets ahead of hefty charges of black powder, loads that bellowed like cannon and sent up billows of smoke big enough to hide a battleship. Starting off at only some 1200-1400 feet per second (fps) muzzle velocity, those bullets arced down so fast that the popular 44-40, sighted for 100 yards, would hit 30 inches low at 200. The 45-70 was not much better — 26 inches.

In contrast, the new "white powder" 30-30's bullet burst out of its barrel with no obscuring smoke, and so fast that it could be sighted point blank at 150 yards and have only 4 inches drop at 200. Metal-jacketed and soft-pointed, the little expanding bullet had an effectiveness on game that amazed hunters hitherto convinced that big-diameter balls were a must. The 30-30 started a cartridge revolution.

Their new baby brought Winchester problems, however. The cartridge and its rifle were not born together. John Browning's design was so obviously a winner that Winchester rushed it into production; Browning got his patent in August, 1894, and Winchester announced the rifle in November of the same year. It was offered only in two popular black powder loads, 32-40 and 38-55.

Why? Some mystery surrounds the 30-30's *accouchement*. In his *Complete Guide to Handloading*, (New York, 1937, 1st ed. 3d ed., 1949, enl.) and rev. Philip Sharpe says that it was originally designed as a black powder load containing 30 grains of propellant, and that some of these were actually

Old style 94 carbine.

The Model 94 carbine in its current style.

made. Hence the second "30" in its popular name, although its makers called it the 30 Winchester or 30 WCF (Winchester Center Fire). James Serven in the 20th ed. GUN DIGEST (1966) wrote that Browning designed the 94 especially for smokeless powder. He may have done so, since smokeless powder loads were produced in Europe in the late 1880s, and the 30-40 Krag rifle, using smokeless military loads, had been adopted by the U.S. Army in 1892.

However, in *Winchester-the Gun that Won the West,* Washington, D.C. 1952. Harold Williamson remarks that "Browning's & Model 94 proved strong enough for smokeless cartridges, but the barrels had to be made of stronger material."

Winchester quickly reacted. A stronger steel that could withstand the 38,000 pounds of breech pressure of the new propellant — 50% more than black powder usually gave — was sought, and found. In August, 1895, Winchester proudly unveiled two new smokeless cartridges, the 30-30 and the 25-35, and gave the 94 the first-ever nickel steel barrels to handle them. (The U.S. Army did not get around to nickel steel rifle barrels until 1927!)

The New Cartridges

The new cartridges had velocities between 1900 and 2000 fps, the 25-35 with 117-gr. bullets, the 30-30 with 160- or 165-gr., according to various authorities. After a few years the 170-gr. bullet became standard.

As the smokeless powder innovation infected the nation, shooters bought Model 1894s, as they were first known, by the thousands, at $14-$18 apiece. Glowing reports poured in of the 30-30's "terrific killing power" on all varieties of big game. The still smaller bullet and lighter recoil of the 25-35 also appealed to many, and their flat trajectories made both cartridges especially popular in the more open country of the West. The Model 94 carbine — short, handy, flat-breeched, and weighing only around 6 pounds — was soon filling more saddle scabbards than any other rifle.

For woods hunting there was still considerable demand for the 32-40 and 38-55, soon loaded with smokeless to their old black powder velocities. Lots of hunters were satisfied with black powder speed and trajectory, preferred big bullets, and suspected that the newfangled cartridges had unnecessary range and speed, probably would just deflect or blow up in thick brush. With its big 255-gr. bullet the 38-55

hit hard at close ranges, and some thought it fine for even moose and elk.

The 32 Special

Winchester introduced the 32 Special in 1902. Just why they wanted another cartridge so similar to the 30-30 is not certain. Maybe it was to offer smokeless speed to those old-timers who wanted it but felt a 30 caliber was too dang small. Maybe the straight taper of the 32-40 case didn't burn smokeless powders efficiently, so Winchester introduced a bottleneck case to get a stronger loading with the .320" bore and 16" rifling twist of the 32-40.

That twist was slow enough to stabilize short lead bullets, so it appealed more to handloaders than the 30-30 with its 1-in-12 twist. Also, factory loads for the 32 Special used at first the same soft-point bullet as the 32-40, which being designed for slower speeds, was inclined to expand more and often kill better than the 30-30. On the other hand, the 32 Special has been accused of losing its accuracy earlier because the slow twist wouldn't stabilize the 170-gr. bullet after the rifling's sharp edges wore off. Incidentally, the 25-35 had the fastest twist of any U.S. sporting rifle, I believe — one turn in 8 inches — needed to stabilize its long 117-gr. bullet.

Anyhow, the 32 Special has always been popular. Because its slower twist and larger bore lessen pressure, giving the gas a larger bullet-base area to work on, it generally gives 50 fs or so more velocity with the 170-gr. bullet than does the 30-30. Some shooters argue that this makes it a better killer on game. Perhaps it was with the older bullets, but now that it has the same type as the 30-30 — and in latest models, the same twist — the two can be taken as twins in killing power.

With the 30-30 as its top scorer, and the 32 Special probably next, the Model 94 became, and has remained, the most popular of all rifles for deer hunting in the U.S. and Canada. In the latter's northern forests it also became a standby for moose. Down Mexico way, too, "treinta-treinta" became synonymous with "meat-getter," and occasionally saw use on other four-legged game. Not only were Winchesters as well as Colts often called in to settle private quarrels, but irregular armies such as Villa's apparently were sometimes equipped with them.

As the years passed the 94 acquired almost as many variations as a Hollywood starlet has husbands. Long the most popular was the 26-inch barreled rifle with an equal-length magazine holding 9 shots, straight-grip buttstock with deeply-curved steel buttplate, weight just under 8 lbs. It looks a bit paleozoic now, but in those days offhand shooting, always important to the hunter, was recognized by target-shooters too — Schuetzenfests were the style — and a crescent buttplate and a bit of muzzle-heaviness are assets when you "stand up on your hind laigs and shoot like a man."

For no extra charge you could buy the gun with a shotgun-type butt or a half-length magazine. For a dollar or two extra came a snazzy octagon barrel. A little more cash would get the extra-light full-length rifle but which weighed only 7 ¼ pounds. And if you had the desire and the dough (it's bread now!) for fancy touches, you could buy choice walnut, checkering, engraving — the flat-faced breech showed off engraving beautifully — or a pistol grip with about as much curve to it as Twiggy! Remember her?

There was also the carbine, cheaper and lighter, with a less-curved buttplate, a 20-

Model 94 chamberings included, from left — 219 Zipper, 25-35, 30-30, 32 Special, 32-40, 38-55, 44 Magnum, H. V. Stent photo.

inch barrel, and a saddle ring, whose actual function has always mystified me. At one time Winchester offered a 15-inch barrel for the carbine.

Any 94 except the carbine could be had in solid frame — permanently screwed together — or take-down design.

The take-down feature was fascinating. Barrel and receiver threads were "interrupted," so that by giving the barrel a quarter-turn you could pull it out of the receiver, the magazine and fore-end coming with it. That made it much easier to pack for traveling. You could also get a different caliber barrel-magazine. The two parts snaped together again in seconds, a safety device locked them in place, and a screw adjustment took up wear. It seemed to work well, for Winchester also offered this system on their 1886 and 1895 rifles, the latter using such powerful cartridges as the 405 and 30-06.

Until 1920 or so, all these variations were offered. Lever actions were riding high, virtually monopolizing the repeating sporting rifle market. But the winds of change were blowing. Veterans of WW I had learned about bolt actions, and wanted some. When surplus military Krags, Springfields, and Enfields were made available at low prices, ex-doughboys all over the land began buying them.

The Bolt Actions Appear

Among the devotees of the 30-06 bolt action sporter, though theirs were usually costly gunsmith-tailored beauties, were most of the gun editors and gun writers. They wrote nothing but good of their favorites — and little but bad about all rival actions and calibers. Everything about lever actions — two-piece stocks, rear-locked many-piece actions, single-pull triggers, barrels with slots for sights, tube magazines — was made fun of. Anything different from the Springfield must be unreliable, inaccurate, and poor, especially carbines and take-down models. The 30-30 and similar cartridges were mere pipsqueaks. Its users and their rifle would soon be quite obsolete.

The old image of the ideal American hunting rifle — a lever action with the over-under look of full-length-magazine-tube-under-barrel gradually gave way to the more slender, streamlined form of the bolt action sporter with flush box magazine, caliber 30, Model of 1906.

To keep up with the style and to bolster sagging sales Winchester developed their own bolt action sporter, the Model 54, in 30-06 and 270 calibers. It came out in 1925. That same year they tried to give the bold

The 94 can be rapidly levered without lowering the rifle or lifting the eyes from aim. H. V. Stent photo.

bolt look to the 94 by bringing out the new Model 55. It had the same action, but a shotgun-style butt, a round 24-inch barrel, and a 3-shot magazine hidden within the forearm. They still cataloged the older models, though with fewer fancy options, but according to George Watrous, in his *History of Winchester Firearms 1866-1966*, (New York, 1971, 3d ed.) when the 55 came out they stopped manufacturing all other models of the 94 except the carbine. They probably had quite a stock on hand.

Neither the 55 nor the 54 sold particularly well; 20,000 in seven years for the lever gun, 50,000 in eleven years for the bolt. Sales of all Model 94s, however, reached the surprising total of 1,000,000 by 1927, an average of 30,000 a year.

Because the Model 55 sold so poorly, the company dropped it in 1932, but came out the next year with a revised version, in Winchester Proof Steel, called the Model 64. This time the magazine projected some 4 inches from the forearm, giving a more graceful appearance and a capacity of 5 shots. The pistol grip had the most daring curve Winchester had yet put on a lever action rifle.

A New Carbine

The carbine got a bit of face lifting too. A shotgun butt was substituted for the old type, the saddle ring was abandoned, a ramp was added for the front sight, the band that holds magazine to barrel was moved from in front of the front sight to behind it, and the forearm was shortened.

Both rifles were available in solid frame only — no more take downs — and these

two, plus a deluxe "Deer" version of the 64, were all that was left to carry the once-voluminous 94 lever action line into the future. With the depression and the overwhelming press dominance of the bolt action, that future looked uncertain indeed.

Calibers were now down to three. Though now offered in high-velocity loads of 1600-1900 fps, the 32-40 and 38-55 were left out, probably because of low sales. The 170-gr. 30-30 had been speeded up to 2200 fs, the 25-35 and 32 Special to 2280 and 2260 with 117- and 170-gr. bullets respectively. Other loads were also introduced to tempt tight-pursed buyers; a 1938 list included an 87-gr. at 2650 and a 100-gr. at 2480 for the 25-35, with 30-30 and 32 Special bullets and velocities ranging from a 110-gr. at 2630 or 2720 fs to the 180-gr. belted Peters at 2120 and 2200.

The 219 Zipper

Even the fastest of these loads, however, looked pretty poky contrasted to the 3000-plus velocities of the 270 and 30-06, or the streaking 4140 fs of the new 220 Swift. So it was with considerable pride that Winchester unveiled, in 1938, a really high speed number for their Model 64. This was the 219 Zipper, its case the old 25-35 necked down, bullets 46- and 56-gr., velocities 3390 and 3050 fs. That's faster than the modern 222 Remington, standard or Magnum.

It looked like an excellent varmint cartridge, but it was in a lever action, so the experts slapped it down at once as too inaccurate to bother with. Whether many of them actually gave it a fair test is doubtful. Philip Sharpe, who did, credits it (op. cit.) as being capable of 1¼- to 1½-inch groups at 100 yards. But the bolt action bugs (who buy most of the varmint rifles) were not interested in any lever gun, and those who were didn't buy many rifles exclusively for varmints. One who did got 16 coyotes in one winter with his 219, according to Don Martin in the 1948 GUN DIGEST, but there just weren't enough buyers. Because of World War II, Winchester stopped making commercial firearms early in 1942; when they resumed in late 1945, the 219 Zipper was no longer listed for the 64.

Model 94 Popularity

By 1948, sales of Model 94s — including 55s and 64s, which have the same action — had reached 1,500,000. Half a million more rifles in 21 years; a little slower than before but, considering those years had included a depression, a 4 ½-year gap in production, and a strong anti-lever campaign, it was again a surprising figure. But what happened after 1948 must have set Winchester's sales staff dancing on the board room tables.

For the post-war years brought a new attitude toward lever actions. Whereas veterans of the first worldwide fracas had returned with an interest whetted for bolt actions, a much larger number came back from WW II in love with a very different arm — the 30-cal. M1 carbine. It was light, short, handy, had no bothersome recoil and no awkward bolt to work.

For hunting big game at home, it had too little punch, so they sought the nearest facsimiles with enough power — and found them in Winchester and Marlin lever carbines. Western movies, first glutting the theaters and then infesting every living room on TV, powerfully reinforced the new interest in the old lever action. Too, a new generation of gun editors and writers, though still favoring bolt guns for their own use, was much more tolerant of other actions and calibers than its predecessors had been.

After 1948 it took *only five years* for Winchester to sell another half-million 94s. Two million now.

Another 8 years, and Winchester's 1961 catalog displayed on its cover the beatifully checkered and engraved Model 94 Number 2,500,000.

Since 1936, when the Model 70 bolt action was introduced, this had been the darling of the magazine writers, and a magnificently-finished example of it was shown on the flip side of the same 1961 colored catalog cover. But it had sold only 500,000 copies, in all its many calibers, in the same time that the little lever gun had sold some 1,250,000.

The 94 can be shouldered quickly for a fast shot. H. V. Stent photo.

Which is not mentioned here to contend that the two are rivals for the same market — the two clienteles are generally different types of shooters — but to make the record clear as to which is more used. The ratio continues roughly the same to this day.

There's little talk today about the lever action becoming obsolete (whatever happened to the Springfield that was to replace it?), or that it is weak or too complicated to work reliably. In fact, the 94 action is simpler and less liable to jams than some of the rotating bolt actions now on the market. Instead of going out of favor the lever gun's single-pull trigger has now spread to its bolt brothers. We no longer believe that light rifles or barrels shorter than 24 inches are inevitably inaccurate.

Model 94 Changes

In 1964 some changes were made in the 94 carbine and, like the changes made at the same time in the M70, they were not for the better. Rising production costs apparently made it imperative that Winchester simplify its manufacturing methods. Pins replaced screws in the receiver, the new cartridge carrier was not an improvement, and the old rounded receiver bottom, so comfortable in the hand, was replaced by a flatter one with sharper corners.

An "Antique" 94 was also brought out, in 30-30 only, with a gay, case-hardened receiver bearing some scrollwork, a brass-plated loading gate, and the old saddle ring revived — God knows why. The standard carbine could still be had in 30-30 or 32 Special, but the 25-35, alas, was no more. It had fallen by the wayside through declining sales in 1955, and the Model 64 had followed it into oblivion in 1957.

For Winchester's centennial in 1966 the company brought back the old 94 long rifle with 26-inch octagon barrel, and a carbine to match, both with gold-plated "Yellow Boy" receivers to commemorate their 1866 ancestor. The next year Winchester gold-plated only the loading gate cover, and called them "The Classics." Other specials and commemoratives have followed almost as regularly as babies in a pre-pill family.

The 94 carbine got a new caliber in 1967, the first for 65 years! It was the 44 Magnum handgun load, with 240-gr. bullet at 1750 fps. The 44's short bullet has a drop from 100-yard zero of 18 inches at 200 yards and 64 at 300. and it takes only a 1-in-38 twist to stabilize it. In 1974 the twist was changed to 1-12.

In 1972 the 94 action was upgraded a bit via solid pins, a better cartridge carrier, a new loading gate and cover. Was it then, too, that Winchester started making receivers of a metal which almost defies re-bluing? It seems a pity, when other changes were for the better.

Best news of 1972, 94-wise, was the return of the fine Model 64 to the Winchester line. To my mind, though not as short and handy as the carbine, the 64 is the handsomest tube-magazine lever action ever made. How its quality compares with the old 64 I don't know, but I've heard that some of the less desirable shortcuts imposed on the carbine are also evident in the 64. It didn't sell well, so it's gone.

Including the 64 and 55, total sales of the Model 94 hit 3,000,000 in 1966. What a record! It must be the most popular and best known sporting firearm ever sold in America and, indeed, in the world.

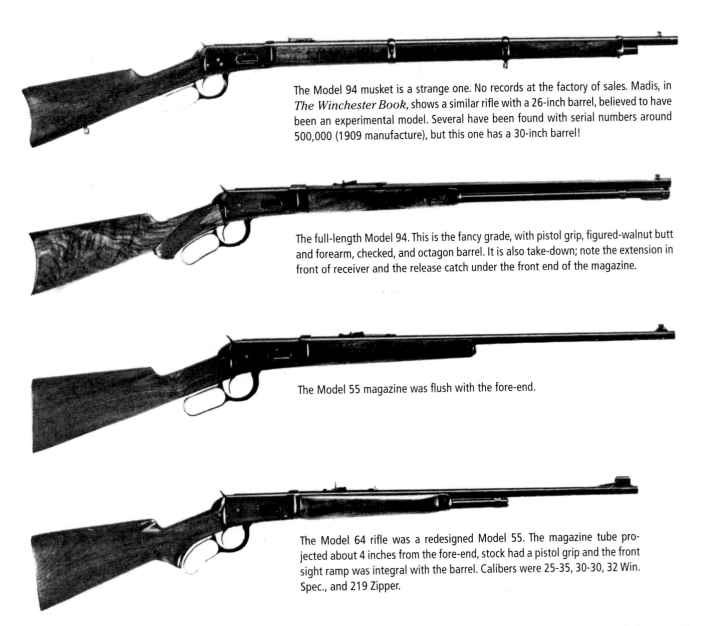

The Model 94 musket is a strange one. No records at the factory of sales. Madis, in *The Winchester Book*, shows a similar rifle with a 26-inch barrel, believed to have been an experimental model. Several have been found with serial numbers around 500,000 (1909 manufacture), but this one has a 30-inch barrel!

The full-length Model 94. This is the fancy grade, with pistol grip, figured-walnut butt and forearm, checked, and octagon barrel. It is also take-down; note the extension in front of receiver and the release catch under the front end of the magazine.

The Model 55 magazine was flush with the fore-end.

The Model 64 rifle was a redesigned Model 55. The magazine tube projected about 4 inches from the fore-end, stock had a pistol grip and the front sight ramp was integral with the barrel. Calibers were 25-35, 30-30, 32 Win. Spec., and 219 Zipper.

Why? No doubt nostalgia and Westerns play a part, for certainly the gun is not perfection personified. But I'd say there are three solid practical reasons back of its universal popularity.

The Reasons Why

First off, the 94 carbine is just about the handiest big-game production rifle ever made. It's short — shorter than any front-locking bolt can be for the same length of barrel. It's light. Its slender steel breech, minus any projecting knobs, makes it easier to carry in the hand all day or slip in and out of a saddle scabbard or a vehicle rack than almost any other rifle. In ease and speed or operation it ranks very high. It whips up fast, the big hammer is thumbed back almost automatically as it comes up, the recoil is not disturbing and, for repeat shots the lever can be flipped easily and fast without moving the butt from the sights.

Relatively inexpensive, its ammunition can be found almost anywhere, the action rarely jams, and it can be relied on to keep working no matter how much it's neglected or abused. Well, almost. The damn things last forever. Two of my shooting acquaintances are still dropping mule deer regularly with 94s over 60 years old.

That's the second reason for its popularity — *ruggedness*. Townsmen who know nothing about gun care, farmers, trappers and prospectors, most of whom treat their rifles roughly, by the nature of their occupation, know it will keep working no matter how little tender loving care it receives.

Harold MacFarlane, gunsmith author of *Gunsmithing Simplified*, (New York and London, 1950-1964, 6 prtgs.) wrote in the *American Rifleman* for January 1949, pp. 33-34:

"Usually I tote a modern bolt gun with the latest in hunting scopes when rambling in the woods, but … when the larder is empty … I reach for the old 30-30 carbine. I know it's obsolete and the shell is a has-been, but for some reason deer die just as dead whether they are hit in the center or the edge of the heart with it. Too, most deer in timber country are killed within 50 yards.

"The point that interests me is the speed of handling of the little carbine. By the time the deer makes two jumps, I can perforate his hide with it …"

Third reason for the 94's popularity is the cartridges it chambers. For the gun's first 20 years or so, its smokeless loads seemed right snappy little numbers, but now they're called anemic, slow, not nearly flat-shooting enough.

But Joe Average Hunter doesn't need siz-

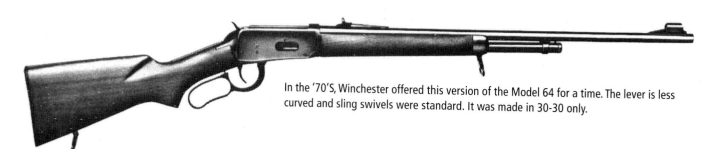

In the '70'S, Winchester offered this version of the Model 64 for a time. The lever is less curved and sling swivels were standard. It was made in 30-30 only.

zling speed, smashing power, and minimum bullet drop any more now than he ever did. He still doesn't practice enough to be an adequate long-range shot, he still shies from much recoil, he still hunts mostly deer. Shots in whitetail woods are still usually hurried, offhand, and well under 100 yards. In western mule deer hunting, too, despite what you read, 150 yards is a long shot and many a chance comes under 50.

Many hunters swore by the 25-35 in the old days. The most infallible mule-deer dropper I've known did all his shooting with a 25-35 till it wore out. But the 94 means the 30-30 and 32 Special, possibly the best deer cartridges ever designed for use by the ordinary meat hunter. They don't blow an animal into bloody burger like the big magnums; they don't whistle through deer at close range without visible effect, either, as some magnum bullets designed for heavy game will. Their bullets are slow, blunt-bowed, with a ballistic coefficient like a bad dream; still, they expand and penetrate reliably at all ordinary ranges, and they don't blow up if they hit brush, or deflect and whine off into the next county.

In a whitetail deer-kill survey taken by the *American Rifleman* in 1947, the 32 Special scored slightly better than the 30-06/220-gr. when it came to dropping a deer in its tracks with a hit in the heart area. The 30-30 170-gr. scored about 15% less. What were the only two calibers which scored 100% when all the others made only about 50%? The 300 Magnum and — wait for it — the 30-30 150-gr.!

What About Game Other Than Deer?

No less an authority than the late great Colonel Townsend Whelen used a 30-30 Model 94 years ago, when both man and gun were young, on Rocky Mountain goats, bighorn sheep, and mule deer. He wrote, (*Outdoor Life, October, 1922.*) years later:

"... I never saw any indication that the rifle lacked killing power for these animals, and in those days I was using the old Winchester soft-point cartridges, the 165-gr. bullet (at) 1960 foot seconds, as compared with the present 170-gr. bullet at 2200."

Colonel Whelen and the almost-as-famous Captain E. C. (Ned) Crossman had a lot of respect for the well-known Rocky Mountain guide, F.H. (Bert) Riggall, a man of vast and varied experience with guns and hunting. Riggall's own favorite calibers were probably the 30-06 and 25-06,

but in 1948 he wrote to me from his home in southwestern Alberta:

"I still have and use a 30-30, and have a great respect for the little shrimp. I have made a lot of clean kills at 150 to (occasionally) 300 yards, and with the latest loads it is a deadly little weapon. I reload for a great many local hunters, and the 30-30 with a 190-gr. 303 Savage bullet and 31 gr. of Dupont No. 3031 powder has killed scores of elk here in the last two or three years and is in great demand. I recently mounted a Weaver K2.5 scope on an *old* 30-30 carbine for a customer, and within a week he had fired two shots and got his buck and a bull. I felt like I was putting a $50 saddle on a $5 horse when I mounted it, but it turned out to be a fine combination!"

Another outdoorsman of wide and varied experience was Jim Osman, for many years game warden at Fernie in some of the best big-game country in North America. He bagged a record bighorn there around 1951 — with a 25-35. In an article in *True's Hunting Yearbook*, 1953, he said that most game in his mountain area was shot under 100 yards. For the occasional farther chance he found the 300 Magnum not enough better than his 30-06 to bother about, the 270 deadly on some shots and poor on others.

My 64 is accurate enough for fine prone shooting, but note that even in open country plant growth makes the prone position difficult. H. V. Stent photo.

Trappers and Indians used 30-30s to get their moose meat. The Indians, though reputedly poor shots, usually had a grizzly hide or two. The trappers, generally better-than-average marksmen, wasted few cartridges. "They seldom shoot beyond 75 yards. They simply sneak along a slough or creek until they find a moose, then pop him in the hump," Osman said.

In the May, 1957 *American Rifleman* S. H. Roberson, who had hunted and studied Rocky Mountain goats in Alaska for years, wrote:

"My personal preference (for goat hunting) is the 30-30 Winchester 94 because of its ruggedness, small size, and all-round convenience. I have used everything from 22 Hornet to 375 Improved Magnum effectively at various times …

"Most goat shooting in Alaska can be done at moderate range if one is willing to stalk his game. My longest shot at goat has been about 200 yards, and the 30-30 handled this very well."

Grizzlies?

A great many black bear have been taken with the 30-30, but how about grizzlies? Jim Osman wrote to me:

"I have shot four grizzlies with a 30-30. One chased my dog, and when he couldn't catch it, turned on me … I blew the top of his head off at about 30 yards, and that was that.

"I shot another big one (at) about 50 yards and the first shot broke his back and the second one finished him." He killed another along the trail once, as he wanted a hide, using only one shot. He shot his fourth grizzly in Yellowhead Pass from about 150 yards. "When hit he came down the slide bawling his head off. I'm afraid I got a little rattled and broke him up pretty bad with 6 shots. A grizzly bear is not as hard to kill as an elk or moose, providing you hit him hard the first time," he wrote.

Famous grizzly guide Jim Stanton, of Knight Inlet, B.C., where the big bears are almost as thick as blackberries, for years had only a 30-30 carbine to protect himself and his clients. His most exciting bear-shoot was probably in his pig-raising days when a mother grizzly chose one of his porkers to give her 2-year-old cub a lesson in killing. The cub was clumsy and the pig screamed bloody murder. Hearing it in his nearby cabin, Jim grabbed his always-loaded carbine and a box of shells, and ran out.

Firing wide to avoid hitting the pig, Jim kept shooting till the cub let go. The mother grizzly charged. Jim aimed and pulled the trigger. The gun was empty. Grabbing for his box of shells he spilled them on the ground. He bent and reached for one, and the grizzly was on him.

Jim swung the carbine up to use it as a club, the bear aimed a big paw to knock him headlong, but the prone pig came to life and darted between them. The grizzly struck at the pig, missed, angrily dashed after it, then stopped, whirled, and charged again at Jim. He'd found one cartridge just in time to drop her.

For moose and elk the 30-30 will certainly do the trick on side or front shots up to 150 yards or so, but something with more poop seems to me desirable for farther ranges.

Admittedly, the unglamorous truth is that in most men's hunting far-off chances at game are rare, and hunters skilled enough to take them rarer. Most of us should either pass them up or stalk to closer ranges, where the 30-30 might well be adequate.

Raking rear end shots on moose or elk probably shouldn't be tried by most of us with any rifle; a gut-shot beast can go a long way and, if not lost, be a helluva mess to clean. It'd be better to shoot high, thus getting a paralyzing spine shot or a clean miss.

Or use my friend Thor Strimbold's trick. In 50 years of woods-wandering and gun-experimenting in northern British Columbia, he has killed many moose and much other game with various small calibers (25-20, 6mm, 222, etc.). Once, using a 30-30 Model 94, he came on two bull moose fighting, and at 45 yards shot the one whose rear was toward him "just below the exhaust port." The bull turned and Thor dropped him with a shot behind the ear. With grouse handloads — a 170-gr. lead alloy bullet at about 1400 fs.

In his lifetime of big-game hunting Thor has lost only one head of game shot at; he believes that bullet placement is much more important than "knockdown power," which he considers largely a myth. Nevertheless, he feels that, generally speaking, once-a-year hunters may be better off with more than minimum power, as long as they are not disturbed by the recoil.

What About 94 Accuracy?

Obviously it's accurate enough for game shooting for most people, but what can it do on targets?

In March, 1933, Colonel Whelen reported in *Outdoor Life* that he had fired 17 groups from a Model 55, 10-shot strings at 100 yards, using 7 brands of ammo and 5 bullet weights. The groups varied from 6.6 to 2.9 inches, with an average of 4.4 inches. Three-shot or 5-shot groups would have been tighter, of course.

Another famous arms authority, Major Charles Askins, also reported in *Outdoor Life* the same year that he had tested a 26-inch barreled, full-magazine 94 at 100 yards with just one brand of ammunition and one bullet weight. His four 10-shot groups measured 2.75, 1.88, 2.63, and 2.0 inches.

I once tested a Model 64 myself, getting some God-awful groups at first. After some practice the 64 made groups as small as 1.63 inches for 5 spaced shots at 100 yards with commercial ammo. With a handload the rifle liked it put 5 into 1.5 inches at 100 yards, 5 into 3.0 at 200, and 4.5 at 300.

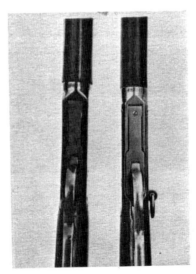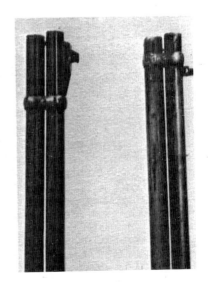

Underside of receivers on old model and post-1964 are different. Note bevelled edges on old model, and the saddle ring, too. Big difference between early and current carbines is the location of sight and band. Early front sight was a blade pinned into a slot in lug. If it got wrecked a coin could be whittled into shape and stuck in. H. V. Stent photos.

For any hunting rifle with iron sights, that's pretty good going, and maybe I crowed a bit to a friend who'd been an exhibition shot for the CIL cartridge makers — he'd perforate a tossed tomato can 3 or 4 times before it grounded, or throw up 3 small oranges at once and blow them into a Sunkist spray in the air, using a 94. He got groups, with a 64, of 1.88 and 1.44 inches. Then he took the old take-down 94 with 26-inch barrel that he used for his exhibition shooting and grouped 1.13 and 1.19 inches. Iron sights, factory ammo.

Mind you, don't expect a 94 carbine off the dealer's shelf to shoot that well, unless you let the barrel get completely cold again after every shot. Some will, but usually when the barrel warms and expands, the front band (and frequently the forearm), becomes too tight. This puts enough pressure on the barrel to change its point of impact, sometimes drastically.

Top: Model 94 with half magazine, fancy grade, take-down. Notice similarity to later Model 64.

Middle: A 300-yard group on a deer-sized target with a 24-inch barreled 30-30, showing accuracy and amount of drop. Aim was a 6 o'clock on big black disc, the rifle sighted to hit point of aim at 150 yards, 2 inches high at 90. H. V. Stent photo.

Bottom: The Model 94 "Antique," introduced a few years ago.

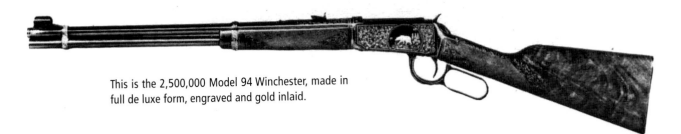

This is the 2,500,000 Model 94 Winchester, made in full de luxe form, engraved and gold inlaid.

A bit of work on the front band and fore-end, as detailed by Helbig and Cain in "Lever Action Rifles" in the 1965 *GUN DIGEST*, will cure this. They found that working over two 94 carbines shrank groups from over 3 inches to 2.21 with handloads and a best group of 1.55. Thor Strimbold has got 100-yard groups of an inch in a worked-over 94 carbine with an excellent barrel and peepsights.

Sometimes the working-over seems unnecessary. Lyman's *Reloading Handbook 45* mentions a 1 ¼ inch 50-yard group with an as-issued 30-30 M94 carbine and open iron sights. John Amber in the 1977 *GUN DIGEST* tells of 5-shot groups measuring .73-and .81-inch made at 50 yards with a Bicentennial 94 and open sights.

So much for the guns. The cartridge will shoot closer yet. In the 1950s Al Barr and Philip Sharpe (Barr related, in a letter to H. V. Stent dated March 26, 1951, that he had shot ½-inch groups at 100 yards, using a heavy-barreled 94. Sharpe's report was in the American Rifleman for March 1952, pp. 47-48.) each gave the 30-30 a real test in a bull gun with target scope, and got groups as small as .55-inch at 100 yards, with their best handloads.

Could — or should — the 94 be updated and improved? Ken Waters has repeatedly argued in GUN DIGEST that the rifle needs more powerful loads. Strimbold agrees, but would like to see the rifle-carbine A) Returned to the old easier-to-carry receiver bottom, and B) The barrel given more "breathing room." A split front band fitted around the front sight ramp, as on the 444 Marlin, would do this. Or changing the encircling carbine-type front band to the sort on the Model 64 and the old long 94, which was, in fact, put on the Yellow Boy carbine for the Centennial.

Still, the old 94 does pretty well on game as it is, and 94 sales are going strong, what with growing hunter demand and a ready response to special issues — no less than 5 commemoratives came out in 1977-78, among them the Cherokee in 44-40.

I'll drink to that, and also to a bit more power. It may easily be obtained in any 30-30 by rechambering it to Ackley's 30-30 Improved. Standard cartridges could still be used, and the reshaped fire-formed cases hand-loaded almost to 300 Savage levels. I've chronographed 2500 fps with 150-gr. bullets and 2325 with 170s in a 20-inch barrel, one which gave only 2200 and 2100 fps for the same bullets in standard factory loads. Too, I've loaded 190-gr. bullets for a heavy elk load a la Riggall.

How about a brand new 94 caliber? Waters and Strimbold suggest a 7mm, and Strimbold would like to see a 33.

Even if we don't get them (and we probably won't), it's safe to predict that the Model 94 will continue to sell well. Some 85 years ago, Winchester, in their catalog introducing the new rifle wrote:

"We believe that no repeating rifle system ever made will appeal to the eye and understanding of the rifleman as this will, and that use will continue to warrant first impressions."

How right they were.

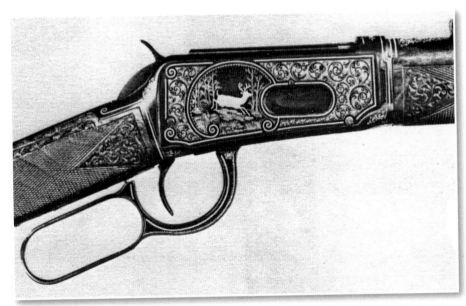

Winchester makes its milestone production guns with all-out embellishment, used to bestow them as gifts, and now sometimes auctions them for good causes. This is a close-up of Model 94 #2,500,000.

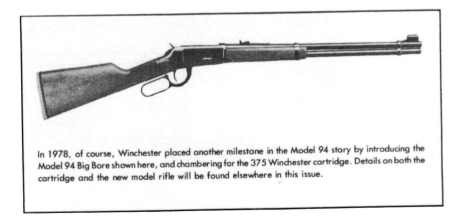

In 1978, of course, Winchester placed another milestone in the Model 94 story by introducing the Model 94 Big Bore shown here, and chambering for the 375 Winchester cartridge. Details on both the cartridge and the new model rifle will be found elsewhere in this issue.

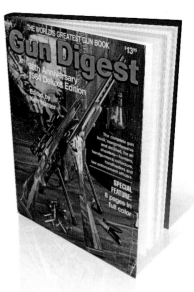

MODEL SEVEN:
A Really New Look

by LAYNE SIMPSON

"Let's build a new bolt action rifle."

"You got to be kidding; we already offer more options than a dog does fleas."

"No; I mean something so new and exciting that it'll have all the mountain stumblers, saddle bums, woods rats and even ladies and kids slavering at our doorstep."

"But we already have the Model 788 carbine and it puts most of its bullets in one ragged hole at a hundred paces."

"No argument there, but let's build a pretty one. In fact, let's sort of resurrect the old Model 600."

(EDITOR'S NOTE: Believe it or not, testing rifles is not always exciting. Thus, Contributing Editor Simpson was not able to resist concocting this conversation between two Remington employees. KW)

"Now I know you're playing with less than a full deck — they almost burned us at the stake for its ventilated rib alone."

"Forget the past and think about this; what would we get if we took the old Model 600; removed its squarish stock; threw away its Delrin trigger guard; turned out its ribbed barrel; discarded its fire-control system and knocked off its dog-leg bolt handle?"

"We'd have a Model 600 receiver and bolt body."

"Right; and we'd also have the foundation for building a rifle which would do everything the Model 600 did and more; and it could be prettier to boot. Here's how we'll do it:

"We'll keep the front section of the Model 600's receiver wall extended out over the bolt, and we'll redesign for smoother bolt operation by keeping the follower from

There is nothing wrong with rifles or ladies that are lady-like.

contacting the bolt body.

"Let's see now, the Model 600's tang is not so shapely so let's flatten it down a bit. Next, we eliminate that dumb bolt release, and we'll can the safety thumb-piece which is a bit larger than it has to be."

"How do we do all of that without busting the design budget?"

"It's easy; we just fit a Model 700 fire-control system which has a bolt release just forward of its trigger piece, as well as a much neater safety lever. And, we'll fix the safety so it doesn't lock the bolt so the fellows can unload with the safety on."

"Now what do we do with the bolt?"

"That's easy too; we merely use one from a Model 700 except we leave the checkering off its knob. Looks kinda nice, doesn't it? Just for good measure, the bolt body might as well be engine turned, and we'll make it a real lightweight by chopping the barrel at 18 ½ inches and tapering it to a .550-inch muzzle. We can top it off with adjustable rear and ramped front sights.

"Now, what about the trigger guard/floorplate assembly, will it be blind or hinged, or aluminum or, heavens forbid, steel?"

"Blind magazines are not quite so popular as hinged floorplates while steel is awfully expensive and besides, only a few old die-hards complain about "pot metal" in rifles anymore, sooo; wait a minute, what if we stamped the unit of steel and yet did such a neat job, it would not be recognized as such from over two feet away? Hey, looks even better than we thought it would. Pretty isn't it?"

"Sure beats the heck out of aluminum."

"Now let's really get fancy and conceal the front guard screw by shifting the floorplate hinge forward. Nice, huh? Wonder what the boys over in Southport will think about that?"

"Oops, you forgot about the floorplate latch."

"Time's awasting, let's just stand on our heads and throw something together. Besides, everything else will be so pretty, who would notice such a minor detail? See, you just push right here with the end of your fingernail and — — well I'll be darned, it worked a minute ago."

"Heck, if we make it perfect, gun writers won't be able to sound objective in their reviews."

"Let's go pure classic with the wood and put a little less drop in its buttstock. We won't even think about such things as Monte Carlo humps and cheek rests. We'll really bug their eyeballs with a cute schnabel forend. How about those smoothly flowing lines? We'll leave off the shine and cut checkering at 18 lines per inch is plenty.

"Holy Ilion, what a beauty we've built, and it weighs less than six and a half pounds too. It handles like greasy lightning. We'll sell zillions of them. What will we chamber it for?"

"222, 243, 6mm, 7mm-08 and 308 Winchester."

"What's the 222 for?"

"Haven't you ever heard of a walking varmint rifle? Let's get tough and strap a 16× Model-T on the 7-08 and see how she does on paper."

"Hey, not bad at all. What should we say when they ask how well it shoots?"

"Oh, I think maybe two minutes of angle with factory loads and one to one and a half with handloads."

"But what about those that measure well under an inch?"

"We'll keep those under our hats because they wouldn't believe us anyhow. Let them find out for themselves."

"What's left to do?"

"We've got to name her. Got any ideas?"

"I don't know; it's the seventh bolt action carbine we've built and all our centerfire models start with Seven.––"

— ONE GOOD GUN —

BROWNING'S T-BOLT I LIKE

by G.N. TED DENTAY

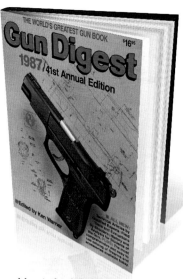

 WHEN dozens of guns go through your hands every year and you keep on turning back to the old standby, you could call it your one good gun. In my case, it's a much-battered-and-used southpaw's Browning T-Bolt which is more than an assembly of steel and wood to me. It's the memories, the whiffs of my history sticking like glue to it. And the certainty that there are going to be more experiences attached to it.

My T-Bolt began life with me as a good deal. When people were discovering that T-Bolts were eminently collectable, I discovered the last bargain. No one wanted the left-handed rifle, so I got it for $95 when they were already $200 and more on the open market. A *goood* deal.

Since that time, a lot of ammo has gone up its spout. Some years saw 10,000 rounds consumed in the ceaseless quest for dragonflies. Other years saw a versimillitude of assorted 22 BB and CB caps for the famous rat hunts. And then, to balance everything out, there were the years of hypervelocity 22s like Stinger and Yellowjacket. They were best at assassinating huge icicles which coated rock faces in winter.

It's hard to say how many rounds in total went into knocking dragonflies out of the sky. Ten years worth of consumption must have totalled in excess of 100,000 rounds. I think we managed a total of ten confirmed kills so the dragonfly population wasn't much reduced.

Hot, lazy summer days spent stretched out comfortably on a hillside overlooking a waterlily-strewn pond. That's the stuff of memories. Darting, dodging metallic-hued dragonflies jinking around small fountains of water thrown up by impacting bullets. They always seemed to be able to predict the Long Rifle's trajectories, but it just added to the fun. The tang of powder smoke hung over the whole area for hours.

The most fun was undoubtedly when we,

being Canadians and 100 miles or so above U.S. law, got hold of a couple of cartons of Gevelot 22 Long Rifle tracers. We awaited dusk with delicious anticipation of the fiery streaks crossing the pond. It didn't matter much if we connected with the darting insect life. Watching the bullet's track was harmless fun enough. There were perfect sandbank butts behind the pond which would satisfy any safety requirements incumbent upon us. The little red-tipped 22s worked flawlessly out of the T-Bolt, but they wouldn't function reliably in a Gevelot semi-auto.

Then there was the season in which the T-Bolt accounted for dozens of dead rats.

Our office was in the second story of a commercial office. Next door there was a construction yard, in which hundreds of pieces of forms, timbers and scaffolding were stored. In the middle of this mess was an office trailer and beneath it the residence-of-record for a large, and unpleasant German shepherd dog.

Every evening when the workmen left, a large helping of kibble mixed with canned food was deposited into his feed bowl. And every evening, when the workmen left, a horde of rats would emerge from under the piles of scaffolding and descend upon the hapless creature's food.

Now, we had no love lost for this miserable example of the canine world, but we couldn't bear to see food stolen out from under its very cowardly nose. So the decision was made to snipe the rats from 50 yards. The technical problem was that we couldn't use standard velocity ammunition of any kind because people lived nearby. We quickly settled on CCI's Mini-Caps, the low-velocity 22 Short look-alike. Its report was absolutely minimal out of the T-Bolt's 22-inch barrel, but it killed with a well-placed shot, unlike the 6mm round-ball and conical-bullet Flobert caps we'd tried before.

When sunset wrapped its roseate mantle around the area, the aluminum-sashed win-

dow would quietly slide back and the muzzle of the rifle would poke out an inch or two. Then the carnage would begin. The brown carpet of rats would predictably flow over the dog's dishes and the diminutive report of the T-Bolt would make itself known.

It took only a few moments of quickly working the action before there were three or four twitching bodies on the ground and an equivalent pile of gleaming brass empties on the carpeted office floor. Then the rest of the lemming-like rush would get the message and melt back into the gathering shadows and the dog would get to eat what balance of his food the miserable creatures had left.

Winter came with monotonous regularity, putting a crimp into usual shooting activities. So, with cross-country skis and snowshoes, we safaried out for icicle shooting. Ice makes the finest of biodegradable targets.

Trap and Skeet shooters like to see the black puff of dust remaining where once a clay pigeon flew. We delighted in the fountains of glittering ice-shards tumbling in the winter's sun following a direct hit with any of the more potent crop of hyper-velocity 22s. No pre-Cambrian rock face was safe and that little T-Bolt took more than its fair share.

After such honorable service, totalling hundreds of thousands of rounds, you'd think the T-Bolt would receive a reasonable retirement. It hasn't. Now it sits behind the door of the new farmhouse, ready to do service in supplying pheasant, pigeon and rabbit for the pot. The experiences of low velocity ammunition and the best of the hyper-velocity gives it the flexibility needed in a constant companion.

Even at that, things don't really change much. That new place has its very own pond, complete with dragon flies. There aren't too many rats around, but the icicles come out with predictable regularity each winter. The T-Bolt has not retired; it may not ever … not ever.

THOSE PLASTIC
REMINGTONS

by DONALD M. SIMMONS

N THE SPRING of the dark Depression year of 1933, E.I. Du Pont de Nemours & Company took a sick Remington Arms Company under its wing. Remington at that time not only made firearms, which were their principal product, but also controlled a large ammunition company and had been dabbling in such things as cash registers, typewriters, and pocketknives.

Du Pont sent over some of its top management people to help get Remington back on its feet. Their first task was to modernize the existing Remington line and all popular Remington rifles went through a face-lifting process. For example, in the high-powered line, the slide-action Model 14 and autoloading Model 8 were cosmetically upgraded to the Models 141 and 81. So, too, in the line of repeating 22-caliber rifles: the autoloading Model 24 was renamed the Model 241 and the popular slide-action Model 12 became the Model 121. All this was accomplished in the Depression days of 1936.

The arrival of World War II more or less put sporting arms on the back burner, but with the coming of peace, new guns began to come out of Remington's Research and Development department. A new philosophy of having an entire line of firearms sharing a large number of parts and even sharing in common some of the more complicated subassemblies was instigated at Remington.

And during the late 1950s, spurred by Du Pont, Remington began to plan an almost entirely plastic rifle. This rifle was to be an autoloading 22 weighing less than five pounds, and was to be priced near to that of competition. Remington asked the chemical engineers at Du Pont to come up with a plastic that could replace both the wooden

WORLD 22 RIFLE
AERIAL SHOOTING RECORD
100,010 WOOD BLOCKS—6 MISSES
SET BY TOM FRYE
REMINGTON ARMS COMPANY, INC.
1959

Model 66MB Mohawk Brown

Model 66AB Apache Black

Model 66BD Black Diamond

Model 76MB Mohawk Brown

Model 11 bolt action — box magazine

Model 12 bolt action — tubular magazine

stock and the receiver. This was a tall order and here are the specs given to the Du Pont chemical development department:

1. The material must be capable of forming any shape desired.

2. It must have a high tensile impact and flexural strength.

3. It must have high abrasion resistance.

4. It must have high resistance to heat distortion.

5. It must be resistant to cold temperatures.

6. It must, if exposed to a flame, not continue to burn when that flame is removed.

7. It must be impervious to solvents, oils, mild acids, alkalis, fungus, rodents, and insects.

8. It must have a finish that is easy to repair.

9. It must be light in weight.

10. It must hold permanent colors.

11. It must have no corrosive effect on other parts.

12. It must be self-lubricating and dimensionally stable.

In less than four months, Du Pont's engineers came up with Nylon Zytel-101. This wonderful plastic had all of those prerequisites and then some. Because of mould cost, the first model was not moulded; instead, a nylon prototype was machined out of bar nylon, and this amazing rifle was able to be fired 75,000 times. This initial testing established the feasibility of using plastic in the manufacture of a gun.

The new Remington family of plastic rifles began with an autoloading 22 rifle called their Model 66. Nylon Zytel-101 only came in basic colors like red, blue, black and yellow but the engineers at Remington found that they could mix these colors and arrive at a wood-like shade. The wood-colored mixture was called Number 66, thus the name of the rifle. Production began in November of 1958. The Model 66 has been so popular that a dead-ringer copy has been imported from Brazil by Firearms Import & Export Corp. (F.I.E.) of Hialeah, Florida.

The Remington Model 66 has a moulded Zylon-101 stock, which is injection moulded in two halves, of which one half has a tongue and the other a groove. They are later bonded together to form a strong hollow assembly replacing three normal sections, the buttstock and forearm, of course, are two; the middle section is the rifle's receiver. Remington calls Color Number 66 "Mohawk Brown." The buttplate, the forearm tip, and the pistol grip cap are all black plastic bonded in place. Each has an attractive white spacer. There are two reinforcing screws with nuts under the receiver cover, and there is one more under the ivory-white diamonds on each side of the forearm. The magazine is in the butt of the rifle, loaded through the butt-plate, holding 14 22 Long Rifle standard or high-speed cartridges.

The striker (hammer) is either an investment steel casting or a forging which requires no machining, except for the two-diameter hole down its center; the bolt appears to be a steel machined forging. The two parts run in grooves in the self-lubricating nylon receiver. The other parts are either stainless steel or mild steel stampings or, like the trigger guard and the trigger itself, are also plastic.

The barrel measures just over 19½ inches, and is clamped to the receiver by a screw-secured barrel bracket in a cradle formed within the stock. When, rarely, the gun needs cleaning, the barrel can be easily removed and cleaned from the breech.

One of the main advantages of the Model 66 from a manufacturer's point of view is that the gun could be assembled with little or no hand fitting. The total weight is about 4½ pounds, and the initial price was $49.95. In spite of the lack of hand fitting, trigger pulls of all the plastic Rem-

Remington's guarantee of the Nylon stock; this decal was on each one.

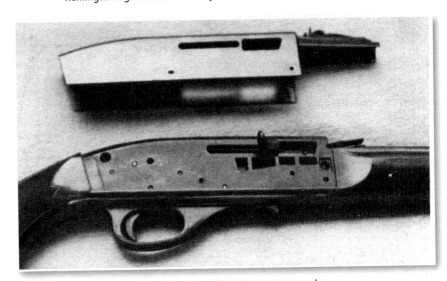

Right side Mohawk 10-C, cover removed.

ington rifles I've seen have been excellent.

In 1959, the Armalite Corporation of Costa Mesa, California, introduced their AR-7 which had a plastic stock, into which the entire rifle could be stored. One of the two big differences between the AR-7 and the Remington 66 is the fact that the 66's bolt runs in a nylon receiver but the bolt of the AR-7 is in a metallic die-cast receiver. The second difference is that the size of the mould required to make the entire Remington stock is much larger. The AR-7 is still made today by Charter Arms Corp. of Stratford, Connecticut.

In the early 1970s, Winchester offered their Model 270, a slide-action, tubular magazine, 22-caliber rifle with a Cycolac

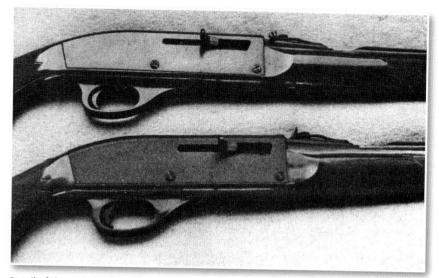

Detail of the early (top) and late covers and rear sights.

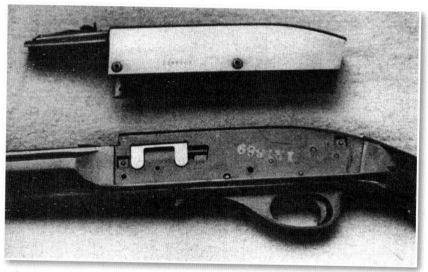

Left side Mohawk 10-C, cover removed.

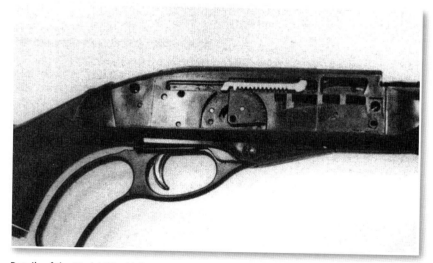

Details of the Model 76 with its cover removed. Notice the rack and pinion action — most ingenious.

plastic stock and forearm. Again, as in the case of the Armalite gun, the mould size of the Model 66 overshadows the Winchester; this rifle never seemed to be very popular with the plastic and was discontinued in the mid-1970s.

Today we hear much about the plastic Austrian Glock 9mm pistols; someone stirred up the feeling they might be able to pass through airport security without detection. However, the Remington Nylon 66 rifle never caused a ripple to the delicate sensitivity of the Ban the Gun groups. It had a steel bolt that recoiled in a plastic receiver, not as in the Glock 17 a steel slide running in steel clips, albeit a plastic frame, too. Both the Glock and the Remington rifle in its later box magazine model appear to have plastic magazines in which only the magazine spring and the cartridges themselves are visible under X-ray. The Glock 17 also has a detectable sheet metal liner while the Remington is all plastic, save for only a small metal "U" clip that holds the top rear of the magazine lips together. The most remarkable point is that the production of the Remington plastic rifle preceded the Glock plastic pistol by almost 30 years!

At the time Remington introduced the Model 66, they still had two other autoloading 22s on the market: the old Model 550-1 and the newer Model 552. The Model 550-1 was on its way out, but the 552 is still in the Remington catalog today. At the time of the Model 66's introduction, the 550-1 sold for $46.75, and the 552 sold for $52.25. The Model 66 acted as a sort of "middle of the line" gun at $49.95.

Sales figures for the Model 66 and its spinoffs are remarkable; at no time through 1981, where my year-to-year production figures end, did it sell under 20,000 rifles per year, and in the year after its introduction, 1959, almost 80,000 were produced. The average yearly production was almost 40,000 rifles. What led to the almost instant public acceptance of this revolutionary rifle? I think the answer is its reliability. Ever since the first 22 autoloading rifle came on the market, there has been a great doubt in the public's mind about performance. The first American autoloader was the Winchester Model 1903 which was a quality rifle, but even with its own special ammo, it could occasionally malfunction, especially if it was not cleaned often enough. The Remington Model 66, dirty or clean, wet or dry, just kept rolling along. With this well-earned reputation, it is easy to see why shooters bought it in large quantities.

The two correct tools for disassembling — a 50 Centavo Mexican coin and a round-ground screwdriver.

The Model 66 has been used to establish endurance records in aerial target shooting. In 1959, Mr. Tom Frye, a representative for Remington, made history as an aerial shooter by firing a set of three Remington Model 66 rifles for 100,010 rounds in 14 days. He only missed six of the hand-thrown wooden blocks in all those shots, a record that still stands today. Each rifle fired 33,000 times and none had a malfunction. This also stands as a testimonial to the sound design of the Remington plastic rifle.

In order to avoid shooter rejection of their PLASTIC gun because of its plastic receiver, the designers at Remington covered the nylon receiver with a blued steel stamping. They must have decided that as long as they were going to disguise the receiver with a steel shell, they might as well make the shell serve some useful purpose. With this in mind, the receiver cover has the rear sight assembly riveted to it. The rear sight is screw-adjustable for both windage and elevation, which is unusual for a rifle in this price range. The cover is grooved so a scope can be mounted. It has been found that when a scope is mounted and the gun is too-rigidly gripped the point of impact may be changed. The steel cover also holds the ejector into the receiver. Finally, the flat spring that tensions the cartridge feed guide is mounted by a rivet to the cover's underside. The original receiver cover had no serial number stamped on it until 1968, when the federal law required that all guns have serial numbers. This requirement must have given Remington a fit, because their receiver was plastic and completely covered. They ended up with the cover stamped instead on the left side.

The serial numbering of the Model 66 and its spinoffs started in 1967 at S/N 400000 and went to 419011, but at that time the number was stamped on the underside of the barrel just aft of the front sight. In 1968 the S/N started with 419012 and went to S/N 473710. In December of 1968, the serial was changed to 2100000, which accounts for the seemingly high serial numbers seen.

When this series of serial numbers reached 2599999 in February of 1977, the letter "A" was added and the S/N went back to A2100000 again. In the last production year of 1988, the serial numbers would be in the A2360000 range. Also, today's numbers are stamped much deeper than they had been previously, for longer and clearer legibility. These serial numbers indicate that even in the last year of production, Remington was making an average of whopping 27,000 Nylons per year!

There is one item on a true blowback action that is nonfunctional — the extractor. When a blowback gun cycles, the shell acts as a piston, driving the bolt rearward without the extractor doing anything. The extractor *is* functional, of course, when an *unfired* cartridge is withdrawn from the gun's breech manually. To verify this, I removed the extractor from one and the rifle functioned perfectly. If the Model 66 is to be fired as a single shot, a loaded cartridge is laid in the ejection port with the rifle slightly slanted. The bolt is retracted and released and the round will automatically

be chambered. Also, no matter if the rifle is held right side up or upside down or any place in between it will keep firing.

The Model 66 was just the beginning of a family of 22-caliber plastic rifles to be made by Remington Arms. The first change, begun in early 1959, was not in the model of the rifle, but rather in the addition of a new color for its stock. "Seneca Green" was the name given to the new stock's mottled dark olive color; this color was discontinued in 1961. The model was called 66SG. Still retaining the basic Model 66, the Apache Black color was added in late 1962, and called the Model 66AB; it was also called the "Presentation" grade. This new variation to the 66 was black-stocked with the receiver cover and the barrel chromium-plated — an impressive combination of colors. The plating of the steel parts was discontinued in 1983, but the black stock was available as the Model 66BD, "Black Diamond."

In the momentous year of 1962, four new models were added to Remington's Nylon gun line. A lever-action repeater in 22

Model	Years Introduced	List Price Then
66	1958	$49.95
66SG	1959	$49.95
66AB	1962	$54.95
66GS	1962	$59.95
76	1962	$59.95
11	1962	$36.95
12	1962	$39.95
10	1962	$25.95
150 Year Commemorative	1966	
77	1970	$54.95
Mohawk 10-C	1971	$54.95
Bi-Centennial Commemorative	1976	$84.95
Black Diamond	1978	$84.95
Apache 77	1987	$109.95

Long Rifle only, the Model 76, was dubbed the Trail Rider. This gun has an extremely short throw on its lever and was available in Mohawk Brown and Apache Black. The internal mechanism is something to behold. The designers of this spinoff had to work with what they had, using the Model 66 stock and bolt. They came up with a locked-breech lever-action rifle starting from an autoloader. They created a very short stroke — about 30 degrees — lever action with a rack and pinion reminiscent of the old Bullard lever-action rifle. The only fly in the ointment of interchangeability was that the barrel, the magazine, and the sights were the only parts borrowed as-is from the Model 66. Could they have gone on from there and substituted a pump forearm for the lever? I would guess Remington had this in mind, but the lack of Model 76 sales changed their plans.

entirely different from the one used in the others.

None of these spinoffs really caught on and by 1964 all four models were dropped. Some rare combinations were also sold; the bolt-action Nylons were occasionally made with Seneca Green stocks, and also unusual was the Model 66, made to shoot 22 Shorts (only) called the "Gallery Special Model".... 66GS; this rifle, in a world that had forgotten the small town carnival. These relatively rare rifles were introduced in 1962 and terminated in 1981. The "Gallery Special" uses a lot of different parts in its manufacture, the bolt and the striker and their respective springs are different for functional reasons, while a counter chain retainer and a cartridge deflector (typical shooting gallery hardware) are added. In 1966 Remington made the Model 66 a Commemorative celebrating

Remington's 150th year; it had an embossed receiver cover. Lastly, and probably the rarest, was the smooth bore 22 Nylon Model 10 single shot, a bolt-action shotgun.

A lot of confusion exists as to which model plastic rifle is which, all of which can be readily resolved by looking at any rifle's black pistol grip cap where the full model nomenclature will be found. There is also the Remington bolt-action single shot handgun with a nylon plastic stock, the Model XP-100, which was introduced in 1963.

The next spinoff from the Model 66 — in 1970 — was the Model 77, a 5-shot box magazine, autoloading Nylon rifle. This magazine, with the exception of its spring and strength clip discussed before, is all plastic. The shooting public seemed to want more magazine capacity and a 10-shot magazine was soon offered as an accessory. In 1971 the Model 77 was renamed the Mohawk 10-C and came with a 10-shot magazine as standard equipment. The original Model 77 was phased out in 1971 and the Mohawk 10-C lasted until 1978. It was a promotional rifle offered to the distributors in large quantities at special discount. At this writing, the only surviving Model 66 is the promotional rifle called the Apache 77 which today is being sold at discount houses such as K-Mart for about $109.95. These latest of the Nylons have their metal parts finished in a jet black with a black sand-blasted painted finish on the external metal parts and the stock/receiver is a dark olive blue-green; there is a 10-round magazine. In September 1987 these new rifles, a cross between the rebirth of the Mohawk 10-C and the Black Diamond were on sale at K-Mart for the low price of $84.97, a real bargain!

One can see by my compilation of list prices that Remington was competitive, but the shooting public didn't take to the other

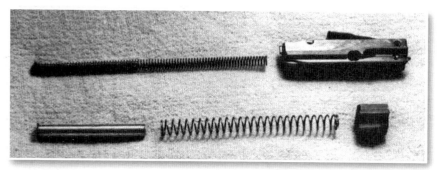

Top: Bolt and hammer, with their springs and guides, in their correct positions.

Plastic trigger guard detail.

The other new models were bolt actions, but with the Model 66 type of stock and sights, and there the similarity ended. The Nylon Model 11 has a steel detachable box magazine, six-shot, 22 Short, Long, or Long Rifle — later there was a 10-shot magazine. The Model 12 is the same type of rifle with a 22 Short or 15 Long Rifle-length tubular magazine under the barrel. In late 1962, Remington announced a low cost Nylon-stocked single shot bolt-action rifle, the Model 10, which, as a safety feature, went on safety each time it was cocked. Strangely, with Remington's great interest in interchangeability, none of the bolt-action rifles shared parts with the Model 66 that could have been the same. As an example, the white diamond that covers the screw in the bolt-action line is

Model	Years Made	Quantity
66	1958-To Date	(By 1981) 956062
66 Seneca Green	1959–1962	42500
76	1962–1964	26947
11	1962–1964	22423
12	1962–1964	27551
10	1962–1964	10670
150 Year Commemorative	1966	3792
77	1970–1973	15327
Mohawk 10-C	1971–1975	(By 1972) 5601
Bi-Cent Commemorative	1976	

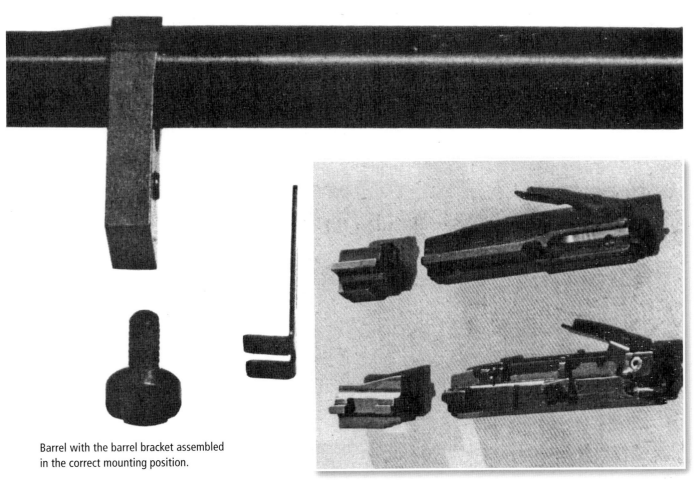

Barrel with the barrel bracket assembled in the correct mounting position.

Bolt and striker of a regular Model 66 over the special lightened parts of a Gallery Special.

plastic rifles like they did to the Model 66. Also note every price was 5 cents short of the next highest dollar.

The two U.S. patents issued to Remington Arms to cover the Model 66 and the subsequent spinoffs are 3,023,527 and 3,027,811, and they cover both the use of plastics to form combination stock/receiver, and the disconnector system used in this fine rifle. Patent number 3,023,527, applied for in January of 1956, was issued on March 6, 1962. It covers the rifle and could be considered the basic specific patent for the whole family of rifles that it eventually spawned. The patent is in the joint names of Wayne E. Leek, of Ilion, New York, which is the town where Remington is located, and Charles H. Morse of Herkimer, New York, which is a smaller town just south of Ilion. These men were the leaders of a design team which put together the Model 66.

The second patent, referred to in detail in the first patent, is number 3,027,811 filed April 29, 1958 and issued April 3, 1962. The patent is in the name of Homer W. Young of Ilion, New York, and covers the ingenious

sear and disconnector system using sheet metal stampings as found in the Model 66 et al.

Both patents were assigned to Remington Arms Co., as these men were employees, and both patents make for very interesting reading, although like all patents, you have to read and reread them to get the meat of their disclosures. In the Leek/Morse patent, there is one section that restates in a few words the entire principle of the Young patent so that you don't have to be looking at the two patents all the time. Also in the Leek/Morse patent there is a very interesting section describing the competitor's plastics that could be used to make the rifle's stock/ receiver instead of using Du Pont's Zytel. Also here we are told that Du Pont's Teflon could be used but it was then too expensive and too difficult to mould.

There is always a lot to learn in reading patents. In all the drawings included in the patents, there is no cartridge feeder guide shown because, obviously, it had not yet been found necessary to the smooth feeding of the autoloading rifle. Also, from the

patents we see that Remington was not sure whether to use a more or less standard cross-bolt manual safety behind the trigger or the top of the pistol grip sliding shotgun-type safety. They ended up with the latter.

The Leek/Morse patent shows an extremely complicated adjustable rear sight that was replaced in production by a much simpler and more efficient one. The patent shows a double screw-adjustable windage setup, while the early production sight had two wheels, one for adjustment of elevation and the other windage; later the windage wheel was replaced by a very small slotted screw. Both the screws are peened over so they can't fall off during shooting.

The action of the 66 is very interesting in that it uses a sear block mechanism. In this system the sear itself is free to pivot out of engagement with the striker against its own spring tension. This is because it is overridden by the much stronger cocked striker spring tension. All this above movement is prevented by the disconnector/ sear block stopping any unlocking movement of the sear. When the trigger is pulled, the disconnector/sear block moves forward and unlocks the sear which releases the striker. When the bolt, after firing, blows rearward driving the striker back, the disconnector/sear block is detached from the trigger, which allows the striker to be locked in the cocked position. In addition to the normal function just described, the disconnector/sear block prevents accidental jar firing of the rifle.

A design patent was also issued to three men, Robert P. Kelly, James S. Martin, and Wayne E. Leek. This type of patent is good for 14 years and this partially explains why the F.I.E. rifle can look so much like the Remington Model 66!

The quantities of these various models of Nylon guns made are very interesting in that the numbers of some of the models are quite, quite low. On the other hand, all the Nylons would have passed 1 million rifles in 1983 at the previously established rate of 40,000 per year.

In writing about the Remington plastic rifles, I really don't need to proof fire them because both I and so many others have tested them so often that everybody knows of their reliability. I did have two Mohawk 10-Cs in my collection that I thought would interest the readers to test. That is because one of them went back to the factory very

every 25 rounds. I cured it by, replacing the entire receiver cover assembly; I suspect the cover-mounted cartridge feed guide spring was not putting quite the required tension on the guide itself.

The other Mohawk is serial number 2417818 made in June of the same year, 1974, and is unmarked as ever having been returned for repairs. It has never malfunctioned in firing hundreds of rounds. Thus we have two Mohawk 10-Cs made within four months of each other; one is a good guy and the other is a black sheep, a rare one.

Changes in the logo stamped on the Nylon Remington barrels: The original logo stamped on the barrel in the open space just in front of the rear sight was "PAT. PEND." over "22 L.R. ONLY" plus the date code and the final inspector's stamp. Later the PAT. PEND. was dropped as the patent was granted and the stylized word "Remington" was added. Most Nylons I have seen also have the oval stamp with "REP" on the right rear of the barrel. This. we understand. means "Remington's English Proofed." In the early 1980s, Remington started to use a much larger stamp on the barrel behind the front sight. It read: "REMINGTON 22 LONG RIFLE ONLY." The date code and inspection stamps remained where they were. Late-manufactured Remington Nylon rifles like

logo changes on the barrel have already been covered. The front sight's material changed in about 1962 from a steel investment casting to a nonferrous die casting. This material change lasted only until about 1964 and then the sight went back to steel again. The front sight cross-sectional shape varied to a more upright line on the sight's post, giving a more conventional sight picture. The barrel at its breech had two gas relief cuts added very soon after production started. In the event of a ruptured shell casing, these cuts allow the hot gases to escape in a vertical direction, thus not hurting the shooter. The bolt's forward face had no spot facing cut as originally fabricated; soon a semicircular end mill cut was added. The original cartridge feed guide piece was held in the bolt through its two hook-like arms by a roll pin. Later on, the surface area of the arms was increased and the hooks became two holes which completely enclosed the pin. The windage adjustment screw on the early rifles up to 1964 was a small coin-slotted knob; because it was so exposed and easily bent, it was replaced by a conventional headless screw. The original striker spring sleeve was made from seamless steel tubing; this was replaced by an open seamed tube in the very early production guns. The earliest strikers were machined all over and appear to have been made from steel bar stock; later the strikers were made from an investment steel casting with little or no machining. The fore and rear ends of the ribs of the striker are much more beveled in the cast ones. In the very earliest Model 66s, the barrel bracket and the later separate barrel support were one piece. Next, in order to use up the stock of thick barrel brackets, a milling cut was taken on one side to make room for the new barrel support. In early examples of the Model 66, on the inside of the plastic stock in the area under the receiver cover, there was a large boss on the right side of the foremost edge of the outer magazine tube which was later deleted from the mould of the right-hand stock piece. Lately, Remington Nylon rifles have their receiver's covers finished in the crinkly black described earlier on the Model Apache 77.

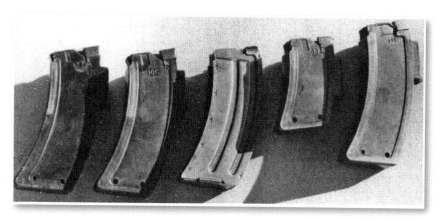

Various magazines for Apache 77, 10-C, 11, 77, 581.

often for repairs and the other is perfect. The older Mohawk is serial number 2398803 and was assembled by the factory in March of 1974. No later than April, 1974, it went back to the factory for repairs; in December of 1974, it returned to the factory again. Again in November of 1978, same old thing — back again. Finally, in March of 1982, it went to the factory again. One would think by this time the rifle would be perfect, but, alas, it was not to be, for the gun still jams occasionally with a loaded 22 cartridge partially in the chamber — about once in

the Model 66 and the Black Diamond, and their newest promotional rifles, the Apache 77, carry the cryptic, and now universal, "Warning — read instruction book for safe operation — free from" (over) "Remington Arms Company, Inc., Ilion N.Y. USA" on the barrel just behind the front sight. At the breech, the Remington logo is replaced with just "22 LONG RIFLE ONLY," with the date code and the approval stamps.

Variations in the Model 66 and its spinoffs are relatively rare. The legend or

The basic differences between the tubular Model 66s and the box magazine Model 77s and others of its ilk are found obviously in the magazines and the area of the stock where those magazines are mounted. The thing not so apparent is that the bolts of the two types of rifles are very different and can't be interchanged. The 77 bolt has a feed rib at the bottom and this rib is not found on a 66. Also, the contour of the ejectors on the two rifles change.

A Mohawk 10-C with a Tasco 4× telescopic sight.

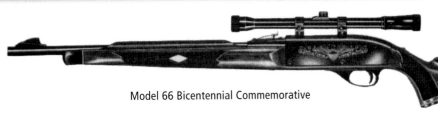

Model 66 Bicentennial Commemorative

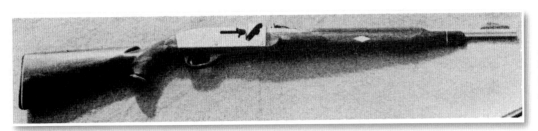

A rare Model 66 Apache Black/Gallery Special, 22 Short only. Note shell deflector, and bracket for counter chain.

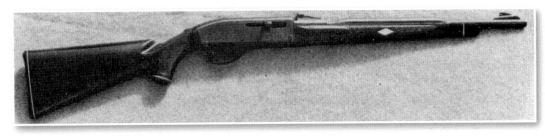

F.I.E.'s Model GR-8 Black Beauty.

To help identify the two items, the one with two holes is used in the tubular Model 66; the one with three is for the box magazine rifles.

F.I.E. (Firearms Import and Export Corp.) of Hialeah, Florida, imported a Remington Model 66 look-a-like from Brazil. The actual manufacturer is CBC (Cia Brasileire Cartuchos, Brazilian Cartridge Company) of Santo Andre, Brazil, SA. The CBC rifle was sold here as the "Black Beauty," usually priced lower than the Remington it was patterned after. In the 1930s Remington Arms owned a minority interest in CBC and with the help of Remington's engineering and production personnel they manufactured Remington guns for the Brazilian market. When, in 1981, the Brazilian government nationalized the company, doing away with Remington's interest in CBC, the Brazilian company was left with the tooling and know-how which enabled them to make a copy of the Remington Model 66.

I have been very satisfied with my Brazilian copy. There are some small differences between the two rifles. The F.I.E. gun has a black stock with black buttplate, pistol grip cap, and forearm tip. Each of these pieces is bonded to the stock with the typical white spacer. There is also a white diamond covering the forearm stock bolt. These add-ons in the F.I.E. are very neatly bonded to the stock with no rough edges at the bonding point. The front sight is a non-steel die casting, without the typical Remington white dot. The rear sight still has a knob on the windage adjustment screw.

Internally, the parts that are in the Remington left in the white are blued in the F.I.E. The fit of the bolt in the nylon receiver in the F.I.E. import is a little more loose than in the Remington, but this seems to have no effect on the function of the rifle. The Brazilian gun's external metal parts are well polished and then blued in a deep black color. Many of the internal parts are steel investment castings including the trigger, and show little or no machining; the rest are, like in the Remington, steel stampings.

While the rifling in the F.I.E. offers the same six lands and grooves and clockwise twist as in the Remington, the actual rifling is quite different in cross-section. The lands in the F.I.E. are rounder on top, and the grooves are deeper. The barrel and the receiver covet are both serial numbered, which is a good idea; the F.I.E. rifle's muzzle is not crowned as in the Remington 66. Like the Remington, the F.I.E. has a bright yellow follower in the magazine that will protrude and can be readily seen when the bolt is drawn rearward. This acts as a very important safety feature, telling the shooter the magazine is empty. F.I.E.'s follower is about ⅛-inch longer than the Remington and can be seen much more easily.

The most remarkable difference, in my mind, is found in the manual that comes with the F.I.E. There are NO instructions on how to field-strip the rifle, let alone disassemble it. Since it is so like the Remington, I just started to take it apart in a similar manner, but things didn't come apart as easily. The receiver cover front retaining screw was very difficult to remove from its hole, and the bolt cocking handle had to be pried from the bolt with two screwdrivers and a great deal of force.

The barrel bracket that secures the barrel in the stock fits very tightly around the barrel, and had to be driven out of the slot in the barrel with a drift punch. Adding to the feeling that this rifle is never to be field-stripped is the fact that the barrel support, which in a Remington is marked "FRONT," is marked "FRENTE," Spanish for front.

I don't know whether the F.I.E. people who wrote the manual don't want the shooter to ever take the rifle apart or if they think that it will never need to be thoroughly cleaned, but I have seen Remington Nylons that were never cleaned by their former owners and they were full of carbon deposits and grit and sand. Although the guns still worked, they are subject to unwarranted wear because of the dirt. In the initial testfiring of the F.I.E. I used both 22 Long Rifle standard and high velocity. The standard ammo had trouble cycling the action with a full magazine on the first two or three series, when the gun was brand-new. After some series of both standard and high speed, the action functioned better.

While in general one would expect the foreign product to undersell our domestic one, this does not seem to be the case in the printed advertising literature for the F.I.E. and the Remington. In the 42nd GUN DIGEST, the Remington 66 was shown at $124 and the F.I.E. Black Beauty at $124.95. Even stranger is the fact that at the recent sale at K-Mart the promotional Remington Apache 77 was $84.97, as mentioned above, and the F.I.E. Black Beauty at that time and store was $96.95.

In preparation for this article on the Remington plastic rifles, I telephoned many people who had advertised a Nylon for sale; almost without exception these were collectors of Remingtons in general and Nylons in particular. In most cases what they had for sale were duplicates. While I knew that these revolutionary rifles interested me, I had no idea how many other collectors were out there. I was also surprised to find that many of these collectors knew much more than I did before I picked their brains.

Jack Heath of Remington Arms wrote me that the Model 66 was to be dropped from the Remington catalog in the year 1988, because the dies that make the plastic stock were wearing out and Remington does not feel justified in replacing them. The Apache 77 will still be available to large quantity buyers. In a gun-using world, where in the military the use of wood is virtually passe, and in a civilian shooting world where walnut stocks have become a luxury and where the climatic stability of plastics is just coming into its own, don't we now see that Remington was way ahead of their time? Don't we also find in a shooting world that no longer feels that gun cleaning and maintenance are important to the function of a firearm that Remington was a quantum jump ahead of its competition? The Remington Model 66 and the type of guns it gave birth to will become more and more common in the near future.

Acknowledgements

Mr. Jack Heath, Remington Arms Co., Wilmington, Delaware.

Mr. Richard F Dietz, Remington Arms Co., Wilmington, Delaware.

Mr. Bud Dumsteg, Remington Arms Co., Wilmington, Delaware.

Mr. Ron Vogel, ELK., Miami, Florida.

Mr. Leonard Hunter, fellow nylonophyle.

Mr. Steve Adrio, who helped.

Mr. J D. Anderson, another nylonophyle.

Mr. Michael Sheehan, photographer.

Mrs. Celeste Kelly, photographer.

Mr. John Raynor, one of the biggest nylonophyles.

Remington Nylons
April 16, 1988

MODEL	CODE	DATE	S/N
66MB	KF	MAY 59	NONE
66MB	OF	JUL 59	NONE
66SG	OF	JUL 59	NONE
66SG	OF	JUL 59	NONE
66SG	BG	JAN 60	NONE
66SG	LG	FEB 60	NONE
66SG	XG	DEC 60	NONE
10	?J	62	NONE
11	BJ	JAN 62	200359
11	BJ	JAN 62	NONE
76MB	LJ	FEB 62	NONE
12	AJ	MAR 62	NONE
76MB	AJ	MAR 62	NONE
11	BJ	JAN 62	NONE
11	BJ	JAN 62	NONE
76MB	J	62	NONE
76MB	J	62	NONE
11	KJ	MAY 62	NONE
11	KJ	MAY 62	NONE
76MB	KJ	MAY 62	NONE
76MB	PJ	JUN 62	NONE
12	PJ	JUN 62	NONE
12	OJ	JUL 62	NONE
76MB	DJ	SEP 62	NONE
76AB	RJ	NOV 62	NONE
12	XJ	DEC 62	NONE
11	BK	JAN 63	NONE
76MB	LK	FEB 63	NONE
11	CK	APR 63	NONE
76AB	PK	JUN 63	NONE
76MB	PK	JUN 63	NONE
12	PK	JUN 63	NONE
12	PK	JUN 63	NONE
76AB	DK	SEP 63	NONE
76MB	DK	SEP 63	NONE
11	BL	JAN 64	NONE
11	KL	MAY 64	NONE
12	KL	MAY 64	NONE
12	KL	MAY 64	NONE
12	PL	JUN 64	NONE
76MB	PL	JUN 64	NONE
76MB	DL	SEP 64	NONE
150TH	AN	MAR 66	NONE
66AB	BR	JAN 68	421705
66AB	LR	FEB 68	425707
66GS	KR	MAY 68	2165148
77MB	KT	MAY 70	2170597
77MB	KU	MAY 71	2207843
10-C	BW	JAN 72	2233022
66MB	CW	APR 72	2253118
10-C	?	?	2273043
10-C	BX	JAN 73	2301825
10-C	PX	JUN 73	2329907
10-C	RX	NOV 73	2362289
66MB	LY	FEB 74	2382331
10-C	AY	MAR 74	2398803
10-C	PY	JUN 74	2401364
10-C	PY	JUN 74	2417810
10-C	OY	JUL 74	2419996
66GS	WY	AUG 74	2421905
66AB	AZ	MAR 75	2486977
10-C	OZ	JUL 75	2515406
10-C	OZ	JUL 75	2521005
10-C	OZ	JUL 75	2522884
10-C	OZ	JUL 75	2523885
66AB	WZ	AUG 75	2537357
BI-CENT	WZ	AUG 75	2538095
BI-CENT	LI	FEB 76	2562604
BI-CENT	CI	APR 76	2590335
BI-CENT	PI	JUN 76	2590747
66AB/GS	LO	FEB 77	2594453
66AB	LO	FEB 77	A2107369
66BD	AQ	MAR 78	A2152054
66BD	EQ	OCT 78	A2152530
66BD	PA	JUN 80	A2211592
66MB	PA	JUN 80	A2211807
66AB	BB	JAN 81	A2227503
66AB	KB	MAY 81	A2241291
66BD	WB	AUG 81	A2250227
APACHE 77	LC	FEB 82	A2261678
APACHE 77	RE	NOV 84	A2305651
66MB	KH	MAY 87	A2335160
66BD	KH	MAY 87	A2335167
66MB	OH	JUL 87	A2341424
66BD	DH	SEP 87	A2366106

F.I.E.

MODEL	CODE	DATE	S/N
GR-8			GR-14918
GR-8			GR-76616

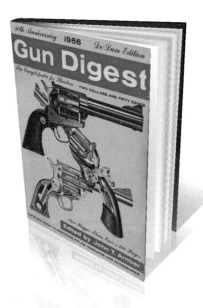

BATTLE OF THE
AUTOMATICS

by JOHN T. AMBER

Some 50 years have passed since the Browning Automatic Shotgun — the first successful autoloader, and the brainchild of that genius of firearms design, John Moses Browning — appeared on the American scene. Continuously made in Belgium since the turn of the century, this most famous of shotguns has had, and still has, a tremendous sale all over the world. Whether it will maintain this leading position in automatic shotgun sales remains to be seen. Certainly, now that there are more competitive autoloading smoothbores available than ever before, the Battle of the Automatics in 1955–1956, and in the years ahead, will be something to watch. You can be sure that the American manufacturers — not to mention the few makers of foreign automatics — will bend every effort to sell you *their* autoloader. Improved models, completely new guns, highly competitive prices and the like will be brought strongly to the shooting public's attention. Well, that means you, and "It's an ill wind ..." as I see it. If you're interested in an automatic shotgun, your gun-buying dollar is going to get

real value this year. Let's review the field as it looks from here.

In 1905 Remington obtained the necessary rights from Browning to make an automatic shotgun, and they have had one on the market ever since, in one form or another. Their Model '11, many thousands of which were sold during a span of well over 30 years, was superseded by their Model 11–48, a streamlined, lighter weight version that is a fine handling, deservedly popular game gun. Offered in two types, which differ chiefly in their shell capacities, and in five gauges — 12, 16, 20, 28 and 410 — the Remington 11–48 (5-shot), and the Sportsman-48 (3 shot) will be strong contenders as always in the autoloader field. In any case, if you want a 28 gauge or a 410 automatic shotgun, your choice will be Remington — nobody else makes them. Prices for the 11–48 or Sportsman-48 start at $110.45.

The patents on the Browning automatic were obtained for the inventor by Winchester's patent lawyers, Seymour and Earl, and a right good job they did! Tommy Johnson, a prolific inventor and long time

employee of the New Haven firm who took out 124 patents assigned to Winchester, is reported to have said that it took him 10 years to design an automatic shotgun that would not infringe Browning's patents. This was the Model 1911, not a particularly successful seller, and it was discontinued in 1925 with few regrets anywhere. Without an automatic shotgun for the next 15 years, the company introduced their Model 40 in 1939. A redesign of the defunct Model 11, the Model 40 was not well received, to say the least — a long, clumsy looking receiver (resulting from the attempt to streamline it), poor handling qualities, and general unreliability, did nothing to endear it to the nation's shooters. The onset of World War II saw it discontinued, of course, and it was not, understandably, revived in the post-war period. Not one of Winchester's happier efforts.

Then came 1954, and Winchester hit the market with an entirely new concept in automatic shotgun design. As most of you know, autoloaders based on the Browning clatter-box — that includes just about all automatics; the Remington Models 11 and 11–48, the Savage auto, even the Italian imports — work on the long-recoil system in which the barrel and the breech block move rearward about 3 inches in the loading-unloading cycle. Not so in the new Model 50 Winchester — the barrel is actually fixed in this gun, with all of the needed energy imparted to the breech block by a floating or independent chamber (as Winchester prefers to term it) that moves a mere one-tenth of an inch! But that small movement is ample to start things going — a rearward extension of the slip-chamber unlocks the breech bolt, thus letting it slam back, unloading the empty, and picking up a fresh round on the return trip. The breech block

Browning Double Automatic in lightweight grade. $133.00 with plain barrel.

J. C. Higgins Model 60 Automatic in de luxe grade, with ventilated rib and "Chokemaster." $99.95.

energy is absorbed by a setup of weights and a buffer spring in the buttstock.

What do these things mean? Well, for one thing, the Model 50 handles any shotshell without adjustment — low base, high base; Skeet, duck loads, the new 2¾" Magnums, you name 'em. No need for friction-ring adjustment on the Model 50; there ain't any. Secondly, you'll notice a softer, slower recoil. Now, any gun expends the same total amount of energy in recoil, but it's going to be *felt* less if that same energy is distributed among several more microseconds of time than are employed in the average shotgun. That's what the Model 50 does, due to that enertia weight and recoil spring in the stock. The factory determined that recoil *effect* at the shoulder was about 25% less than with other guns of similar weight, and my own shooting of the Model 50 bears this claim out. A third point, perhaps not so important to the average user, is the quick and easy interchangeability of barrels — a quarter-turn of the interrupted breech threads, and the spare barrel is in or out.

The Model 50 is not quite a lightweight, what with a 7¾-8 pound average heft — an alloy receivered 12 and a new 20 gauge are rumored in the works — and its balance point feels a bit strange, at least at first. The recoil machinery stashed in the buttstock accounts for this last item, and the result, of course, is a faster pointing barrel. Anyway, that's something you soon get used to — I did, and I now like the handling of the Model 50. I've even shot pretty well with it.

Next to enter the lists in this struggle for supremacy in the auto-loading mart was the oldest maker of them all, the Browning Arms Company of St. Louis (Mo.) and Ogden (Utah). Their latest candidate, hight the Double Twelve, was introduced early in 1955, and a sweet handling gun it has proven to be. This new 12 gauge, featuring several interesting and important innovations, will not replace the regular Browning autos, of course. Rather, as Browning puts it, the new gun is designed for those who want the fine quality of the double barreled shotgun at a price something less than half the cost of the latter. This they have done — the fine finish, the careful fitting together, the nice touches indicative of good workmanship are all there, as they are in all Browning products. The same subleties of good craftsmanship have been lacking, unfortunately, in the post-war products of more than a few of our arms makers.

The new Double Twelve was developed by Val Browning, a son of the immortal John M., over a period of eight years — eight years of intensive testing and trial until the gun was really ready. There are no "bugs" in the 12-12 that I have been able to discover. These are the new features of the Double Twelve: most important, a patented short action, cushioned in the loading and unloading cycle against balanced springs. This absorption of the recoil energy by springs reduces the recoil effect where it counts the most, at the shoulder of the shooter. This shorter action is housed in a receiver smoothly rounded at the rear, noticeably shorter than those in the usual autoloader, and the result is a handsome gun on the whole — the rather stubby looking pistol grip, not as cleanly radiused in its lower curve as it ought to be, is a minor jarring note, but I'll readily admit that it feels pretty good.

The most visually prominent aspect of the new Browning is the loading system, a complete departure from normal loading operations with a standard Browning type automatic. The loading port of this new 2-shot gun (there is no magazine tube in the forearm) is on the *left* side of the receiver. With the breech block open — the factory says to leave the block open when the gun is empty — the fresh shell is inserted in the loading port, and is instantly whisked into the chamber by the closing breech block. The second loaded round is then shoved into the same place, where it remains in sight until the first shot is fired, when it in turn is carried into the chamber. As you can see, another shell can be quickly placed on the loading tray as soon as it is empty — you won't get 3 to 5 shots off quite as rapidly as you can with the regular autoloader, but this new loading system is fast, faster than usual, especially with a bit of practice.

Quick takedown is another feature of the new Browning — the forearm, which remains permanently attached to the gun, is flipped down by the release of a catch, and the barrel is pulled out. That's all there is to it. Last but by no means least, the Double Twelve handles all standard length shotshells, from the lightest quail loads to the heaviest duck and goose loads (including the 2¾"Magnums) without adjustment. On my first session with the new gun, one cold and wet afternoon at the local Skeet range, I ran through some hundred rounds of old and new, light and heavy shells, not a one of which caused any trouble — functioning was perfect. My sample was the light weight model with alloy receiver, satin finished in a light gray, going several ounces under 8 pounds, and even with the heavy standard length Magnum loads the recoil wasn't too punishing.

All in all, a fine gun, but I've been wondering just which segment of the shooting world it will appeal to — it will hardly be the choice of the man who wants the capacity of the regular autoloader, especially when prices are considered. Browning's standard auto sells for $121.50, while the new 2-shot in standard weight with blued steel receiver costs $123.00. Yet it *is* an autoloader, and as such I can't quite see it making much of a dent in the ranks of the side-by-side or over-under gun devotees. It will sell, of course, but for volume sales, I think the Browning Arms Company will have to rely on their original masterpiece, the Browning Automatic.

Only one other American made autoloader derives from the original Browning design, the Savage Model 755 and its light weight counterpart, the Model 775. These were introduced in 1949, modified from the parent pattern to the extent of a rounded receiver at the rear. These have shown themselves to be quite reliable, adequate guns and, in view of their comparatively low, highly competitive price range, they have been able to capture a sizable number of the shotgunner's dollars. Prosaic, workaday specimens of the old mechanism, these Savages, but they're sound, serviceable guns, and I have a hunch they will continue to be bought in fair numbers.

The latest and newest automatic shotgun to reach the market — and the most spectacular from a design standpoint — will be the *gas operated J. C. Higgins Model 60 Automatic*. If I have left this exciting news to the last, it's been for darn good reasons — in the first place, the highly confidential dope on the new gun didn't reach me until a short time ago. This advertising man's puff read swell, but I wanted to get my hot little hands on the actual gun and see for myself! A few days ago — this is mid-1955, and the target release date to the public is next September — I latched on to one and immediately poured several dozen rounds through it. Now I can tell you all about it!

The first and only gas operated automatic shotgun on today's market, the new Model 60 functions in much the same way as the Garand or M-1 rifle — of fond (?) memory to millions of ex-GIs. Briefly, this is how it works — on firing, and after the shot charge has passed the gas ports in the barrel, gas passes through the ports to impinge on a piston. This piston and action bar are driven to the rear, compressing the action spring and moving the bolt slide a short distance to the rear *before the breech bolt starts to unlock*. This delayed unlocking insures that the shot charge is well out of the muzzle and the gas pressure reduced before the bolt is carried all the way back. All of this extracts and ejects the fired shell, and releases the next round from the magazine. The action spring forces the piston and action bar forward, picking up a fresh load and locking the breech bolt. All clear?

	Gauges Available	Capacity	Approx. Weight, standard grade	Alloy Parts	Takedown	Raised Rib available	Vent. Rib available	Stock Dimensions	Safety	Price Range standard grades	Features
Breda	12	5	7¼	None	Yes	Yes	No	14x1½x2⅝	Lever or Tang	$179.50–189.50	Full length sighting plane; double extractors; moving parts chromed; action can be stripped w/o tools.
Browning Standard	12, 16	5	8	None	Yes	Yes	Yes	14¼x1⅝x2½	Cross Bolt	121.50–141.50	Straight sighting plane; magazine cutoff; forged bbl. guide ring; large head safety; 32" bbl. available; hand fitted parts, hand engraved.
Browning Light Weight	12, 16	5	7¼	None	Yes	Yes	Yes	14¼x1⅝x2½	Cross Bolt	131.50–151.50	
Browning Double Auto Standard	12	2	7¾	None	Yes	Yes	No	14¼x1⅝x2½	Vert. Slide	123.00–133.00	Shorter receiver; new recoil mechanism; new convenient safety; new recessed rib; fast loading and takedown; hand engraved, hand fitted.
Browning Double Auto Light Weight	12	2	6¾	Rec.	Yes	Yes	No	14¼x1⅝x2½	Vert. Slide	133.00–143.00	
Franchi	12, 20	4	6¼	None	Yes	No	Yes	14x1½x2⅝	Cross Bolt	158.00–176.00	Superchromed barrels; auto. magazine cutoff; sling swivels.
J. C. Higgins Model 60	12	5	7½	None	No	No	Yes	14x1⅜x2¼	Cross Bolt	89.95–99.95	Gas operated action; reduced recoil; factory vent. rib, with or w/o combination variable choke-comp device.
Remington 11-48	12, 16, 20, 28, 410	5	7½	None	Yes	No	Yes	14x1⅝x2½	Cross Bolt	110.45–132.55	Streamlined design matches other Remington guns; interchangeable barrels. Compensating recoil system.
Remington Sportsman-48	12, 16, 20	3	7½	None	Yes	No	Yes	14x1⅝x2½	Cross Bolt	110.45–132.55	
Savage Model 755	12, 16	5	8¼	None	Yes	No	No	14x1½x2⅝	Cross Bolt	99.50–109.00	Factory installed choke device available; receiver-top matted.
Savage Model 775	12, 16	5	7¼	Rec.	Yes	No	No	14x1½x2⅝	Cross Bolt	105.00–114.50	
Winchester Model 50	12, 20	3	7¾	Guard	Yes	No	Yes	14x1½x2½	Cross Bolt	120.50–	New "independent" chamber and fixed barrel; reduced recoil; easy takedown; faster pointing.

This operating cycle takes a lot less time than it took you to read about it, and the Model 60 can be fired about as fast as you can pull the trigger. Few of us ever want to shoot quite that fast — after all, it takes a little time to recover from the recoil, no matter how soft, and get back on the target — but the high cyclic rate of fire is certainly no disadvantage. And the recoil of this lightest of *standard* grade guns — my sample goes exactly 7½ pounds — is noticeably softer and easier than you'd ordinarily expect from a gun of this weight. I was soon convinced of that the other day — I put over 100 shells through the Model 60, my shoulder protected only by a lightly padded Skeet jacket, and there was no pain. I could easily have shot as many more, and my Model 60 is the plain barrel version, no choke device fitted.

Incidentally, those four boxes of shells I shot up were a mixed lot — Skeet, trap, 1 oz. quail loads, and a box of the 2¾" Magnums — and the Model 60 stuttered 'em off without a protest. No load adjustment of any kind is needed.

There is no takedown as such on the Model 60 — the barrel and receiver are permanently locked together, which means that this gun can't shoot loose. It also permits the factory installation of a ventilated rib, the first time this feature has been offered on an autoloader.

I'm going to confess to a feeling of pleased surprise when I first picked up the Model 60 — after all, the J. C. Higgins guns are made in the highly modern, mass production plant of High Standard, and an evidence of machine production in the Model 60 would not be amiss. Instead, this new auto is a handsome piece on all counts — the barrel and receiver reveal a fine, smooth polish, well blued; the top of the receiver has a glare-proof matt finish, while the breech block and shell lifter are damascened, or engine turned. The walnut buttstock, with capped and nicely checkered pistol grip, is well proportioned and good looking. The beavertail type forearm of matching walnut makes a good handful, and is also checkered.

The jointing up of wood and metal, the inletting, is excellently done, and the gun as a whole has a good feel, taut and solid. There is even a name plate inlet into the underside of the stock, termed silver by the factory, but which looks like stainless steel to me. But silver or not, it's a nice touch, and one rarely found on guns in this low price range. At $89.95 (standard grade) this is a lot of gun for the money, and at $99.95, which includes the factory installed ventilated rib and the Chokemaster (a combined recoil compensator and variable choke),I think it's an even better value. It doesn't take much of a soothsayer to predict that the Model 60 is going to sell, and sell well, in the Battle of the Automatics.

The foreign autos available here, the Franchi and Breda, etc., don't have much chance of achieving mass sales, in my opinion, because of their relatively high prices, and won't be commented on here for that reason. Basic specifications and price ranges for all of the automatics mentioned above will be found in the chart below, which is arranged so that a side-by-side comparison may be made. For your final choice, pay a visit to your local gunshop or sports store, where you ' can examine and handle them to see which pleases *you*.

Check Chart of Automatic Shotguns

THE REMINGTON
MODEL 10
First of the Streamlined Slide Actions

by LARRY S. STERETT

N JUNE 12, 1901, John D. Pedersen, residing at Denver, in the county of Arapahoe and State of Colorado, filed an application with the United States Patent Office for an improvement in Magazine-Guns. Subsequently he was granted Patent No. 719,955, on February 3, 1903, for a Magazine-Firearm. Production drawings were completed in 1905, and in 1907 the Remington Arms Co. began production of a slide-action or pump-action shotgun based on this patent. Although not the first pump-action shotgun ever manufactured, it was the first hammerless solid-breech repeating shotgun ever produced, or literally 'the first of the streamlines.' Later, when Remington catalogs included a listing of the many Remington accomplishments, heading the list was the famed Model 10.

In production for nearly 25 years, at least 12 different grades of the Model 10 were manufactured, along with variations within the grades. Three noticeable receiver changes took place during this time, as might be expected when a gun is in production over a span of many years. The stock

---

Designed over 50 years ago, this trim, graceful Pedersen design compares favorably in handsome appearance with today's latest offerings — and it still performs well. Ask any Model 10 owner!

---

design also changed, as is shown in fig. 1.

Two things did remain unchanged — the basic design of the one solid piece receiver without any opening at top or sides, and the method of takedown. The absence of the usual receiver openings prevents dirt, snow, rain, and other foreign substances from entering the mechanism, thus offering the shooter protection no other gun could then offer. Shells were loaded and ejected from the bottom of the receiver. The Model 10 should have been a salesman's delight for left-handed shooters, since even the safety, which was located in the forward part of the trigger guard, could be worked with ease from either side.

Fig. 2. Model 10 parts section from a 1923 Remington catalog. Note trigger guard perforation and straight fore-end.

The 1910 Remington Arms Co. and Union Metallic Cartridge Co. catalog has this to say of the new Remington Repeating Shotgun:

"The Remington 1908 Model, solid breech, hammerless take-down, 6-shot repeating shotgun is an example of the highest development of the gun-makers' art. It embodies many new and novel features and eliminates those which are objectionable in repeating shotguns of the present day. Beauty of design, perfection of workmanship and finish are strikingly apparent. Absence of projecting parts adds symmetry to its altogether pleasing and graceful lines. It handles fast and balances perfectly, due in large measure to the grip of stock being more nearly in line with the barrel than any other design of repeating shotgun yet produced. Operation of the mechanism causes no change in the exterior appearance of the gun, excepting in the position of the slide-handle or fore-arm, which is not unsightly."

Fig. 1. Top to Bottom: A 1909-made No. 1 "Standard" grade, differing in several details from later Model 10s. The stock shows the most noticeable difference. With the rounded semi-pistol grip, slightly fluted comb, and flattened wood behind the receiver, it appears very similar to the buttstock on the Remington M1900 hammerless double-barrel shotgun. (The recoil pad is not original.) The fore-end is also slightly different, having 17 grooves and being almost cylindrical its entire length. Note triangular cutout in rear of trigger guard — a common design of double-barrels. The trigger guard screw, below the slide release button, has no lock screw. The barrel is the original 30" full choke type.

This 1922 Model 10A, now with a 20" cylinder bore riot barrel, is not a 10R, as the barrel was a replacement for the original 30" full choke type. The 16-groove fore-end is slightly fuller in the mid-section for a more hand-filling grip. The trigger guard is no longer cut out and the guard screw has a lock screw.

This 1931 Model 10A has a solid ribbed barrel. It had originally a 30" full choke barrel, but a Cutts Compensator has been installed to give a barrel length of 26" with the full choke tube. The receiver does not differ much from gun 2 above, except that the serial number is on the left side instead of the bottom. The buttstock again has a fluted comb — the buttplate is original. The fore-end has only

12 grooves and an even greater swelling in the mid-section.

This is the Model 29B — short-lived successor to the Model 10. The receiver, basically the same externally, has several internal changes. The safety is now a push-through type and has been moved to the rear of the trigger guard. The slide release button has been made solid and ringed. The checkered grip and fore-end are similar to that of the Model 10B. The barrel on this model was originally a 30" full choke, but the barrel was refitted after a previous owner had jumped a ditch, jamming the barrel into a snow drift, and then fired it without checking the barrel.

Model 1910's Described

Note that the shotgun is called the 1908 Model in this 1910 catalog. However, no shotguns have ever been examined by this writer with the 1908 designation, even guns manufactured in 1908, although in later years the Model 10 designation did actually appear on the shotgun.

The 1910 catalog lists 8 different grades of the Remington Repeating Shotgun as follows:

"No. 1 'Standard' Grade, 7¾ lbs. 6 shot repeater, 26", 28", 30" and 32" Remington steel barrel, any desired choke. 30" full choke sent unless otherwise specified. Half-pistol grip stock and fore-arm of American walnut, regular dimensions 13¾", drop at heel 2¾", drop at comb 1⅝". Any other length or drop of stock made to order at an advance of $10. List, $27.

"No. 2 'Special' Grade, 7¾ lbs. Same as No. 1 Standard grade with the exception that the stock and fore-arm are of selected Imported walnut, neatly checked. Will furnish made to order, without extra charge, lengths from 13½" to 15", drops 2¼" to 3¼"at heel. Any other length or drop of stock made to order at an advance of $10. List, $47.

"No. 3 'Trap Special' Grade, 7¾ lbs. A 6 shot repeater designed especially for trap shooting purposes. This grade differs from No. 3 'Trap' in that the stock and fore-arm are American Walnut, the stock being furnished in but one dimension which is 14" in length, drop 2" at heel and 1½" at comb. The majority of trap shooters have found these dimensions to be the best adapted for trap shooting purposes. The barrel is of Remington steel and the top surface is neatly matted its entire length (and is) especially selected for trap loads and guaranteed to shoot over 70% of the load in a 30" circle at 40 yards. List, $45.

"No. 3 'Trap' Grade, 7¾ lbs. 6 shot repeater designed especially for trap-shooting

purposes, 26", 28", 30" and 32" Remington steel barrel, any desired choke. We guarantee the full choke barrel to shoot over 70% of the load in a 30" circle at 40 yards. Straight grip stock and fore-arm are of selected curly Imported walnut and are neatly checkered, regular stock dimensions 14"×1½"×2". Will furnish made to order, without extra charge, lengths from 13½" to 15", drops from 2" to 3¼" at the heel. Any other length or drop of stock made to order at an advance of $10. List, $47.

"No. 4 'Tournament' Grade. 6 shot repeater, 26", 28", 30" and 32" Remington steel barrel any desired choke. Stock and fore-arm of specially selected Imported walnut, neatly finished by hand with attractive checkering. Receiver and barrel finished in a rich scroll hand engraving. All working parts are hand polished. Pistol grip stock 13¾" long, drop at heel 2¾", drop at comb 1⅝". List, $60.

"No. 5 'Expert' Grade. 6 shot repeater, 26", 28", 30" and 32" Remington steel barrel, any desired choke. Stock and fore-arm are of the choicest Imported walnut, handsomely checkered by hand, silver name plate inlaid in stock. The barrel and receiver are finished with a beautiful deep scroll hand engraving with panel on left side of receiver. All working parts are hand polished. List, $90.

"No. 6 'Premier' Grade. The No. 6 'Premier' grade Pump gun … is a work of art, no effort being spared to produce the finest gun in both workmanship and finish as it is possible for a factory to turn out. The receiver and barrel are finished in a beautiful deep scroll hand engraving which brings out the game panels in relief. Owner's initials engraved on name plate, if so desired. List, $140.

"No. 0 'Riot' Grade. Furnished with 20-inch Cylinder Barrel Only. The Riot grade pump is bored especially to shoot buckshot. It is being used in a number of State prisons, also by express messengers and watchmen. It is a 6 shot repeater made in 12 gauge only. Stock dimensions same as No. 1 Standard grade. List, $27."

The stock dimensions for the No. 4, No. 5, and No. 6 grades were the same. However, special stock dimensions would be made to order without extra charge. A straight grip was also available on these three grades. Unless specified otherwise it would be furnished 14"×1½"×2" drop at heel.

Grades 1 and 2 would be furnished with a matted-rib barrel instead of plain at an advance of $6.75 list. Grade 3 (both models) could have a solid ribbed barrel instead of plain at an advance of $6.75 list. Grades 4, 5, and 6 would be furnished with a raised solid ribbed barrel instead of plain at an advance of $6.75 list.

The 1911–1912 Remington - UMC catalog lists the "Remington - UMC Model 10" for the first time, yet the introductory paragraph begins: "The Remington-UMC 1908 Model …" The same eight grades cited above were offered at the same list prices. The only difference was that instead of the two companies operating under the same ownership

The name of John Douglas Pedersen — once called by John Browning "the greatest gun designer in the world" — although not as well known as that of Browning, is recognizable to many as being that of a very able gun designer, particularly of military weapons. The Pedersen Semi-automatic Rifle, which almost became our service rifle during the 1930's, and which was tooled up for by the British and copied by the Japanese; the 276 Pedersen cartridge, which was approved for adoption as our service cartridge and vetoed by the then U. S. Army Chief of Staff, General Douglas MacArthur; the Remington 45 pistol, recommended for adoption by a Navy Board at the beginning of World War I; and, of course, the ill-fated Pedersen Device, 65,000 of which were manufactured in 1918 along with sufficient supplies of ammunition, and later destroyed without ever having been in service.

For some reason these military designs of John D. Pedersen never quite made it. All were adopted or recommended for adoption, but none was actually put into service. His commercial designs, however, were something else. Many shooters are familiar with Pedersen guns, such as the famous Model 12, a 22 caliber repeating rifle; the Model 51 automatic pistol; the Model 25 slide action repeating rifle, the Model 14 and 14½ high power slide action repeating rifles and later Models 121 and 141, all of which were produced by Remington Arms Co. (His military designs usually bore his name, his commercially produced design never did.)

The author wishes to thank the Remington Arms Company, Inc., Mr. S. M. Alvis, and Mr. Frank Wheeler for their assistance in the preparation of this article.

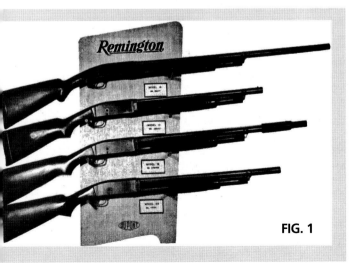

FIG. 1

COMPONENT PARTS

and management, but using separate names, as they had done for years, they were now functioning as the Remington Arms-Union Metallic Cartridge Co., and the Model 10 is listed as the Model No. 10. This is also the first year in which the Remington-UMC ball trade mark appeared on the lower tang. This particular trade mark was ordered removed in May, 1924.

In the 1913–1914 catalog, mention of the 1908 Model has disappeared. The Remington-UMC Repeating Shotgun had become simply the Model No. 10, and so it would remain in catalogs for nearly another 15 years. The designation of the various grades had also changed, although the specifications basically remained the same. The grades available at this time were much as before, but prices were changed slightly, and the model designations altered. The No. 10A "Standard" grade was still $27, the "Special" and "Trap" sold at $45, the "Tournament" was shown at $55, the "Expert" and "Premier" at $80 and $120 (these 3 last made only to order), while the "Riot" gun cost $27.

Several changes in the Model 10 became evident in the 1915–1916 catalog. All grades, other than the 10S Trap Special and 10C Trap grades, had been illustrated up to this time with the rounded half-pistol grip, as shown by gun 1 in fig. 1. In the 1915–1916 catalog the 10A, 10B, and 10R grades have the flat-bottomed pistol grip typical of most modern shotguns. (Even more evident is the change in price. Catalogs previous to 1915–1916 contained the following statement: "All prices subject to change without notice. Prices

quoted in this catalogue are 'list' prices. Dealers will furnish our arms at regular retail prices, which are considerably less than 'list' prices.") The 1915–1916 catalog is stamped "Retail prices on parts and extras 15% above catalogue list. We have had to advance our prices because of the great increase in the cost of material and labor. Your dealer will quote you the new prices. They are higher than the list prices in the catalog." (The prices actually shown are the same as in the 1913–1914 catalog.)

By 1918 the Model No. 10 had become simply the Model 10 Repeating Shotgun. The same array of grades was still available, at higher list prices, with an added number of extras. Notable changes in the 1918–1919 catalog were announced. For example, the No. 10A "Standard" was now $42, the 10B "Special" was $70, and the 10S "Trap Special" was $61, including a matted-rib barrel. The "Premier," or 10F was up to $183.50. The latter was made only to order, as were also the 10D and 10E versions, these costing $81.50 and $122.25 respectively. Grades 10A, 10B, 10S ("Trap Special"), 10C, 10D, 10E, and 10F were available with solid raised rib barrels for $9.25 extra, or with a matted top surface barrel) except the 10S) for the same price. Barrels only were available, plain, for grades 10A, 10B, 10S, and 10C, for $21.55; a matted top or raised solid rib was $9.25 more. Extra barrels for the 10D grade were $27.50 for the plain, and $36.45 for the deluxe version; for the 10E, extra barrels were $34.45 and $43.70; for the 10F, $40.85 and $50.10. A note regarding ribbed barrels stated:

"Ventilated rib barrel NOT furnished on Model 10 guns. The barrel and rib are made in one solid piece, consequently we cannot fit a rib to a plain barrel."

Any length or drop of stock was available on special order for grades 10A, 10B, and 10C, at an advance List of $13.40, requiring 6–8 weeks.

The illustrations of the Model 10 in the 1918–1919 Remington-UMC catalog all have the skeleton trigger guard and the early receiver, as shown on gun number 1 in fig. 1. The fore-end on the 10A and 10R is the 17-groove version.

The 1923 catalog of Remington Arms Company, Inc., (note the name change) has the same parts illustration as the previous catalog, showing the skeletonized trigger guard, early receiver, and 17-groove fore-end. There are, however, many noticeable changes. For one thing there are no list prices printed in this catalog. There are some pencilled-in prices, apparently put there by a former owner of the catalog, for several of the shotguns and rifles. The Model 10A, if we can assume the prices to be correct, was selling at $50.90, or

$10.60 less than the Model 11A Autoloading Shotgun. This price is questionable, however, in view of the fact that the Model 11A was retailing for $56.75 in 1931. Grades A to F, plus S and R, are priced the same as previously, but a new No. 10T "Target" grade with Ventilated Rib, described thus, was introduced:

"The ventilated rib and barrel are machined out of a solid bar of steel. This makes it impossible for the rib to become loose, as often happens when the rib is simply brazed to the barrel. To prevent shooting under the target this gun is constructed to shoot center if sighted close to the receiver.

"The long extension fore-end will suit either the short or long-armed shooter. It is extra full and shaped to permit a firm and steady hold, to give better control over the swing of the gun on sharp angles and to add to the ease with which double targets may be shot. For those who prefer it a short, full fore-end … will be supplied instead."

"The shooter who is hard to fit will appreciate the wide variation of stock dimensions supplied without extra charge."

"Specifications and options: A raised matted, ventilated-rib barrel, 28, 30, or 32 inches, furnished to any choke specifications, metal rear sight fitted at no extra charge. High-grade imported walnut stock and fore-end, both neatly checkered and with oil finish. Recoil pad of any make desired. Straight-grip stock, regular dimensions, 14"×1½"×2" at comb. Will furnish made to order, at no extra charge, but subject to 6–8 week's delay, half or full pistol grip, lengths from 13½" to 15", drops 1¼" to 3¼" at heel and 1¼" to 1¾" at comb. Stock dimensions outside of these limits or stocks with castoff or of Monte Carlo type, subject to extra charge.

"This model also supplied in Nos. 10TD, 10TE and 10TF Grades with engraving, checkering and quality of wood same as supplied on Tournament,' 'Expert' and 'Premier Grades of the regular Model 10 …"

Model 10T Introduced

The Model 10A is shown in the 1923 catalog with solid trigger guard, guard-screw check screw on the receiver, and 16-groove fore-end as shown on gun number 2 in fig. 1. The newly introduced No. 10T also has the solid trigger guard and the guard-screw check screw. The other grades are still illustrated with the skeleton trigger guard, no check screw and the 10R still has the 17-groove fore-end. It is rather interesting to note that the 10R grades (circa 1917–1918) shown in figs. 3, 4 and 5 have the 17-groove fore-ends, but solid trigger guards and the early receiver design; particularly when an original 1905 production drawing of the trigger guard assembly shows it to be solid, with no record of it being al-

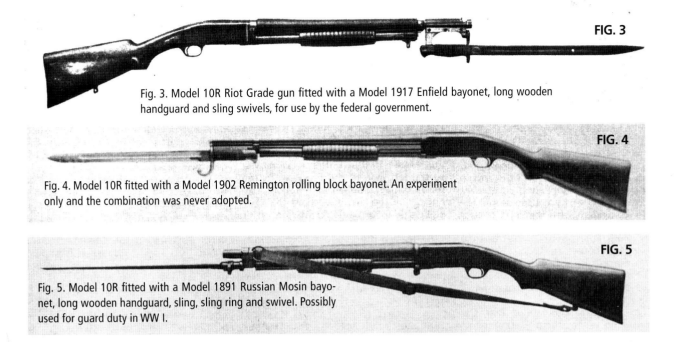

Fig. 3. Model 10R Riot Grade gun fitted with a Model 1917 Enfield bayonet, long wooden handguard and sling swivels, for use by the federal government.

Fig. 4. Model 10R fitted with a Model 1902 Remington rolling block bayonet. An experiment only and the combination was never adopted.

Fig. 5. Model 10R fitted with a Model 1891 Russian Mosin bayonet, long wooden handguard, sling, sling ring and swivel. Possibly used for guard duty in WW I.

tered up through 1922. Actually all the 10A grades observed by the author, up to number U38,277 (top gun in fig. 1), have the skeletonized guard. The sectional views in catalogs through 1923 also show the pierced guard, while an undated brochure thought to have been published around 1930, when the last of the Model 10's were being sent to warehouses, shows the solid guard.

The 1925 Stoeger catalog listed the Model 10A and 10R at $52.50 each and the 10B at $85. The illustrations are of the early design with skeletonized trigger guard and 17-groove fore-end. The specifications are the same as those listed in previous Remington catalogs, but the weight of the 10A is given as 7½ pounds. Only full, modified, or cylinder bore barrels were available at the listed price. Stock modifications were available for $16 and a raised solid rib cost $9.60 extra. The 10B specifications were the same as previously also, with the weight listed at 7¾ pounds. Extra barrels for either the 10A or 10B models could be obtained, complete with yoke and barrel lug, for $24.75.

How many Model 10 shotguns were produced is not exactly known. The factory believes that number 275,452 was the last one produced, and this during the year 1931. Yet the author has owned number 275,706 for several years and in the fall of 1963 found an original Model 10R, number 276,128, at a gun show. My 275,706 originally had a 30-inch full choke barrel with solid ribbed barrel and was produced in 1931. The 10R, number 276,128, was probably finished in 1932.

And so it goes. The majority of the Model 10's were probably of the 10A and 10R grades. At least most of the Model 10's passing through the author's hands, or which he

has observed at various gun shows and elsewhere, have been of these two grades, with the full choke 10A being the more common. Although a few of the 10B "Special' and 10C "Trap" grades have been examined, not one of the 10D, 10E, 10F, or 10T grades has been located.

Model 10's at War

No doubt the Government purchased a fair quantity of the 10R grades before, during, and after World War I for use on guard duty and possibly in the trenches. However, a search of the records of the Office of the Chief of Ordnance has failed to locate the number of such purchases. Apparently Government purchases of the Model 10R were made on at least two different occasions. Several local veterans who served with the A.E.F. have mentioned seeing the Model 10R in France back in 1918. These would be of the grade illustrated in figs. 3 to 5. That a later purchase was made is indicated by War Department "Technical Manual 9–285 Shotguns, All Types," dated September 21, 1942, in which the 12 gauge Remington M10 is listed. (A later manual, TM9-1285, dated 25 November 1942, does not list the M10. This is understandable since the Model 10 had been out of active production for 14 years, and during a war nothing could be much worse than having a gun for which repair parts were not available.) In TM9-285 the Model 10 illustrations are of the late type with 12-groove fore-end, guard-screw check screw, solid trigger guard, and model designation and serial number on the left side of the receiver (fig. 1, gun number 3). The serial number on one of the Model 10's pictured in the manual is 267,709, which would place its manufacture between 1926 and 1931, too

late for WW I. There is one different feature in this manual, which reads as follows:

"Paragraph 36. Description. A. Identification marks on this gun (Model 10) are generally to be found as follows: ... (3) The words "REMINGTON (trade mark)," on left side of action slide bar."

This marking is visible on the action slide bar in some of the illustrations and is of the later type. The unusual part is that beginning with number U222,148 (1924), which was a "Riot" grade, none of the guns observed by the author have had any markings in this location.

The particular gun mentioned above as being pictured in TM9-285 does not have a bayonet attachment, but does have sling swivels located on the butt-stock and forward of the fore-end on the magazine tube. Mention is made that some of the guns will have a bayonet attachment and handguard attached to the muzzle, in which case the forward swivel is on the bayonet attachment. The attachment is not illustrated, but is probably of the perforated metal type, currently being sold by some surplus dealers. Except for the swivel and possible Government markings the military M10 "Riot" type is the same as the commercial Model 10R.

The M10 was manufactured concurrent with the M29 for a few years, but this was probably simply a matter of runout of work in process on the M10, coincident with the start of production for the Model 29 — short lived successor to the M10. The last significant year for production to warehouse for the M10 was 1928. In 1929 the M29 was manufactured in quantity and about 3,000 M10's were finished up to warehouse. In 1930, 1931, and 1932, there were a few dribbles of the M10 going to warehouse, but these were probably assembled from parts manufactured earlier.

The 1929 Stoeger catalog lists the Remington M29 Pump Action shotgun in grades 29A, 29B, 29T, and 29R, at $49.30, $79.65, $140.00, and $49.30 respectively. The grades correspond to those of the M10, which was available previously. The brief description of the Model 29, along with specifications, appeared as follows:

"This gun embodies many new and novel features. It handles fast and balances perfectly. The operation of the mechanism causes no change in the exterior appearance of the gun. The receiver is ABSOLUTELY SOLID. The hammerless feature and safety trigger mechanism prevents the explosion of the shell until the breech is full locked.

"Hammerless; solid-breech; take-down; bottom ejection; coil springs that cannot break used throughout; checkered grip and fore-end; cross bolt safety; Remington steel barrel, 26, 28, 30 or 32 inch, full choke, modified choke, or cylinder bore. Top of receiver matted. American walnut stock and fore-end. Half pistol grip stock, regular dimensions 13¾" long, 2¾" drop at heel 1⅝" drop at comb; magazine holds five which, with one in the chamber, gives a capacity of six shots without reloading. Weight about 7½" pounds; length over-all, 49"; taken down, 30" with 30" barrel."

A *Dealers Price List*, effective January 2, 1931, does not list the M10; instead it lists the Model 29A-F, plus R, S, TA, TC, TD, TE, and TF. The 29A "Standard" Grade was retailing at $48.95, with the newly introduced Model 31 available in the same grades at the same prices.

Identifying M10 Shotguns

The serial number of the Model 10 was located on the bottom of the receiver, ahead of the breech opening, and was preceded by a U, up through at least number U224,463 (1924 manufacture). This letter (U) was used to identify the Model 10, since many customers corresponding with the factory failed to identify the proper model number of their gun. (BO was the prefix used to indicate the 20 gauge Model 17 Shotgun.) This practice is no longer followed as the model designations are placed on the gun. The actual designation "Model 10" did not appear on the receiver until sometime between gun number U224.463 and gun number 242,554 (made in 1926). At this time the "U" was dropped and the serial number and Model 10 designation were moved to the left side of the receiver, in the lower center. The serial numbers also appear on the barrel, without the "U," right side or left side, right-side up or upside down, just ahead of the receiver, and on the right side of the trigger guard. This latter location is not visible until the gun is disassembled.

At least 8 different barrel markings have been observed for the Model 10. They are listed below, along with the highest year of manufacture of the guns observed with that marking.

1911 Remington Arms Co., Ilion, N.Y. U.S.A. Patents, Feby. 3, 1903, May 16, 1905.

1913 Remington Arms — Union Metallic Cartridge Co. Remington Works, Ilion, New York, U.S.A. Patented February 3, 1903 and May 16, 1905.

1914 The markings on this particular gun, the only one of its type observed, are the same as the following one, except for the designation "Model 10-A," instead of "Model 10."

1920 MODEL 10 The Remington Arms Union Metallic Ctg. Co. Inc. Remington Ilion Works, Ilion, New York, U.S.A, Patented February 3, 1903, and May 16, 1905.

1924 MODEL 10 Remington Arms Com pany, Inc. Successor to the Remington Arms U.M.C. Co. Inc. Rem ington Ilion Wks. Ilion, N.Y. U.S.A. Patented Feb. 3,03, and May 16,05.

1926 Remington Arms Co., Inc. Remington Ilion Works, Ilion, N.Y. Made in U.S.A. Patented Feb. 3, 1903 and May 16, 1905.

1931 Remington Arms Co., Inc. Remington Ilion Works, Ilion, N.Y. Made in U.S.A. Patented Feb. 3, 1903, May 16, 1905 and Mar. 30, 1926.

1932 Remington Arms Co., Inc. Remington Ilion Works, Ilion, N.Y. Made in U.S.A. U.S. Patent Numbers 1579177-1660216. Other Patents Pending.

Sometime between U205,107 (made 1922) and U216.914 (made 1923) the RP or R.P. on the right side of the barrel was changed to R.E.P. These are proof marks and are abbreviations for "Remington English Proof." The R.E.P. continues to be the standard Remington proofmark. It is understood that the E was incorporated in the marking at the time the procedure was changed or modified to fully conform with British requirements, so that firearms exported by Remington would be acceptable to British standards.

During its years of manufacture various marks, other than the serial number, gauge, and degree of choke, appeared on the Model 10 near the breech end of the barrel. A few of these marks are illustrated below.

P, PS, WS', RX, RW, AK2. ¤ ☼ ⚓ ♀

The various letters are production code marks which continue in use today, but in different forms. With such markings it is possible to identify the particular year and month that a firearm was produced.

The various symbols or characters are inspection marks. It is understood that in the early years and to some degree today, each inspector had his own particular design for the punch marking.

Contrary to what some people would have you believe the little anchor does not indicate a U.S. Navy gun. This mark appears on the Model 10 from about 1926 on to 1931, when it was no longer being produced. It also appears on other Remington arms of this period, such as the M51 automatic pistol. Although shotguns seldom receive much notice at gun shows, automatic pistols are something different. The author has been to a number of shows where some of the exhibitors have hiked the price of a $20 M51 up to $45–50 with the comment:

"See that anchor. This was a Navy gun, you know. It's worth more."

Don't you believe it. Sure, some naval officer may have purchased a Remington M51 or even a Model 10 for personal use, and it may have had an anchor on it, or not, depending on when it was produced, but the little anchor does not indicate previous ownership by the U. S. Navy.

Tales of Model 10's

As with most guns many interesting tales could be told concerning the Model 10, without a doubt, but we'll only mention here incidents involving two of the guns actually checked by the author.

Under the buttplate of a Model 10 examined there was a small green hunting license, No. 11792, issued at Tishomingo, Oklahoma, on Sept. 7, 1928, to a 22-year old. (The duck season then lasted from October 1 to January 15, with a limit of 10 per day, 50 per season, while the squirrel season was seven months long with a 6-per-day limit!) A few years later this shotgun was sold to a college student, a cousin of the Oklahoma hunter. When the author examined this M10 in 1962, its owner was having it re-blued and a new buttstock fitted, after 30 years of good service. Model 10 owners are a dedicated lot.

The second tale also concerns a second-hand Model 10A with a 30-inch full choke barrel. Originally it had belonged to a doctor, but was sold to its present owner around 1930. For many years in the 1930s it saw service around a farm where one of the favorite pastimes was shooting rabbits from the platform of a huge Minneapolis-Moline combine, one of the first such machines in western Illinois. How many rabbits this particular Model 10

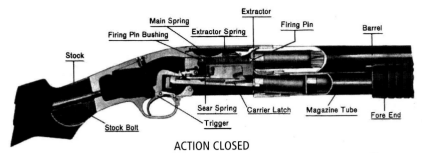

Cross-section of the Remington Model 10 shotgun, mechanism in the "Action Closed" position.

ACTION CLOSED

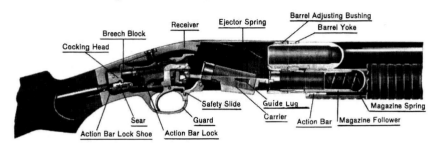

ACTION OPEN

Cross-section of the Remington Model 10 shotgun, mechanism in the "Action Open" position.

accounted for is unknown, but the total must have been in the hundreds. From a vantage point 8 feet up any rabbit that moved was meat in the larder, and some of the claims made for it were just short of fantastic. Many times the author has heard the claim made that it would shoot like a rifle. Then came the 1963 hunting season. The owner was pheasant hunting with some friends in Iowa. About 10:00 a.m. a big cock arose, the Model 10 was swung, the trigger squeezed, and a tremendous roar was heard. The pheasant flew on, but the Model 10 now had a ventilated barrel. The owner had left his cleaning rod in the barrel! The barrel contained the pressure for nearly 20 inches, then it let go. A hurried trip to a nearby farmhouse and a few minutes diligent work with a hacksaw and the Model 10 returned to the field minus several inches of its original full choke barrel. On close shots it is deadly, or so they say, but it no longer shoots like a rifle. The cleaning rod? It was never found. Maybe it struck the pheasant, and if so, the hunter who bags this bird is going to wonder. A few cases have been recorded of pheasants being shot, and when retrieved were found to have an arrow stuck in them, but a cleaning rod?

Details and Assembly

Thus far little has been said of the Model 10 in regard to functioning and assembly. In operation the M10 functions much the same as any pump or slide action shotgun or rifle. The action release button is on the right side of the receiver and pushing in on it, while pulling back on the fore-end, will withdraw the breechblock, allowing a shell to enter the action from the magazine (assuming the gun has been loaded). The gun

is now in the position shown in the sectional view "Action Open."

The action release button also serves as an indicator button. When it projects from the receiver the gun is cocked and in firing position. If flush with the side of the receiver, the gun has been fired or the breechblock is not fully locked in the forward position. As a safety precaution the Model 10 is designed not to fire if the breechblock is not locked fully closed.

Pushing forward on the fore-end will chamber the shell and lock the breechblock. The safety can be put on by pushing it to the rear, thus preventing the trigger from being pulled. Pushing forward on the safety as the gun is shouldered will release it and allow the gun to be fired. Assuming that the gun has been fired, it is now in the position shown in the sectional view "Action Closed." The fore-end can then be pulled back without pushing in on the action release button.

The extractor, located on the top front edge of the breechblock, grasps the rim of the shell and withdraws it as the breechblock moves to the rear. The shell is held in the top of the receiver by two ribs until it has been fully withdrawn from the chamber. The extractor, extractor spring, and ejector spring, then push the empty shell straight down and out the bottom of the receiver.

The Model 10 was manufactured only in the take-down version, and can be disassembled and assembled without tools for cleaning, carrying, or interchanging of barrels. With the gun unloaded and in an upright position, press down on the magazine lever detent on the left front end of the magazine

and swing the magazine lever to the right until it stops. Grasping this lever, rotate it clockwise a quarter-turn, or until straight down, to release the magazine. Next shove forward on the fore-end until the action bar and magazine tube are free of the receiver. Grasp the barrel and magazine near the receiver with the left hand, rotate it a quarter-turn clockwise and pull forward out of the receiver.

If the gun is to be stored in a leg-of-mutton type gun case, draw the magazine back until stopped and hold the fore-end forward of the stop lugs on the magazine. Using the lever, rotate the magazine a quarter-turn counterclockwise and push the lever back into its locked position. The action bar is now protected from sliding out and possibly getting bent.

If the barrel is being changed for one of a different length or choke, it is also necessary to transfer the magazine, and fore-end, action bar assembly. To do this swing the magazine lever fully down and forward by releasing the magazine lever detent from the inner edge of the magazine tube. Now push magazine to the rear to clear the barrel lug. As soon as the magazine is free of the barrel lug, tilt the front of the tube downward and pull the entire assembly — magazine and action bar with fore-end — forward away from the barrel yoke. Magazine, etc., can now be transfererd to another barrel by reversing the above procedure.

To assemble the M10, press magazine detent lever downward again — assuming gun has been stored in a case — and swing the lever to the right. Rotate magazine until lever is straight down and slide magazine and fore-end forward as far as possible. Pull the trigger to uncock the firing pin — this is not detrimental to the gun and difficulty will be experienced in assembling the gun if it is cocked. If the breechblock is not in its forward position, jar it into place by holding the receiver downward and striking the front end against the palm of the hand. Gripping barrel and magazine firmly in the left hand, insert rear end of the barrel into the receiver so that the magazine projects straight out relative to the left side of the receiver. Be sure barrel yoke is snug against the receiver and rotate barrel a quarter-turn counterclockwise, or until the small lines on the bottom of the barrel yoke and receiver coincide. Although not always necessary, it sometimes helps to grasp the receiver in an inverted position with the right hand, so that the thumb can be placed in the opening, pressing the breechblock forward and against the top of the receiver. If this method is used the barrel is inserted into the receiver with the magazine projecting away — still the left side of the receiver, however.

Barrel is rotated as before until the lines on the bottom of the barrel yoke and receiver coincide. Move the fore-end rearward to enter the action bar into the receiver and engage it with the breechblock; open the action part way. Push the magazine rearward into the receiver until it stops and rotate it a quarter-turn to the right, or until the lever is horizontal. Swing the lever back into its locked position.

The barrel has square threads which are not apt to be crossed by careless handling, but several thousand takedowns may cause a certain amount of wear and subsequent looseness. However, there is an adjustment bushing in the receiver to take up any looseness which might develop. The instructions to be followed, quoted from an old Remington catalog, are:

"... take down the barrel; loosen by a few turns the screw which holds bushing lock on face of receiver until lock can be moved back under head of screw, thus unlocking the bushing. Then turn adjusting bushing in direction of arrow using screwdriver or any piece of metal in the slots provided for that purpose in the bushing. Turn until the notches in the bushing will match the notches in the lock. Push lock into place and tighten screw. If notches do not match do not force the lock against the bushing, but turn bushing until they do match. Ordinarily an adjustment of one or two notches will be sufficient to take up the wear ..."

To load the M10 it is necessary to shove the fore-end forward and turn the gun upside down so that shells may be placed on the breechblock and pushed into the magazine. The magazine holds 5 shells, and after chambering a shell from the magazine an additional one may be inserted.

If it becomes necessary to remove a loaded shell from the chamber this can be accomplished by pushing the action release button on the right side of the receiver and pulling the fore-end slowly to the rear until the shell from the chamber is ejected, but without completing the stroke. Returning the fore-end to its forward position will close the breechblock on an empty chamber. If the magazine is to be unloaded, it can be done without having to chamber each shell; remove the shell from the chamber as before, followed by *completion* of the rearward stroke to allow the next shell to pass from the magazine to the carrier. Moving the fore-end forward slightly will lift the shell to the level of the barrel, and allow the carrier to be pressed up against the side of the receiver with the finger, causing the shell to drop down into the palm. Pulling the fore-end to the rear to release the next shell and repeating the above motions will empty the magazine. Be sure to keep the gun right side up when doing this.

RESTRICTED SELLING PRICES

FIG. 6

Remington-UMC Repeating Shotguns, "PUMP ACTION."

Model No. 10.

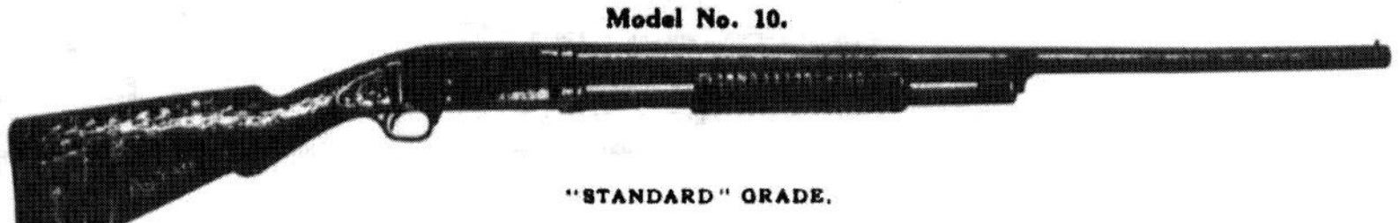

"STANDARD" GRADE.

Made in 12 Gauge only. Standard Lengths, 26, 28, 30 and 32 inches.

Cylinder, Modified Choke or Full Choke.

		WHOLESALE	RETAIL
No. 0.	"Riot" Grade, 20-inch barrel	$19.25	$22.75
	Extra barrel	10.13	11.25
No. 1.	"Standard" Grade, 30-inch barrel, weight about 7½ lbs	19.25	22.75
	Extra barrel	10.13	11.25
	Made in 12 gauge only, standard length 30 inches, also furnished in 26, 28 and 32 inches any desired choke; weight about 7¼ pounds; drop, 2¾ inches at heel, 1⅝ inch at cone; standard length, 13¾ inches. Any other length or drop of stock made to order at an advance of $10	25/10%	List Net
No. 2.	"Special" Grade	33.00	39.50
	Extra barrel	10.13	11.25
	Remington fluid steel barrel, blued finish. Selected English walnut pistol grip stock, with full cone, stock and forearm finely checkered, rubber butt plate, matted rib on receiver, chambered for 2¾-inch shells. Standard dimensions of stock 13¾ inches long, 2¾ inches drop at heel, 1⅝ inches drop at cone. Will furnish made to order drops from 2¼ inches to 3¼ inches and lengths from 13½ to 15 inches, **without extra charge.** Any dimension other than given above will be subject to additional charge of $10	25/10%	List Net

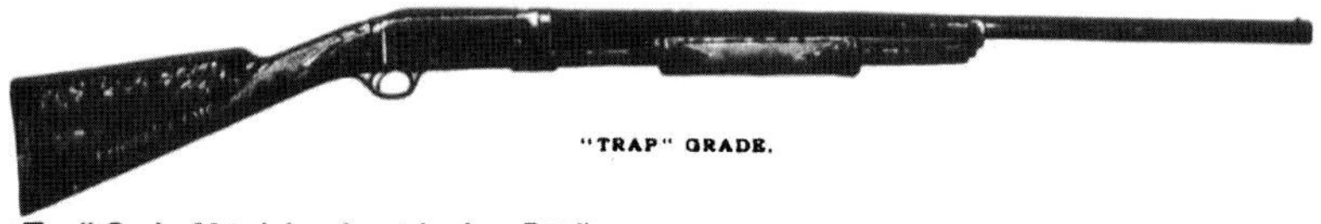

"TRAP" GRADE.

No. 3.	"Trap" Grade, 30-inch barrel, weight about 7¾ lbs	33.00	39.50
	Extra barrel	10.13	11.25
	Remington fluid steel barrel, blued finish. Selected English walnut straight grip stock, with full cone, stock and forearm finely checkered, rubber butt plate, matted rib on receiver, chambered for 2¾-inch shells. Standard dimension of stock 14 inches long. Drop 2 inches at heel and 1½ inches at cone. Will furnish made to order stocks for the "Trap" grade pump gun from 13½ inches to 15 inches long, drops from 2 inches to 3¼ inches, **without extra charge.** Any dimension other than given above will be subject to additional charge of $10	25/10%	List Net
No. 3S.	"Trap Special" Grade	28.68	33.75
	Dimensions of stock, 14 inches in length, drop 2 inches at heel and 1½ inches at cone. Any other length or drop will have to be made to order and therefore will be subject to extra charge of $10	25/10%	List Net
No. 4.	"Tournament" Grade	38.46	45.25
	Extra barrel	12.83	14.25
No. 5.	"Expert" Grade	57.59	67.75
	Extra barrel	16.20	18.00
No. 6.	"Premier" Grade	86.46	105.25
	Extra barrel	19.24	21.38

Nos. 4, 5 and 6 Grades supplied with any length or drop desired without additional charge.

EXTRAS.

Repeating Shotguns, Model No. 10, furnished with raised *Solid matted* rib full length of barrel.........Extra	4.00	5.00
Matting Top Surface of Barrel	4.00	5.00
"Ordnance Steel" Barrel furnished instead of "Remington Steel" at extra charge	4.00	5.00

Fig. 6. The price list of February 1st, 1912. Notice that retail prices are not the same as in the 1911–1912 catalog, and there is a No. 3 and a No. 3S grade, instead of two No. 3 grades. This "S" version appears in the next catalog as the No. 10S, because of designation changes.

If the gun is one of the last Model 10s produced — those with serial numbers above approximately 230,000 — the shells can be removed from the magazine without opening the action. With the gun inverted, pressing in on the carrier latch will release a shell onto the breechblock where it can be rolled into the palm by turning the gun slightly. Repeating the process will empty the magazine, but it is still necessary to remove the shell from the chamber in the conventional manner.

A few Model 10s turn up in gun-shops, at gun shows, and at some auctions from time to time, in conditions ranging from abused (poor) to nearly new. Most of these guns are the "Standard" grade, and since few people collect shotguns, particularly the pump models, even the nearly new guns seldom bring much more than $30. Just "good" ones can usually be obtained for around $20. The other grades, of course, bring more money, with the "trap" grades generally going for around $60 in good condition. For the most part, however, Model 10 owners are a loyal lot and even though it has been out of production for over three decades, many of these guns can still be seen in the duck blinds and fields, on the trap range, doing in general what a good shotgun should, scoring when it counts.

Designed over years ago, it is difficult to tell which is the more modern gun, whether seen in action in the game fields or viewed side by side in a gun rack — the 1964 models of any brand or the Remington Model 10, first of the streamliners.

The
DARNE GUN

Despite little advertising and less fanfare, the makers of this unique, handsome and elegant double gun have sold nearly a half-million of them throughout the world. They must be doing something right!

by JOHN T. AMBER

Do you know the Darne side-by-side double gun? This decidedly unusual shotgun, truly unique in its action design, has had small sale and distribution in the United States despite its several virtues and, in view of its quality construction-even in the lowest-cost grades – its moderate selling price. In point of fact, there isas far as I can determine, no difference in quality of workmanship metal-to-metal fit, jointing of wood and metal, polishing and finish of all components-between the lowest-priced Darnes and the highest. There is, though, good value in the extra-cost versions — stocks of better-quality, fancier-figure walnut, a

greater expanse of finer-line checkering, plus various degrees and extents of engraving. There is a basic design difference, too, but a relatively unimportant one — removal of the barrels is made a little easier on the higher grades, but that's a matter, mostly, of convenience.

It's the action of the Dame that sets it apart from all other shotguns. An action that, at the same time, makes it one of the trimmest and streamlined of shotguns, yet the basic design of the action was evolved some 80 years ago — Darne guns of that age look, in their essential form and style, identical with their latest productions. One could, I suppose, look on this adherence to

long-established form and design elements in two ways — one, that the makers of the Darne have resisted change and modernization, remaining locked into the original concept through inertia or worse. Or it might be said that, once having brought the Darne design to its ultimate development, the makers looked on their efforts and found them good, even perfect, virtually. I hold to the second view, for offhand I can't think of anything that could materially improve the current Darne design — not and keep the Darne design intact. O, there are those who would like the safety repositioned — it's on the left side of the action-but there are some shotgunners who prefer through-bolt

The elegant Darne V22, light, graceful, superbly balanced.

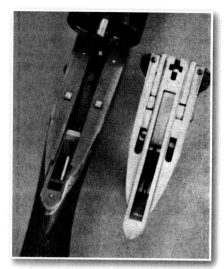

The bright "squares on the receiver *are*, in effect, the sears of the Darne action. At right is the actual receiver turned upside down.

safeties to top-tang types. There is another Darne aspect, a style point, that isn't completely to my liking, and that's a stock form Darne furnishes — and one that is, I'll admit, quite popular in Europe.

This particular Darne stock has a semi-pistol grip — a long, sweeping form, with rounded end, that looks much like the type found on vintage Browning autoloaders. I'd bought my first Darne some 25 years ago, at which time this stock style was common and popular on a number of shotguns. I didn't know much then, either, though of course I thought I did.

I've used that Darne a good bit over the years, but in this job there's almost always a new shotgun to try out, sometimes several a year or season — and in recent years

The Darne breech face, showing the obturator disks, the extractor hooks (at 6 o'clock) and the ejector pins. The large hole receives the round barrel lug, the latter secured by a vertical bolt. However, the main bolting is done by the toggle arm actuated by the operating lever, seen raised here.

more than ever. For that reason I've used the Darne less and less, but that's also true of some three or four other smoothbores I own — the shorter seasons in recent times account for some of that, too.

During all that long usage I've never had a moment's trouble with the Darne — nothing ever broke, nothing malfunctioned.

Visit to St. Etienne

I'd always wanted to visit the Darne plant in southern France (I can't think of any arms factory I wouldn't like to see), but I'd never done more than pass through that area on previous visits. Last year, however, knowing that I'd be returning to that section of France from Budapest, to spend a few days with Raymond Caranta (our Continental editor), I planned a call on Darne. Caranta lives at Aie-en — Provence, only a short drive from St. Etienne, site of the Darne factory.

The general manager for Darne, Jean Bruyere, made Raymond and me welcome and escorted us on a tour of the buildings and shops. I don't know what, exactly, I expected to find, but I've got to say that both of us were hardly prepared for what we saw! Imagine a one-story, long and narrow shop — perhaps 50 feet wide and maybe 400 feet or more deep. The ceilings, about 20 feet above us, were dark with the soot and grime of years. Down either side of the long room, high above the workers, ran shafting and pulleys — lots of pulleys. Leather belts, small and large, fell to the machines, driving them. Here was a shop where Samuel Colt, Philo Remington or Oliver Winchester would have felt at home. The slap and clatter of the belts and pulleys would have been familiar music. The lighting was dim, the corners dark — one had a sense of what the oil-lamped factories of a century earlier might have been like.

There *was* a touch of progress, if that's the right word. Standing in one area were two ultra-modern machines — high speed, tape fed automated milling machines. An incongruous sight, to be sure, but both were in operation. These new tools, with others perhaps to follow, may — one day — see the Darne factory a fully up-to — date plant, but for now the Darne shotgun is still fabricated, fitted and finished by hand. Men wielding files — and women, too — are there in force, particularly at a long row of benches in the final fitting and assembly stages.

Make no mistake, I've not described the Darne plant to criticize or deplore — far from it. An old pappy myself, and one who has always delighted in the genuine excellence that trained and dedicated hands can produce, I was gratified — if surprised — to view the Darne approach to gunmak-

ing. Quality of materials and workmanship, close attention to the perfect assembly of even minor components-these are the norms at Darne.

As I've said, Darne guns are not highly expensive, even in the embellished grades. Some $500-$750 will buy their top model, I believe; compare that with certain English and Italian shotguns! No, what puzzles me — now that I know how they're made-is how they can be sold at such attractive prices.

The Dame is a solid-frame double gun, there's no dropping down of the barrels, released to open by means of a top-snap lever. For this reason the stock can be — and is — a one-piece affair. If the inletting at and around the receiver is examined it'll be obvious that here is a hell of an inletting job. I don't think there are a dozen stockmakers here who'd want to replace a busted Darne stock — not without an aggravation bonus!

The Darne breechblock is a sliding one; the side-projecting "ears" are grasped between the thumb and first fingers, drawing it back, and the operating lever — swinging vertically in a central channel in the block — is pulled smartly upward and backward. That movement pulls fired cases fully out of the chambers; unfired cartridges are extracted only for a short distance. A roll of the gun to either side, after fired-case extractions, lets the empties fall to the ground or, if you're a reloader, into your hand. Darne calls this "automatic ejection," but cases are not kicked clear and away, as we know happens with the usual ejectors. Semantics, maybe, nevertheless their system works.

All double-gun barrels converge from breech to muzzle. In all other doubles but Darnes, as far as I know, the loaded shotshell lies in a slightly cocked position because the standing breech is not at 90° to the long axis of the barrels. In the Darne this has been fixed-each half of the standing breech carries an obturating disk, these angled a small amount, just enough to bring them into exact square

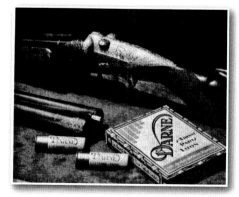

Elegant is the word for this delightful Darne birdgun, a 6-lb. 12 bore.

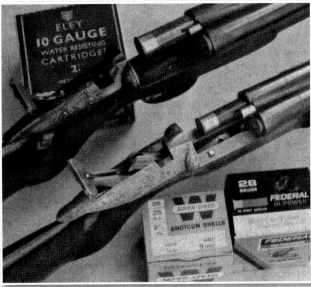

with each converging barrel. Not very important? These flanged disks, completely encircling the shell rim, are an aid to gas containment if a rim lets go. In addition, and because Darne guns are carefully gauged to have minimum chambers and headspace, Darne claims reduced recoil, increased gas thrust on the shot charge for more velocity, and better patterns. In fact, Darne fully guarantees that their barrels, in whatever gauges and lengths, will pattern 72% to 82%. That "warrenteed" performance, note, was made before the advent of plastic shotshells and their enhanced patterning qualities.

All Darne guns, by the way, are fully guaranteed against defects in materials and workmanship for 5 years! They're also approved by "Quality France" (an honor not lightly obtained), an organization which makes sure that French products live up to their manufacturer's claims — sort of an industrial ombudsman.

The single trigger is not highly regarded in Europe, so Darne guns, like the others, have two triggers, but with the front one hinged. Trigger pulls are, in my experience, crisp and of moderate weight. I snapped some 7 or 8 guns during the factory visit, none of which showed any drag or excess heaviness. My sample Darne (which I'll describe later) has triggers that weigh, consistently, about 4–5 lbs. rear and front-and they're snappy.

Darne barrels are sleeved, that is, mounted into the breech sections via the "monobloc" system, a long-tested technique that offers various advantages — greater strength because the breech sleeve can be heat treated to better properties than conventional systems, and for less heat in assembly than is the case with brazed lumps.

Two styles of top ribs are furnished — a normal raised rib (not ventilated) and their "Plume" rib, the type sometimes called "swamped" also. This one drops away from its level position at the breech to lie between the barrels all the way to the muzzle — in effect, there is no top rib. The Plume rib is the type to specify if you want the Darne gun to be ultra light. As you'll see, you can get them that way from Darne — no problem.

Darnes are made in all gauges extant — 10, 12, 1⅔", 16, 20 and 28, plus one you won't want — 24! I don't think the 24s are very popular in France, either. Barrel lengths — standard is 27.6" (70cm), but lengths in 25.6" (65cm), 26.8" (68cm), 28.4" (72cm), 30" (75cm) and 32" (80cm) can be had. All Darne barrels, price range regardless, are given the heaviest French proving-the Triple Proof Test — equal to 8¼ tons psi, and the fully finished guns are again proved at chamber pressure ranging from 5.4 tons to 7.7, the exact psi depending on chamber length.

All of the specs cited apply to standard Darne guns — those that can be bought over the counter from any of Darne's world network of agents. However, Darne has long been geared to a custom gun setup-they'll make one up with virtually anything the customer wants — stock woods, engraving, barrel lengths and chokes, whatever. All you have to do it name it — and, of course, pay for it!

As I've said, Darne guns are elegant and graceful, light and excellently balanced — yet they're tough, too, and made to take it. The V22 grade gun loaned to me (while my special order Darne is being made) weighs just 6 lbs., and that's a standard weight for them. Heavier ones can be had, of course, and lighter ones as well in the smaller gauges. The Model V22 has Darne's standard stock dimensions — 1½" at the comb nose,

Left: The Darne V22, action partly opened, sliding safety lies above guard.

Right: The 28 gauge Darne has a "silvered" action, the stronger 10 gauge (rear) has a black receiver. One is the best-handling quail or grouse gun imaginable; the big bore is also light and lively enough for carrying many a mile without tiring the shooter.

2¼" at heel, and a pull of 14¼"-15¼" to the rear and forward triggers. I need a pull of 14¾", and I like a comb cut to 1⅜" or a hair less, hence my special order — it hasn't arrived yet, unfortunately, so there won't be any pictures of it here.

The V22 has 27.6" barrels, and for that reason it hasn't been as handy as I'd have liked in the woodcock thickets I got into last fall. The one on order will have their 25.6" tubes, which I think will help in like conditions. On the other hand, managing to get in a few days of pheasant hunting last year, I found the Dame a delight to carry and to shoot. I'd worked up some 2¾ dram loads, using an ounce of 6s, and when I was on 'em they fell. That light load produced no bothersome recoil, either, but I had slipped on a Pachmayr rubber pad to lengthen the pull. That doubtless helped. Recoil, it seemed to me, felt about like a 3¼-1¼ load would in a gun of 7-7½ pounds.

Stoeger marketed the Darne until recently — and they may still have some on hand-but now there's a new importer — Firearms Center, Inc., 113 Spokane, Victoria, TX 77901. They'll have basic models in stock, they say, but any of the many grades may be ordered. FCI hasn't established firm prices, so far, but they are selling the Darnes on the company's standard 5-year warranty. How can you go wrong?

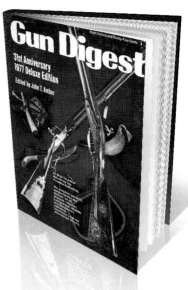

ITHACA'S MAG 10

by WALLACE LABISKY

AT LEAST a half-hour before legal shooting time we began to hear their gabble as strings of blue and snow geese flighted across the refuge boundary into enemy territory. Being some two miles away, the sounds came only faintly at first, but then with spine-tingling clearness as several large flocks angled past our field. But the early morning light was still too murky to make them out.

As always there were the eager-beaver types, willing to run the risk of a stiff fine and possible loss of license. "Outlaws!" I muttered under my breath as I listened to sporadic clusters of shotgun fire in the distance. Then, after many long moments of impatience, I heard my partner speak softly. "Heads up," he said. "Zero hour." I pulled back the bolt on Ithaca's big MAG-10 autoloader and let one of those long, green handloads slam into the chamber. Then I

In spite of its weight and long length the first autoloading big bore magnum handles and swings surprisingly well — and the gas system tames the recoil.

---

thumbed another into the magazine to bring the gun to full 3-shot capacity.

An attractive decoy spread, plus the fact that a large percentage of the big webfoots would be trusting juvenile birds straight off the Arctic nesting grounds, were two points in our favor. Yet I knew from years of experience that the MAG-10 wasn't going to be too much gun for the task. Education would be a quick thing as the geese ran the gun-bristling firing line at the refuge edge, where gunners were packed in elbow-to-el-

bow. While our decoys would get the attention of passing flocks, drawing an occasional gaggle within range, we had no illusions of those classic, calendar-type approaches where the birds coast in with cupped wings and lowered feet. No, there was none of that. The shooting that followed was the kind that puts a magnum gun and specially-developed handloads to the supreme test.

At this time Ithaca's MAG-10 wasn't exactly a stranger in my hands. In the months preceding this opening-day goose shoot in northeastern South Dakota, I had fired nearly 300 rounds through the big tube, testing for pattern and functioning. So I was fully aware of the gun's capabilities but, equally important, how would it measure up under actual hunting conditions?

There's a lot of wood and steel in this Ithaca. It measures 54 inches from muzzle to stock toe and, when fully loaded, the scale says nearly 12½ pounds. Was it going to point like a two-by-four, be cumbersome and sluggish to swing?

Chalk it up to first-morning jitters, the initial chance to score was foiled by my failure to fully release the safety when a juvenile blue drifted past, just outside the decoys. Then, following a brief lull, things got hot. Another lone blue came through and, when the MAG-10 boomed, this one plummeted like a sack of meal. Before I could retrieve that first kill, the big gun chopped down three snows — all singles, all very crisp kills at long range, and I admit to shooting twice at one of these.

The crowning touch came about an hour later when a massive wave of blues and snows, flushed from a distant field, hightailed it for refuge safety. There was a moment or two of indecision. The birds were marginally high. Seventy, possibly 80 yards overhead? Who could say for certain? But an inner voice kept insisting I try.

With a total length of 54 inches and weighing close to 12½ pounds fully loaded, Ithaca's MAG-10 is a big armful. Although the gun handles and points surprisingly well one must learn to put extra effort into one's swing to keep from shooting behind. A carrying strap makes good sense for lugging this big autoloader to and from the shooting site.

It took two loads to establish the proper lead, the second one pulling a tuft of tail-end feathers and signalling the need for more daylight between gun muzzle and bird. On the third try the big adult blue let go all holds and fell, and fell, and fell…

Field Notes

As I write these lines, I have before me my gunning log, and here are a few pertinent comments I entered after the above shoot:

"MAG-10 possesses good balance; points and handles surprisingly well considering its length and weight. Those shooters using a sustained lead will have no problem staying ahead, but those who employ the swing-through method will probably have to put forth a little more initial effort to attain proper gun speed. No malfunctions, and recoil with 2-oz. loads at 1,250 fps is in no way bothersome."

Ah, yes — recoil. Here is where the MAG-10 really pays its way. The gun's weight and Ithaca's "Countercoil" gas system are highly effective in taking the bite out of the bark. However, don't be misled — there's a sizeable amount of recoil sensation with this big fowling piece. But it is a prolonged push, much less noticeable than the abrupt, jarring punch delivered by a fixed-breech gun of the same weight and firing identical loads. As an additional advantage, the more manageable the recoil, the quicker the shooter's recovery in getting off follow-up shots.

I was, of course, fully aware of the way the MAG-10 damps apparent recoil long before I put the gun to work on waterfowl. I routinely pattern-test shotguns by firing from a sand-bagged rest and, when using a double gun, about 20 rounds of the 3½ fodder is all that I can take at a single session. Even then I tend to come away a bit hazy, often with a nagging headache, and always with neck muscles that complain loudly. But with the MAG-10 there was none of this torture — I found I could run off a string of 30 to 40 rounds without the slightest discomfort.

The MAG-10's gas system will probably go down in firearms history as one of the major milestones in gas-gun design. Its most striking aspects are simplicity and ease of maintenance.

"Uncluttered" seems to be the best word to use in describing the system. There are only two major parts (both of stainless steel) attached to the barrel ring, and only one of these moves — the gas cylinder.

Powder gas is taken off through a single barrel port located 10¾" forward of the breech. The gas travels downward through the barrel ring, enters a combination chamber/piston, then jets to the rear through a ⅟₁₆" diameter hole to act directly against the cylinder. The stationary piston is of two-diameter design, the much smaller rearward section being the part on which the gas cylinder moves. When in-battery position, the hollow cylinder completely surrounds the much larger, forward part of the piston.

On firing, cylinder force is transmitted to the bolt slide by means of a "transfer sleeve" which moves back and forth on the magazine tube. The rear of this sleeve has a pair of rod-like fingers which mate with "tunnels" in the front of the receiver and deliver an equalized thrust to the bolt slide.

Maximum travel distance for both gas cylinder and transfer sleeve is ⅝", the travel terminating when the sleeve butts against the forward end of the receiver. At this point in the cycle, the camming action of the slide has permitted the rear of the bolt to drop and disengage from its locking mortise in the barrel extension. The bolt and slide now carry through on their own to handle extraction and ejection. The action spring, which furnishes the power for chambering a fresh round and for returning the gas system to battery position, is conventionally housed in the buttstock.

Early Problem

The linkage connecting the action spring and the bolt slide is strictly heavy duty, as it certainly should be in a magnum-class gun. However, I have to report here that, in my sample gun (SN 879), that the pin which ties the forward end of the bolt link to the slide gave up rather early in life. After 116 MAX handloads had been fired, this forward pin drifted out about 1/16" and, on the 117th shot, the action jammed tightly when the rear of the bolt overrode the projecting pin and was prevented from fully unlocking. Believe me, this could not be easily corrected in the field. Happily, the only damage was to the pin itself.

Back at my work bench, I discovered that both the front and rear bolt-link pins were of questionable construction, being simply a strip of thin sheet steel formed into a tight roll. The replacement pins Ithaca furnished are of solid steel, as they should be, and with these there has been no problem.

But getting back to the "Counter-coil" gas system, my test gun has not been the least bit finicky about digesting a wide variety of loads. The system has functioned most reliably with handloads ranging from 1⅜ to 2¼ ounces of shot, and using about all of the propellant powders suitable for 10-ga. use. This certainly amounts to a big "plus" mark, considering that the system was primarily designed around the 3½" factory round.

This is not to say that the gun will handle the standard 2⅞" load, because it won't — not reliably. The gas system will do its part, but feeding and chambering problems can be expected with the shorter shell. At least this was the case with my test gun. If "light" loads are desired for a preseason warm-up or for easy-range duck shooting, the trouble-free approach is to handload the 3½" shell.

Ithaca has made no claim as to how many rounds can be fired before it becomes necessary to clean the gas system. They say only that the system should be inspected and cleaned "regularly," which is good advice because most powders used in 10-ga. loads will leave considerable fouling behind.

I suppose I should have totally neglected the gas system on my test gun to see how long it would remain in "go" condition, and I might have done so if the system had been difficult to service. On the contrary, maintenance of the barrel-attached parts is so easy that they were given a going-over each time I cleaned the bore, which is to say about every 25 to 30 rounds. Removal of the retaining ring at the rear of the gas piston allows the cylinder to slide free, and a few wipes with a solvent-soaked patch usually removes the accummulated carbon and other crud. In warm, humid weather the fouling build-up is likely to be slightly heavier, and a bit more gummy, than it is when atmospheric condi-

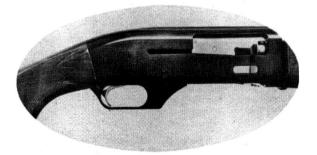

Smooth, flowing lines do much to tone down the massiveness of the MAG-10's 9-inch-long receiver. The bolt and several other key action parts are made of stainless steel, the receiver of 4130. Checkering on the pistol grip runs 18 lines per inch. The forward part of the aluminum-alloy trigger guard houses the coil-type mainspring.

tions are cool and dry — assuming the same amount of firing.

Like the major gas-system components, the MAG-10 breech bolt with its integral locking lug is also of stainless steel, as are the operating handle, shell carrier, action release and trigger. The trigger housing is of aluminum alloy, black anodized, and the massive 9-inch-long receiver is machined from a solid block of 4130 steel.

The MAG-10 bolt has very few parts. There are two crosspins — one to retain both firing pin and polyethylene recoil buffer that nests at the bolt's rear, encircling the firing pin, and another that works in conjunction with the bolt-slide cam for locking/unlocking. Most interestingly, the single hook-type extractor is tensioned by the firing-pin spring through the use of a small two-armed piece positioned on the back side of the bolt face. This tension bar, by means of a hole through its center, is held in alignment by the firing pin, and the pin's spring keeps it snugged up against the extractor at all times. This unique design seems to work perfectly well — with this qualification.

Extraction/Ejection

During my early pattern testing, the sample gun frequently failed to eject the fired shells, in which case the empty hull invariably remained in the ejection port, lengthwise. It was mistakenly thought at first that the handloads involved were not compatible with the gas system. Later, after carefully examining a number of empties, it was determined that the extractor was slipping over the shell rim on ejector contact, and that the shell was being nudged ahead instead of being turned outward at right angle to the port. Even though extraction from the chamber was always 100% complete, it was clearly a matter of insufficient tension on the extractor.

The corrective measures involved increasing the force by altering the bend in the tension bar, and then heat-hardening the part so that it would not "relax." It was also discovered that the extractor itself was quite blunt and, in comparison with the replacement sent out by Ithaca, it was amazing that the original worked as well as it did. The additional tension, along with the new sharp exterior, completely eliminated this particular malfunction.

Since then I have talked with several MAG-10 owners, and have received letters from others, but none has reported an extractor-related problem; nor to my knowledge has any other reviewer made mention of it. So apparently my sample gun was pretty much an isolated case in this respect.

Another parts failure appeared during my load development work — the polyethylene

From the top — MAG-10's stainless steel breech block locks into barrel extension via integral lug at top rear. Small crosspin retains firing pin and polyethylene recoil buffer; large crosspin is part of the camming system that works with bolt slide to raise and lower bolt rear for locking/unlocking. •MAG-10's "Countercoil" gas system is the epitome of simplicity. The gas cylinder is the only moving part — seen here in-battery. Gas bleeds off through single barrel port, enters chamber in piston, then jets out through a rear-facing orifice to act against the hollowed-out cylinder. Cylinder is then propelled rearward on stationary piston. The snap ring seen serves only to retain gas cylinder when barrel is removed from action. • Here the MAG-10 gas cylinder has ended its ⅝" of rearward travel, at which point residual gas exhausts. The cylinder propels a sleeve on magazine tube, transferring cylinder thrust to bolt slide. The gas system attaches to barrel ring by large, round nut seen at right. • Detachable sling swivels are standard on MAG-10. Forward swivel/loop screws into fore-end nut, rear swivel is near stock toe.

recoil buffer at the rear of the bolt developed a partial crack, first noticed after firing about 250 rounds (mostly very stout packages generating up to 12,000 l.u.p.). The damage may have occurred earlier, of course. Even though the original buffer might have remained serviceable for several hundred more shots, it was replaced to avoid a possible snafu while hunting.

A final bit of tinkering was to remove a burr inside the magazine tube, which prevented inserting more than one shell if the rim diameter ran over about .925." (Remington 10-ga. rims run .918/.922" diameter, but some Alcan and Winchester rims go as big as .932.")

The burr was located at the rear of the magazine slotway, which accommodates the shell-follower retaining screw. My diagnosis is that much pattern testing with only one shell in the magazine (as a check on such matters as feeding and chambering) permitted the retaining screw to peen the metal at this point. At any rate, a few judicious file strokes took care of the matter, but not without first unscrewing the magazine tube from the receiver.

Like all Ithaca shotguns, the MAG-10 has a "Roto-Forged" barrel, meaning the tube is hammer-forged around a mandrel from a hot billet of steel, then stress-relieved to retain its straightness. But, unlike other Ithaca models, the bore is not chromed — a concession, I'd guess, to those shooters who might want to customize the bore by altering the choke, lengthening the forcing cone, et cetera. There is no choice as to barrel length or choke — all are 32" Full.

Bore diameter of my sample gun is exactly to industry standards at .775" and the choke constriction amounts to .041." The 2½" long choke section is of the conical type — no muzzle parallel. As near as I can tell, the MAG-10's forcing cone is of "standard" length at about ½" or ⅝" Barrel wall thickness at the muzzle is about .080" this being some .020" under several European-built side-by-side 10s I've checked.

Sitting atop the big tube is a ⅜ inch-wide ventilated rib, its flat surface engraved with straight, longitudinal lines for glare suppression. The front sight is a Bradley type with a .132" white bead. There is no center bead. A "rib extension" of matching width and height, integral with the receiver top, stretches the dead-level sighting plane to nearly 38." This receiver rib, however, is not grooved or dulled in any way to combat reflected light.

Floating Vent Rib

The vent rib, it's worth noting, is of the floating type. Dovetailed to rectangular supports, it is anchored only at the two rearmost posts. This permits the barrel and rib to move independently of one another and, if continuous shooting heats the barrel to a point of expansion, rib warpage does not occur.

At the outset, the test gun's trigger pull went a shade over three pounds, and my considerable shooting has not brought about any change. But, alas, the let-off is preceded by a l-o-n-g stretch of travel — not rough travel, just lengthy. Although a pull such as this would be abominable on a rifle nowadays, in shotgunning it is something you can learn to live with.

The clean, harmonious lines of the MAG-10 make it a right handsome piece, and the weight distribution places the point of balance (the gun empty) at the bolt operating handle, or about 6 ¾" ahead of the trigger. As such, the gun feels just about right in my hands — no pronounced muzzle heaviness, but rather just good steadiness.

The American walnut Ithaca uses on this gun has to be seen to be appreciated. Tight-grained, with an attractive figure accentuated by a modern, gloss-type finish, these MAG-10 buttstocks easily meet, and in some cases surpass, the semi-fancy classification.

The pistol grip and fore-end carry 18-line checkering, the diamonds cleanly cut. The area covered is more than adequate to provide sure, non-slip control — all this far outweighing the touch or two of less-than-perfect workmanship at the borders. Also functional is the 12-inch-long fore-end, somewhat U-shaped in section. It has a comfortable, contoured "groove" at its upper sides to accommodate the thumb and fingers.

In section, the husky pistol grip (capped with a polished aluminum oval encircled by black plastic) is a flattish oval with a minimum circumference of 5½" The stock comb is fairly broad and nicely fluted, while the butt end of the wood wears a "Presenta tion" recoil pad by Pachmayr. Stock measurements for the sample gun are 14⅛" × 1 7/16" × 2¼", with about ⅛" cast-off and a downpitch of 2 ⅛." For this shooter, who wears a 35" sleeve, these dimensions are very close to being a custom fit; those with shorter arms would doubtless be happier with a slightly shorter pull, especially when wearing bulky, cold-weather garments.

Standard with the MAG-10 are detachable 1-inch sling swivels. The front swivel screws into the fore-end nut, the rear one attaching in the same way to an inletted base 3½" forward of the stock toe. This very practical approach would benefit many duck/goose/turkey guns. Most waterfowlers can find use for about 6 pair of hands in getting their-paraphernalia out to pit or blind, and being able to hang ye olde fowling piece on one's shoulder is a big help at such times. Most shooters will prefer, as I do, to detach the sling once they're settled in and ready for action, but in a pinch the gun can be used with the sling in place, yet handling and pointing won't suffer markedly.

Somewhat puzzling, Ithaca doesn't include a carrying strap with each MAG-10. Among the several accessories offered by the firm is a dandy 1-inch carrying strap in natural russet or oiled leather that would be eminently suitable. I know, because I'm using one.

Pattern Tests

My pattern-test work with the MAG-10 was a long-winded episode. All told, I fired 215 3½" loads — practically all of them fold-crimp handloads that were assembled, predominantly, in the Remington SP plastic shell.

As for the Remington factory round, with 2 ozs. No. 2 chilled and its old style card-and-felt wad column and antiquated roll crimp, it made a rather sorry showing. Only one individual pattern exceeded the full-choke minimum standard of 70%, and the average efficiency at 40 yards was pretty sour at only 63.8% — just tight modified-choke performance. (Note: Remington announced late in 1975 a new 10-ga. Power Piston loading with extra-hard shot in 2⅞" and 3½" lengths. This upgrading, long overdue, should produce a large improvement over the former loads in all guns.)

It really came as no surprise to find that this MAG-10 barrel wasn't fond of BB shot. Using a 2⅛-oz. charge of chilled shot, for example, the best 40-yard average was just a fraction over 70% with a PGS, fiber fillers and a plastic sleeve topping 52.5 grains of AL-8 powder. For really tight, strong-dense-center patterns with non-buffered BB loads, the .041" choke is probably a bit too much constriction.

However, when 40 grains of white household flour was used as a buffering agent with a 2-oz. charge of Lubaloy BBs, the 40-yard average jumped dramatically to 88.6%. Powder charge for this Remington-cased package was 47/HS-6 (MV 1,255 fps), and again the wad stack consisted of a PGS, et cetera. But on moving back to the 75-yard marker, the load shed much of its glamor. It averaged only 35 pellets in a 30-inch circle. None of this brought big, salty tears to my eyes because I usually let the other fellow play with BBs.

With handloads using No. 2 shot this MAG-10 did right well. Almost all suitable powders were tried with 2-and 2⅛-oz. payloads and, except for a few prescriptions with the new Ballistic Pattern Driver (a plastic shot-cup wad from Ballistic Products, Inc., 16230 Fifth Avenue North, Wayzata, Minn. 55391), the wad column drill was the PGS, fiber fillers and a plastic sleeve.

For the non-buffered chilled-shot packages, the 5-shot 40-yard averages ranged from 71% to just over 83% — good full-choke performance. Before this I'd always regarded AL-8 as a hard-to-beat 10-ga. propellant, but in these tests with non-buffered shot loads, Hodgdon's HS-6 invariably came through with the highest efficiencies.

Turning now to the buffered shot loads, 40 grs. of ordinary household flour was used to fill the pellet interstices to reduce shot deformation. The most readily available of the suitable materials, flour does a good job in this role.

The 40-yard averages with a 2-oz. load of chilled 2s zoomed to *91.8%* with 47/HS-6, and to *92.4%* with 48/Blue Dot. These high-velocity loads placed an average of 122 pellets in a *20-inch* circle at 40 yards. At 75 yards both gave 70-pellet averages for the 30-inch circle — certainly more than adequate pattern coverage for even a small, 5-pound goose. As you may have guessed, these two buffered handloads were called on to handle the bulk of my goose busting with the MAG-10, and both did a consistently outstanding job at extreme range.

Incidentally, you may have read or heard about the shot charge's rate of drop, and how this necessitates a hard-to-execute "hold over" when confronted with a crossing shot at long range. This matter of drop was checked out very carefully when running pattern tests at 75 yards. I found there was only a 5 to 17 inch difference between pattern-center impact when using the very same "sight picture" I used at 40 yards. That's a long way from the two feet of drop frequently mentioned out at 75/80 yards.

Next, using chilled 4s in search of a far-reaching duck load, the MAG-10 averaged 74.2% with a 2 -oz. charge pushed by 50/Blue Dot, the wadding being a PGS multi-wad stack with a plastic shot sleeve. Using 43.5/SR-4756 behind the Ballistic Pattern Driver wad and 2 ozs. of Lubaloy 4s, the 40-yard percentage was much the same, but with stronger center density.

Finally, 42/HS-6 with the BPD wad and 1⅞ ozs. of Lubaloy 4s delivered 83% patterns with even stronger center density than the preceding load. Shot charges of 1⅝ and 1¾ ozs. were also tried with the BPD wad and HS-6, with results in the 82/84% bracket. But, considering all aspects of pattern worth, the 17/8 oz. loading got the nod for long-range

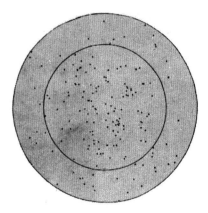

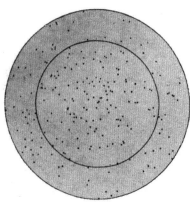

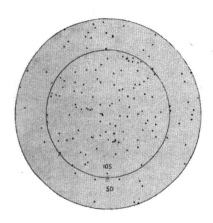

Exceptionally strong core density usually results when a buffering agent (here 40 grains of white household flour) is used to fill the pellet interstices to lessen deformation from jaming. This 40-yard (92.4%) pattern has 125 pellets in the 20" core, with only 46 in the 5" annular area. A strong 40-yard imbalance in pellet distribution, such as this, is necessary for sure coverage on geese at 70/75 yards range. This pattern represents average performance for the AAAG-10 with a 2×2 chilled payload powered by 48 grains of Blue Dot for 1,295 fps MV.

This 40-yard pattern counts 84.7% and represents near-average performance for Labisky's Ithaca MAG-lOwith the 1⅞x4 Lubaloyshot loading using the new Ballistic Pattern Driver plastic wad. A charge of 42/HS-6 powder in the Remington 3½" SP plastic case shows 1,270 fps. Strong density in the 20" pattern core (here 135 pellets) insures adequate hits on large ducks at greatly extended ranges.

Forty-yard efficiencies ranged from 78.4% to 89.2% when the MAG-10 barrel was fed a 2-oz. charge of chilled 2s pushed by 48/HS-6 for a MV of 1,280 fps. Wad column in the Remington hull was the Alcan PGS, two ⅜" fiber fillers and the Kwik-Sert sleeve. This 83.3% pattern represents average performance with 105 pellets in the 20" core and 50 in the 5" annular area. Of the many non-buffered handloads tried, this loading, with CCI-157 primers, was one of the better ones.

duck busting, and it handled the task with much authority. Load details and ballistics for this handload and others field-tested appear in an appended table.

Following my opening-day shoot, many more geese fell to the MAG-10, but it wasn't until very late in the season that I found time to work the big gun on highballing mallards. And on one such hunt, the unexpected happened.

The temperature that day was in the low 20s, and a light covering of snow plus a numbing wind had the quackers on the move, looking for a good, square meal. To reach a promising pass-shooting spot I had to follow a narrow, half-mile-long strip of standing corn and, as I walked along, I began to notice fresh web-footed tracks. Suddenly a big greenhead was flailing the air less than 20 yards ahead. I

came unglued in time to settle his hash at no more than 40 paces. By the time I reached the far end of the corn strip the hunt was over. I had three more drakes in hand — all taken on the jump. And if this little episode doesn't effectively attest to the MAG-10's good handling, I'll eat my duck call, reed and all.

Not every waterfowler, or turkey hunter, will have a crying need for Ithaca's big 10-bore autoloader, but from what I've been able to gather, considerable interest has been generated all across the country. So much interest, in fact, that MAG-10's are still mighty hard to come by. Most dealers, I understand, haven't been able to discard their waiting lists, and it may be yet another year before the supply exceeds the demand.

Field-Tested Hand loads
Ithaca MAG-10 Autoloader

Remington 3½" SP plastic shell
CCI-109 primer*
42.0 grs. HS-6
BPD + 20-ga. ⅜" + ⅜" fiber
1⅞ ozs. No. 4 Lubaloy 6-point fold crimp
Av. MV: 1,270 fps
Av. pressure: 10,500 l.u.p.
Av. 40-yd. efficiency: 82.8%

Remington 3½" SP plastic shell
CCI-109 primer*
45.0 grs. HS-7
BPD + 20-ga. ⅜" +¼" fiber
2 ozs. No. 2 Lubaloy 6-point fold crimp Av. MV: 1,225 fps
Av. pressure: 10,500 l.u.p. Av. 40-yd. efficiency: 81.0%

Remington 3½" SP plastic shell
CCI-157 primer
48.0 grs. HS-6
PGS + B card + ⅜" + ⅜" + Kwik-Sert
2 ozs. No. 2 chilled
6-point fold crimp
Av. MV: 1,283 fps
Av. pressure: 10,300 l.u.p.
Av. 40-yard efficiency: 83.1%

Remington 3½" SP plastic shell
CCI-157 primer
46.0 grs. HS-6
PGS + .070" NC + ⅜" +¼" + Kwik-Sert
2⅛ ozs. No. 2 chilled
6-point fold crimp
Av. MV: 1,220 fps
Av. pressure: 10,150 l.u.p.
Av. 40-yd. efficiency: 83.6%

Remington 3½" SP plastic shell
CCI-157 primer
47.0 grs. HS-6
PGS + .070" NC + ⅜" +¼" + Kwik-Sert
2 ozs. No. 2 chilled
40.0 grs. white household flour
1" square onionskin paper
6-point fold crimp (paraffin sealed)
Av. MV: 1,255 fps
Av. pressure: 10,000 l.u.p.
Av. 40-yd. efficiency: 91.8%

Remington 3½" SP plastic shell
Rem. 57-Star primer
48.0 grs. Blue Dot
PGS + .070" NC + ⅜" +¼" + Kwik-Sert
2 ozs. No. 2 chilled
40.0 grs. white household flour
1" square onionskin paper
6-point fold crimp (paraffin sealed)
Av. MV: 1,295 fps
Av. pressure: 10,600 l.u.p.
Av. 40-yd. efficiency: 92.4%

*Enlarge primer pocket by first seating a fired 209-size primer.

Sixty pounds wad-seating pressure used for all loads.

PGS = Alcan plastic gas seal; NC = Nitro card.
BPD = Ballistic Pattern Driver plastic wad.

The Collectible
WINCHESTER
42 ... a shooter's choice, and
a collector's joy

by WILLIAM S. SNYDER

 HERE IN THE world the 410 shotgun fits into the scheme of things is perhaps a philosophical question best left to, well, philosophers. Other gauges are and always have been more popular in this country as well as abroad. Those shooters and collectors who are partial to the 410 are not all interested in *why* they like it. And for the user it is strictly a question of utility. If, on the other hand, you collect 410s, then other considerations come into play; or you may fall into the category of user *and* collector.

If you were to take a poll of gun buffs and ask the question, "What 410 shotgun would you consider not only functional but collectible as well?" it would seem likely the Winchester Model 42 would be well toward the top of the list. Indeed, for the Model 42 enthusiast, other types, makes and models simply won't do. The Model 42 is a much different shotgun from a finely crafted side-by-side or an expensive over/under. It was a mass-produced scattergun, but it has attracted a following over the years. And in that perspective we're going to take a close look at its history and the variations in

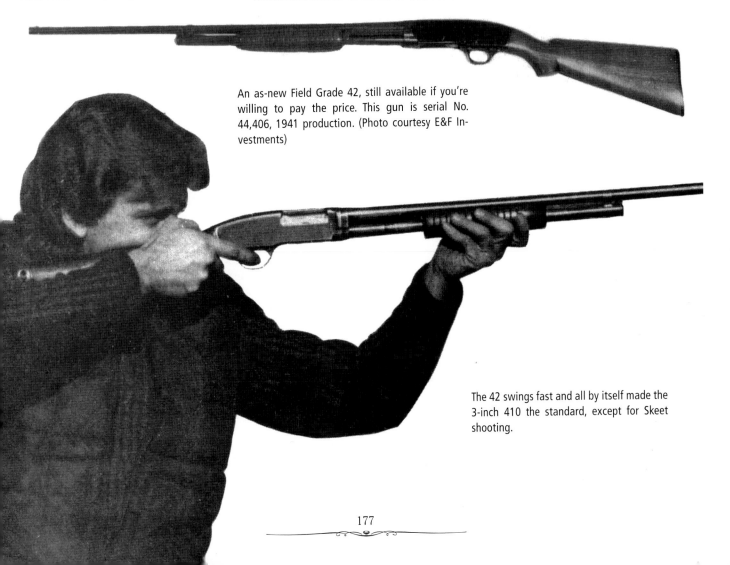

An as-new Field Grade 42, still available if you're willing to pay the price. This gun is serial No. 44,406, 1941 production. (Photo courtesy E&F Investments)

The 42 swings fast and all by itself made the 3-inch 410 the standard, except for Skeet shooting.

which it was produced, as well as some of its more common mechanical problems.

The Model 42 offered something different in a 410 shell-the 3-inch length. Like so many other new things for rifle or shotgun, the 3-inch 410 was not an innovation, but an evolution. The 410 evolved from the 44-40 rifle shot cartridge — he shot was contained in a paper enclosure — and at the early stage even the mild bottleneck shape of the 44-40 case was still present. The next step in the evolution was a straight brass case, 2 inches long.

At first, Winchester designers were preparing the Model 42 design for the 2½-inch shell. And by 1932, the Model 42 designed by Thomas C. Johnson would have been in production had it not been for John M. Olin. The Olin interest had recently purchased Winchester Arms, and Olin had been a long-time admirer of their firearms. John Olin was adamant that the Model 42 be introduced as a shotgun which offered something new, one which would utilize a 3-inch shell. Changing the shell length was responsible for holding up production though in the long run it proved worthwhile considering the popularity the gun would enjoy.

Early in 1933 the 42 was in full production, and a 1934 Winchester catalog gave a lengthy description of the Model 42's physical characteristics along with an account of its virtues.

The new Model 42 Winchester Slide Action Hammerless .410 Repeater is of completely new design and construction. It has a general similarity in appearance to the famous Model 12 Winchester, but in each and every part, it is a .410 shotgun.

Here are 2-inch, 2½-inch and 3-inch 410 shells, of which only the latter two survive.

Model 42 is the first American made .410 repeater to handle a 3-inch shell and the first pump action gun designed for such a shell. The chambering for 3-inch shells makes the Model 42 a unique achievement in American gun making.

Model 42 is made in two styles, the Standard Grade gun and the Model 42 Skeet Gun. Both stles are chambered ex-

pressly for 3-inch shells, but in addition will also handle the regular two and a half .410 gauge shell.

The Standard Grade is furnished with either 26 inch or 28 inch full choke, modified choke or cylinder bore barrel of Winchester Proof Steel, pistol grip walnut stock, hard rubber butt plate and round slide handle with circular grooves. The Skeet Gun is fur-

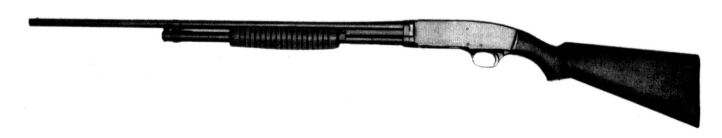

This is the original factory prototype of the Model 42. It bears no external or internal markings of any kind, and the receiver is pieced together, as opposed to production models which had one-piece receivers. Records indicate that it was made in the Winchester model shop in August of 1932. (Photos courtesy of Buffalo Bill Historical Center, Cody, Wyoming.)

nished with 26-inch Skeet Choke Barrel of Winchester Proof Steel, straight grip walnut stock, checkered, hard rubber butt plate, and extension action slide handle, checkered. The magazine of each gun has a capacity of five 3-inch shells or six 2 and a half inch shells.

This early catalog description continues with other features of the gun such as its weight and makes note of the gun's balance and appearance, amongst other things. It also made note of the fact that the gun, in its first year of production, already held the 410-bore world's long-run record at Skeet.

The year after the gun was introduced a third variation was added, the Trap Grade. Standard accessories were a checkered pistol grip stock and a smaller

And there is one more type within the Model 42 series, the DeLuxe, which was probably first offered in 1950 and remained available through the end of production in 1963. A full range of engraving was offered for the DeLuxe, a feature which is noted primarily in distributor catalogs. Winchester records up to 1941 reveal that only seven guns in Pigeon Grade were produced. Records which closely detail the production of the Model 42 are incomplete following 1943, so it is impossible to say how many were made between that year and 1963. Their number, whatever it was, make the DeLuxe a seldom-seen item.

The DeLuxe had many special features such as hand-finished working parts and jeweled breechbolt and elevator. Wood

balance between the different chokes is another story: Full-61 percent; Modified-27 percent; Skeet-8.3 percent; and Cylinder bore at 2.8 percent. Thus, my experience searching high and low over the years for Model 42s with chokes other than Full is revealed for what it really was, mostly an exercise in futility.

And the following figures are also revealing, again from 1933 to 1943: Of the almost 51,000 guns produced, 46,577 were Field Grade guns! That doesn't leave much, does it? The remainder breaks down as follows: 3,558 were Skeet Grade; 231 were Skeet guns in Trap Grade; and the remainder, a paltry 466 pieces, had "special features."

Even a cursory glance at the above numbers makes it quite clear that the vast

A well-used Field Grade Model, as most are. (M. Morse photo)

slide than that found on the Field Grade. Also standard was the 26-inch barrel in Full choke. If the customer desired a 28-inch barrel or a different choke, there was no extra charge. One merely had to tell them what was wanted. This policy, of course, allowed Winchester to sell many more guns and, as will be seen a little later here, would eventually create some very scarce combinations of choke and barrel length within the different types. It would seem that the Trap Grade was a variation which did not produce a great deal of enthusiasm with the gun buying public as it was no longer offered in the 1939 catalog. Another type was introduced in 1934, the Skeet Gun-Trap Grade, though I do not consider this piece to be a separate type and, in fact, it didn't last. The only real difference between it and the regular issue Skeet gun was that the customer could order specific stock dimensions and the quality of the walnut was generally better. After 1939 the Skeet gun was no longer offered in Trap Grade.

was of the highest grade walnut and often had checkering in diamond-shaped panels.

There seems little doubt that the DeLuxe is the rarest of the 42s, especially so if it carries factory engraving. But what of the other guns, the Field and Skeet Grade? The scarce guns which exist among those two types are the result of three little words which the long-time Winchester collector is very familiar with: *Special-order features*. All of a sudden, once that phrase enters the picture, we no longer have the simplicity of only three major types of Model 42. Before we begin to outline those features, it might be helpful to look at some production records that break down the numbers and types of Model 42s and which tell an interesting story by themselves.

Of the slightly under 51,000 42s made up to 1943, the production of 26-inch and 28-inch barrels is almost evenly divided. In the same time period (1933-1943) the

majority of Model 42s encountered by any collector will be Field Grade guns in Full choke and either 26- or 28-inch barrels. That is not to say that the Field Grade doesn't have some interesting (and rare) variations, however. Foremost amongst these is a 42 set up for 2½-inch shells. Remember, this was the first repeater which would handle a 3-inch shell. Nevertheless, there were 37 made (again, up until 1943) with 2½-inch chambers. The Skeet gun was normally chambered for the 2½-inch shell, but the fact remains that, as a special-order item, it could be (and was) made with 3-inch chambers. If this special-order thing seems to be getting out of hand, bear with me, the end is in sight.

There are two other noteworthy special-order features and both are quite rare: Any Model 42 with a vent rib; any Model 42 with a Cutts Compensator. Winchester offered both, but very few, in relation to the number of guns produced, were made. If you find either one at a garage sale, buy it.

Indeed, unused — let alone unfired — Model 42s of any sort are rare birds. (M. Morse photo)

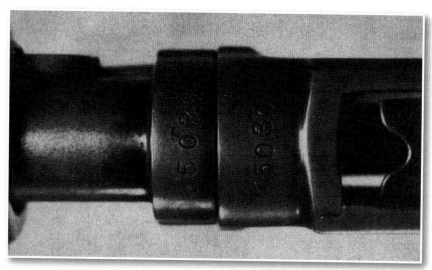

Matching serial numbers are the best proof that one gun has not been pieced together from two.

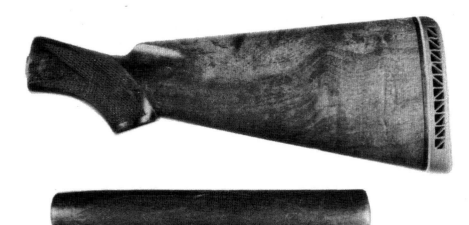

Used wood, such as this Skeet-style stock and slide handle, can still be found at gun shows and occasionally in the parts inventory of your local gunsmith.

The "Winchester Special Ventilated Rib" was first offered in 1954 and probably was available until the last year of production, though it seems that of the few which were produced most were made before 1960. Up until 1954, the standard barrel configuration was round with the raised matted rib usually offered as an option. The matted rib was not advertised after 1954, and it is only encountered in a very few guns, though it's not as scarce as the vent rib. Many people are under the impression that the vent rib was a Winchester factory item. The truth of the matter is that a majority were installed by Simmons Gun Specialty Company and returned to the factory for bluing. As for the Cutts Compensator, very few were ordered and by 1956 it was discontinued.

No figures are extant for the numbers of vent ribs and Cutts Compensator-equipped guns. The only way to get an accurate idea of their remaining numbers is to start looking for them. It will soon become apparent that the search will be a long one.

As becomes increasingly obvious, it would be a virtual impossibility to assemble a complete collection of the Model 42s. From the standpoint of the collector, it is the various chokes which present the greatest problem. It would, for instance, not be impossible to find an example fitted with a Cutts Compensator. Time consuming perhaps, but not impossible. On the other hand, it would be something else again to find individual chokes. Or,

try and find the DeLuxe in all the different chokes. It would be much more practical to assemble a collection which represents the major types and then add other pieces which show a different feature than those guns you already have-a pistol grip stock as opposed to the straight grip, for example.

The following list details some of the more academic points of items which are not only useful in identifying the various models but are also useful in dating the guns and making sure that they are original. An illustration of the value of this trivia involves a collector who brought a Model 42 to me several years ago. He contended that the gun was an early one, a fact which held up after dating the gun from the serial numbers. He also thought that the gun was unaltered. This, however, proved to be wrong. The forearm was almost flat on the bottom with a length that was a bit over 8½ inches. That forearm was not used until after 1945, so it was safe to assume that it was a replacement. Not that such a detail radically affected the value of the gun. It's just that any gun is either original or it isn't, plain and simple. Here's the list:

1. The majority of DeLuxe guns had grip caps on pistol grip stocks.

2. Skeet guns in Trap Grade were nearly always fitted with pistol grips.

3. Beginning in 1939, cheekpieces and Monte Carlo stocks were offered.

4. Extension slide handles were standard for Skeet guns though they were also fitted to Field Grade guns at the buyer's option.

5. Front sights were steel, brass and monel; steel, followed by brass seem to predominate.

6. Straight grips were offered between serial numbers 21,000 and 64,000. They are also seen on guns with lower and higher numbers, though not with any frequency.

7. Several different recoil pads were used, including Jostom, D-W, Hawkins and Goodrich.

As with any group of guns, misconceptions are harbored by many concerning how many of which model were made and in which variations. A friend recently informed me that the Model 42s were made primarily in Full and Skeet chokes, and it's interesting to note how people acquire

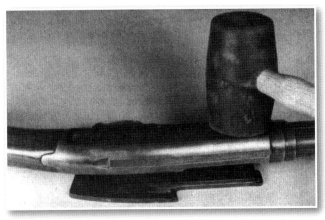

The usual method of removing the sideplate is striking the other side of the gun. Use a soft hammer and strike both *ends*, not the *middle*. Note position of hammer.

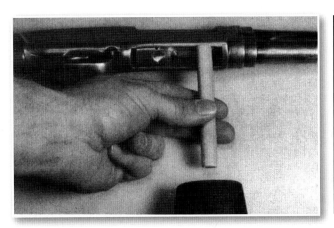

An ill-advised method for removing a tight sideplate. If you are forced to try this, proceed with caution, gently.

The sideplate comes off in one piece as shown. Always return the two screws to the holes they came from as they will seldom interchange. (M. Morse photo)

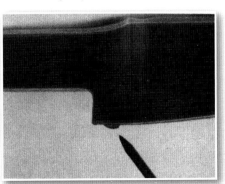

This small extrusion on the sideplate has a corresponding notch in the frame. Make sure it's in place before trying to force the sideplate on.

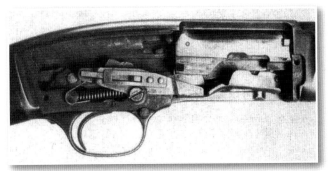

With the sideplate off, the action can be moved back and forth, making the internal parts visible enough to determine a broken or misplaced part. The bolt is closed at upper right.

The small spring just above the trigger that looks like a bent paper clip doesn't break very often, but does come loose quite often. If the carrier loses its tension, this spring is probably the culprit.

Knowing that the screw which retains the carrier mechanism is loosened by turning it *clockwise* helps, if you don't want to break it.

Even a slightly bent carrier can cause feeding problems. They are easily straightened if you go slowly, gently.

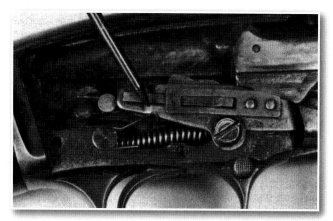

The carrier spring in its proper position as noted by the pointer.

The J-shaped carrier spring (behind and above the trigger) in its OFF position. Carrier will not work when the upper end of the spring is unattached as shown here.

The right-hand extractor is generally a trouble-free part.

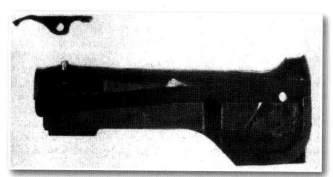

The left-hand extractor (top, left) above the pin and slot in the bolt.

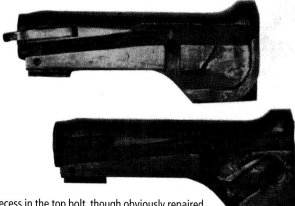

The recess in the top bolt, though obviously repaired, still retains the proper shape. The bottom one, in spite of the unsightly repair, was still in working order (M. Snyder photo)

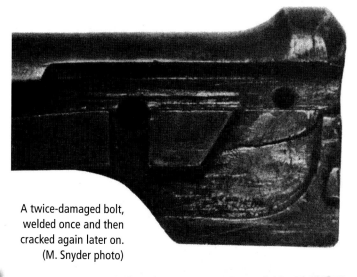

A twice-damaged bolt, welded once and then cracked again later on. (M. Snyder photo)

To replace the headspace ring simply remove the screw and slide the lock (slotted piece) away from the barrel and unscrew the headspace ring.

A new headspace ring is one of the more easily found parts for the Model 42. Other parts are not so easily acquired.

some of their impressions. In this particular instance, the man who told me this is an avid trap shooter and hunts not a lick. Thus, he was in a position to see more Skeet-choked guns in the possession of friends and fellow shooters than any other choke, accounting for his notion that the Skeet choke is common.

For those who are inclined toward working on this gun, a few points are of interest. If you haven't spent much time repairing firearms, bear in mind the two following scenarios. First, we have the fellow who enters the local gunsmith's place with shotgun in hand. It is a simple matter to explain to the gunsmith what the problem is, find out about when your gun will be ready to pick up, then be on your way. The second scenario is somewhat more grim since it involves a fellow who brings the gun in with the stock under his arm, the barrel in one hand and a sack or shoe box full of parts in the other hand. The gunsmith begins frowning as this ugly sight walks through the door and chances are good that he will still be frowning when it leaves, maybe *with* the gun.

A short text and some photos of the inner workings of a particular firearm may do nothing more than get you in trouble. Now, with that in mind, let's take a closer look at some of the mechanical problems which afflict the Model 42.

One common failing is the broken left-hand extractor, an easily remedied problem *if* you can find the part. Lefthand extractors can be found without a great deal of trouble, unlike other Model 42 parts. Bolts, for instance, are scarce as are most other parts.

With the action closed, remove the sideplate and carefully lift the bolt out. Before doing so, make a careful visual inspection of the action, noting what goes where. The left-hand extractor requires removing the small pin which holds it in place after which it is a simple matter to lay the new one in, align the two holes and replace the pin. When replacing the bolt, make sure it sets properly before setting the sideplate on it. Laying the sideplate on and trying to tap the bolt down by using a small hammer will usually result in a

broken bolt and/or sideplate. Remove the sideplate with care. It's not at all uncommon to find a gun which hasn't had the sideplate removed in many years, if at all. Most fit very tightly anyway, so any undue force can break them.

The bolt is easily removed with the sideplate off which allows access to another common problem-a broken carrier spring. It's not unusual to dislodge the carrier spring when removing the sideplate, but it's simple to re-attach by bending the U-shaped upper end back over the carrier. This spring is one of those parts which relies on its own tension to remain in place.

Broken or cracked bolts are often a problem in the Model 42, and if the one in your gun is still intact, it's easy to keep it that way by not working the action with a lot of force. Shells can be loaded or ejected just as easily when you don't slam the gun open or shut and the softer practice will contribute many years to the life of the bolt. Bolts are hard to replace because they're hard to find, accounting

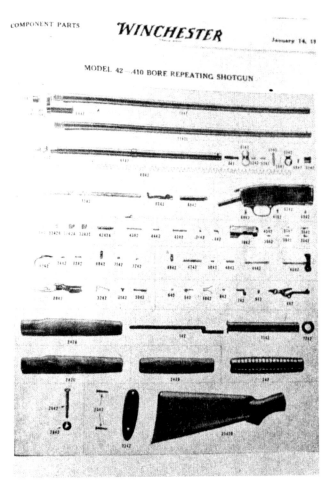

Component parts for the Model 42 from the 1949 catalog. (M. Snyder photo)

This 1949 catalog shows the specifications for the Field Grade Model. (M. Snyder photo)

for the large number that have been welded or brazed. A crack, certainly, and *some* breaks can be welded by any competent unsmith should you be so unlucky as to damage one.

If you have a part which can't be repaired, the logical steps are to inquire at your local gunsmith or peruse the offerings of the parts dealers which always frequent the gun shows. When you are forced into this situation, carefully examine any parts you buy with care as they are often badly worn. With a bolt, for example, it is critical that the area around the recess have sharp and clearly defined edges. Anything less will be a temporary solution.

More people get into trouble with gun repairs in the assembly or disassembly than in replacing a part. With the Model 42, these problems come from not aligning the tab on the upper part of the sideplate, using too much force in seating it, or taking it off or discovering too late that the single screw which retains the carrier is loosened by turning it clockwise.

Another problem that requires a lot of disassembly is tightening or replacing the headspace ring. If you choose to do it yourself, the adjustment is made by moving the ring sometimes a very little bit. Before it will move, however, you must locate the small screw at its base, remove it and slide the small keeper away from the ring. At that point, the ring can be taken completely off or turned the needed amount for adjustment. Be sure and slide the keeper back to its original position and replace the screw tightly. How do you know if the headspace needs adjusting? Most often it will become noticeable as a slight (sometimes severe) looseness between barrel and action.

One last thought on this home repair route: I have one old Field Grade 42 I shoot regularly and when it malfunctions I have no qualms about tearing into it. If, on the other hand, it were an as-new Field Grade or a nice Skeet or DeLuxe model, it would be carted off to the gunsmith if it needed work. Bear that in mind before you begin work on one you own.

Model 42s are a lot of fun for an occasional round of trap and even better for upland game birds such as quail, grouse and chukar as well as rabbit, and interesting to collect as well. The Model 42 is suited best to that purpose for which it was designed, specifically, to be shot. Owning one or a dozen without an adequate supply of 410 shells would be a tragedy.

Acknowledgements

My thanks to Mark Beinke of Mark's Gun Shop, Klamath Falls, Oregon, for his help on the inner workings of the Model 42 and for the numerous items he provided for many of the photographs. Thanks are also due to the Buffalo Bill Historical Center for their photos of the prototype Model 42.

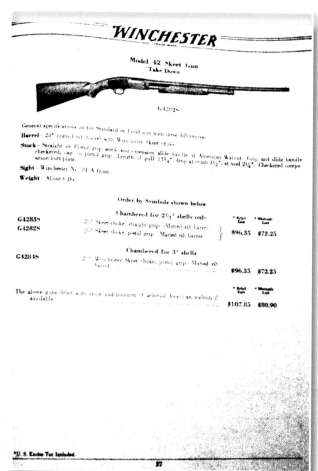

This Skeet Model listing (1949) offers both shell lengths at the same price, though very few Skeet Models with 3-inch chambers were made. (M. Snyder photo)

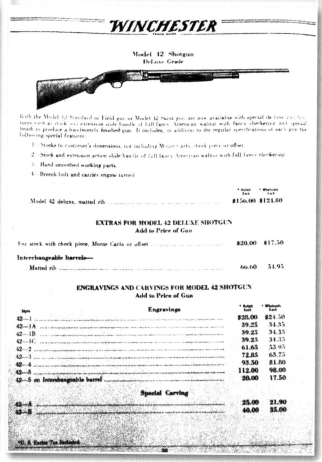

Note the subtle difference between the slide on this Deluxe Model 42 as compared to the photo which shows the Skeet Model. (M. Snyder photo)

The THOMPSON SUBMACHINE GUN
WEAPON OF WAR AND PEACE

A complete history of the fabulous "Tommygun" from the few handmade Model 1919's through the 2000-per-day production of World War II. Made infamous by gangsters, beloved by Marines and GI's, for almost three decades the Thompson was on the front line of every war. Now "obsolete," it still holds a top place in fighting men's hearts

by RAY BEARSE

ENTUCKY BORN John T. Thompson (1860-1940), who grew up during a period when wars were fought with single shot muzzle-loaders and early bolt and lever action repeaters, had no inkling in his early days that his name would become synonymous with what is probably the deadliest hand weapon ever devised by man — the Tommygun. "Thompson" … "Tommygun" … "Typewriter" … "Burpgun" … "Chopper" — these are universal terms for any SMG, be it a Schmeisser, Sten, Beretta, Solothurn, or whatever.

General Thompson (West Point class of 1882) did not invent the submachine gun nor even discover the principle used in the weapon bearing his name, but he was a co-designer of what is probably the most reliable, rugged, and expensive production SMG ever manufactured.

The Thompson, beginning with the bootleg battles of the '20's and through the heyday of Dillinger's ilk, gained an undeserved reputation of being the major weapon in

M1921 Thompson Submachine Gun, serial #45, manufactured by Colt. The M21 was normally equipped with a front sight, Lyman adjustable rear sight and a type XX (20-round) magazine. This is #1047 in the Colt Collection, Connecticut State Library, Hartford, Conn.

the arsenal of scoundrels — and one used by almost no one else. In truth, 999 of every 1000 Thompsons have been used for law and order, under circumstances ranging from U.S. Marines landing in Nicaragua to lonely peace officers shooting it out with BAR-equipped highwaymen, and from G-men busting up Baby Face Nelson's Wisconsin hideout to the Allies fighting the tyranny of Hitler and Hirohito. Even today, almost a half-century after its first public appearance on the peaceful greensward at Camp Perry, Ohio, "obsolete" Thompsons are belly-busting Red guerrillas in the far reaches of the globe.

The first Thompson was not a true SMG but an unsuccessful 30-cal. auto rifle developed about 1916–17. The first Thompson SMG, made by the Warner & Swasey Co. of Cleveland, reportedly was designed in late 1918. Developers included Gen. Thompson his son Col. Marcellus Thompson, and T. E. Eickhoff, later chief engineer, Cleveland Ordnance District. A news story at the time Eickhoff retired in 1955 described him as the chief Thompson design engineer (1916–25). In late 1919 or early 1920, the Auto Ordnance Corp., with offices at 501 Fifth Ave., New York City, and later with manufacturing and assembly facilities at Bridgeport, Conn., was formed to manufacture and distribute Thompson SMG's.

The Thompsons left Auto Ordnance after the death of major stockholder Thomas Fortune (The Buck) Ryan in 1928. and during the 1930's the firm was taken over by Russell Maguire of Maguire Industries.

After World War II, guns, spare parts, and accessories passed through several hands. In December, 1951, George Numrich, Jr., president of Numrich Arms Corp., West Hurley, N. Y., acquired the name "Auto Ordnance" and a large stock of guns and parts. "Tommy Gun" is the registered trade mark of the Numrich Arms Corp.

Operating Cycle

The basic operating cycles for both the retarded blow-back (when the Blish lock

is installed) and simple blow-back Thompsons are practically identical. With the safety in the forward (fire) position and the fire selector switch in the rearward (semi-auto) position, the retracted bolt, held by the sear, is released and moves forward under pressure of the recoil spring. The bolt drives the top cartridge in the magazine forward into the chamber, at the same time camming the Blish lock into the receiver's locking grooves. *(Commercial Thompsons, most experimental models, and the M1928A1 utilize the so-called "Blish adhesion principle," patented by Captain John Blish, U.S.N., on June 30, 1913. Blish, a naval ordnance expert, maintained that the locking surfaces of a breech mechanism, if set at the proper angle to the direction of force, will resist the application of high pressure; that such pressure, in fact, will cause them to adhere for an instant; and that when pressure drops the adhesion is lost and the breech mechanism opens. Many engineers deny the Blish-principle exists. During tests in 1928 the British discovered that no one could tell, when firing, whether the Blish lock was in or out of the gun. The same observation was made later by Thompson-armed British soldiers at Tobruk. When they had trouble keeping the locks free of desert sand, they found the weapon would keep on firing, even a little faster possibly, if they took out "the bloody lock" and pitched it at the Jerries.)* Bolt and receiver are now locked together in the forward position; the hammer falls forward and the firing pin indents the cartridge primer.

Gas pressure from the fired cartridge presses against the bolt face, is transmitted upward and unlocks the bolt. Both bolt and actuator are driven rearward, extracting the fired case from the chamber and ejecting it. The still-moving bolt compresses the recoil spring against the buffer pilot collar and the sear locks into one of two bolt notches. The loading-unloading cycle is now completed.

If the fire control lever is set at full-auto the sear doesn't engage the bolt cocking notch but remains depressed. As long as

the sear is disengaged the weapon continues to fire until the trigger is released or the ammunition is exhausted.

Model 1919

The M1919, the "basic machine mechanism" without the later refinements of sights and buttstock, originally used a belt feed and is characterized by twin pistol grips, square actuator handle, and the very high cyclic rate of 1500 s.p.m. (shots per minute). Eight toolmaker's models are reported to have been made. Each weighed 7 lbs. in 45 ACP caliber and had 30 parts.

The M19 was test fired at Springfield Armory in late 1919 or early 1920; its first reported public appearance was in August, 1920, at the National Matches at Camp Perry. The late Captain E. C. (Ned) Crossman, early firearms identification expert and pioneer gun editor, wrote the first known detailed report on the M19: "A Pocket Machine Gun," (Oct. 16, 1920, the *Scientific American*). His comments on the Thompson's potential as a "peacemaker" include the following:

"The adoption by the New York police of the wicked little submachine gun is of course interesting to those who wish to see the customary New York brand of gunplay made less one-sided.

"Without a doubt the early future will see a happy coincidence of a policeman skilled in pointing of the new weapon and an automobile full of yeggs willing to engage in the customary running gunfight.

"The result will be the worst shot up assortment of crooks that has come to the attention of the coroner."

According to Crossman and 1920 Auto Ordnance advertisements, the New York police department adopted the Thompson in 1920. This raises the question of whether there was a 1920 model, as no known Thompsons other than the eight M19 pilot models were manufactured until 1921. The Cross-man article, Auto Ordnance advertisements, and a November, 1920, Popular Mechanics article, "The Submachine Gun," show several Thompsons which differ in detail from the belt-fed M19 and the first production model, the M1921. Observed variations include:

(1) A left-side full section drawing of a Thompson without sights, stock, or provision for attaching a stock.

(2) A Thompson with no sights or shoulder stock (held by a N.Y.P.D. sergeant). The magazine is a type XX (20-round) box.

(3) A Thompson equipped with a type XX magazine and a front sight but no

shoulder stock (held by a N.Y.P.D. patrolman).

(4) A Thompson with a type C (100-round) drum magazine, a very small front sight, and a shoulder stock of a different design than that of the M21.

(5) A Thompson with no sights and no shoulder stock or provision for one. The pivot plate has a different exterior design than that of the M21.

What model were these guns and what model did the New York police adopt? This writer believes they were modified M19's; that the Thompsons and their associates hoped to obtain publicity which would lead to orders and financial backing for production. Although records are unavailable, it is probable that the N.Y.P.D. agreed in 1920 to purchase the Thompson once it was in production. (Although the M19's 1500 s.p.m. cyclic rate was excessive, it made great promotion material. The 1920 Auto Ordnance ads stressed that the gun should be fired full-auto without shoulder stock and from the hip; that for semi-auto fire the weapon could be fired with stock from the shoulder. In fact, however, even with a reduced cyclic rate the Thompson or any other SMG is more effective when used with a shoulder stock — even when hip fired.)

Model 1921

The M21 is a modified M19 with the cyclic rate reduced to 800 s.p.m. It has a 10.5-inch circular finned barrel (a questionable cooling feature, possibly derived from the Hotchkiss MG's), a Lyman adjustable rear sight and a blade front sight. It is characterized by the classic front and rear pistol grips with finger grooves. With detachable shoulder stock the gun weighs 9.75 lbs. and is 31.8 inches overall; without shoulder stock it weighs 8.5 lbs. and is 23.3 inches long.

The M21 could be quickly set for full- or semi-auto fire by means of the fire selector lever (rocker), located near the magazine catch and safety on the left side of the frame above the trigger guard. The maximum deliverable rate of fire at full-auto is about 275–300 s.p.m.; at semi-auto about 100 s.p.m. Rate varies with magazine capacity, the gunner's proficiency and his ability to change magazines.

Four types of 45 ACP magazines could be used with the M21: the 100-round type C, the favorite of gang-land's "Chopper Charlies"; type L drum (50 rounds); type XX (20 rounds), and type XVIII for the Peters-Thompson shot or riot cartridge. Types XXV and XXX, introduced in WW II,

can also be used with the M21.

Early Auto Ordnance press releases said that the M21 would be produced in calibers 22 LR, 32 ACP, 38 ACP, and 9mm Parabellum (Luger) as well as the 45 ACP. Thompsons in any caliber other than 45 ACP were produced in very limited numbers. The late Captain Philip B. Sharpe, author of The Rifle in America and Complete Guide to Handloading, reported that at least one M21 was produced for the 351 Winchester Self-Loading Rifle cartridge. Three only are reported to have been made for the 9mm Luger cartridge.

In 1952 Numrich Arms sold Thompson finned barrels in 9mm Luger, 7.63 Mauser, and 30 Luger calibers. The three barrels, which were 12.5 inches long when Cutts Compensator-equipped and 10.5 inches without, may have been made for the M21 or for the later M26 and M29 Birmingham Small Arms Thompsons; possibly they were designed for the M21 but used on the M26 and M29.

It should be noted that the Thompson SMG, with its high cyclic rate and resultant excessive muzzle-climb, was not a very accurate weapon until the Cutts Compensator was introduced in 1926. This device, designed by Col. Richard M. Cutts, USMC, and his son Richard (later General Cutts, USMC), is a short, top-slotted tube attached to the muzzle that directs escaping gas upwards, thus forcing the muzzle down. This permitted accurate burst firing (the SMG's reason for existence), reduced recoil and stabilized semi-auto fire. Cutts-equipped Thompsons were designated by "AC" after the model number. So far as is known, all U.S. military Thompsons were Cutts-equipped from about 1928 until the pressure of wartime production caused discontinuance of the muzzle device.

The M21 was the favorite tool of quick death connoisseurs like Al Capone's chief gunner's mate "Machine Gun" Jack McGurn. "To a gangster," wrote newsman Fred Pasley, "a Thompson is never anything but a 'typewriter' and the 50- or 100-round drum is always a 'ukelele.'"(Al Capone; the Biography of a Self-Made Man. by Frederick D. Pasley, New York City, 1930.) The M21 was the so-called "machine gun" in news stories on Chicago's decade-long Battle of the Bootleg Marne; and it carried out its peak executions during the reigns of Mayor William Hale (Big Bill) Thompson, 1915–23 and 1927–31, who was elected and reelected on campaign slogans such as "Keep Chicago Wet" and "Keep King George out of Chicago."

The Capone front man who purchased Thompsons, usually in lots, was known as Frank Thompson — perhaps the alias of a humorous hood. His job must have been a snap, since there were no federal restrictions on SMG sales in those happy days, when "choppers" were sold over-the-counter in sporting goods and hardware stores for about $200.

The writer has been able to verify only these four large-scale Chicago gangland shootings involving the Thompson, but each was so spectacular that it was inevitable the Thompson would be tarred as a gangster's tool:

April 27, 1926: Cook County Assistant State's Attorney William H. McSwiggin and two companions, both bootleggers, killed while making the rounds of speakeasies.

Sept. 20, 1926: In broad daylight, eleven black touring cars — the classic gangland transportation — carrying Thompson gunners unsuccessfully invaded Capone's home bailiwick in suburban Cicero. Police estimated more than 1,000 rounds were fired. Results: one bystander injured, no gunshot wounds and nobody killed. "This is war," said the Chicago Examiner's editorial.

Oct. 11, 1926: Hymie Weiss, the hood who had staged the Cicero raid, and two companions were shot dead in front of a church.

Feb. 14, 1929, date of Chicago's most horrible gangland killing: seven Bugs Moran mobsters machine-gunned in a north side garage, the infamous St. Valentine's Day massacre. Firearms identification pioneer expert. Col. Calvin Goddard, brought to Chicago by a "Blue Stocking" coroner's jury foreman Bert A. Massey, identified the 70 fired 45 ACP cases and bullets as having been fired from a Thompson with a 50-round drum and from a Thompson with a 20-round box magazine. Col. Goddard later tied the cases and bullets to two Thompsons abandoned in the Holland, Mich., hideout of Fred Burke, a member of the Egan's Rats mob of St. Louis. "It was Goddard's work on the evidence." wrote editor Walter J. Howe in the January, 1963, American Rifleman, "that advanced his stature and also the stature of firearms identification."

The M21, after gangsters had demonstrated its deadly utility, was bought by the Marine Corps for use in Nicaraguan jungle combat, where most of the fighting was at ranges of 50 yards or less. Many an eight-man squad was equipped with four Thompsons and occasionally a BAR.

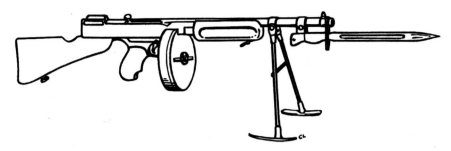

M1923 with Springfield bayonet, bi-pod and early version of horizontal fore-end; used special 45-cal. cartridge which reportedly had twice the punch of standard 45 ACP.

B.S.A. Models 26 and 29 were chambered for 9mm Luger, 45 ACP, 9mm Bayard and 30 Mauser. Note placement of grip and trigger guard.

After this fighting against the Nicaraguan bandit — or patriot — Sandino petered out to a rare skirmish, the average Marine squad was equipped with one Thompson, one BAR, and six M1903 Springfield 30-cal. rifles.

1923 Military Models

In 1923 Auto Ordnance offered two variations of the M21. Thompson buffs refer to either as the Military Model of 1923. The M23 was available in two calibers, 45 ACP and the Remington-Thompson 45 Military cartridge. The latter round had a 1.0-inch case, compared to the 0.895-inch case of the 45 ACP, and used a 250-gr. (sic) metal jacketed bullet with a reported muzzle velocity of 1,450 fps — nearly twice the velocity and more than twice the energy of the 45 ACP. It is the most powerful SMG cartridge known to the writer. The Army summarily rejected this fine round because it would have added another cartridge to complicate ammunition supply problems — but so did the inferior 30 carbine cartridge adopted in 1940.

The M23 also came in two barrel versions. One had a 14.5-inch barrel, measured 36 inches over-all, weighed 12.5 lbs. with bipod, and was equipped with a horizontal fore-end (a modified version of which was used on the later M1928A1). A barrel stud for holding the 16-inch Springfield bayonet was available. Unlike the M21, this M23 had no cooling fins but used a heavier barrel as compensation. (Final production M1928A1's — sometimes called M1928A2 — and all M1's and M1A1's utilized this cooling meth-od.) The other M23 was merely the M21 with the standard 10.5-inch circular finned barrel plus a horizontal fore-end and sling. Only a few M23's were manufactured, and most of them — if not all — were used for demonstration purposes.

1926 B.S.A. Model

The Birmingham Small Arms Company, Ltd., Birmingham, England — World War I manufacturers of the American designed Lewis gun — made at least two Thompsons in 1926. At least two because "Model 1926" and the serial number "2" are stamped on a Thompson described by Rich Lauchli of Collinsville, Ill. The writer never has seen any previous mention of the M26.

The M26, as reported by Lauchli, is of 9mm Luger caliber, weighs 7.5 lbs. without magazine and is 32 inches over-all with a 12.5-inch barrel and 9.625-inch receiver. The action is a modified M21, capable of full-auto fire only, with trigger guard moved to the extreme rear of the receiver and buttstock attached to the back rather than to the bottom of the receiver. Cyclic rate (not given) is probably about 800 s.p.m. The M26 is reported to have used either a drum or a curved box magazine, capacities not given.

Model 1927

The Model 1927, probably made only in 45 ACP caliber, was later called the 27AC when Cutts-equipped and 27A when not Cutts-equipped. The M27 can deliver semi-auto fire only but except for the absence of the fire selector switch it is identical in outward appearance to the earlier M21 and the later M28.

All other U.S.-made Thompson models were capable of full- and semi-auto fire.

Auto Ordnance nomenclature for the M27 is slightly confusing in that both advertisements and catalogs use the designation "Automatic Carbine" and "Semi-Automatic Carbine" indiscriminately for the semi-automatic model. The M27 fire rate is the same as for the semi-auto fire of the M21 and M28, about 100 s.p.m.

A different rocker and rocker pivot were substituted for similar M21 parts, and three parts (rocker spring, rocker plunger, and rocker pin) were added. All other M27 parts, including magazines, are interchangeable with the M21 and M28. When parts were available, M27 owners could readily convert the weapon to full-auto fire by replacing the M27 rocker and rocker pivot with full-auto model components and removing the extra parts.

Only a few M27's were made and many of these were converted to full-auto fire. Of seven M27's the writer has examined, five had been converted to full-auto fire.

Model 1928

In late 1928 or early 1929 Auto Ordnance introduced a modified M21, the Model 1928. The only difference was a lower — 600 s.p.m. — cyclic rate. This was achieved by substituting a heavier actuator, a longer recoil spring, and a single-unit pilot and buffer. Externally there is no difference. Model markings are unreliable because many M21's were converted to M28 with no change in model markings. The only positive method of identification is to field strip and examine the parts concerned.

The M28, like the M21, is characterized by the twin front and rear vertical pistol grips, and is usually termed the "commercial" model. Magazine types XVIII, XX, and L can be used with the M28, along with WW II types XXV and XXX. The 100-round drum magazine should not be used on the M28 because its spring tension does not properly coordinate with the M28's slower cyclic rate, and occasional malfunctions can result. The best customers for the 100-round drum, the Chicago gangsters, used the Thompson very little after the St. Valentine's Day massacre. Manufacture of the type C drum was soon discontinued.

1928 U.S. Navy Model

Auto Ordnance, except for a few Navy and Marine Corps sales of Cutts-equipped M21's, had been unable to gain U.S. military acceptance of the early Thompson for two reasons: (1) Excessive cyclic rate of fire and its accompanying disadvantages; (2) inability of the average military mind to recognize the tactical vistas opened by the new weapon. However, the slower cyclic rate of the M28 together with the Cutts made that model immediately attractive to the Marine Corp.

The 1928 U.S. Navy Model — the Auto Ordnance designation — is the M28 equipped with a horizontal fore-end, sling swivels, sling, and a Cutts. The horizontal fore-end replaced the classic vertical foregrip because the latter cannot practicably be equipped with a sling, a military prerequisite. The Navy also purchased Thompsons for landing force operations.

M1928A1

The Army almost immediately adopted the U.S. Navy Model but called it the M1928A1. "A1" stands for "Alteration 1" — the changes previously described on the M28 resulting in the Navy Model.

Until WW II, the Army generally confined Thompson issue to tank units, armored scout car and some motorcycle personnel. The writer remembers that the scout cars attached to the Headquarters Company, Third Cavalry (a horse outfit), stationed at Fort Ethan Allen, Vt., during the 1930's were Thompson equipped. During WW II Thompsons were issued to infantry units, transportation outfits, paratroopers, and special units such as the Rangers. M1928A1 Thompsons were issued with 50-round drums and 20-round magazines. The Thompson proved to be a superb weapon for Pacific Island fighting.

1929 B.S.A. Model

Auto Ordnance designers in cooperation with Birmingham Small Arms developed the M29 as an entrant in the Belgian government's 1929 SMG tests. The 1929 Thompson was not adopted. The M29 is basically the M26 with a fire-selector switch for full- and semi-auto fire.

George Numrich reports M29 calibers in 9mm Bayard (Belgian SMG cartridge), 9mm Luger, and 7.63mm Mauser; Rich Lauchli reports on three M29's: a 45 ACP, serial No. 2, cyclic rate 700 s.p.m., weight 10.5 lbs., over-all length 35.37 inches with Cutts-equipped barrel; 7.63mm Mauser, serial No. 7, cyclic rate 800 s.p.m., weight 9.75 lbs., over-all length 36 inches with 12.5-inch Cutts-equipped barrel; 30 Mauser (7.63mm Mauser), serial No. 8, weight 9.5 lbs., other data same as for the M29 serial No.7 *(M29, serial No. 7, is stamped "7.63 Mauser;" M29, serial No. 8, is stamped "30 Mauser." The former was equipped with a*

M1927 Semi-Auto Thompson carbine, also called Auto Machine Carbine. This model can be readily converted to the full-auto fire of the M21 or M28. Ownership requires Federal $200 tax.

M1928 Thompson made for Service Armament president Val Forgett, Jr., has custom stock, gold-plated trigger and selector lever, engraving and gold inlays. Type L drum magazine.

M1928A1 Thompson is identical with U.S. Navy model. It is commercial M28 with horizontal rather than vertical foregrip. Made by Auto-Ordance Co., and Arms for U. S. Army, Navy Marine Corps. Many were shipped to the United Kingdom after the Dunkirk debacle.

Chinese copy of M1921 reportedly made in or around Shanghai. Note finger grooves in fore-end and method of sling attachment.

forward-curved box magazine, capacity not known but probably 30 or 32 rounds.)

Foreign Acceptance of the Thompson

Made aware of the Thompson through motion pictures and gangster news stories, plus Nicaraguan use by the Marines, Argentina, Brazil, China, Greece, Mexico, Norway, Poland, Sweden, and the Soviet Union gave Auto Ordnance orders.

Numrich told the writer that a Red Army SMG manual calls the Thompson a "Chicago Typewriter." Several editions of the late W. H. B. Smith's *Small Arms of the World* but not the latest (1962) edition reproduced the illustration and caption which Numrich mentions. The Soviets equipped their Thompsons with a 20-inch scimitar (curved) bayonet.

The Nazis purchased Thompsons to analyze the basic design. The Allies subsequent-

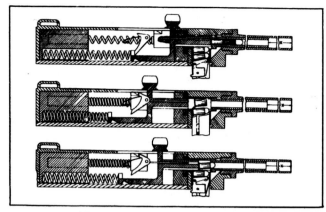

THE CONVERSION UNIT IN ACTION

Thompson 22-cal. conversion unit. Top — the device in the act of firing. center — Fire case being ejected. Bottom — Cocked and ready to fire. SMG can easily be reconverted to 45 ACP.

ly found detailed pre-war drawings of the Thompson. Hugo Schmeisser, greatest of all SMG designers, headed Nazi Germany's extensive SMG research and design program.

The Thompson won quick acceptance among some countries south of the Rio Grande where *bandidos*, both in and out of office, appreciated its lethal qualities.

The Phoney War

Great Britain, whose military leaders believed the SMG to be a "gangster's weapon, not to be used by gentlemen," made no effort to design its own SMG's or to procure Thompsons until after the German Wehrmacht blitzkrieged Poland.

The French ordered too few Thompsons too late. A small number was on the New York docks awaiting shipment to France when Marshal Pétain pulled down the once glorious tricolor.

During the political-military debacle and the sweat and guts miracle that was Dunkirk, the British Purchasing Commission ordered "All immediately available Thompsons and all you can manufacture." It didn't matter the model — unsold commercial M21's, semi-auto M27's, commercial M28's with vertical foregrips, and M1928A1's from U.S. Ordnance warehouses and arsenals (along with the last pre-war Single Action Colts) were shipped in the first available bottoms — anything to stave off the expected invasion. Winston Churchill, by now prime minister, knew the Thompson. An unemployed statesman in the 1920's, he had covered the American scene as a working journalist for the Hearst press.

Wartime Thompsons

Meanwhile, Auto Ordnance executives had realized additional Thompson production was immediately required on a huge scale. On Dec. 15, 1939, Savage Arms Corp., then at Chicopee Falls, Mass., and WW I manufacturer of the famed Lewis gun, signed a contract to produce Thompsons. Four months later the first one came off the assembly line. Savage production of the M1928A1 eventually reached 2,000 acceptable weapons every 24 hours.

Commercial Thompsons are beautiful weapons. The quality of workmanship, the fine walnut buttstocks and high-blue finish, the precision manufacture of milled parts and skilled fittings, probably never has been approached by any other production SMG. War, however, places utilitarianism and fast production above aesthetic considerations. Auto Ordnance and Savage production personnel began a survey to see what steps could be taken to save time and material.

Savage Arms Vice President O. M. (Jack) Knode, Jr., described some of these wartime changes for the writer:

"The first model Thompsons we built had the pistol grip fore-end. This was discontinued fairly early in production and somewhat later the finned barrels were also discontinued, since the cooling effect of the fins seemed no greater than the cooling effect of the added mass of barrel steel when the fins were omitted. During the production of these Thompsons, many minor changes and improvements were effected. The Cutts Compensator was discontinued at an early date and the Lyman rear sight did not last too long. Other changes included the substitution of punch press and screw machine parts for such (machined) components as the pivot plate, safety, and rocker arm."

The 1941 M1 Thompson

Designers, knowing the Thompson would function without the Blish lock, discarded it, along with the now-unnecessary breech oiler and actuator. The redesigned weapon, with other modifications, became the Thompson M1. The receiver was reduced in size, the buttstock made non-detachable, and the operating handle and its slot moved from the top of the receiver to the right side. The M1 weighs 10.5 lbs. without magazine.

The M1 was approved by U.S. Army Ordnance in 1941 and went into production the same year. Because of the quick changeover from M1928A1 to M1 production, early M1's used the earlier rocker pivot and safety; the later M1 rocker and safety are interchangeable with those on the M1928A1.

As drum magazines were discontinued with the advent of the M1, the M1 safety catch needed no provision for the drum; however, as a result of the changeover, M1928A1 catches with drum capability were used on early M1's. The later M1 safety catch is interchangeable with the M1928A1 but drums cannnot be used in M-1928A1's so equipped.

M21 and M28 parts interchangeable with the M1 are: pivot plate, trigger and spring, disconnector and spring, sear and spring, sear lever and spring, frame latch and spring, and extractor and trip.

The M1A1 of 1942

The M1A1 resulted from a basic change in the M1. The two-piece firing pin (firing pin and firing pin spring) was replaced by a simple metal pimple machined onto the bolt face. It worked well.

As to the U.S. Ordnance adoption date of the M1A1, Knode told the writer, "During contract number 15, dated Dec. 15, 1942. calling for 100.000 Thompsons, the changes resulting in the 42M1 and the M1A1 were made. Less than 100 of the former (those with movable firing pins) were made, as I recall, before the fixed firing pin became standard. 515,000 guns were produced subsequent to the change."

No further information was available on the limited production 42M1. Nor has the writer been able to confirm reports of a tubular receiver Thompson, the T-2.

Auto Ordnance reportedly switched from M1 to M1A1 production at the same time as Savage. Thompson production ceased in early 1944 when U.S. Ordnance apparently determined that the supply of SMG's was ample for all services. There were plenty of Thompsons, the production rate of the recently adopted M3A1 was satisfactory and stocks of the M3A1's predecessor, the M3, and the Marine Corps issue Reising were adequate. The Thompson was categorized as "Limited Standard."

Reisings and Grease Guns

Some writers have implied, and many GI's believed, that the Reising SMG, designed by Eugene Reising, replaced the Thompson as the standard Marine Corps SMG. The Reising, in fact or affection, never supplanted the Thompson. The Corps. in 1940, had adopted the Reising as a "Limited Standard" to supplement the inadequate supply of Thompsons. Most production Thompsons of that period were shipped to the British.

The Reising utilized a delayed blow-back action. The M50, with a one-piece conventional rifle-type stock, was 35.75 inches over-all; the 11-inch barrel was equipped with a Cutts-type compensator. The M55, with a folding wire stock, was 22.25 inches over-all with the stock folded; the 10.5-inch barrel was not compensator-equipped.

The Reising had one notable feature: light weight. Without magazine, the M50 weighed 6.75 lbs. and the M55 6.25 lbs. Ultra-light weight, however, is a questionable advantage in a full-automatic weapon — and the Reising. capable of semi- and full-auto fire, had a cyclic rate of 450–600 s.p.m. Two magazines, a 20-round box and a 12-round box (not very practical for an SMG), were available.

Reising told the writer, "Between 1940 and 1943 about 70,000 M50's and 30,000 M55's were manufactured."

The Thompson was replaced by the U.S. Ordnance-designed M3 and its modified successor the M3A1, the familiar "grease guns." The M3's comply with Hugo Schmeisser's basic principles of simplicity, reliability, durability, and ease of mass production by non-arms manufacturers. Primitive people, with no mechanical or firearms experience, can readily be taught to operate the weapon.

The M3's are design-derived from Schmeisser's MP38 and the British Sten (also MP38 derived). The M3A1 is better than the Sten but probably not quite so good as the MP38. Nevertheless, it fulfills the role of an SMG far better than the M14 rifle replaces the BAR, Garand, carbine, and SMG!

The M3A1 is a full-automatic air-cooled, blowback operated SMG made largely from stampings. It weighs 10.25 lbs. with loaded 30-round magazine, 8.15 lbs. without. It has an 8-inch barrel, is 29.8 inches

M1 Thompson, developed early in WW II, discorded Blish lock, acted as a straight blowback weapon. Many parts interchange with M28 and later M1A1. M1A1 Thompson was replaced by M3 and M3A1 SMG's, but many Thompsons of all models are still used throughout the world.

The M3 "greasegun" which, with its successor the M3A1, replaced the Thompson as standard SMG of U.S Armed Forces.

over-all with wire stock extended. The cyclic rate is 450 s.p.m.

How Many Thompsons?

Auto Ordnance in 1920 sublet the manufacture of the first 15,000 receivers and other parts to Colt. About 6,000 complete Thompsons reportedly were sold by 1930. After the Army adopted the M1928A1, production zoomed, and in November, 1939, Russell Maguire presented Gen. C. T. Harris with the 250,000th M1928A1.

George Numrich, Jr., told the writer that about 2.5 million Thompsons were made, including 1.24 million which Jack Knode reports Savage produced during WW II. A few Thompsons have been made up by Numrich Arms since the early 1950's.

Not all Thompsons shipped overseas reached thheir intended destination. Knode reports: "During the war we heard a rumor that a large quantity (200,000) were on a ship sunk in Tobruk harbor, but I have never heard this verified nor do I know whether they were salvaged." Numrich says: "About a half-million M1A1's are resting off the shores of Norway due to German U-boat action."

Wartime scuttlebutt being what it was, perhaps the above-reported incidents were the same.

Sights

Early Thompson pilot models intended for hip-firing had no front or rear sights.

After a detachable stock was added, a blade or bead front sight was supplied. The original rear sight was just a slot cut in the actuator handle. All commercial Thompsons observed (except an M21 with serial number 45 — a Colt Museum specimen) have been equipped with a blade front sight; bead sights have also been reported. Both standard blade and bead type front sights have been observed on the M1 and M1A1.

Auto Ordnance, beginning with the M21, equipped Thompsons with what was probably the most expensive and elaborate rear sight ever placed on an SMG. The sight, manufactured by Lyman, had a folding leaf adjustable for elevation (up to 600 yards) and windage. The sight was protected by Enfield-type "ears." (Gen. Thompson had supervised construction of the Remington Enfield plant at Eddystone, Pa.) This sight was discontinued during late M1928A1 production.

The M1 and M1A1 were equipped with several types of simplified rear sights. The most common was a nonadjustable L-shaped piece screwed to the receiver. The aperture was a punch-pressed hole. Some wartime Thompsons had the rear sight protected by forward sloping ears.

45 ACP Thompson Magazines

The type XVIII holds 18 Peters-Thompson 45 ACP riot shot cartridges. Each cartridge contains approximately 120 No. 8 pellets.

Some Thompson magazine carriers (from left): U. S. Armed Forces carrier for 8 Type XXX magazines now used for 30-round M3A1 magazines; British Army metal carrier of WW II vintage for 12 Type XX magazines; Woven web carrier for 5 Type XX magazines; woven web carrier for one Type L drum.

The writer never has been able to locate one of these magazines. Bill Toney, Chief Firearms Inspector of the Border Patrol and former national handgun champion (who has never seen this magazine either), has told the writer that he uses shot cartridges in the standard 20- and 30-round Thompson magazines. Toney has probably had as much if not more experience with the Thompson than any other lawman. The Peters-Thompson riot cartridge was slightly longer than today's 45 ACP shot cartridge, and the type XVIII magazine is reported to have been slightly longer front to rear than the standard Thompson magazines.

Type XX, a 20-round box or "stick" magazine; fits all Thompsons; weighs 6.4 ounces empty and 14.8 ounces loaded.

Type XXV is a 25-round box or stick magazine. Many Thompson writers and collectors seem unaware that this magazine was made, but the Seymour Products Company, Seymour, Conn., made 25,000 type XXV's in 1940. George Numrich, Jr., suggests that type XXV may have been made on special order for the British or French. The writer believes it might have been an experimental version between types XX and XXX because, at the time, the adoption of a Thompson that would

not use the 50-rounddrum was being considered and the cartridge capacity of Type XX was considered too small. Most Nazi SMG's had 30- or 32-round magazines. Another factor favoring the experimental transitional theory is the small number of XXV's made. During 1940–44, Seymour made approximately 1.2 million type XX and one million type XXX magazines, yet Seymour was but one of several firms making WW II Thompson magazines.

Type XXX, an unofficial designation, is a 30-round box or stick magazine that was designed when the M1. without provision for the 50-round drum, was adopted. It will fit all 45 ACP Thompsons; it weighs 13 ounces empty and about 36 ounces loaded.

Type L, a 50-round drum magazine introduced with the M21, weighs 2.5 lbs. empty and 4.6 lbs. loaded. It will fit all 45 ACP Thompsons except the M1, 42M1 and M1A1. Feed and functioning problems were encountered when the L drum was first used on the M28, the result of incorrect magazine mainspring tension. The tension was applied to the mainspring by turning the magazine key. Experiments showed that when the magazine was wound to 11 "clicks" — a sound heard as the key was turned — it would feed satisfactorily.

Use of this drum was discontinued for several reasons. Weight was a factor. Including the carriers, 150 cartridges in 30-round magazines weigh only 80 per cent as much as in drums. In addition, the box magazine is easier to load and handle, does not rattle like the drum, and is less inclined to jam.

Type C (sometimes called type 0) is a 100-round drum that weighs 8.5 lbs. loaded or almost as much as the Thompson itself. This drum was discontinued with the advent of the M28. Every specimen observed by the writer carried a serial number on the top cover and bottom pan of the magazine. Serial numbers rarely matched.

Few details were available on experimental Thompson magazines. Numrich reported his No. 7, cal. 7.63mm Mauser Thompson to have a curved type box magazine.

Magazine Carriers

Here are some magazine carriers. There are undoubtedly others.

(1) Woven 5-pocket belt carrier for type XX magazines.

(2) Canvas pouch for 8 type XXX magazines. It can be worn over the shoulder or on a belt, and is now used for the 30-round "grease gun" magazines.

FISCHETTI

© 1963. New York Herald Tribune Inc.

The honeymoon's over.

Reputation of Thompson even led to its use in cartoons on international politics, as at left.

THOMPSON SMG

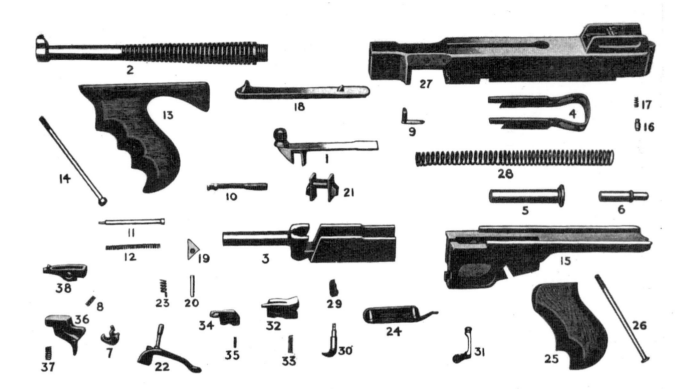

Parts List

1 Actuator
2 Barrel with front sight
3 Bolt
4 Breech Oiler (including felt pads)
5 Buffer (including fiber discs)
6 Buffer Pilot
7 Disconnector
8 Disconnector Spring
9 Ejector
10 Extractor
11 Firing Pin
12 Firing Pin Spring
13 Fore Grip
14 Fore Grip Screw

15 Frame
16 Frame Latch
17 Frame Latch Spring
18 Grip Mount
19 Hammer
20 Hammer Pin
21 Lock
22 Magazine Catch
23 Magazine Catch Spring
24 Pivot Plate
25 Rear Grip
26 Rear Grip Screw
27 Receiver with Sight Guard Base
28 Recoil Spring
29 Rocker

30 Rocker Pivot or Fire Control Lever
31 Safety
32 Sear
33 Sear Spring
34 Sear Lever
35 Sear Lever Spring
36 Trigger
37 Trigger Spring
38 Trip

Numbers 1, 5, 6 and 28 illustrate M21 parts only. Parts 7, 8, 10, 16, 17, 24 and 32 to 38 are interchangeable among M1, M21 and M28.

Horse owners with a Thompson can use this outfit.

Web carrying case held one M21 or M28 Thompson with pocket for dismounted stock and four Type XX magazines.

(3) Woven carrier with belt loop; some for one type L drum.

(4) Woven carrier with shoulder strap for two type C magazines.

(5) British Army metal carrier with handle for 12 type XX magazines.

(6) Woven belt carrier for one type L drum.

Gun Carriers

During the late 1920's and early '30's, whenever innocuous violin players appeared in public toting their instrument cases, they were almost certain to be greeted with the quip, "Got your Tommygun, I see." The violin case Thompson carrier, favored by gangsters, is now passé, but a saxophone type case is liked by many lawmen. Bill Toney, who says it is easier to teach a recruit to effectively handle the Thompson than to shoot a six-gun, toted his M1928 Thompson, spare magazine and type L drum along with cleaning gear and spare parts kit, in such a case.

The Army during the 1930's issued a beautiful oak-and-leather saddle scabbard for carrying the Thompson in scout cars, motorcycles, and on horseback. In WW II a canvas zipper case was issued for the M1 and M1A1.

Auto Ordnance in 1920 designed a stout woven carrier for toting the Thompson with a separate pocket for the detachable stock. Four pockets held type XX magazines. This carrier could be slung over the shoulder or strapped to a saddle.

Accessories

The Thompson was provided with a full, if not extensive, complement of accessories. Some were produced by or for Auto Ordnance while others were offered by outside firms. Accessories such as spare parts and the cleaning kit were necessities; magazines and gun cases were convenient. Accessories such as the aircraft unit holding 28 Thompsons which could all be fired at once may have existed only in pilot form or in the fertile imagination of Auto Ordnance personnel. This affair was pictured in a de luxe pre-WW II Thompson catalog. Had the U.S. adopted this weird contraption, the gunner would have needed a substantial crew to change and load the 100-round drums.

Odd-ball accessories included a deck mount for sea-going Thompsons and a gadget, which the cavalry once experimented with, that clamped a Thompson to the handle bars of a motorcycle. "One hand for the bike — one hand for the Thompson trigger." There was also a mount for installing Thompsons on the bow of motorcycle sidecars so chasing cops could gun down running robbers.

Sometime before WW II, Am-Ro Distributors, Cincinnati, O., offered the Robbins-Thompson sub-caliber 22 LR adaptor. This device, including a 22 LR drum, a breech mechanism, and a chamber with barrel extension, was apparently based on the Williams Floating Chamber for the 22 Colt Service Ace. This very scarce item is much sought by Thompson collectors. The writer used one about 1940, but it was not my own. One was also seen at a New York police dept. range before WW II.

The Cutts Compensator eliminated the need for the "muzzle strap brake" — a leather strap with a slot at one end through which the muzzle was placed while the gunner held the other end under one foot.

The New York Police Dept. was an early purchaser of this forerunner of the Cutts. The writer does not know who produced this item.

During the 1920's, Auto Ordnance offered Springfield bayonets and stud adapters, flash hiders, silencers, canvas breech-covers, and a muzzle device which is said to have operated the action when blank cartridges were used.

The most practical accessory probably was Auto Ordnance's combination spare parts and cleaning kit. The Thompson chamber was difficult to reach, and a bent handle chamber brush was used to keep it clear. A pull-through thong and brush was included. Spare parts included extractor, firing pin and spring, hammer pin, sear and sear lever spring, and trigger spring. This kit came in a metal box of dimensions identical to a type XX magazine. Auto Ordnance literature suggested it could be handily toted in a magazine carrier pocket. (Imagine a gunner's reaction if, during the course of a shootout, he tried to replace a magazine with the spare parts kit!)

Taps for the Thompson

"All Thompson Submachine Guns in the Zone of the Interior (United States) and in the Pacific Theater have been replaced with M3 and M3A1 Submachine Guns. Approximately 60% replacement of the Thompsons with M3 and M3A1 types had been accomplished in the European Theatre when shipments were suspended due to VE Day," read a January, 1946, Army Ordnance memorandum. Thompsons became officially obsolete in March, 1946. Ten months later another memorandum read, "The book of standards shall be revised by the elimination of the Gun, Submachine, Caliber .45, Thompson, M1928A1, M1 and M1A1."

Thus, in a sparsely worded communique, was the Thompson, hardy survivor of countless global engagements and trusted comrade of nearly 2 million Allied fighting men, retired to the status of a relic.

The communique also noted that 25,526 serviceable and 15,791 unserviceable Thompsons were in Field Stores while 259,000 were in overseas theaters of operation. Only 161 were in the hands of stateside troops.

The communique valued the M1928A1 at $72 and the M1 and M1A1 at $44. Today a Dewat (Deactivated War Trophy) M1928A1 brings between $175 and $200, and Thompson Dewat prices are still going up. Prices have doubled within recent years.

The Dewat program, which allowed ownership of deactuated full-automatic

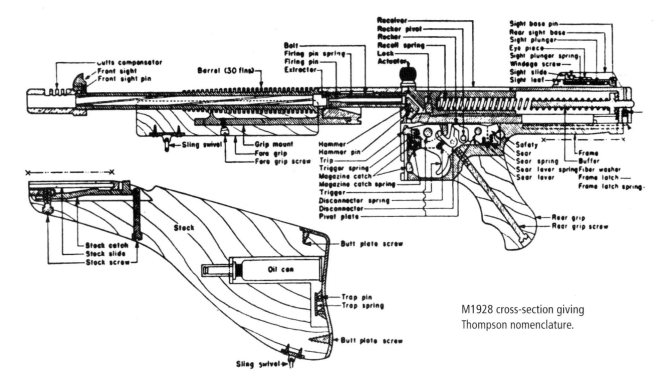

M1928 cross-section giving Thompson nomenclature.

weapons without registration or the transfer tax provisions of the National Firearms Act, was suspended on July 1, 1958.

The Thompson Today

During the 1950's, Numrich Arms assembled Thompsons from spare parts, calling these the M1921/28. Assembly of the M21/28 wa discontinued in early 1961. Today, Numrich sells assembled M1A1's. Most go to law enforcement agencies and State Department-approved foreign customers.

"We also sell," says Numrich, "about 10 to 12 guns per year with the payment of the $200 federal transfer tax, and some of these are used to shoot at prairie dogs from Piper Cubs in Texas and also for shark shooting off the California coast."

The Number One civilian Thompson buff was probably novelist Ernest Hemingway, who is reported either to have paid $1,000 for his Thompson or to have won it in a poker game from a millionaire sportsman. His ostensible purpose was to shoot sharks attempting to eat his big game fish, but actually he just enjoyed "shooting for the hell of it."

Numrich Arms in 1954 made several Thompsons for the 30 Carbine cartridge. "The experiment worked out very well." Numrich said. Several 9mm Luger Thompsons were made up at about the same time.

Rich Lauchli furnished the following data on a 30 Carbine Thompson which may have been one of the Numrich experimental models:

Weight without magazine, 9.75 lbs.; over-all length with 14.5-inch barrel, 36.25 inches;

full- and semi-auto fire. The M28 action had no markings on the right side of the receiver but the left side was marked:

THOMPSON SUBMACHINE GUN/CAL. 30
SHORT RIFLE M1/SELF LOADING CARTRIDGE

The 30 Carbine cartridge was known in the early 1940's as the 30 Short Rifle Self Loading Cartridge. No magazine details were available.

An Auto Ordnance experimental carbine for the 30 Carbine cartridge (not a Thompson) was rejected early in the 1941 Army Ordnance tests.

Numrich has been attempting to design a semi-auto Thompson with a foolproof disconnector. In March, 1963, John Martin, president of Tri-State Tool and Die Co., Frostburg, Md., sent the writer photos of a semi-auto Thompson which, he said, has been approved by the Treasury Department's Alcohol and Tobacco Tax Unit. According to Martin, his "Guerrilla" will use the 1928 action modified for semi-auto fire only. Its specifications: weight 11 lbs.; over-all length 37.3 inches with 16-inch Cutts-equipped barrel. The "Guerrilla" will be adapted to all 45 ACP Thompson magazines with the possible exception of the Type C. Martin says he will make his own frames and receivers — the most difficult Thompson parts to get — and the remainder, except for Martin's semi-auto feature and barrels, will be Savage or Auto Ordnance manufactured components.

(As the Gun Digest goes to press, word has reached us that Numrich has designed, but

is not in production on, a semi-auto Thompson with 16½" barrel which is not easily convertible to full-automatic. Numrich states that, since his company holds the patents, trade-marks, etc., on the Thompson SMG, it is doubtful if any other company could produce a Thompson of any kind. — Ed.)

(Late in 1964 the Eagle Gun Co., Stratford, Conn., announced their Eagle Carbine, a semi-automatic. 30-shot arm resembling the Thompson SMG in general appearance. Chambered for either the 45 ACP or 9mm Luger — barrels can be interchanged — it weighs 9 lbs., is 36½ inches over-all with a 16½-barrel. — Ed.)

So deadly is the Thompson's reputation that for many years the federal government forbade the manufacture or importation of any arm, even a single shot, if it resembled the classic Thompson. This ruling has been rescinded.

Since the Treasury Department curtailed the Dewat program, it has been reported that thousands of serviceable Thompsons have been destroyed at the government's order by burning through the receiver with a cutting torch. This is a wanton and deliberate destruction of a proven asset to America and her weapon-hungry friends. True, the Thompson has been replaced by cheaper and easier to make weapons, but it is still capable of rendering valiant service in the cause of free men everywhere. On too many occasions in the past America has been caught with her munitions cupboard empty. It should not happen again.

Specification Data of Thompson Submachine Guns

Model[1]	Weight (lbs.)	Barrel[2] (inches)	Over-all (inches)	Cyclic Rate (s.p.m.)[3]	Magazine Types	Calibers	Notes and Comment
M1919	8.25 See notes	10.5	31.8	1,500	See notes	45 ACP, 22 LR, 32 ACP, 38 ACP, 9mm Luger, 351 Win. S.L.	Basic machine mechanism. Weight, 7 lbs. without stock. Originally belt feed; modified for type C, L, XXVIII and XX magazines.
M1921	9.75	10.5	31.8	800	C, L, XXX, XVIII, XX	45 ACP, 22 LR, 32 ACP, 38 ACP, 9mm Luger, 351 Win. S.L.	First production Thompson. First 15,000 made by Colt. Characterized by classic twin pistol grips.
M1923	See notes	10.5, 14.5	31.8-35.8	800	XXX, XVIII, XX	45 ACP; Rem.-Thompson mil. ctg., cal. 45	Experimental. First Thompson with sling and horizontal fore-end. Weight, 12.5 lbs with 14.5″ bbl., stock and bipod; 9.75 lbs. with 10.5″ bbl. (less bipod?)
M26 (BSA)	7.5	12.5 with Cutts	35-36	800 (?)	See notes	9mm Luger	Experimental. Modified action by Birmingham Small Arms. Forward-curved magazine, capacity unknown.
M1927	9.75	10.5	31.8		C, L, XVIII, XX	45 ACP; Others (?)	Semi-auto. Easily converted to full-auto.
M1928	9.75	10.5	31.8	600	L, XXX, XVIII, XX	45 ACP	Same as M21 except for slower cyclic rate. Experimental use in 30 Carbine and other cals.
M1928 Navy Model	9.75	12.5 with Cutts	33	600	L, XXX, XVIII, XXV, XX	45 ACP	Same as M28 except always Cutts equipped and has horizontal fore-end and sling.
M1928A1	9.75	12.5 with Cutts	33	600	L, XXX, XVIII, XXV, XX	45 ACP	Model number is Army nomenclature for U.S. Navy M28.
M29 (BSA)	See notes	12.5 with Cutts	35.37-36	700-800	See notes	45 ACP, 9mm Luger, 9mm Bayard, 30 Mauser, 30 Luger (?)	Experimental. Very limited quantity made by Birmingham Small Arms. Weight, 9.5-10.5 lbs. depending on cal. 45 ACP uses standard magazines; details of other cal. magazines unknown.
M1928A2	10.5	10.5	31.8	600	L, XXX, XVIII, XV, XX	45 ACP, others	Same as M28A1 except: heavier unfinned bbl., no Lyman rear sight; some specimens have vertical forward grip instead of horizontal fore-end.
M1	10.5	10.5	31.8	700-750	XXX, XXV, XX	45 ACP	Blish lock, actuator and breech oiler eliminated. Will not take 50-round drum.
42M1	10.5	10.5	31.8	700-750	XXX, XXV, XX	45 ACP	Transitional model between M1 and M1A1. Experimental firing pin (?). Less than 100 made.
M1A1	10.5	10.5	31.8	700-750	XXX, XXV, XX	45 ACP	Similar to M1 except for fixed firing pin.
T-2							No data available. Reportedly a tubular receiver model.
M1921/28	9.75	10.5	31.8	600	L, XXX, XXV, XVIII, XX	45 ACP	Made up of prewar parts by Numrich Arms.

1. All Thompsons were air-cooled. All had delayed blowback actions with Blish locks except the M1, 42M1 and M1A1, which were straight blowback designs. All were both full- and semi-automatic except the M26 (full-auto) and the M27 (semi-auto).

2. All Thompsons had finned bbls. except: M23 with 14.5″ bbl., M28A2, M1, 42M1, M1A1. Reising M50 and M55 had finned bbls., SMG's M3 and M3A1 had unfinned bbls. The Cutts Compensator, developed in 1926, ap-parently first was used on the BSA Thompson M26, it was used on all later Thompsons except the M28A1 until WW II exigencies caused its discard on the M1 and subsequent military models. Data for Cutts use on civilian Thompsons is wanting.

3. Maximum deliverable fire rate at full-auto was approximately 225 to 300 shots per minute (s.p.m.).

Chart by Ray Bearse

THOMPSON SUBMACHINE GUNS

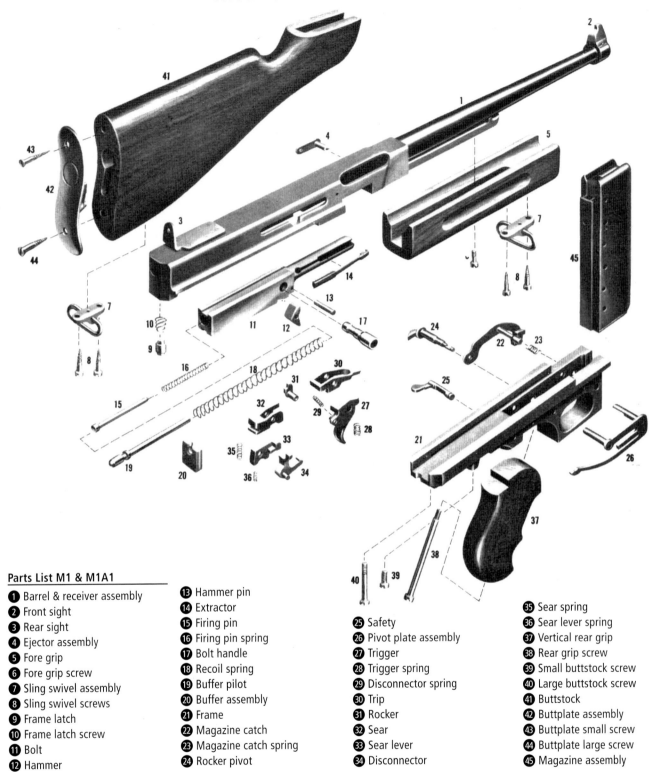

Parts List M1 & M1A1

1. Barrel & receiver assembly
2. Front sight
3. Rear sight
4. Ejector assembly
5. Fore grip
6. Fore grip screw
7. Sling swivel assembly
8. Sling swivel screws
9. Frame latch
10. Frame latch screw
11. Bolt
12. Hammer
13. Hammer pin
14. Extractor
15. Firing pin
16. Firing pin spring
17. Bolt handle
18. Recoil spring
19. Buffer pilot
20. Buffer assembly
21. Frame
22. Magazine catch
23. Magazine catch spring
24. Rocker pivot
25. Safety
26. Pivot plate assembly
27. Trigger
28. Trigger spring
29. Disconnector spring
30. Trip
31. Rocker
32. Sear
33. Sear lever
34. Disconnector
35. Sear spring
36. Sear lever spring
37. Vertical rear grip
38. Rear grip screw
39. Small buttstock screw
40. Large buttstock screw
41. Buttstock
42. Buttplate assembly
43. Buttplate small screw
44. Buttplate large screw
45. Magazine assembly

Disassembly M1 & M1A1 — Retract bolt handle (17) and check action to be sure gun is unloaded. Press up magazine catch (22) and remove magazine (45). Unscrew two butt stock screws (39, 40) and remove butt stock (41) from frame (21). Grasp retracted bolt handle and pull trigger, allowing bolt to slide to its forward position. Set safety at "FIRE" and rocker pivot at "FULL AUTO." Place gun upside-down and press in frame latch (9). Tap frame toward rear of barrel and receiver group (1) a short distance. Squeeze trigger and slide frame off to rear. Press buffer pilot (19) into receiver and remove buffer (20). Remove pilot and recoil spring (18) carefully to prevent forcible ejection of pilot. Slide bolt (11) to rear and tip back end of bolt until bolt handle rests in semicircular cut on right side of receiver. Press bottom of hammer (12) rearward and remove bolt handle. This completes disassembly of major assemblies necessary for all normal cleaning purposes. Further disassembly is not recommended unless necessary for replacement or repair of damaged parts. Reassemble in reverse order.

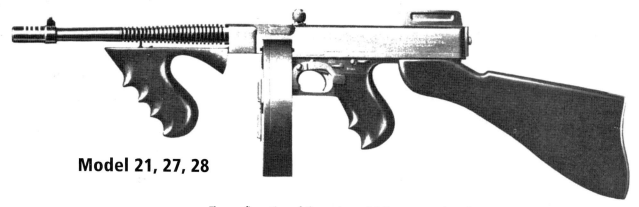

Model 21, 27, 28

The configuration of the early model Thompson submachine guns is shown here (basically the same in models 1921, 1927 and 1928) with Cutts compensator and type L 50-round drum magazine.

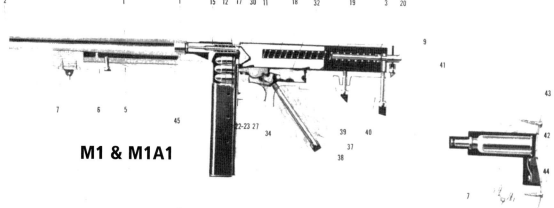

M1 & M1A1

The cutaway illustration shows the baste M1 Thompson submachine gun with the Blish lock eliminated. The M1A1 mechanism incorporated a firing pin integral with the bolt head. This M1 is shown with the type XX standard 20-round box magazine.

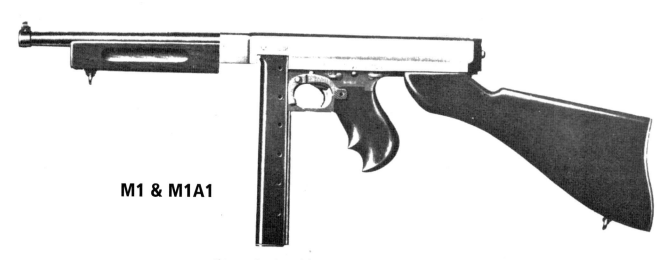

M1 & M1A1

This exterior view of the M1 Thompson shows the differences in configuration with the earlier models. This model is shown with the type XXX 30-round box magazine.

ODDBALL HARDBALLS

by MASON WILLIAMS

IN SHOOTERS' parlance "hardball" refers to the GI cal.-45 Colt automatic pistol that fires GI ammunition — loads with full metal jacket bullets. Usually these handguns are pretty much as-issue jobs, or else they are the finely finished Match Target pistols available from the Director of Civilian Marksmanship via the National Rifle Association. Seldom has a better dollar value been offered the American handgun shooter. This article, however, is not about match target handguns, regardless of their capabilities. Rather, I would like to ramble on about some of the goofed-up 45 ACP pistols that I have run into.

In most businesses it takes a lot of brains and initiative to foul up on a production piece, and when such happens the result is customarily sold at a premium price as a "one in a million" item. The rate of goof-ups in the arms industry, I believe, ranks as one of the highest in the world, particularly during wartime when the primary object of production lines is to get as many pistols as possible into the hands of our men. When the scrap is all over, Ordnance sits down and sorts through those which remain, then picks out the unusual items and does something with them. Now and then one gets through them, though, and that is what this article is all about.

Now, I'm sure that somewhere among my readers there lurks an over-zealous policeman or Federal officer who wants to get a Medal of Commendation. Let me state for the record that all the oddballs mentioned here are strictly — but strictly — legitimate. So relax and forget about the medals. Also, at this point, a word to collectors. None of these is for sale. If anyone has a real oddball I sure would like to hear about it. I'm not an avid collector but when an unusual

> For well over a half-century we have been blessed — or bemused — by the 45 ACP, so there's little left to say about it, right? Wrong. This collector describes in detail a number of unusual GI 45s, guns few shooters know exist

Model 1911 cal. 45 ACP comes my way, I buy it if it will add to my basic collection and to my over-all knowledge of 45s. Many 45s that have been reblued, altered, etc., have no value to me. I am interested only in the more unusual "as-issue" oddballs. The thing that fascinates me is how these pistols get through the countless Government checks, inspections, etc., to finally fall into the hands of the American shooter. A lot of these pistols are simply curiosa, while others are genuine collector's items. Often it is difficult to draw the line. I will not attempt to do so.

I must be vague about certain details here, because the entire history and background of the 45 ACP pistol is filled with grey areas. Records no longer exist or have been lost. Many of the men who worked on the original 45s are no longer with us. Much of the information is secondhand. So please do not be too critical if I appear to sluff off some details. Most of the time I will come right out and say I just don't know. Bear with me and let's have some fun trying to figure out some of the goofs that I know about.

Rem-UMC

Let's start off with one I purchased from the Director of Civilian Marksmanship. Now the DCM is about as official an agency of the Government as one can find — and anything that is officially an agency of the U.S. Government dislikes anything that does not fit the prescribed specifications. Let me try to trace — theoretically of course, because no one really knows — the origin of this particular 45 Model 1911 and/or Model 1911A1.

Way back around 1917 the U.S. Army needed 45s, so among other contractors they authorized Remington-Union Metallic Corp. to manufacture as many 45s as they could. Remington-UMC was given a block of serial numbers entirely separate from the

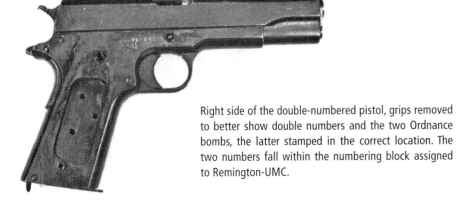

Right side of the double-numbered pistol, grips removed to better show double numbers and the two Ordnance bombs, the latter stamped in the correct location. The two numbers fall within the numbering block assigned to Remington-UMC.

regular run of numbers. These commenced with number 1 and ended with number 21,676. This much is known.

The frame of this 45 meets every requirement as one of the Remington-UMC frames, starting off with the inspector's initials, "EEC," just above the magazine release on the left side of the receiver. The phrase "United States Property" is in the correct place (for this specimen) on the left side of the frame ahead of the trigger guard. So far all is well.

The numbers on these pistols should be stamped just above the trigger on the right side of the receiver. Mine has No. 1545 all right, which is correct for a Remington-UMC. Two Ordnance bombs are stamped side by side partially over and partially below the "No." preceding the serial number. Directly below these ordnance bombs and a bit to the left is stamped 10210, in slightly smaller numerals. This is the only instance I have ever run into of a firearm carrying two numbers. The interesting point is that both numbers fall well within the numbering series assigned to Remington-UMC back in 1917.

My thought on this double numbering is that this receiver came off the line for issue, and then for some reason was held out and possibly used as an instruction control receiver. This could well have been the case because the low number 1545 shows this was one of the first production receivers off the line. Later on, pressure for more and more pistols could have forced the company to re-number the receiver and re-issue it for service. This is all guesswork. I don't know. I have examined all the stampings under a glass and they appear to be of the same approximate vintage. This receiver came to me completely equipped as a Model 1911 frame with the short safety spur, flat mainspring housing and every indication that it was original throughout.

If you think one error is plenty for one pistol — hold on to your hats. The slide is

standard, of Colt manufacture, and meets all specifications of the Model 1911A1 slides. On the other hand, all slide parts appear to be Model 1911 type. The left side carries all the correct stampings for such a slide, but there is absolutely nothing on the right side of the slide — not even serrations, despite the fact that the left side does carry serrations. I have miked the slide and it meets specifications. Obviously someone failed to put this slide through the final stamping on the right side, but how the serrations were left off remains a mystery. It's a weird looking pistol viewed from the right side.

This pistol was obviously brought in after World War II for rebuilding. The finish, a relatively new and perfect parkerizing, is clean, light and unused. Plastic grips were added. How such an odd combination ever got through without someone picking it up I don't know. As I mentioned above, this pistol was purchased by an NRA member from the DCM just a couple of years ago. No other pistol that I own has so many oddball things wrong with it.

45 Dummy

Compared to this one-in-a-million pistol let's look at another weird 45. To confuse the issue even more, this 45 is not a pistol at all. What is it? It's a dummy 45 pistol made of hard rubber, plus solid lead, to give it weight so that it duplicates the hang and feel of the conventional 45 ACP. The butt is stamped U.S. Navy. I spent four full years in the Navy during the Second World War and I saw just one of these pistols. It was kept by the Executive Officer for training purposes. Every now and then some fortunate seaman would be permitted to drop it into his empty holster and go on guard duty. I have heard men speak of these dummies, and I understand many were used for hand-to-hand combat training during the war. As far as I am concerned these dummies are so realistic that if the lights were low or visibility bad I certainly would not argue with a man

shoving one at me. Despite the fact that they cannot fire they make an excellent blackjack or pacifier. I would hate to be clobbered by one. One of my friends back from China in 1947 gave it to my son to play with. One day he and a friend were repulsing Indians — the odds were something like 6000 to two — and he threw it at the screaming savages. I happened to witness this and, on picking it up, realized what it was. Unfortunately, the hammer broke off during the breaking up of the Indian charge. Since then it has been carefully protected. Being martially marked it will remain in my collection of 45 ACPs.

Lunch Pail 45

I now come to a real fouled-up 45 ACP — one that I have named my "lunch pail" 45. This pistol also started out in life as a Remington-UMC handgun — at least to the best of my knowledge. The slide meets every requirement of that brand, including all component parts of the slide assembly.

The odd thing about this pistol is the receiver. It has the customary "United States Property" stamping on the left side of the receiver, ahead of the trigger guard, but that is the only mark on the frame. No serial number, no inspector's initials, no marks of any kind appear. Again the receiver has been assembled with parts that meet the specifications of a pistol of that manufacture and age.

The outside shows considerable holster wear, a police officer having carried it for nearly 30 years. I doubt if it has been fired more than a hundred times. The inside parts show little or no wear and they all appear to be original.

The slide and the receiver assembly appear to have been together for a good many years — in my opinion they are the original assembly. I can't be certain, of course, but I imagine this receiver was "borrowed" from the line after completion but prior to final acceptance and stamping. The parts were probably also brought home piecemeal in

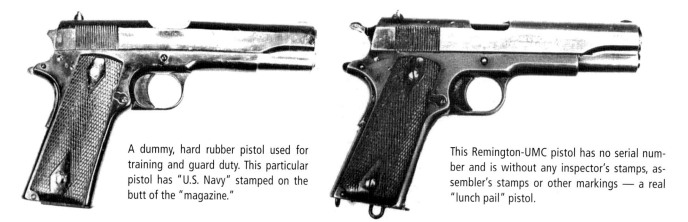

A dummy, hard rubber pistol used for training and guard duty. This particular pistol has "U.S. Navy" stamped on the butt of the "magazine."

This Remington-UMC pistol has no serial number and is without any inspector's stamps, assembler's stamps or other markings — a real "lunch pail" pistol.

the lunch pail every evening. With the millions of parts then coming off the line each day it's a wonder more of this style don't turn up. If you ever run into one I suggest you take it to a local authority and ask them to assign it a number; then you will be in the clear. A lot of these pistols — so I am told — were given to foremen and heads of departments after the war as a token present or as a momento so don't assume that every one was stolen.

Savage 45

Another oddball that you will run into occasionally is the "Savage" variation of the Model 1911 45 pistol. Now this has nothing to do with the Savage Arms Corp. in Westfield, Mass. In 1917–1918 the demand for 45 pistols was so great that the government gave contracts to any firm which could produce them. The records are a bit fuzzy but it appears that the A. J. Savage Munitions Co. of San Diego, Calif., was given a contract to manufacture complete Model 1911 pistols. From what I can find out they only made slides before the contract was cancelled in 1919. It would appear that these slides, or at least some of them, were accepted by the government so that, after the war, these slides were incorporated into rebuilt pistols. You can identify these Savage slides by the lettering, all in one block, on the left side of the front part of the slide. This reads:

Patented Dec. 19, 1905
Feb. 14, 1911, Aug. 19, 1913
Colt's Pt. F. A. Mfg. Co.

Directly to the rear of this lettering is a flaming bomb with a large S inside the bomb circle. The right side of the slide carries the standard stamping "Model of 1911 U. S. Army." While this variation may factually be considered a "production" model they are seldom encountered. Few people have ever seen one.

X-Number 45s

Another seldom-seen variation is the X number pistol. As I understand it these pistols were brought back into certain government armories, stripped down and rebuilt. From what I can determine all of the receivers were machined flat and cleaned on both sides to remove all lettering and numbers. After blueing the receivers were stamped on the right side with an X followed by a new serial number. Those serial numbers I have seen were low, mine being 1923. This new number is found above and behind the trigger. Above the number is the phrase "United States Property."

On the left side of the receiver — at least on my pistol — is a sitting eagle. Below this is S17. The eagle and the lettering are quite small and you need a good glass to make out the details. They are located directly above the magazine release, slightly higher than the spot where the regular inspector's initials are customarily found.

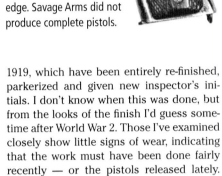

The Savage Arms "slide" pistol, rarely seen today. To the author's knowledge, Savage Arms did not produce complete pistols.

I have seen these pistols with the receivers machined so much that the naked eye can readily see the difference between the thickness of the X frames and a new frame. If you run into one of these X numbered 45s, examine the slide for machining — it might well be original and legitimate.

Low Number 45s

Every now and then you will see one of the original low number Model 1911 pistols. The first 50,000 or so were superbly finished. They stand out like a flashlight among candles. The very early ones, carrying numbers down around 10,000 or lower, are beauties — too good to shoot, in my opinion. So far I've seen only one with a misplaced serial, that one number 6324, so-stamped far ahead of the trigger guard. This on the right side of the receiver, of course, directly opposite the legend "United States Property" stamped on the opposite side.

I have run into quite a few of the old World War I pistols carrying serial numbers that date them back to 1916, 1917, 1918 and 1919, which have been entirely re-finished, parkerized and given new inspector's initials. I don't know when this was done, but from the looks of the finish I'd guess sometime after World War 2. Those I've examined closely show little signs of wear, indicating that the work must have been done fairly recently — or the pistols released lately. These are good buys for the man who wants a rugged handgun.

In conclusion I'd like to point out that many 1911 and 1911A1 pistols may be found in variations that add considerably to their value for collectors. If you find one of these oddballs ask a collector about it — it may be of some worth.

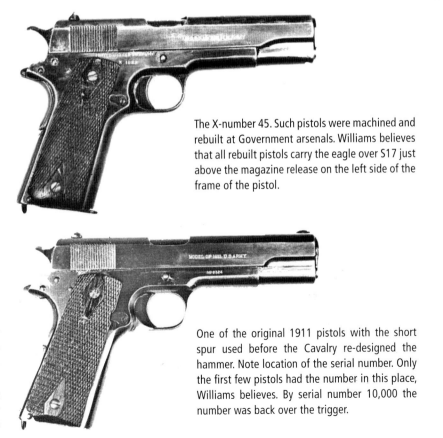

The X-number 45. Such pistols were machined and rebuilt at Government arsenals. Williams believes that all rebuilt pistols carry the eagle over S17 just above the magazine release on the left side of the frame of the pistol.

One of the original 1911 pistols with the short spur used before the Cavalry re-designed the hammer. Note location of the serial number. Only the first few pistols had the number in this place, Williams believes. By serial number 10,000 the number was back over the trigger.

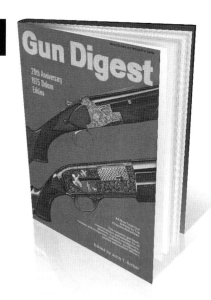

THE 1903 SPRINGFIELD

An interesting and detailed account of the most famous military rifle in United States history — including the numerous variations made since its birth.

by AL MILLER

HETHER OR NOT the Springfield 03 was the best military rifle of its time is still open to argument; Mausers, Lee-Enfields — each has its protagonists. Regardless of their respective virtues though, there can be little doubt that the 03 was the best prepared and finished. No service arm, before or since, ever enjoyed so much painstaking care during its manufacture.

Stocks were made out of good, solid walnut, superior to many found on commercial sporters today. Although machine-inletted, the marriage of wood to metal was unbelievably close, especially on those rifles fashioned between the wars when quality, not time, was the watchword. Metal fittings, all machined from forgings, were carefully polished before bluing. Bolt heads were knurled, triggers serrated. For a while, even buttplates were machine-checkered. Tool marks were rare. Each rifle was a "finished" product when it left the armory.

They were accurate, too. National Match Springfields ruled the target ranges both here and abroad for many years and the service model was no slouch in that department, either.

Every 03 in my racks, including the World War II versions, will keep five shots inside 2½" at 100 yards. This, of course, from a rest and using match ammo, but with issue sights. Perhaps I've been lucky but I've never owned or fired an inaccurate Springfield; nor one which could be described as "just so-so."

The oft-repeated charge that the 03 made a better sporter than a military arm may

have some justification. Many of its design features — the excellent finish, the close tolerances — hint of a conception by riflemen, target shots and hunters, rather than by soldiers.

The inherent sporting qualities of the Springfield were noticed shortly after its birth. Teddy Roosevelt had one armory-altered in late 1903, a special stock fitted (serial number 0009), which he took to Africa in 1909. He characterized it as "the lightest and handiest of all my rifles," and he managed to kill an impressive number of animals with it, including both hippo and rhino, using the original 150-gr., full-patch bullet at 2700 fps.

Stewart Edward White, the sportsman-novelist, was another of the early Springfield users. He collected upwards of 400 African trophies using one or another of his 03 sporters, among others, and judged the new rifle-cartridge combination ideal medicine for lions.

White's first Springfield sporter was made up by Louis Wundhammer about 1910, this first rifle one of four that had been ordered by Capt. E. C. Crossman. The first Stewart. Edward White rifle, serial number 166,346, has a Hock Island arsenal barrel dated February, 1910. Made by Louis Wundhammer of Los Angeles, it is one of four such Springfield 1903 sporters ordered by Capt. E. C. (Ned) Crossman. One was for Capt. Crossman, the other two for Robert C Rogers and John Colbv. See Grossman's Book of the Springfield *(Georgetown, S. C, 19511 or the Gin Digest, I5th edition. Later, Owen, Griffin & Howe, Hoffman, Linden and several oth-*

ers made them. These were handsome rifles, a bit heavy by modern standards but each a thing of beauty: choice wood, tasteful engraving and checkering — and if they were not too well used, still capable today of formidable accuracy. Until the middle 'thirties, when Winchester brought out their Model 70, Springfield sporters set the standards by which other hunting and target rifles were judged.)

For years, the 03 was this nation's official service rifle. It lost that title to the Garand in 1935, but with the advent of World War II the 03 and its descendants, the A3 and A4, saw active duty as late as the 1950s. The Springfield's battle honors include campaigns in the Phillipines, Central America, the Caribbean, Mexico, the Western Front during World War I, every theater in World War II and, finally, Korea.

Turned out to pasture, the Springfield's career is far from over. During the past two decades, thousands have found their way into the hands and gunracks of American sportsmen. The NRA offered them, via the Director of Civilian Marksmanship, to its members at bargain rates over the years; surplus stores sold them; every sporting goods store of any stature at all tallied some in its inventory. Today these veterans, most civilianized by fancy stocks, scopes and professional blue jobs, can be seen by the score each fall when the red-coated hordes invade mountain and forest. The 03 isn't dead yet.

But they're getting scarce; at least, the "as issued" specimens are — and the gun collecting fraternity is becoming aware of it. During the past year, Springfield prices have soared. If a man has any ambition to collect them, the time to start is now.

The Early Models

"Sired by Mauser, out of Krag" is the way one wag described the Springfield. Its official birthday was June 18, 1903 when the Chief of Ordnance accepted it, the official designation: *U.S. Magazine Rifle, Model of 1903, Caliber .30.* It came with a 24" barrel, rod bayonet, ramp type rear sight and an odd looking blade with two large holes drilled through it for a front sight. The bolt handle was curved but wasn't swept back. The forward barrel band was located right at the nose of the stock.

The 1903 cartridge, which came into being at the same time, was slightly longer than the current '06 round and fired a 220-gr., full-jacketed round nose bullet at 2200 fps.

In 1905, the rod bayonet was shunted aside in favor of the knife type and, about the same time, an improved leaf rear sight, resembling that used on the Krag, was mounted in place of the unsatisfactory ramp.

Meanwhile, the ever-busy Germans had opened their bag of tricks again, surprising the shooting world by introducing a radical pointed bullet they called *spitzges-choss*. This new pointed shape enabled them to send the 154-gr. bullet from their 8mm service round at the then astonishing speed of 2800 fps. Quick to see the advantages of the new design, our ordnance people got busy in their ballistics labs and whipped up the now famous 30-06 cartridge.

Pushing a 150-gr. pointed bullet out of the muzzle at 2700 fps, the 06 case was reduced to 2.49" long, necessitated by the 03 case having been too long for the new spitzer bullet by .070". Several thousand 1903 rifles had been produced by this time but, rather than re-barrel them, it was decided, in the interests of economy, to shorten and re-chamber the existing barrels. Two-tenths inch (.200") was shaved off the breech, the chambers altered for the new cartridge, and the threads cut two turns deeper. This operation left the barrels 23.79" long (chamber and bore) and all Springfield 03 barrels made since then have measured the same. Over-all barrel length became 24.006".

The next major change took place in 1918 when the steel used to make receivers and bolts was strengthened. Those critical parts were double heat treated, a process which made the surface metal extremely hard while allowing the core steel to remain relatively soft. Actions fabricated in this manner have weathered test rounds devel-

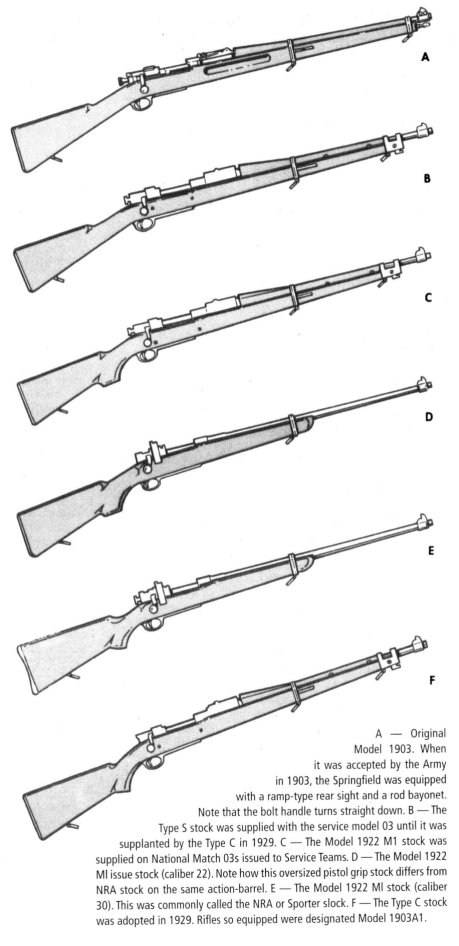

A — Original Model 1903. When it was accepted by the Army in 1903, the Springfield was equipped with a ramp-type rear sight and a rod bayonet. Note that the bolt handle turns straight down. B — The Type S stock was supplied with the service model 03 until it was supplanted by the Type C in 1929. C — The Model 1922 M1 stock was supplied on National Match 03s issued to Service Teams. D — The Model 1922 MI issue stock (caliber 22). Note how this oversized pistol grip stock differs from NRA stock on the same action-barrel. E — The Model 1922 MI stock (caliber 30). This was commonly called the NRA or Sporter slock. F — The Type C stock was adopted in 1929. Rifles so equipped were designated Model 1903A1.

oping pressures of 125,000 psi without a whimper. The tough surface not only wears well but with a little use, cams and runways smooth to a mirror-like glaze, making those particular actions the slickest Springfield ever built.

Despite the time, effort and expense which must have been spent creating the new process, nobody bothered to record the exact point when the change was instituted. Authorities agree it took place somewhere around receiver No. 800,000, but nobody's really sure. Nevertheless, 800,000 is the magic number, it being generally accepted that actions made subsequently are the stronger. Although "low numbered" Springfields, that is, those with serial numbers under 800,000, are regarded as weaker and less desirable, it should be remembered that each was subjected to 70,000 pound test loads, and that these were the same rifles which created the Springfield's reputation in the wars and on the game fields. Nevertheless, it is true that the shattering of several of the earlier case-hardened actions brought on the change in heat treatment in early 1918.

Rock Island 03s received the improved double heat treatment starting with receiver No. 285,507. From No. 319,921 on some R.I. receivers were made of a nickel steel similar to that used later in producing the wartime A3s and A4s. Springfield Armory didn't adopt nickel steel until 1928 but again, no one there in Massachusetts noticed the exact time of the changeover. In all probability rifles produced after No. 1,290,266 boasted nickel steel actions.

Variations in the quality of steel are primarily of interest only to purists. It goes without saying that any high-numbered 03 — always assuming good condition — will accomodate modern loads with perfect safety.

The Pedersen Device

To back up slightly: Shortly after the U.S. declared war on Germany in 1917, a well known arms designer of the day, one J. D. Pedersen, approached the War Department with an intriguing invention. The Pedersen Device, as historians call it, was essentially an automatic pistol mechanism with a stubby, integral barrel which could be slipped into the 03's receiver in place of the regular bolt. Once locked in place — this was accomplished by a flip of the magazine cutoff to "Off" — a long box magazine containing 40 cartridges resembling the 32 ACP was inserted into the right side of the bolt and — presto! The Springfield was converted into an instant semiautomatic rifle!

Only three alterations to the rifle were necessary: an ejection port had to be cut into the left side of the receiver; the magazine cutoff had two grooves milled in it, and a small "kicker" was added to the sear. None of these modifications prevented the rifle from using the regular service round when the original bolt was in place.

Although the pistol-sized cartridge fired an 80-gr. bullet at a mere 1300 fps, General Pershing recognized its lethal potential and ordered 100,000 Pedersen units. Some 65,000 had been completed when Armistice Day arrived but none were ever issued to troops. A few years after the war, most of the devices were destroyed. A few, as usual, managed to escape the crushers and are now eagerly sought after by collectors.

It's easy to recognize the 03s modified for the Pedersen unit. There is a small, lozenge-shaped ejection port on the left side of the receiver, and to quell any further doubts the legend, *U.S Springfield Armory Model 1903 Mark I* is inscribed on the receiver. Records concerning this variation are sketchy but it's believed that one rifle, appropriately modified, was produced for each of the Pedersen devices manufactured.

When World War I ended, the Battle Reports and recommendations concerning the various weapons used were reviewed. The 03 came through with flying colors. Complaints were few and suggested changes even fewer. One, that was accepted, concerned the bolt handle. It was angled backwards slightly to bring it more in line with the trigger.

The Marine Corps, always marksmanship oriented, altered the sights of their rifles: the width of the front blade was increased to .10" and undercut, while the diameter of the rear peep was doubled. In addition, the triangular-shaped open sight in the rear leaf was dispensed with. 03s with Marine Corps sights are very much in demand by collectors.

Type C Stocks

After a considerable amount of experimentation, a new service stock, the Type C was chosen in 1928. The original Type S stock had been criticized for its abrupt drop at the heel and because many felt it was too short. The new stock was straighter, its buttstock contour reminiscent of those found on good shotguns. A hand-filling integral pistol grip had been added and the finger grooves, so pronounced on the old S stock, were deleted. Rifles with the new stock were designated Model 1903A1s.

Although the semi-automatic M1 was chosen to succeed the 03 in 1935, almost a year passed before the last bolt action rolled off the production line at Springfield Armory.

A few more were assembled in 1937 and another handful, the last, were produced in 1939. With receiver No. 1,532,878, the 03 became just another obsolete military rifle — or so everyone believed at the time.

Just before production ceased, a second gas escape port was drilled through the forward receiver ring. Up to this point, only one port, about ⅛" diameter, had pierced the ring on the right. Why an additional hole was put on the left is anyone's guess. I've only noticed a handful of 03s so made, all with serial numbers above 1,500,000. When the wartime A3s and A4s appeared, only one port was evident, this time on the left side.

Late in 1941, sensing the hot breath of war and unable to supply our rapidly expanding military forces sufficiently with the new M1, the War Department issued a contract to the Remington Arms Company to begin production of the 03. Except for the name Remington and the serial numbers, which started with No. 3,000,000, this version of the 03 was a faithful replica of the Armory model in every respect.

With an eye toward increasing production, Remington's engineers took a critical look at the old design. After a few months of fiddling with slide rules and handmade prototypes, they came up with the *U.S. Rifle. Caliber .30. Model of 1903A3.*

Why not A2? Because a Model A2 had already been approved and was in service. Not really a rifle, it was simply a modified barreled action, altered to fit inside the breech of a tank cannon and used for practice to reduce training expenses.

Old-timers howled in anguish when the first A3 appeared. Barrel bands, floorplate and trigger guard were made of stamped metal. To add insult to injury, the barrels, most still bearing lathe scars, had only two grooves instead of the traditional four. Critics admitted that the rear-mounted receiver sight might offer some advantages but most insisted that the rifle would never stand up under battle conditions.

Despite the outraged cries and dire predictions, the A3 performed creditably throughout World War II, seeing service in every theater and adding new luster to the name Springfield. It was sturdy, as dependable as its famed forefather, and just about as accurate.

This last surprised everyone. The ability of a 4-grooved barrel to group better than a two-groover, if any, must be slight. From a rest, my 03s and A3s deliver the same accuracy: 2" to 2½" at 100 yards with match ammo. The life of a 2-grooved tube is reputedly shorter than the four if AP ammunition

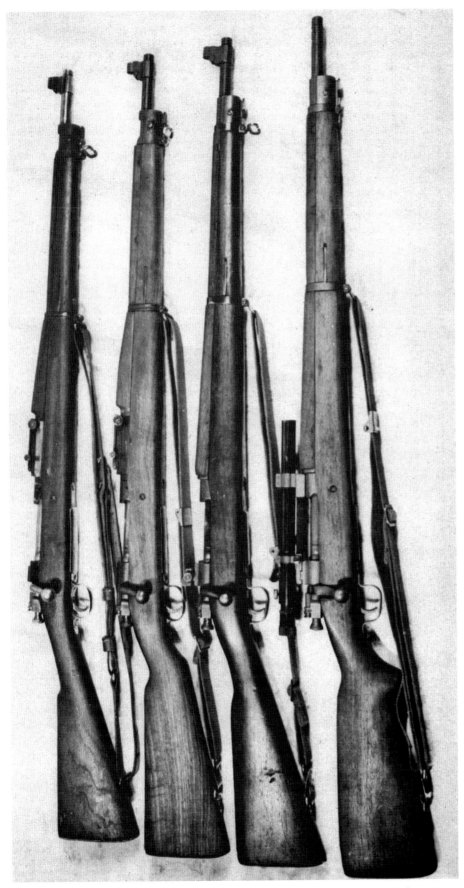

1903 Service. Left to right: 1903 with S stock; 1903A1 with WW II semi-pistol-grip stock; 1903A3; 1903A4, the sniper's model with a modified Type C stock.

is used, but evidently the Army felt the difference in longevity was more than offset by lower manufacturing costs and greater production.

Two Million A3s

Remington turned out most of the two million A3s but Smith-Corona also added another 200,000 or so to the total. A number of the latter will be found with 4-groove and, occasionally, 6-groove barrels which were supplied by High Standard, Savage and several other sub-contractors.

The A4, the sniper's model, made its bow in 1943. It was simply an A3 equipped with a Weaver 330C telescopic sight (the Army called it the M73B1 carried in a Redfield Jr. mount. The bolt handle was altered to clear the scope and no iron sights were fitted.

To the best of my knowledge, Remington took no special pains with bedding or action but the A4 sniper standing in my rack is blessed with what must surely be one of the smoothest actions ever made. Its condition indicated that it had never been issued yet the trigger is crisp and light — almost too light — and the rifle will consistently group all shots within 1¼"

The number of A4s produced was very small, something on the order of 28,000 all told. Few were issued before 1944 but many were still in action as late as the early 1950s. The Marines used them in Korea, mounting 8- and 12-power target scopes on them.

There's no way of knowing how many survived but the number must be small. The rarest of all have serial numbers beginning with a "Z" prefix; fewer than 2900 were made.

Of all the Springfields produced, the cream were the target and sporter rifles which trickled out of the Armory during the quiet years between wars. Less than 2000 ever saw the light of day in any given year but each was a handcrafted marvel.

Assembled from carefully selected parts, with cocking cams, bolts, sight leaves, extractors and runways polished, stocks fashioned from first-class, straight-grained black walnut, equipped with star gauged barrels and target sights, the National Match Springfields, NRA Sporters and the other limited edition models represented the Armory's finest achievements. Little wonder they dominated the target ranges for so many years.

When I was a boy, the word "star gauged" had a magic ring. This interesting device was a feeler gauge used at the Armory to measure the uniformity of a barrel's bore. If land and groove measurements were within one ten-thousandths of an inch

(.0001") from chamber to muzzle the barrel was judged match grade, and a small "star mark" was stamped on the lower edge of the muzzle crown. In U.S. shooting circles a star gauged barrel was regarded as the ultimate.

Target-Sporter Models

More than a dozen different match, target and sporting models were created by Springfield Armory between 1921 and 1940. (Some 1000 or fewer National Match versions of the A3 rifle, purportedly equipped with Redfield micrometer rear sights, were produced from about 1953 through 1956, but I haven't been able to find a photograph of one of these or a specimen.) Some were designed exclusively for service teams; most were made available to NRA members. In addition, a series of full-fledged 30-caliber target rifles was issued. They were characterized by long, heavy barrels, micrometer sights on the receiver, globe sights at the muzzle, mounting blocks for telescopic sights — some were even decorated with adjustable buttplates and other match-rifle equipment. These remarkable rifles, weighing from 12 to 13 pounds, were just about unbeatable on the range.

During one period, the Armory even made up a few "free rifles" for the International Teams. These had longer, heavier barrels, set triggers, long hook buttplates and palm rests. They were about as good as anything Europe had to offer, and they tipped the scales at a hefty 14 pounds.

Some of those old rifles are still floating around, most of them pretty worn now. I'd never pay extra money for one myself unless it is accompanied by the original Ordnance Dept. bill of sale and its star gauging record.

Needless to say, a clever gunsmith can counterfeit a National Match model without too much trouble. A bit of judicious polishing, a close fitting stock, a homemade star mark on the muzzle, the rifle's serial number engraved on the bolt — as always, it pays to be prudent when purchasing a used firearm.

Chances are, if you do run across one of those old specials, it will be an NRA Sporter. Several thousand were made and quite a few, relatively speaking, seem to have survived.

The Sporter, like the other specials, was put together from near-perfect parts and given the same care as a National Match rifle during production. The barrel — star gauged, of course — was slightly tapered; a Lyman 48 receiver sight was mounted on the bridge but the standard service blade was retained up forward; the stock contour

A — The 1903 Springfield in early standard-issue forms. It has the original S stock with grasping grooves and greater drop, at heel. B — The 1903A1 was simply the standard 03 mounted in a Type C stock. C — 1903A1 in a wartime C stock. Notice the blunted pistol grip, the general absence of clean stock lines. D — The 1903A3. The World War II version of the 03 has a receiver peep sight and is characterized by the use of stamped parts and a two-groove barrel. E — The 1903A4. The sniper's model is equipped with a Weaver 2y2X scope in Redfield Jr. mounts and the Type C stock. No iron sights were fitted.

An ejection port on the Mark I Springfield allowed the small Pedersen-designed cartridge cases to escape the semi-automatic bolt. Note the slight stock cutaway beneath the port.

An ejection port on the Mark I Springfield allowed the small Pedersen-designed cartridge cases to escape the semi-automatic bolt. Note the slight stock cutaway beneath the port.

Those Mark I 03s modified to accept the Pedersen device were plainly marked as such on the receiver ring. Mark I parts. Top, sear and cutoff from a standard 03; bottom, sear and cutoff from a Mark I Springfield modified to accept the Pedersen device.

was distinctly different from the service style, resembling those on commercial rifles.

While on the subject, it should be noted that the Armory developed several different stocks. The S and C stocks, which have already been mentioned, were relegated to the service rifles, including the N.M. models, but there were various other supplied for the specials.

The Model 1922 or NRA Model as it was popularly known, featured a shotgun-style butt, a well-turned pistol grip and short, sport-er style fore-end. This was used on the 22 rimfire Springfields and on the 30-06 Sporters when these (and other later versions) were sold for civilian use through the DCM.

This same M1922 NRA stock — except for having finger grooves — was used on the 1922 "Match Springfield," a 30-cal. rifle

introduced that year. This rifle was a fore-runner of the "Style T" Match 03 rifle first offered in late 1929 and made in limited numbers for a few years.

The M1922 Ml stock, in its NRA form, differed little from the M1922 stock, but the "issue only" version was considerably different — while a half- or sporter stock, the fore-end had finger grooves, the pistol grip profile showed a flatter angle, and the rear of the buttstock looked like the service rifle or S stock in drops, dimension and form. There were numerous other stock styles over the years, some experimental, others of limited production. For full and complete information on all of these — and for the finest account of Springfield rifles extant, see *The '03 Springfield*, by Clark S. Campbell, published by Ray Riling Arms Books Co., 6844 Gorsten St., Philadelphia, Pa. 19119.

The Springfield Sporter

To get back to the Sporters: They're heavy by today's standards, scaling pretty close to 9 pounds. Weighty though they may be, those I've fired were very accurate with actions as smooth as silk.

A great number served as the basis for some of the classics turned out by such people as Nied-ner, Shelhamer, Griffin & Howe and Stoeger during the 1920s and the early '30s.

The first 22 practice rifle based on the 03 action was a single shot. It was fitted with a 24-inch barrel bored off-center at the breech so that the regular firing pin would hit the rim of the small case. The cartridge, by the way, was a special 22 Long Rifle featuring a Pope-designed bullet. It was manufactured by Peters for a limited time and called the "22 Stevens-Pope Armory." Only a few of these arms were produced. Except for the bores, their appearance was indistinguishable from the service rifle.

Another chip off the old block was the Gallery Practice Rifle, Model 1903. Except for chamber and barrel, it too was a duplicate of the issue rifle. Although some of its design features smacked of genius, its accuracy left much to be desired.

Rather than fashion a new bolt or firing pin assembly, Springfield engineers (Majors J. E. HofFer and J. T. Thompson) created an adaptor cartridge. Made entirely of steel, they were deliberately made shorter than the standard 06 round to prevent one of the latter from being chambered by mistake. Each adaptor contained an integral firing pin and a tiny slot in the side which permitted a 22 Short cartridge to be inserted. The devices could be loaded into the magazine, worked through the action and extracted exactly like the service cartridge. From a training standpoint, the approach was ideal, especially for those ROTC and National Guard units located far from regular outdoor ranges. It meant that the troops could train with a rifle of standard size and weight, shoot from all positions and even practice rapid-fire on indoor ranges.

Clever as the idea was, the adaptors proved impractical. When fired, the bullet enjoyed about half an inch of free travel before it struck the rifling. After a few rounds, lead and grease built up at this point. Accuracy suffered accordingly. In addition, the adaptors tended to rust in short order, requiring an exasperating amount of maintenance to keep them in operating condition. Most aggravating of all — as far as the shooters were concerned — was the fact that unloading the spent 22 cases was a miserable and frustrating chore.

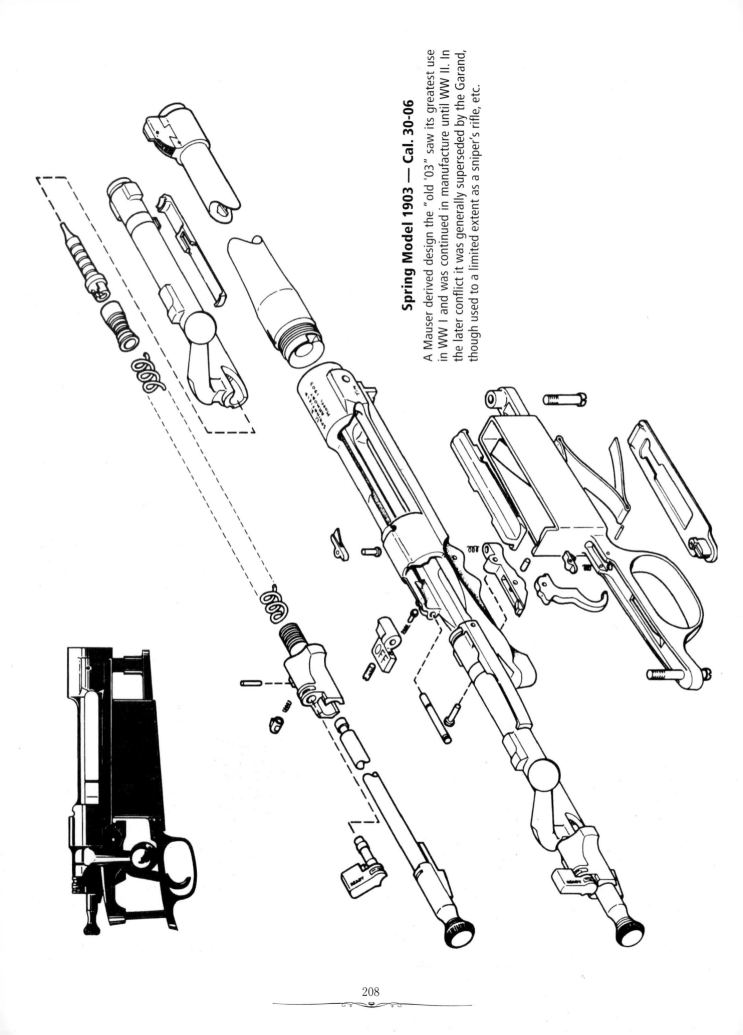

Spring Model 1903 — Cal. 30-06

A Mauser derived design the "old '03" saw its greatest use in WW I and was continued in manufacture until WW II. In the later conflict it was generally superseded by the Garand, though used to a limited extent as a sniper's rifle, etc.

The NRA Sporter. Assembled from carefully selected parts, fitted with star-gauged barrels and stocked with dense-grained walnut, these rifles sold for $41.50 forty years ago. They were heavy but superbly accurate.

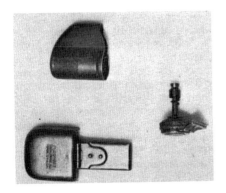

Curiosa. Relics of the days when the 03 ruled the target range. Top, front sight protector; lower left, rear sight protector; right, rear sight micrometer adjuster.

Despite these shortcomings, it wasn't until 1919 that plans for a new 22 trainer were started. More like the target rifles we know today, its bolt was two-piece and a 5-shot magazine jutted below the floorplate. It still looked in 1920 like the issue rifle except for a Lyman 48 micrometer sight mounted on the receiver. Chambered for the regular 22 Long Rifle cartridge, these prototype versions were the first really accurate 22s that Ordnance had ever developed.

Micrometer sight adjustor. One of the accessories offered the serious competitor of the early 1920s when the 03 dominated the ranges. These tools permitted accurately controlled small changes in elevation.

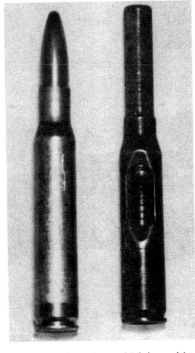

22 Short cartridge adaptor (right), used in the Gallery Practice Rifle of 1907. A 30-06 Military round is shown for comparison.

The Model 1922

Two years later (in June of 1922) a refined version, called the *U.S. Rifle. Caliber .22. Model 1922*, was issued. It was the first Springfield to have the half-stock style that was soon to become famous as the "Sporter" stock. By mid-1924 some 2000 M1922 rifles had been made, their price just over $39.

The improved-mechanism Model 1922 Ml which followed also had — in its "as issued" form — a half-stock with an oversize flat-angle pistol grip. These had an excessive amount of drop at the heel. The NRA version had the graceful Sporter stock, as before. Bolt travel was still as long as that of the standard 03, a full 3.3 inches, but chamber dimensions were better, the 5-shot magazine was now flush, and the Lyman 48 C receiver sight had ½-minute clicks.

The 1922 M2s, introduced in late 1932, wore a new stock. While a half-stock, it was not the Sporter NRA style used earlier; instead, it had finger-grooves in the fore-end

and a buttstock profile about like the N.M. stock. These M2s had a short bolt throw, speed lock ignition and provision for headspace adjustment. That last was incorporated in the locking lug assembly on the final production models.

M2s can still be found hard at work on small bore ranges around the country. Many carry the letters "A" or "B" after their serial numbers. Those markings signify that the rifles were originally issued as M1922s or M1922s Mis and later arsenal modified to M2 specifications.

The *International Match Rifle, Caliber 30, Model 1924*, carried a checkered pistol grip stock, a hooked buttplate, a ball-type palm rest, a Lyman 48 receiver sight and a heavy 30" barrel. These also had double-set triggers of one type or another (see Campbell's book). An identical rifle was made in 22 Long Rifle, using the Model 1922 Ml action, for our successful U.S. International teams, but with the action considerably re-designed. Twelve of the 1924 match Springfields in 22 caliber were made in 15 days, the result of a last-minute order for them!

The old 03 wasn't perfect. Its sights were too delicate for battle conditions; the two-piece firing pin, which failed on occasion, affected lock time adversely; the high bridge made for an overly tall sighting plane and the Springfield action could never cope with escaping gas as well as the Mauser. Nonetheless, it was the best rifle that ever came out of the Armory — and it could shoot. The average 03 was more accurate than any of its contemporaries. Regardless of its shortcomings it looms high on the list of the world's great rifles.

The 03 helped make a lot of history during the first half of this century; on target ranges, battle ground and game fields. More than four million were produced but age, wear and tear, combat, lend-lease and sporterizing have taken their toll. The 03, in military dress, is rapidly disappearing from the scene.

Tribute and Epitaph

But not entirely. A handful are still on active duty. While watching General Eisenhower's funeral, I noticed the familiar silhouettes when the Presidential color guard hove into view. Sure enough, they were armed with the old bolt actions. Some months ago I saw the Army Drill Team in action. They too were equipped with 03s. I've no idea why they carried them but it was a nostalgic sight to a guy who learned to shoot and run through the Manual of Arms with one.

I remember crossing the English Channel one gray day in June of '44. The ship rolled

A "long-slide" Lyman 48 micrometer sight, here seen on a Sedgeley sporter.

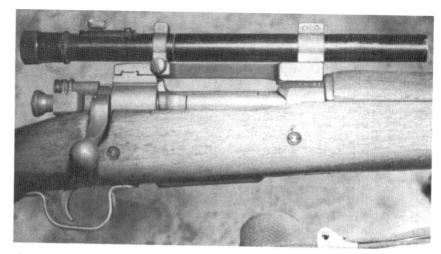

This 1903A4 Sniper rifle has a 2½ X Weaver telescopic sight in a Redfield Jr. mount, saw active duty as late as the Korean conflict. Note the altered bolt handle.

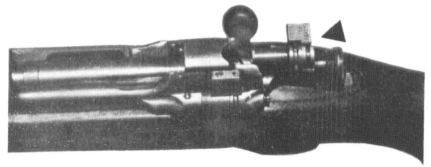

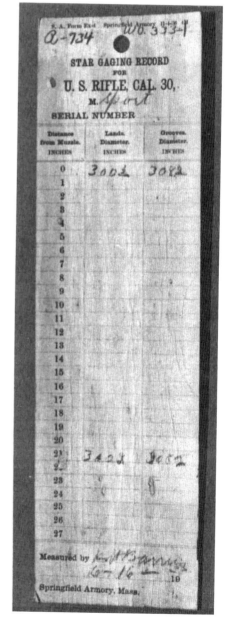

sluggishly as the helmsman threw the wheel hard over to avoid a floating mine. Several of the troopers broke out their M1s and emptied them at the shiny, dark globe without result. A lanky, tobacco-chewing sergeant muttered an apology as he elbowed up to the rail, cradling a weatherbeaten 03 tenderly in his arms. Balancing easily against the ship's gentle heave, he slid into the leather sling and sighted carefully for what seemed to be an eternity. The Springfield's bark was lost in the dull boom of the exploding mine and, as the echoes lost themselves over the tortured water,

Above: The reversed safety on the above rifle (arrow) must have been taken from a match rifle, for the serial number on the bolt doesn't match that on the receiver. It pays to be cautious when shopping for collector's items.

Right: "Star Gaging Record" card used to indicate bore and groove dimensions of selected 03 barrels.

the marksman cast a scornful glance at the M1s. "Firepower, hell! I'll stick to my 03!"

If the 03 ever needs an epitaph, that should do as well as any.

Sighting tube. A small number of "sighting tubes" made at Springfield Armory and issued to service rifle teams. The minimum sight setting was 600 yards.

THE
M16A2
NEW WORLD STANDARD FOR INFANTRY RIFLES...

...out-pentetrates the M1 rifle shooting M2 ball at 800 yards

by C.E. HARRIS

HE M16A2 is the new standard to which past and future military rifles will be compared. This second-generation 5.56mm rifle is the product of cooperation between industry and U.S. forces to develop, test and field a product-improved rifle which should meet their needs to the end of this century. The M16A2, standardized in November, 1983, is a wonderful example of how the military development and procurement system is *supposed* to work. The efficiency with which this work proceeded from concept to production and fielding is a tribute to military-industrial cooperation.

When the M16A1 rifle was first adopted by U.S. troops in 1967, the Marines were the most vocal opponent of a "small caliber" rifle. At that time there were valid complaints about the reliability of the M16 and its M193 ammunition and its range and lethality. Although changes in the rifle and ammunition corrected the functional problems, by 1970 it was apparent the sights and the ballistics of the 55-gr. M193 cartridge reached their limits in combat at about 500 yards. To many critics, even 500 yards pushed credibility.

Adopting the 5.56mm NATO SS109/M855 cartridge in 1977 brought ammunition ef-

fective to well beyond 600 yards in lethality and accuracy and penetration. Standardization of this NATO cartridge brought a need to adapt the M16 rifle to it, and provided the opportunity to correct the known tactical deficiencies in the M16A1. The USMC Firepower Division, at Quantico, VA, was tasked with this development in cooperation with Colt Industries, under supervision of the Joint Services Small Arms Program (JSSAP).

The product-improved rifle was identified as M16A1E1 during operational testing which preceded formal type classification. Operational testing of 30 M16A1E1 rifles

Production version of Colt M16A2: Obvious changes visible are heavier barrel, new muzzle-brake/compensator, improved sights and hand guard, integral brass deflector on receiver and contoured pistol grip.

M16A2 barrel marking gives caliber and twist as "1/7."

The AK74 5.45mm cartridge and the AK47 7.62mm cartridge — the competitors — are shown to the left of the 5.56mm NATO M855 cartridge, our new standard.

Right side of receiver shows the integral brass deflector on the receiver behind the ejection port which prevents lefthanders from being struck by ejected cases. Aluminum device sandwiched between pistol grip and lower receiver inhibits inadvertent automatic in non-combat situations, such as marksmanship training, where this photo was taken.

served to evaluate the changes and provide input for further refinements which would be incorporated in the production version of the M16A2. The Modified Operation Test (MOT) began on November 23, 1981, and was completed on December 11, 1981. Supplemental tests continued through August, 1982, to confirm the validity of some proposed improvements and to confirm their production feasibility.

The M16A2 is now in full production, having been adopted by the U.S. Marines to replace their entire complement of M16A1 rifles within the next five years. The Army has also decided to adopt the M16A2. The Canadians are also adopting it, but without the new sights or burst control, as the C7.

The test findings summarized in the MOT Final Report conclude the M16A2 performs as well or better than the M16A1 in all areas. The advantages of the M16A2 over the

M16A1 are listed below:

- *Increased effectiveness*: higher hit probability, greater lethality and penetration, improved range through use of NATO standard SS109/M855 ammunition.

- *Better durability and handling* with improved, stronger handguard, and buttstock, longer buttstock, new buttcap, contoured pistol grip.

- *Reduced barrel jump and muzzle climb* during full automatic or sustained semiautomatic fire with new muzzle-brake-compensator.

- *Reduced dust signature* as well when fired over sandy or dusty ground.

- *Heavier, stronger barrel*, to resist bending, with 7-inch twist to exploit advantages of new NATO ammunition.

- *Better sights*: improved contrast and less glare with square post front sight, faster

target acquisition of moving targets, better detection of targets in low light, and improved accuracy at long range by use of two optimized rear sight apertures.

- *Better fire control* and more effective use of ammunition with 3-shot burst option.

Operational firepower effectiveness was evaluated by comparing the M16A1 and M16A2 in tactical scenarios. These included base of fire, assault and counterattack, ambush, long range and mid-range defensive fires, final protective fires, defense against ambush, area target suppression, and night firing.

There was no appreciable difference in base of fire effectiveness between the M16A1 and M16A2, but in the assault and counterattack, test results from the Small Arms Remoted Target System (SARTS) showed the A2 obtained a significantly greater percentage of hits in burst fire.

The contoured pistol grip is intended to provide more secure grasping; backstrap is deeply grooved, and frontstrap has deep finger groove to provide secure hold. Selector lever offers choice of semi-auto or 3-shot bursts. Rear sight has minute of angle clicks for windage and elevation, matched to M855 or SS109 ammunition.

When fired semi-automatic on the field range and Infantry Tactical Training (ITT) course simulations, no significant difference was noted. In the ambush scenario, using high volume semi-automatic fire no appreciable difference was noted. Firing in the burst mode at night the data were inconclusive, but when the same course of fire was fired in daylight on the area target suppression test, the A2 delivered 7 percent more hits at 100 meters than did the M16A1.

When firing in the burst mode at multiple targets at 100 meters the A2 gave a significantly higher number of hits, but at 50 meters this difference was not apparent. All persons firing the M16A1 used for comparison were firing short bursts of 2 or 3 rounds, which may or may not be what would happen in the high stress of actual combat. In the simulation of a patrol being ambushed, requiring quick reaction, immediate action and firing in bursts or automatic fire, the A2 obtained 19 percent hits, compared to only 12 percent for the M16A1.

The A2's increased ruggedness was evaluated through user assessments and inspection of rifles for damage after an exercise in which several squads conducted an operation clearing seven buildings in "combat town." Rifles were used as steps and to gain access to second stories of buildings. Each participant attacked a rubber dummy stabilized by ropes, executing the vertical butt stroke, smash, parry and horizontal butt stroke, in the same sequence with each weapon. Participants also fixed bayonets and attacked a simulated enemy, bayonetting and slashing it twice. The handguards of the A2 were more durable and appeared to offer better control in close combat, and for urban or builtup area operations.

Portability of each weapon was compared for tactical and non-tactical methods of carry, including the manual of arms while marching. Test participants marched to and from the range with both weapons, and carried them through the combat town course, day movement course and other subtests which included a forced march. User comments indicated no preference for carrying either the M16A1 or A2.

Vulnerability of the weapons to detection and countermeasures were assessed by comparing the noise generated when being carried, and while being operated, as well as the muzzle flash and/or dust signature produced when each weapon fired in day or night conditions. Photographic presentations of the muzzle flash or dust produced were obtained to provide an accurate assessment. Personnel in the butts also answered questionnaires assessing their ability to identify which weapons were being fired based on sounds heard in the butts.

Conclusions indicated no difference in the amount of noise generated by either weapon when being carried or operated. No difference was indicated in muzzle flash in day or night conditions. No significant dust signature was noted due to cold weather conditions, although when firing over new snow less disturbance was noted under the muzzles of the A2s. No essential difference in shape that could be used as a characteristic to identify units can be noted at any distance without the aid of binoculars or a telescope. Personnel in the butts could distinguish which ammunition was being fired at ranges beyond 600 meters, because the NATO SS109 and M855 ammunition remains supersonic to a far greater range, producing a distinct crack as it passes overhead, whereas the 55-grain M193 bullet goes subsonic shortly beyond 600 meters, producing only a muffled pop.

A limited test compared the M16A1 and the new A2 as to any interference generated while carrying the weapons caused by changes in center of gravity, or methods of carry when engaged in airborne, amphibious or helicopter operations. Participants carried both rifles in operation scenarios wearing full combat gear. There was no meaningful difference between weapons regarding their compatibility or suitability while entering or exiting landing craft, vehicles or aircraft.

The human factors evaluation, or "man-machine interface" characteristics of the two rifles were compared as they might affect operating safety (including hot or sharp parts), useability and adjustability of sights and controls in terms of speed, accessibility, and accuracy of adjustment; and recoil, as it affects recovery time, in burst fire or sustained rapid semiautomatic fire, accuracy in precision fire, comfort and confidence. The effects of the redesigned handguard and buttstock were also evaluated as they affected accuracy, control in automatic fire and hand to hand combat.

Test participants preferred the sights on the M16A2 to those on the M16A1 because they were easier to adjust and provided a greater range of adjustment, which effectively doubles the useful engagement range of this rifle with SS109/M855-type ammunition compared to the M16A1 with M193-type ammunition. The sights on the A2 are safer to adjust when the weapon is loaded than those on the M16A1, because the front sight is not used for routine sight changes. Ranging adjustments are made on the elevation dial of the rear sight after the front sight is initially adjusted to obtain a battlesight zero. Refinements were made in the size of the front sight post and rear

The small aperture leg is used for precision daylight fire at ranges beyond 200 meters. The large aperture is used for snap shooting at ranges less than 200 meters and for low light level use near dawn or dusk. Elevation drum moves sight in minute of angle clicks.

M16A2 front sight is square in cross-section with parallel sides to provide a more distinct sight picture. After first zero adjustment, rear sight offers all adjustments normally required.

Table I
Accuracy Comparison of M16A2 vs. AK-74

Weapon/Ammunition	Range (yds.)				
M16A2 with 55-gr. M193	100	300	600	800	1000
Mean Radius (ins.)	1.87	4.18	13.2	18.3	no hits
Extreme Spread (ins.)	5.25	13.4	31.4	46.5	no hits
Hits On "E" Silhouette 39" high x 19" wide	20x20	20x20	11x20	10x20	no hits
Score on NRA decimal target SR and MR	99-6X	93-1X	81-1X	79	no hits
M16A2 with M855/SS109					
Mean Radius (ins.)	1.95	5.22	10.98	11.78	15.95
Extreme Spread (ins.)	5.5	15.75	32.75	43.0	73.9
Hits on "E" Silhouette	20x20	20x20	15x20	12x20	6x10
Score on NRA decimal target SR and MR	99-5X	90-1X	91-2X	82-1X	79-1X
AK-74 with 5.45 mm PS					
Mean Radius (ins.)	1.87	8.47	15.9	20.3	no hits
Extreme Spread (ins.)	7.25	21.6	44.0	74.5	no hits
Hits on "E" Silhouette	20x20	17x20	9x20	7x20	no hits
Score on NRA decimal target SR and MR	99-6X	79-0X	69-0X	57	no hits

M193, followed by the M16A1 with M193 and finally the AK-74 with Type PS ammunition. Accuracy results for the various weapons and types of ammunition tested are summarized in the accompanying tables.

In penetration tests the M16A1 rifle with M193 ammunition, the M16A2 with SS109, M855, M193 and Olin Penetrator (commercial approximation of the SS109), and the AK-74 with Type PS ammunition were fired against 3.5mm thick mild steel plates at various ranges. In addition, the 7.62mm M40A1 Remington sniper rifle with M118 Special Ball (Match, 175-2.0 gr. bullet at 2575 fps) and M80 standard Ball (148.0-2.0 bullet at 2750 fps) were fired for comparison. Maximum ranges at which penetrations of the test plate occurred were 500 yards for the M193, 600 for the AK-74 and 7.62mm M80, and 800 for the 7.62mm M118, 5.56mm SS109, M855 and Olin Penetrator. Results are summarized in an accompanying table.

sight apertures based on these tests to optimize precision of fire in daylight conditions, and target acquisition for close range snap shooting and firing in morning or evening nautical twilight conditions.

The M16A2 production sight is adjustable from 300 to 800 meters and has indexing marks on the dial and receiver which align when the sight is turned all the way down or within one click. The 300- and 800-meter settings are co-located on the same position, marked with an indexing line on the top of the dial. Remaining ranges are marked on the dial in 100m increments: i.e., 4, 5, 6, 7. Range markings on the elevation dial align with the following detents 8/3 (800/300 meters) at 0 or 25th click, 4 - 3rd click, 5—7th click, 6—12th click, 7—18th click. The short range rear sight aperture is used for ranges up to 200m, has an outside diameter of .375-in. and an inside diameter of .20-in. It is marked "0–2" at the base and has a windage reference point at the top which is used for precision fire with the long range aperture.

The long range aperture is used for firing beyond 200m and has an outside diameter of .375-in. with an inside diameter of .070-in. It is marked "3–8" at the base. The rear faces of both sight apertures are concave and heavily phosphated to reduce glare. One quarter-revolution (one movement/detent) of the front sight moves point of impact approximately 1.4 moa, one click of the elevation dial on the rear sight moves point of impact approximately 1 moa, and one click of the windage knob on the rear sight moves point of impact approximately ½ moa. Firing tests indicate that point of impact is not significantly different with

M193 or SS109/M855 ammunition when using the same sight settings at ranges less than 500 meters.

Accuracy and penetration of the M16A1 with M193, the A2 with M193 and SS109/M855 and the Soviet AK-74 with 5.45mm Type PS ammunition were compared at ranges from 100 to 900 meters. The Soviet AK-74 was found to be reliable and accurate at short ranges, but its sights were a limiting factor beyond about 200 meters — it has a short sighting radius, open rear notch sight and no windage adjustments. The M193 ammunition was found most accurate at ranges less than 300 meters, but the SS109 most accurate at ranges beyond 500 meters. The most accurate rifle overall was the M16A2 with SS109 ammunition; the next most accurate was the M16A2 with

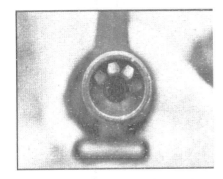

New muzzle-brake/compensator has closed bottom to reduce dust signature produced when rifle is fired from prone position. It also dramatically improves hit probability in burst fire by reducing muzzle climb.

Familiar M16A1 features such as take-down mechanism and bolt-assist knob coexist with new things like brass deflector at right on M16A2.

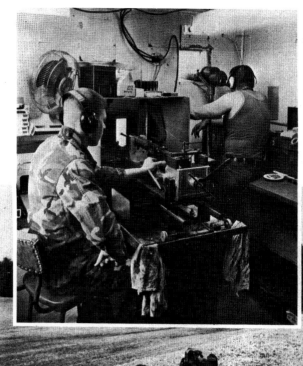

Extensive testing of the M16A2 from machine rests indicates that it compares very favorably to the 7.62mm M14 and earlier M1 rifles at ranges beyond 500 yards. Scoped M16A2 was fired in terminal ballistic tests; M40A1 is in no danger of replacement, but there may be scoped M16A2s.

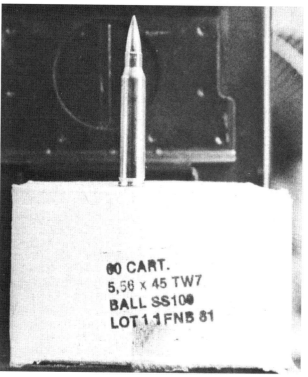

Far Right: All the old infantry hardware is present — sling swivel and bayonet lug — on the M16A2 but the barrel is noticeably heavier than the M16A1 and the new muzzle brake is a boon.

20 CARTRIDGES

5.56 MM

62 GRAIN PENETRATOR

E.O. 4443

WINCHESTER GROUP
OLIN CORPORATION
EAST ALTON, ILLINOIS, U.S.A.

00 CART.
5,56 x 45 TW7
BALL SS109
LOT 11 FNB 81

NATO 5.56mm ammunition is made in the U.S. by Olin Corp. and by Lake City Ammunition Plant FN production is the standard by which others are compared. Ballistics are approximately 3100 fps for a 62-gr. steel core bullet from the M16A2, capable of perforating a 3.5mm steel plate at 700 yards, and capable of defeating soft body armor to 1000 yards. Accuracy of this ammunition from the M16A2 is approximately 2 minutes of angle at ranges less 300, and about 3 minutes to 1000 yards.

The question of lethality and effectiveness of the M193 cartridge fired from the fast twist rifling in the M16A2 was of concern because existing stocks of M193 ammunition will be used until sufficient supplies of type M855 ammunition can be produced to replace it. Previous testing had already established there was no loss of precision when M193 ammunition was fired in the M16A2. However, since some nations had adopted faster twists of rifling for supposed humanitarian reasons, this factor had to be investigated. Test firings were conducted with M193 ammunition in both the M16A2 and M16A1 at ranges of 100, 300 and 500 yards, shooting into 20 percent gelatin blocks of U.S. DoD standards, 50cm thick. Testing indicated there was no significant difference in the lethality of M193 ammunition in the M16A2 as compared to the

Writer Harris is well-known as a shooter who will shoot all of what's handy anytime there's a chance. Here he shoots an Egyptian AKM; he has fired the AR15 and the various M16 options in about all the variations there are and created some of them himself. Indeed, the USMC officially commended Harris for his work with them on the M16A2.

M16A1 at any range fired. The SS109/M855 was equivalent to the M193 at ranges up to 300 yards, and it was significantly more effective at longer ranges, such as 500 yards.

Brief tests were conducted to determine the compatibility of the M16A2 barrel with 22 rimfire ammunition used in the M261 Conversion Unit. This sub-caliber training device is used by Army and Air Force units for preliminary training and by reserve units not having year-round ranges. The conversion unit replaces the standard bolt carrier assembly and converts the weapon to blowback operation, firing 22 LR ammunition from 10-round magazine inserts which are loaded into standard M16 magazines. The device is made under contract to the U.S. Army by Saco Defense Systems, Inc., Saco, Maine, USA.

The normal accuracy expected of 10-shot groups with 22 rimfire ammunition fired from the M16A1 with M261 Conversion unit is about 4 MOA at ranges up to 50 meters. Although this is about twice the dispersion of M193 or SS109 type ammunition, it is deemed adequate for training purposes. Side-by-side comparisons with two M16A2 and M16A1 upper receivers, used alternately on the same lower receivers, firing the same M261 unit showed no significant difference in precision, the mean extreme spread of ten consecutive 10-shot groups with each being 2.25-in. and 2.37-in., respectively, at 50 yards.

Testing to date indicates that the M16A2 preserves the strong points of the M16A1 system, while correcting most, if not all of its deficiencies. Since the M16A2 has been adopted by the U.S. Army and U.S. Marine Corps, as well as by the Canadian Forces, it is sure to become a new standard against which future gen erations of small caliber weapons will be compared.

Table II
Performance Of Typical Military Rifles Against NATO 3.5mm Thick Mild Steel Test Plate

Weapon	Cartridge	Range (yds.)	Performance*
Carbine, M1	Ball, M1	100	CP
		200	FP
AKM	7.62×39 PS (steel core)	300	CP
		400	50% CP, 50% PP
M16A1	Ball, M193	400	CP
		500	50% CP, 50% PP
		600	FP
M16A2	Ball, M855	600	CP
		700	CP
		800	50% CP, 50% PP
		1000	FP
AK-74	5.45×39 PS	600	CP
		800	FP
Rifle, M1	Ball M2	500	CP
		600	FP
Rifle, M14	Ball M80	700	CP
		800	FP
Rifle, M21/M40	Ball M118	800	CP
		900	50% CP, 50% PP
		1000	FP

*Explanation of terms:

CP - complete perforation in which major portion of the projectile exits the armor

PP - partial penetration in which a hole is generated but the major portion of the projectile does not exit the armor

FP - failure to penetrate, the plate may be dented but is intact

THE MOST IMPORTANT RIFLE

by JIM THOMPSON

REATNESS IN firearms is a pretty subjective judgement. But when a gun is nearing its hundredth birthday, hasn't been out of production for much longer than somebody's coffeebreak, and is still a favorite of hunters and precision shooters everywhere, calling it great may be an understatement. About the closest estimate one can acquire of the quantities of the Mauser Model 98 produced thus far is somewhere between 91 million and 125 million. It's hard to come up with a firmer figure, for the rifle was produced in twenty or more countries, most of which used it as a military rifle, and another large group of nations produced clones, copies and ripoffs of the original, often in quantities so vast they couldn't give a production figure if they wanted, and they don't want.

Only the Russian AK-47 design comes anywhere close to the production figures of the Model 98. It's probably not that close, but no one knows for sure. The Chinese and Japanese produced Model 98 rifles and copies in vast quantities, both for themselves and for client states. The Belgians, Poles, Austrians, Czechs, Iranians, Yugoslavs, Turks, Spaniards, Argentines, Brazilians, Mexicans and others produced military M98s in quantity; others produced near-copies and "improvements" for military use like the U.S. M1903 and '03A3. (Yes, the Mauser firm was paid at least $400,000 inroyalties until at least 1914.) There were also the U.S/British P17/P14 "Enfields" and the late French MAS derivatives in this category.

And that's just the military rifles. Handmade Model 98s in calibers up to 50 Browning are still being turned out by builders like Fred Wells of Prescott, Arizona. French, Dutch, British and Italian sporting rifles and actions have been

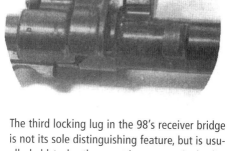

The third locking lug in the 98's receiver bridge is not its sole distinguishing feature, but is usually held to be the most important single distinction between the M98 and its predecessors.

Marking on standard German K98k of WWII vintage, circa 1944.

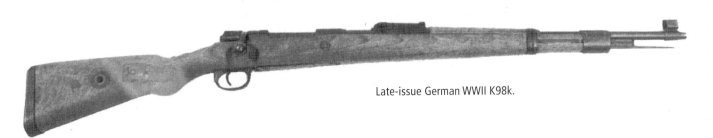

Late-issue German WWII K98k.

made in standard, miniature and magnum lengths. The Finnish Sakos and the Swedish Carl Gustaf and Husqvarna are all 98-type actions. Many of the countries which used the 98 as a military rifle produced and most *still* produce the action as a hunting piece. The famous Swiss annual *Waffen Digest* recently (1992 edition) carried a couple of unusual announcements: One was descriptive of a "new" product called *Mauser Jagdrepetierer Modell 98*, a rather familiar model introduced by the mother firm, Mauser-Werke, Oberndorf-am-Neckar, absent from the thriving market for their most famous product for 46 years. Waffen Frankonia also introduced their new K98k military rifle, actually a reworked and specification updated military rifle with new parts and stocks, as and where necessary.

So why introduce — at fairly high prices, incidentally — technology almost a century old as a new product at a time of worldwide economic recession? Simply put: demand. The Mauser 98 is closer to a true basic product than nearly any other firearm, and though the analogy seems strained, it occupies a market position similar to eggs, flour or rice. If one needs an accurate rifle for hunting, sniping, experimenting or target shooting, the

ancient three-lug "safety" action is a fine place to start. Indeed, structurally, there's little to choose between any M98 and the latest bolt guns from, say, Weatherby or Remington; there have been refinements, but the nuts and bolts have been very similar for a long time, and almost anything in the way of doo-dads one can imagine or concoct for a Model 70 Winchester can be acquired, built or purchased for the Mauser.

Of course, for civilians, even purchasing an old military action for very little money and doing the full custom job on it doesn't save a penny over a top-of-the-line commercial product. The main difference is, when the consumer reworks his own Model 98, he gets *exactly* what he wants — no more, no less — and if he can do some or all of the work, he really can save a few bucks. What is unique about this time-honored process is that such rifles can be built up slowly, on a sort of self-regulating installment plan, adding a new trigger in January, scope or mount in March, stock in June or July, total refinish some other year. That you cannot do with a new rifle which comes in a fancy box.

But there's more to the Mauser 98 saga. From 1898 to about 1962, military Mausers were built in considerable variety. All

specifications called for minimum vise-secured accuracy level *under* two minutes of angle. Most performed better. Of course, given the limitations of a broad V rear sight and skinny front blade, or pyramidal "barleycorn" post, shooter-limited factors meant such a level of accuracy was seldom maintained in the field. There were no mystery alloys used in Model 98 Mausers, and if the odd stamped or roughly soldered or welded part found its way onto a wartime K98k, it was always someplace where it bore little stress. The 98s were made for so long that whole metallurgical techniques changed, but, surprisingly, this had almost no impact on the rifle's quality or durability. Even the military finishes of the rifles generally exceeded the workaday qualities of most of today's civilian firearms.

Most original specification rifles from about 1898 through World War II used what are today considered rather primitive ordnance steels, but carefully heat-treated so that while the core remained very soft, the surface was often as high as 62 on the Rockwell C scale. FN rifles and many from Eastern Europe used tighter dimensional tolerances overall, used far more sophisticated metallurgy, and show lower hardness figures. However, this latter group comprises generally superior actions, far more durable. I am often compelled to repeat to shooters and collectors that hardness very decidedly *is not strength*; most materials in use today develop their strengths at hardness levels way below the vogue of forty years ago, and are, in fact, dangerous at high hardness levels. Hardness is relevant in any respect only to a given material in a given application and lately, more often than not, optimum strengths are obtained at levels far below what was popular thirty to forty years ago. When someone in a gun store begins to talk hardness level as some kind of quality determinant, your best response is to turn on your heel and leave. The very strongest bolt actions in the world, the Japanese Arisakas, are quite soft. Dimensions, design, venting and strength determine the overall safety and quality of a

This assortment is only a part of the new cornucopia of Mauser 98 delight brought to us by the changing world picture. The author's point is that any one of them in barely decent condition is a fine rifle for real rifle work.

rifle action; hardness alone as a factor is bunk. Read *Hatcher's Notes* to get a more specific idea of how these matters translate to reality.

The engineering factors which made the M98 a landmark were simple progressions from the M1892–1896 designs, but they were significant enough that few countries could avoid discarding whatever they had been using to adopt the new system. Rifles just three to ten years old in military service became second-line materiel in most of the world. The third or "emergency" locking lug, the inside receiver ring collar, and the vastly improved, safer, more reliable firing mechanism with its lockout to prevent premature ignition with a broken firing pin, combined with a conglomerate of earlier Mauser evolutionary features

and improved metallurgy to produce a rifle which looked and worked very much like its predecessors. In terms of safety under rough conditions and rapid-fire, though, the Model 98 stood alone.

It surprises many collectors and shooters that relatively few Mausers were actually built by the designing firm. "Few" is, of course, a relative term: The Oberndorf factory produced millions. But almost from the beginning, demand was so vast and deep that firms in Europe and elsewhere were licensed to produce the guns. Loewe, DWM, Steyr, Sauer and Son, Fabrique Nationale, the Czech works at BRNO, Radom in Poland, all the German government arsenals and all their subcontractors, and as many as a hundred small factories in Central Europe were producing actions and/or complete rifles by the mid-1920s.

If one wishes to analyze the impact Paul Mauser had on the world, he should dig through the cartridge specifications in one of the better reloading manuals and refer back to Paul Mauser's 1880s and 1890s cartridges. He'll find almost every currently popular medium-power rifle cartridge owes much to the compatible cartridges Mauser designed from their inception to be quickly and cheaply adapted to standard rifle actions. The Mauser originals — 7.92×57, 7×57, 7.65×53 (sometimes called 7.65×54) — and the Brenneke cartridges developed in direct consultation with the Mauser firm do not resemble the 308, 30/06, 270 and others by accident; from case heads to bottlenecks, modern cartridge configurations are virtually all derived from original Mauser ideas.

Before World War I, the Turks, Argentines, Chileans, Mexicans, Brazilians and many others had adopted the military 98. By the mid-1980s, there were already so many Model 98 Mauser versions and variants that a complete listing would've been almost impossible. And by the late 1940s, another World War later, such a catalog was literally impossible. Many countries had ordered rifles in that period from several manufacturers and in several configurations and lengths. Rifles were also refurbished, of course, and calibers were sometimes changed.

Brazil, at one time or another, for example, ordered quantities of rifles from virtually all the major European manufacturers and in 1954 began to manufacture receivers at Itajuba Arsenal. So when one says "Brazilian Mauser," he may be describing a Model 1908 29-inch long rifle, similar to the German Gew.98 or K98a revision built by DWM; a Czech 08/34, almost identical to the Nazi K98k but with a 22-inch barrel and in 7mm; the Oberndorf-built M1935 long rifle, essentially a later clone of the original Model 1908, the "2nd Variation" 08/34; various rifles shortened to 24 inches and barrels rebored to 30-06 and appropriately modified; the M1954, a 30-06 rifle receiver built as such, but completed with parts left over from all kinds of surplus rifles, including German 98ks; or as many as a dozen other fairly obscure variants ordered in small quantities for special purposes or from firms unwilling to advance normal credit to the Brazilian government and therefore delivered only on a cash in advance basis.

The most common general action configuration of the M98 Mauser is the so-called "large ring, standard length." The receiver ring measures 1.410 inches. The "small ring" rifles measure 1.3 inches. There are also differences in overall configuration, but the ring size is readily discernible and is, therefore, the main identifier. The standard action is 8.75 inches long; the "short" action measures 8.5 inches in length and, at 43 ounces, is 2 ounces lighter than the standard length. There are also large ring, small thread actions which accept M93/95-style barrels, and these — especially those built by FN — are very handy to gunsmiths who wish to stock actions that can be delivered in a variety of configurations.

However, the differences in size are minimal; a person chooses one or the other usually based upon aesthetics or, more commonly, what's available at a

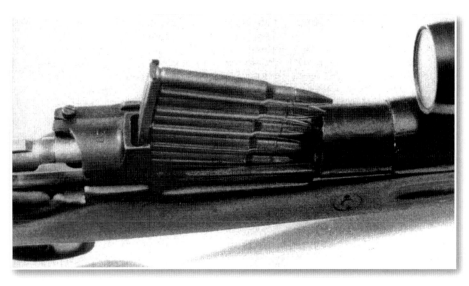

FN-built Peruvian M1946 short rifle accepting five rounds in a stripper clip of the 30-06 for which these post-WWII rifles were chambered.

given time. The truly short or miniature actions and the magnum length units are either carefully modified and sectioned militaries or civilian actions. Virtually any Model 98 action that has been checked for cracks and has been rebarreled with correct headspace is quite safe for any standard cartridge which can be stuffed into it. Smiths have become adept at opening up magazines and adapting receivers even to the longer magnum rounds.

But I have always been fond of shooting military rifles, in general, and Mausers, in particular, in their original configurations. The performance is surprising, the variety amazing, and the original cartridges are at least as good as the 30-06 and 7.62×51mm rounds to which many were later converted.

In the six years or so since GCA '68 was modified to allow curio and relic firearms to enter the country again, quite a variety of Mausers have entered. The pictures accompanying and the information with them will supply some specifics, but I'll relate some general data here.

The first big batch of Mausers to enter the U.S. recently arrived from China, and encompassed virtually all eras and nearly all manufacturers. The Chinese ordered millions, made more millions, apparently bought used specimens of other country's service rifles after both World Wars, and may have gotten some from the Soviets. So the variety was startling. I saw several hundred rifles, which ranged from truly oddball 16½- to 17-inch barreled 8mm carbines to standard German-issue Gewehr 98s from World War I, German Standard Modell rifles, K98ks in German-issue style and complete with World War II fits and

codes, and just about everything else one can imagine finding its way to that part of the world. Since these rifles saw as much as sixty years of hard duty, most were pretty beat up, though some were far better than average.

Springfield Sporters (Penn Run, PA) brought in most of the Model 98 Mauser supply from Yugoslavia. These were mostly rebuilt in Yugoslavia, and to very high standards. There were several variants, including the enormous quantity of VZ.24/G.24t rifles captured from the Waffen SS; K98ks and refurbished G.98s from the same source; Yugoslavian-built pre- and post-World War II rifles; Czech contract rifles from the late '20s and the '30s; and oddments of other Central European Mausers captured by the Yugoslavians.

These rifles, in addition to being well-maintained and beautifully rebuilt, contain more of the "if this rifle could talk" history collectors appreciate than most other hardware on the market and genuinely deserve a place in any European Mauser collection, despite — maybe because of — the applied Yugoslavian markings. They're also good actions for conversion, although most bear mint-like 8mm barrels, and throwing them out would be foolish. Century International Arms supplied virtually all the Latin American Mausers pictured within this article. If the close-ups reveal anything, it's that the "export" guns were often made to higher standards than those for German domestic consumption. And why not? Foreign contracts were open to competitive commercial bid and nothing was locked in automatically. Most were made to very high standards, like the best sporting rifles of the period. And since I

A composite "Kar.98b," made in 8mm to approximate the interwar German specification, bearing parts from at least six countries, but primarily comprising a Greek-issue FN 24/30 action, German M1936 "Olympic" target barrel and Argentine stock, with fittings from Turkey, Austria and elsewhere. Shoots well.

had an opportunity to compare directly with German rifles of the same years, it was pretty obvious that finish quality was higher on the DWM, Steyr, and even Mauser/Oberndorf guns for Latin America. What was interesting was the shooting quality delivered down-range.

Before developing that data, however, let me note that every Mauser I shot that's pictured here was in the very best available condition. This cost me extra; it'll cost you extra, but it's dollars well spent. It always pays off. Of course, this caution does not apply so much if you're doing a full-house sporter conversion; Century sells actions in various conditions, already stripped of their barrels and wood; often, complete rifles in fair to good condition cost less than the actions. But if you mean to do any shooting as-is, get the best condition available. If you're a collector, this is especially true. Pay the extra money, and it'll always be reflected in the gun's long-term value. It also always costs much more to restore a clunker than to purchase a better rifle in the first place.

It's also wise to shoot the best ammo you can. Surprisingly, the quality of surplus ammo is now very high. The FN Belgian 7.65mm Argentine and the San Francisco (Argentina) 7.65 shot as well as any military ammo I've ever shot. Yugoslavian PrviPartizan and Yugoslavian surplus 8mm, also from Century, performed beautifully and very accurately, as did the Yugoslavian 7×57.

Several of the rifles shot very close to MOA, and the Peruvian M1935 7.65 — which looked quite rough but sported a superb bore — actually delivered a ⅞-inch group at just over 100 yards. The 7mm long rifles also performed exceptionally, especially the two M1935 Brazilian Mausers, one of which was the proverbial gnat's eyelash below the Peruvian gun in on-target performance. The Chilean Steyr M1912 was not far behind. Even the ugly M1954 Brazilian — as rough a rifle as I've ever seen and dared to fire, but sporting a pristine bore and perfect head-space even by commercial standards — performed right up to the standards of my National Match M1 in 30-06. The Yugoslavian PrviPartizan 7mm 175-grain loading shot to point of aim in the Brazilian M1935 at 300 yards, but with the sights set for 100 meters. The trajectory suggested high velocity and excellent power, but I determined — since there were no signs of high pressure — chronographing was unnecessary.

The little Argentine M1909 carbines — one an Argentine-built DGFM, the other a DWM from Germany — delivered 1½-inch groups at 100 yards. Those are five-shot groups. I fired three rounds of Norma's excellent softpoints per gun and did a little better.

Again, as noted early on, these were best groups. No Model 98 sight is quite discriminatory enough to deliver this sort of accuracy anyway, except from a rest, and even then, eyesight limitations and the hard realities of real shooting don't allow the shooter to do that consistently. But the potential is there. I've lately been recommending B-Square's long eye relief scope setups because they don't demand anything be drilled or ground up, and the military Mausers thus retain their collector's value. Also, the stripper loading capability is maintained, and the bolt handles need not be modified.

I'd be remiss if I didn't mention the tradeoff equation with high-powered rifles. That is, the little 6½- to 7½-pound carbines are light and handy, but the Mauser buttplate is downright abusive, and short barrels generate serious muzzleblast. The 29-inch barreled long rifles are cumbersome, but sweet to shoot and easy to balance, even over long sessions. The 22- to 24-inch barreled guns, as one might expect, are about midway between the two. Military ammo in 7mm and 8mm is loaded stiffer and shoots better than most American commercial ammo; in fact, I recommend RWS or Norma factory loads in 7.92×57JS (8mm) or handloads. American 8mm is so underloaded that European publications list it as a whole different caliber.

Paul Mauser died in 1914. But you can bet on it: Come 2014, his last major rifle design will be alive, well, and living almost everywhere.

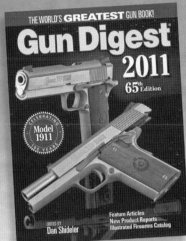
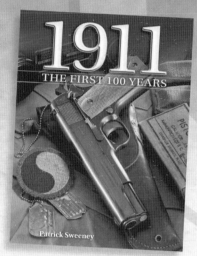

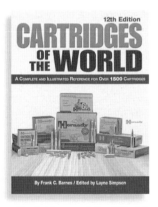
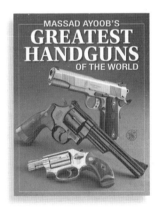
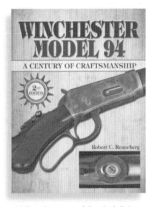
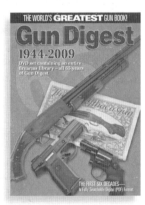